INDIA'S INCLUSIVE GROWTH IN THE AGE OF GLOBALIZATION

India's Inclusive Growth in the Age of Globalization

Edited by

Dr. Amalesh Banerjee

KANISHKA PUBLISHERS, DISTRIBUTORS
NEW DELHI-110 002

KANISHKA PUBLISHERS, DISTRIBUTORS
4697/5-21 A, Ansari Road, Daryaganj
New Delhi-110 002
Phones : 2327 0497, 2328 8285
Fax : 011-2328 8285
E-mail: kanishka_publishing@yahoo.co.in

First Published 2009

ISBN 978-81-8457-131-8

PRINTED IN INDIA

Published by Madan Sachdeva for Kanishka Publishers, Distributors, 4697/5-21A, Ansari Road, Daryaganj, New Delhi-110 002, Typeset by Sunshine Graphics, Delhi, and Printed at Rajdhani Printers, Delhi.

Preface

After fifty years of planning Indian economy has now reached to the phase of high growth. The expectation now is that by the end of the Eleventh Five Year Plan, the economic growth will touch the two digit level. However, this phase of prosperity is attended with all pervading despondency at the lower stratum of the population. The widespread belief, based on current empiiical studies, is that the benefits of this growth has not reached to the needy and poor segment of population. The tricle-down has failed. Hence the emphasis is on the inclusive growth. This implies that planning for growth has to be designed in such a way so that left out segment of population, particularly the SC/ST and minorities can participate in the production process and can earn their livelihood through higher income. This volume has directly addressed this pragmatic issue. Having discussed the character of the present capital intensive type of planning both theoretically and empirically, the volume has put forward the suggestions for planning for rural development. Most of the scholars are of opinion that extensive investment in the rural sector for revamping the traditional rural industries and extension of modern industries in the rural sector can significantly open the employment opportunities in the real sector. This will relieve the debt-ridden farmers and provide more employment to the hudge unorganized rural labour force. The research papers are path-breaking in this respect. The volume has grown out of a group discussions held under the banner of the 'Global Centre for Development Studies'. Part–I of the volume presents the theoretical models and the characterization of our present economic growth. The nature of inflation and instability was assessed minutely. Employment aspect of the economy, and the empowerment of left out social groups and women are discussed in the Part–II. Finance, is an important tool of development. Micro-credit and financial inclusion is examined in the Part–III. Decentralized planning and the Gandhian Path of

Village Welfare are treated in the Part–IV. The volume thus finds out the ills of the system and explores the possible way out of the agony of the present growth process.

Dr. Amalesh Banerjee

Contents

PART – II
EMPLOYMENT AND EMPOWERMENT

PART – III
MICROCREDIT AND FINANCIAL INCLUSION

PART – IV
DECENTRALIZATION AND GANDHIAN ECONOMICS

List of Contributors

Dr. Anupam Gupta, Professor of Economics, Visva Bharati University, Madhulipi, Kolkata.

Dr. Durgadas Roy, Professor of Economics, Rabindra Bharati University, Kolkata.

Dr. Rabin Mukherjee, Formerly of Reserve Bank of India, 2, Satrughna Ghosh Lane, Kolkata.

Dr. Mithilesh K. Sinha, Reader and Head of the Department of Economics, Nagaland University, Lumani, Makukchung, Nagaland.

Dr. Birendra Kumar Jha, Reader, H.O.D. Economics, D.B.K.N. College, Narhan, Samastipur, Bihar.

Dr. Rakesh A. Joshi, Reader, Department of Economics, Sourashtra University Rajkot, Gujarat.

Dr. Ashok Kumar Maji, H.O.D. Economics K.B. College, Bermo P.O. Jarangdih, Dist. Bokaro, Jharkhand.

Manoj Kumar Singh, Economics Department, Peoples' College, Mokukchung, Kohima, Nagaland.

Kuntal Chakraborty, Principle, Pathar Pratima College, 24-Parganas (S), West Bengal.

Dr. Sankar Chatterjee, Dy. Director, NIRD, Rajendra Nagar, Hyderabad.

Sujata Bhadra, Sr. Lecturer, Peoples' College, Kokrajhar, Assam.

Dr. Deb Kumar Bhattacharya, Reader, Santipur College, Nadia, W.B.

Dr. S.N. Tripathy, Professor of Economics, Gokhale Institute of Politics and Economics, Pune.

Dr. D.K. Ghosh, SDO (W), Purulia, P.O. Kalyani, W.B.

Dr. P.K. Roy Barman, United Bank, Bhattacharya Para Road, Barisha, Kolkata.

Dr. Sukhendu Majumdar, Principle, Management Institute, Dimapur, Assam.

Dr. Ram Naresh Thakur, Professor, Samastipur (P.G.) College, Samastipur, Bihar.

Part–I : MACRO DIMENSION

1

Introduction: Planning for Inclusive Growth

AMALESH BANERJEE

India has been pursuing economic plan for last fifty years. Each of the past ten five year plans had a package objective, primarily for rapid growth and eradication of poverty and expansion of employment. However, now the Eleventh Five Year Plan makes specific focus on the inclusive growth of the economy. It implies that the growth process that experienced over the years were not sufficiently inclusive of all poverty-striken sections of the population. Although there had been substantial reduction of poverty over past few decades during the five year plans, the core content of the rural poverty remained intractable. Current national sample survey reveals that certain sections of population appears as hard content of poverty-striken people and some special actions are imperative for addressing this hard content of the poor people. It is envisaged that the Eleventh Five Year Plan will directly take up intervention actions to alleviate the poverty of these left out segments of population. In fact last Ten Five Year Plan envisaged balanced regional development and equality and employment. But the growth of population and urban biased industrial development have left out the backward section of population and the rural sector in general unaddressed. Hence, the most vulnerable segment of population comprising SC/ST and the Muslim, still remain deeply entranced in poverty. We have been basically following a high-tech industrialization which provided employment to the technically skilled personnel. This trend has been further strengthened with the advance of the Information Technology Sector. Thus economy achieves higher rate of growth to the extent of 6-8 per cent GDP but the employment generation has been lagging behind. In fact over last fifty years from 1947–87 the task of inclusion has been slow. On the 50th year our Ninth Five Year Plan started the voyage with the objective of higher rate of growth, ensuring food and nutritional security for all, particularly the vulnerable sections of society. The plan promised to usher in an era of growth with social justice and participation in which the poor can become effective instruments of a participatory planning process. Till now, when we launched the Eleventh Five Year Plan, the welfare of the vast masses of population remain deplorable. The decadel growth rates of GDP and per capita income reveal unsatisfactory picture. Only after 1980–90 per capita income and GDP growth rates show some tenable progress. NSS data of 2004-05 indicate that poor and vulnerable section of population is about 77 per cent. Hence it is natural that the Eleventh Five Year Plan envisages as inclusive growth of the economy.

The poor and vulnerable section of population is mainly in the rural area and are wrapped up in agriculture. The main components of this segments are SC/ST and Muslims minorities. With small piece of land holding or landless, the poor and vulnerable section has no formal training of skill so as to switch on to alternative non-farm occupation. It require two-pronage attack. First is to improve the agriculture through diversification of output. Secondly, the non-farm rural activity structure has to be modernized for greater absorption of labour force. Let us see what course of action the Eleventh Five Year Plan envisages for reduction of poverty and participation of the under-privileged in the production process. The budget (2008-09) proposal has declared Rs. 71 thousand crores loan waiver. This more will be benefit the farmers. Besides, a number of other special scheme (Central) prevails. As stated largest number of poverty-ridden people are SC/ST, Muslims and landless rural people. How can they be included in the production process? They have to be attached with non-farm subsidiary activities. For that purpose nominal skill has to be transmitted to these assetless poor people. In course of time they will be involved in the earning structure and their learning of technique of production will continue or they will be what in other terms tell as 'learning by doing.'

The budget of 2008-09 has eliminated the burden of indebtedness of small farmers for once only. But what is essential is to develop a financial structure which will support the farmers in weal and woes. A well-neat financial structure, a remunerative price of product of farmers and insurance against risk and calamities and regularization of money lenders together will save the farmer's.

Farming has to be remunerative and the non-farm work opportunities have to be developed so that farmers may fall back upon in times of distress for alternative employment. However the approach to Eleventh Plan does not indicate this salvation grid.

However, now micro-finance revolution is going on throughout the country. However this micro-finance movement has to be regulated and monitored carefully.

But one most remember that micro-finance revolution is not second green revolution. Second green revolution involves, raising the productivity of land, diversification of crops and cultivation. This means sustainable production and development. Inclusive development means empowerment of weaker sections, SC/ST and women. Eleventh Five Year Plan and budget 2008-09 falls short of that ideal comprehensive perspective plan for food security and agricultural development. It is not only one scheme of employment guarantee but similar such scheme of production and marketing has to be evolved for extensive inclusive development programme. What is required is financial and market inclusiveness. Attention has to be concentrated equally both supply and demand side issue. Effective implementation of the scheme like SGSY, NREGA are important.

Another area of inclusive development is the social sector which has been although weak in our planning. The vulnerable section of population which we referred to above is not only weak in terms food security but also deprived in terms of education, health and nutrition for child and mother. Given the fact that India figures at a very low level in terms of Human Development Index, the social sector has attracted major attention of the government. 2008-09 budget also made substantial allocation for Aam Admi. As proportion of the Central Government's total outlay (Plan as well as non-plan) on social services went up from 10.97 per cent in 2001–02 to 16.42 per cent in 2007-08. Of this the education and health attracted major share. The Sarva Shiksha Abhiyan and National Rural Health Mission (NRHM) are the flagship programmes.

However, the performances of the Indian states are wide apart. Agricultural sector and the social sector growth determine the status of different states in the national growth process. Regional disparities is an important issue in Indian economic growth. Apart from current economic policy of the government this has a long historical reasons. It requires a bold step to overcome those long entranced factors. Apart from human resource development, infrastructure, manufacturing and services are the major determinants of contemporary economic growth of India. It is the contribution of services and manufacturing that pushes up Indian economic growth. States which are endowed with these facilities reflect higher and rapid rate of growth.

In respect of poverty line, Uttar Pradesh has highest number of people (19.6%) below poverty level. This is followed by Bihar (12.2 %) and Maharashtra (10.5%). In terms of growth rate also Bihar, Uttar Pradesh, Orissa and Rajasthan have low rate of growth. This vide regional differences in growth among states has resulted in persistence of poverty and social problem in some states. If we look at the states it will appear that inter regional differences are as vivid as the intra-regional differences within states. Position of the region will be glaring if one looks at the North-Eastern States, N.E. region is as a whole appear to be isolated from the mainland. After sixty years of Independence for the first time rail line has entered in Tripura state. However the present programme of vision North-East envisages railway connectivity with every state capital in the N.E. region. The airport are being built in every state capital. The political and natural limitations are being reduced. However, for the growth process to take momentum in this region, following important works are needed to be taken up on the priority basis: *(a)* spread of technical education, *(b)* connectivity, *(c)* development of agriculture including zoom cultivation, *(d)* extension of financial support, *(e)* improvement of law and order. After decades of isolation the North-East is now getting special attention like the 'East Look Policy' of the government. Eleventh Five Year Plan envisages a rapid development of the region.

Growth targets of the different states in the region during the Eleventh Five Year Plan almost at par with advance states.

These targets are modest and the states are capable to achieve those rates of sectoral growth.

The 'Vision 2002' has set up a strategy with following components for development of the region: *(a)* participatory development through grassroots planning, *(b)* capacity development, *(c)* augmentation of physical infrastructure, *(d)* requisite investment to come from Central

Government, *(e)* protecting the tribal rights to land; and *(f)* providing market—friendly governance and environment.

Table–1
Growth Targets for the Eleventh Plan (in per cent) for N.E. States

States	*Agriculture*	*Industry*	*Services*	*Total*
Arunachal Pradesh	2.8	8.0	7.2	6.4
Assam	2.0	8.0	8.0	0.5
Manipur	1.2	8.0	7.9	7.3
Mizoram	1.6	8.0	8.0	7.1
Nagaland	8.4	8.0	10.0	9.3
Sikkim	3.3	8.0	7.2	6.2
Tripura	1.4	8.0	8.0	6.9
India	4.1	10.0	9.9	9.0

Source : Planning Commission.

Intra-state regional disparities prevail in almost all states. Sometime angry reaction to these inequality find expression in destructive terrorist activities. Take the case of inter district variation in development in West Bengal, one of the leading states enjoying sustained high rate of growth over sometime. Northern region and Western regions of the state of W.B. are now engaging special attention of the State Government. Historically backward region of Western districts are now coming up in respect of education, and infrastructure. Industries are now moving in this drought-prone region. Regional disparities and dissention led to the division of Bihar, Madhya Pradesh and Uttar Pradesh. However, more division of States and formation of new small states does not ensure development. Growth story of small states does not indicate resolution of backwardness along that line. States must pay attention to the development of leading development parameters.

II

Present volume brings together various issues of inclusive growth as envisaged in the Eleventh Five Year Plan, both at macro and micro levels. Problem of inclusive growth have been discussed on theoretical plan which indicates both the potentiality and problems of Indian economic growth in contemporary phase of planning. Scholars assessed the potentiality of the present economic growth rate and indicated the strength of the components of this growth and its sustainability. The volume is divided in several parts. The part on presents the theoretical issues of present economic growth. The message of the theoretical study is that present strategy of growth is unlikely to be sufficiently inclusive of different depressed social groups. In fact capitalist development process is inherently exclusive. With this extensive observation Rabin Mukherjee stressed that the extraction and exploitation is the in-built character of capitalist development. Unless strong intervention, the inclusive development will fadeout. Anupam Gupta examined the growth potency in the Kalackian framework. It has been pointed out that incourse of economic growth structural imbalance will entail instability. Michael Kalacki propounded that structural imbalance between the food grains producting sector and the rest of the economy would generate inflation and would increase inequality in the distribution of income. He has formulated the Kalacki model in the context of India. The present inflationary condition of the economy sufficiently attest to this proposition of Gupta. Durgadas Roy expressed apprehension that this high growth phase of the economy may lead to a state of high unemployment. That the present high growth rate is largely exclusionary and characterized as jobless growth is clear. In his evaluation of National Rural Employment Guarantee Programme (NREGP) he pointed out that the programme has reached out to the most needy house-holds in the states. It is also pointed out that the distribution of the benefits of accelerated growth has been palpably uneven. Interclass, inter-sectoral and inter-regional disparities have widened.

India is now poised for a rapid growth in a liberalized position. This situation combines the domestic and international sources. While domestic liberalization encourage the private (monopoly) capital, globalization enhances exports and attracts the foreign capital flow. Banerjee pointed out that these combination of forces favourably impacted the India economy. While aggregate growth pattern is highly attractive, the attended sectoral imbalance failed to provide sufficient employment and equally failed to raise agricultural output. The high liquidity and parasitic supply situation generated inflation which is now highest in 13 years. Banerjee pointed out that under such situation macroeconomic policies are failing. It requires intervention measures to arrest the inflation. Contemporary experience of economic growth in many Third World Countries indicate that globalization has enhanced the economic growth. M.K. Sinha emphasized that globalization also has enhanced. The channel of growth in this contest is the export-led growth supported by inflow of foreign capital.

However the fall out of such growth experience in India raised some important issues for consideration. Impact of growth on the social sector is not happy. R.A. Joshi was concerned about several forms of inequality prevailing in Indian. This is aggravated by the present liberalized growth process. He considers that a redistributive system can meet these inequalities. On employment area, the present growth process has a disappointing effect. Casualization and informalization are certain aspects of the issue. With the help of district level study of unorganized non-farm activities in rural Bengal, Kuntal Chakraborty concluded that with the adoption of intermediate technology, training and marketing network the informalization of labour force can be considerable attended.

It is ironical that Indian economic growth, basically neglected agriculture. The manufacture and service sector-led growth has not only produced imbalance and inflation in the economy, this has also brought misery to the farmers. With low productivity, low price of farm products and growing burden of debt, farmers in several states (even in Green Revaluation belt) are committing suicides. Rakesh Joshi has addressed this serious and soul-searching issue of Indian economy. He suggested that inputs of agriculture should be supplied to the farmers at a subsidized rates. Particularly better irrigation facilities should be made available at low cost. Finally bank finances should be made available at low cost.

Modern economy is basically knowledge-based economy. Economic growth in the South-East Asian Countries are mainly knowledge based. With the expansion of scientific knowledge the old structure of manufacturing industry and the service activities have undergone a radial change. In our country higher education is limited and is often beyond the reach of tribal population. Banerjee held out the proposition that modern scientific education must be all-inclusive so that disadvantaged people may come up in technical occupation and new profession. As a part of inclusive development strategy, Eleventh Five Year Plan particularly emphasized the extensive development of education facilities for all section, particularly the under previlized section of population. We have heard of regional balance as an important objective of plan. We have seen above the inter-state differences. Bihar is one such backward state. What the Eleventh Five Year Plan proposes for Bihar? B.K. Jha deplores that decline of Bihar began from 1960s and has come to be treated as one of four least developed states. Jha has rightly pointed out that Bihar needs new vision. New target of growth rate, has been fixed for different sectors. He was rightly observed that key to prosperity of the state lies in higher productivity at farm and factories. Eleventh Plan has provided Bihar a unique restructure policy so as to include all sections of depressed people of the state.

The state of employment has been examined by Manoj Kumar Singh. Based on NSS data he first examine the population distribution between urban and rural segments and then workers division between the urban and the rural sectors. It has been found that women's employment has increased in low paid jobs. Another phenomenon is that nearly 50 per cent of men and 70 per cent of women do not have designated places of work. Given this state of employment in urban and rural sector, the incidence of poverty in the rural sector is very acute. Ram Naresh Thakur took pain in identifying the rural-urban divide in respect of various demographic indicators. The study showed that the vicious circle of poverty is very strong in the rural sector.

Having examined the employment status and the poverty intensity in both urban and rural sectors, we shall now turn to examine remedial measures suggested by scholars. There are four specific areas suggested by the writers in order to enhance the process of inclusive growth. These areas are: *(a)* financial inclusion, *(b)* small industry expansion, *(c)* rural and agricultural diversification and development, *(d)* decentralization of planning.

Financial Inclusion has Various Dimensions

(a) Structural aspect: Extension of the formal financial structure in the rural area is not sufficient so that the underprivileged section of population can avail of the institutional credit; *(b)* the micro finance for micro enterprises and empowerment of weaker section; *(c)* credit facility for Small and Medium Enterprises (SME).

By different index, financial inclusion in India is low, even lower than China. The financial index comprising C-D ration, per thousand adults, availability of bank services indicate that India rank at a very low level. If we look to the different states of the country, one will be surprised to know that in West Bengal one third of Panchayat area do not have any bank branch. It is identified that there are 108 areas where there are no bank office within 10 km radius. On the other hand in 2005 C/D ratio in West Bengal was 55, in 2006, 60 p.c.

Mithilesh has elaborately examined the issue in different aspects–structural and functional. Even banks support to priority sector is declining recently. At present micro finance revolution is going on through out the country. Functions of millions of S.H.G. indicate that micro finance, where properly monitored, is likely to strengthen the inclusive growth process, women empowerment and employment generation in the informal sector. D.K. Bhattacharya made a case study of Nadia district of West Bengal. Micro credit facilities extended to millions of poor and vulnerable section of population can turn their misery, and can raise their productivity. Bhattacharya particularly pointed out that self-employment programme for different rural activities can be strengthened for employment generation. Shankar Chatterjee outlined the success of Swaranjayanti Gram Swarozgar Yojana (SGSY) in the state of Jammu and Kashmir. The study pointed out that these programmes have been successful with the support of micro finance. Another success story of micro finance in Boroland which has been examined by Sujata Bhadra. Bodo ethnic groups in Assam have earnestly adopted the S.H.G. Programme and Bodo Women have substantially benefited from the micro finance scheme.

The micro finance programme has developed here both financial and social intermediation. 2009 is the 40th year of commercial bank nationalization which started with the formation of SBI 58 years ago. Inclusive finance started since 1955 on the recommendation of Gorwala Committee. Earlier Rural Banking Enquiry Committee come out with a broad programme of inclusive finance. SBI operation has been on outstanding success. By extension of branches, in the rural sector, and extending credit to the weaker segments of the population and to the backward areas of the country (like North-East India) the SBI family has become a saga of success of inclusive finance. Micro finance is also supplied by Regional Rural Banks and N.G.Os. Regional Rural Banks of SBI, more than one third of total RRB, set up by the commercial banks, are set up in the remote and tribal areas. Micro finances coverage of the SBI – sponsored RRBs are extensive and inclusive. Current Micro finance Regulation Bill is of course not comprehensive. NABARD has to take more attention to the regulation and proper functioning of the S.H.G. Programmes.

Current NSS findings indicate that multiple social groups in the country are locked up in the rural and in the furflung areas of the country who are devoid of minimum amenities of modern level of well-being. The formal structure of administration and finance do not have access to those areas. It is therefore proposed that voluntary organizations, N.G.O. in the civil society have important role in human resource development and to enhance the prospect of inclusive development. P.K. Roy Burman explored this fundamental issue of social structure. However, as a socially responsible organization N.G.Os have to work in close union with the Panchayats.

Decentralized development machinery or Panchayat Raj is constitutionally devised as an effective machinery for inclusive development. When different ethnic groups and disadvantaged social groups have the due share in dispensation of decisions for development, that will certainly strengthen the basis of participatory or inclusive growth. Dilip Ghosh and S.N. Tripathy have explored this area of inclusive development. Ghosh made a penetrating analysis of decentralized planning experience in West Bengal and identified the area of success and pit fails of the Panchayati system of West Bengal. Tripathy specially emphasized that when decentralized planning is correctly implemented the marginalized tribal population will have an effective presence in the growth process of the economy.

But one must remember that the disadvantaged social groups are mainly associated with agriculture and rural informal activities. The agricultural sector and the non-farm rural small enterprises have to be modernized with the adoption of innovation. This is a package consisting of adoption of modern technology and building up of production and marketing organization. When this net-work of structure of production, marketing and finance work together, rural economy will become vibrant and the indebtedness of the farmers will be eliminated. Ashok K. Majhi has outlined such a small scale industry structure for Jharkhand people, when more than 50 per cent people are down—trodden and deprived. Examining the employment and women participation in non-form activities in West Bengal, Prabir Biswas, Sudeshna Biswas and Amal Goswami asserted that SSI sector offers more employment to women and empower them in economic life. In West Bengal the urban industrial sector cannot provide full-employment. But along with the urban industries, the labour intensive SSI units can offer better chance of development. But along with the urban industries, the labour intensive SSI units can offer better chance of employment to women. Thus as a part inclusive development strategy, the SSI units should be encouraged. It is also proposed that agriculture is the backward sector and huge population are aligned with agriculture. Hence agriculture has to be diversified in terms of crop and non-crop production. Modernization of entire rural economy implies transformation of entire production structure on the principle of profitability and marketability. This is far greater than conventional Green Revolution. The second green revolution therefore encompasses transformation of the entire rural economy.

Inclusive development implies participation of all sections of population—male, female, tribals, non-tribals in the production process. Where this participation of all productive agents are based on skill productivity, production will increase and the development will augment social welfare. When one goes for industrialization of backward areas, say Bihar, as Jha has pointed out, the principle of development should be revamping the traditional rural industries on the one hand and on the other hand innovating new modern small and medium enterprises in the rural sector. What is this kind of strategy? Majumder reminds us that we should not forget the Gandhian strategy of development. He, however, is not obsessed with that. He proposed that our modern inclusive development must combine the traditional and modern medium and information industries. New generation, new skill, new industries and new products is the modern production cycle for inclusive development and welfare.

2

Growth and Inflation in a Structural Macroeconomic Model

ANUPAM GUPTA

Introduction

Preliminary estimates show a rate of growth higher than 9 per cent in India in 2006-07. This has been the highest rate of growth in any year so far. However, such high rate of growth of the economy was associated with a very low rate of growth of food grains output and a creeping inflation that has not been abated even now. The rate of growth of food grain output was 2 per cent, against a planned growth of 4 per cent, in the financial year 2006-07. The rates of inflation estimated by the wholesale index number occasionally crossed 6 per cent in recent times. The rate of increase of price level was relatively higher for the food grains. Among the three cost of living index numbers—those of the agricultural workers, industrial labourers and the urban non-manual employees—that of the agricultural workers was the highest followed by successively the next two. Shortage of food compelled import of wheat and edible oil in the year 2006-07. A high rate of growth with disproportionate impact on structure generates structural inflation. There is no doubt that a certain degree of structural change is a welcome aspect of economic growth. However, structural change beyond a certain order disturbs the balance of the economy.

In the present context the following observation of a Minister is significant. "A few weeks ago the newspapers reported that the number of Indian billionaires had exceeded the number of billionaires in Japan, and there was a considerable amount of self-congratulation on this. ...We rank eighth in the world in the number of our millionaires and we stand 126th on the Human Development Index. I am glad to report that last year we were 127th."

(Edited extracts from a speech of Shri Mani Shankar Aiyar at the CII Northern Region Annual Meeting 2006-07, New Delhi, April 4).

Approximately 20 million workers are in the organized sector and 300 million workers depend on the unorganized sector in India. Out of this 300 millions at least 60 millions together with their dependents live below the poverty line. The poverty line in India means consumption at bare minimum of subsistence. Rise in food price makes their distress more acute. A high rate of growth would be happy to all if it was combined with a balance in the growth of the various sectors. The tertiary sector has been growing at the highest rate since nearly three decades. The rate of growth of the primary sector, on the other hand, had been lagging behind the desired level. Even at such low rate of growth of the primary, particularly agricultural sector, demand was inadequate for lack of employment opportunities of the people. In a regime of very high and rising rate of growth of output, the rate of growth of employment gradually decreased from more than 2 per cent to a level even less than 1 per cent over the last decade.

A group of economists led by Professor B.B. Bhattacharya analyzed the inflationary impact of a disproportionately high rate of growth of the tertiary sector. However that is not the subject matter of this chapter.

In course of his review of the development process of the Indian economy in the early fifties, Michael Kalecki propounded that structural imbalance between the food grains producing sector and the rest of the economy would generate inflation and increase inequality in the distribution of income. For large country like India, the problem of shortage of food grains cannot be solved through international trade. Presently India is the second largest producer of wheat and rice in the world. The peculiar phenomenon is that, with one fourth of India's population languishing below the poverty line, India is the highest exporter of rice among all countries of the world. Total food grain output in India has reached a stalemate at a figure around 200 million tons over the last decade. Share of pulses and oilseeds in the total output has declined over the last two decades. Unless the total output is increased by 15 to 20 per cent, food requirement of the existing population cannot be satisfied. This is a large quantity and particularly for the most basic consumer good of the people. Such large shortage of food grain can not be covered by international trade. Here increase in production is an imperative and fertility of soil is the essential precondition of foodgrains supply. The question of justifiability of surrender of fertile land to non-agricultural activities like manufacturing and real estate construction is obviously the most debated issue in Indian politics at present.

Under such circumstances a review of the economic model of Kalecki formulated in the context of India has a topical significance. It is a closed economy model. An exercise on that model is presented in this chapter.

II

In the early phase of literature on the Theory of Economic Development till the end of the fifties capital accumulation was taken to be the main requirement for regeneration of an underdeveloped economy. 'Vicious circle of poverty' identified by Nurkse needed to be broken by a 'Big Push' of initial investment. The same theme was presented in various types of approaches like 'condition of Take Off' of Rostow, 'critical minimum effort thesis' of Libenstein and 'Low Level Equilibrium Trap' of Nelson. The issue of allocation of resources between consumption goods producing industries and capital goods producing industries was taken to be a matter of choice. Economics worked out this problem of choice in terms of the choice of the time horizon of planning. In such an intellectual ambience of economists concerned with development of the underdeveloped countries the policy makers in India quite naturally gave considerable emphasis on capital formation. Problem of economic development was thus treated as a problem of organization of supply of commodities.

Since the early fifties, however, another stream of thought on the theory of economic development was taking shape. According to this approach demand for manufactured goods will be lagging unless the need for food at the subsistence level is satisfied. The initial clue to such a possibility is derived from the writings of Kalecki.[1] In the approach of Kalecki the commodities are classified between consumer goods for the labourers and the rest. Foodgrains constitute the major part of the consumer goods of the labourers. With capital accumulation demand for labourers increase over time. Total wage payment to the labourers increase with increase in employment.

In an economy in which the subsistence of a large section of population is not satisfied, the inevitable and immediate consequence of rise in total wage will be a corresponding increase in the demand for foodgrains. Unless supply of foodgrains can be increased adequately to match the increase in demand, prices of foodgrains will rise.

Some economists formulated models of economic development under hierarchical demand.[2] In its extreme form it is supposed that demand for other consumer goods will not arise until the demand for basic consumer goods like foodgrains is satisfied. In a more general form of formulation of the problem, elasticity of demand for foodgrains is assumed to be very low for the poor people. Thus as total wage increases and demand for foodgrains increases price of foodgrains would rise. As a result, share of wage spent of foodgrains by any labourer would rise. Such a phenomenon may lead to contraction in demand for other consumer goods of the poor people.[3] However, the nature of effect of capital formation on the demand for consumer goods other than food, namely clothing, depends upon two opposing forces. Capital accumulation would create new employment opportunities. In an economy with a large section of population craving in basic subsistence, creation of new employment opportunities does not raise the real wage rate. These newly employed people generate additional demand for both food and nonfood consumer goods. Consequent rise in the price of foodgrains would increase the share of foodgrains in the total consumption expenditure of those labourers who were in employment since before. Share of expenditure on clothing of these labourers who have been in employment since before this new dose of capital formation, would fall. This aspect is taken as an argument for demand constraint on the development of an economy with surplus labour. However, it is necessary to note that even at the higher price of foodgrains an additional amount of demand for nonfoodgrain consumer good, like clothing, is created by the additional labourers employed on the new capital. The net effect on the total demand for clothing is the difference between the additional demand for clothing of the new labourers and the loss of demand for clothing due to reduction of the share of expenditure on it among the labourers who had been continuing in employment since before.

A rise in the price of foodgrains in an economy with a large population at bare subsistence level creates problem for various reasons. The adverse effect of rise in price of foodgrains on the level of demand for nonfoodgrain consumer goods is not inevitable. But for most of the political systems rise in price of foodgrains would put pressure on the budget of the state. This is particularly true for a country with low per capita income and a large proportion of population suffering from poverty. The government of an underdeveloped economy has to take initiative for capital formation and development of material and social infrastructure. The government has to maintain law and order, provide administration for protection of rights and for safeguarding the implementation of contracts. The efficiency in the implementation of such functions depends on the quality of life of the people. A population suffering from widespread malnutrition and with a low literacy rate can not provide the proper social condition for efficient administration of the functions of the state. Any rise in the price of foodgrains, however small it might be, increases the danger of malnutrition of the poverty-stricken people. The governments in underdeveloped countries in most cases have to subsidise supply of foodgrains and generate employment opportunities for the very poor with rural public works programme. Although the rural labour force are generally not organized in trade unions, attempts to protect their level of living from further deterioration on the part of the government lead to increase in public expenditure corresponding to rise in the price level of the foodgrains.

Increase in public expenditure on subsidies on foodgrains and also on the cost of employment of surplus rural labour on public works programme may be taken as a case of rise in money wage due to rise in price of foodgrains. Although there is no trade union to immediately press for protection of real wage against rise in the prices of foodgrains for the rural labour force, nevertheless the democratic system and the media response in the world to a large extent serve the purpose. In a large number of labour surplus economics governments have to take the responsibility of providing essential foodgrains at a subsidised price to the people. A public distribution system has to be maintained for the purpose. Governments are also politically constrained in the matter of raising the issue price of foodgrains. Moreover, in the occasions of crisis and sometimes on humanitarian grounds the governments have to bear the entire cost of issue of foodgrains. The public distribution system has to procure the required amount of foodgrains from farmers with big stock of marketable surplus. The procurement price is politically negotiated between the organization of the farmers and the state. So any increase in the cost of production is immediately transmitted to a rise in the procurement price. Any corresponding upward revision in issue price may reduce demand for foodgrains and result in accumulation of stock with the public distribution system. Since the procurement price is generally taken as the support price and since the whole matter is politically negotiated, the state has to remain prepared to purchase unlimited quantity from the farmers. The lobby of big farmers with substantial share in the marketable surplus resist any downward revision of procurement price even in the years of good harvest. Thus maintenance of the public distribution system and generation of employment on rural public works account for a big amount of expenditure in the public budget.

In an underdeveloped economy overwhelmingly large proportion of population is employed in the informal or the unorganized sector. On the other hand the public sector has to provide employment to a large section of the work force in the organized areas of activities. Employees in the organized sector have trade unions and their emoluments are determined by collective bargaining. Again, in the organized sector while the private sector firms can be virtually plunge into a stalemate under business loss, public sector units can not cancel or postpone the disbursement of emoluments to the employees. The employees collectively protect their real income against erosion of value under inflation. So expenditure of the government increases as a result of rise in the emoluments of the employees in the organized sector.

We have already emphasized the special role of the foodgrains sector and have also referred to the practice of division of the economy into the foodgrains and the nonfoodgrains sectors in the literature on economic development. In a labour surplus economy foodgrains account for major part of consumption expenditure of a very large section of the total population. In the absence of employment opportunities and low income a large section of population might be forced to forego their basic needs of food and the demand for food may be low as a result. Under inelastic demand for food in this situation rise in the price of food may lead to deficiency in demand in the nonfoodgrains sector of the economy. Under given technology rate of growth of population sets the limit to the maximal rate of growth in a one sector growth model. The rate of growth of foodgrains can be taken as the limiting factor on the maximal growth with stable prices in a two sector model of a labour surplus economy.

Foodgrains are supplied to the market by a very large number of farmers. Even if the supply is taken to come from farmers with large volumes of marketable surplus, the total number of such farmers must be very large in an underdeveloped economy. Left to themselves the farmers would constitute a competitive market. In a labour surplus economy, under scarcity of land and foodgrains, returns to capital and land would be high in a free market. But given the large number of farmers with the homogeneous commodity of marketable surplus of foodgrains of any type, no farmer can independently command a market power. Intervention of the government for provision of food to the large section of population leads to formation of a farmers' lobby as a political force. The foodgrains market can be taken as a competitive market. Due to homogeneity of the product the farmers can unite into a strong political lobby in order to promote their interest in their negotiation with the state.[4]

Question arises about the nature of the nonfoodgrains market. Nonfoodgrains consists of various types of commodities and homogeneity of product can not be assumed in this case. In the non-agricultural sector informal types of business may account for a large section of employment and a fairly good share of the product in a labour surplus economy. The raw materials of the nonfoodgrains producing units in the informal sector, like yarn for weaving cloth, may be taken to come from the production units in the organized sector. Due to heterogeneity of products, the producer of neither the organized sector nor the informal nonfoodgrains production units can form a single political lobby. But the different producers in the organized sector may be taken to independently wield market power. Instead of a competitive market the producers in this case may be taken to operate under oligopoly with conjectural variation in prices. Any producer would not think of unilaterally changing the price. But under a common exogenous event like rise in the rate of tax or increase in the cost of energy a firm may raise the price of the product without any fear of losing market.[5] In the similar way a rise in the wage rate following from a rise in the price of foodgrains may be taken as a common cause for raising the price of the products in the nonfoodgrains market.

III

Relationship between rate of growth of foodgrains and the rate of growth of the nonfoodgrain output under stable prices was demonstrated by Kalecki. This approach was of a very general nature. The effect of the relationship among the growth rates on the price level and the distribution of income was indicated without any specification of details of the mechanism of functioning of the various constituent markets. In the following presentation the details of relationship between the rates of growth and the price level are worked out under certain explicit assumptions. These assumptions are derived from the characteristics of a labour-surplus economy discussed in the previous section. In a number of approaches to the study of effect of scarcity of foodgrains on the price level of the economy, analysis were done in a comparative static framework.[6] But in such cases the imbalance would arise as a problem of time lag, arising out of relationship between variables related to different periods of time. A dynamic process analysis is appropriate methodology for the analysis of the particular problem under consideration. Such a methodology was followed in its essential elements by Kalecki. The following is an elaboration of that elementary approach. In the following exercise foodgrains sector is identified with agriculture and the nonfoodgrain sector is identified with manufacturing.

There are two markets. One for foodgrains and the other for manufactured goods. Foodgrains are demanded by the labourers employed in the manufacturing sector. The foodgrains market is assumed to be a competitive market. The quantity of foodgrains demanded by a representative labourer in the manufacturing sector at time 't' (q^a_{dt}), is a function of the price of foodgrains, (p^a_t), and the real wage of the labourer in the manufacturing sector, (w_b). The form of the function is taken as follows.

$$q^a_{dt} = A(p_t^a)^{-\eta_d}(w_b)^{v_d} \qquad \ldots\ldots(1)$$

Here η_d is the price-elasticity of demand and v_d is the income-elasticity of demand for foodgrains. These are taken as parameters and 'A' is a constant. The ratio of dependent population to gainfully employed population is taken to be given in this exercise. So, the rates of growth of the two would be identical in any sector. The population dependent on the manufacturing sector and performing as demanders of foodgrains is N^b_t, and is assumed to increase at the rate 'n' over time. So, $N_t^b = N_0^b(e)^{nt}$. Total demand for foodgrains is,

$$D^a_t = q_{dt}{}^a . N^b_t = [AN^b_o(e)^{nt}](p^a_t)^{-\eta_d}(w_b)^{v_d} \qquad ......(2)$$

At a given price of foodgrains and a given real wage, the rate of growth of demand of foodgrains is $\hat{D}_a = n$.

Proportion of foodgrains output marked by a representative farmer with marketable surplus depends on the price in the following manner.

$$q^a_{st} = h(p^a_t)^{\eta s} \qquad ......(3)$$

Where η_s is the elasticity of proportion of marketed surplus with respect to price. h and η_s are parameters, and $h(p^a_t)^{\eta s} < 1$. The aggregate output of foodgrains, $S_t^{a'}$ is assumed to increase at an exogenously given rate 'm'. So,

$$S_t^{a'} = H(e)^{mt} \qquad ......(4)$$

Aggregate amount of marketable surplus offered as supply of foodgrains to the market, S_t^a, in this case should be,

$$S_t^a = [h.H(e)^{mt}](p_t^a)^{\eta s} = B(e)^{mt}(p_t^a)^{\eta s} \qquad ......(5)$$

At a given price of foodgrains $\hat{S}_t^a = m$.

In a competitive market of foodgrains the market is cleared in equilibrium. So,

$$D_t^a = S_t^a \qquad ......(6)$$

Taking logarithm of both sides and eliminating log p_t^a, we get,

$$\log p^a_t = \frac{\{\log(AN_o{}^b) - \log B\} + (n - m)t + v_d \log w_b}{\eta_d + \eta_s}$$

Differentiating both sides of above with respect of time, 't', we get the rate of change of price level p as follows:

$$\hat{p}_1{}^a = \frac{n - m + v_d \hat{w}_b}{\eta_d + \eta_s}$$

Here a distinction has to be made between the direct effect of a rise in price on the real wage and the effect of collective bargaining, induced by a rise in the price of foodgrains, on the real wage. In the second case collective bargaining neutralizes the effect of rise in price on the cost of living of people dependent on wage income in the manufacturing sector. If the time lag in wage revision corresponding to the rise in the cost of living is ignored, the real wage would remain as given. If 'n' and 'm' are respectively replaced by $\hat{D}_t^a$ and $\hat{S}_t^a$, the expression for the rate of change of price of foodgrains in (6) would be as given below.

$$\hat{p}_t^a = \frac{\hat{D}_t^a - \hat{S}_t^a}{\eta_d + \eta_s} \qquad \text{......(7)}$$

In the next stage let us introduce relationships between the inputs and the outputs of the two sectors. In a labour surplus economy at a given state of technology output of foodgrains would depend upon capital and technology in that sector. However, taking a general form of production function in the foodgrains sector total output $S_t^{a'}$ may be expressed as,

$$S_t^{a'} = \phi\,(K_t^a,\ N_t^a,\ t) \qquad \text{......(8)}$$

At a given price of foodgrains rate of growth of marketable surplus $\hat{S}^a$ and the rate of growth of output $\hat{S}^{a'}$ are equal and both of them may be expressed as $g_a = m$. From the above production function such rate of change may be expressed as follows.

$$m = g_a = \hat{N}^a{}_t\, \xi_a \qquad \text{......(9)}$$

Here $\hat{N}^a{}_t$, is the rate of change of employment in the foodgrains sector and ξ_a is the ratio of relative change in foodgrains output to relative change in employment in this sector.

$$\xi_a = \frac{m}{\hat{N}^a{}_t} = \frac{\phi_K \hat{K}^a{}_t}{\phi}.\frac{\hat{K}^a{}_t}{\hat{N}^a{}_t} + \frac{\phi_n N^a{}_t}{\phi} + \frac{\phi_t}{\phi}.\frac{1}{\hat{N}^a{}_t} \qquad \text{......(10)}$$

Employment in the foodgrains producing sector $N^a{}_t$ is related to the total employment in the economy. Let $N^b{}_t$ be the employment in the manufacturing sector. Under proportionality between dependent population and gainfully employed population in every sector it is immaterial whether total population or total number of gainfully employed population $N^a{}_t + N^b{}_t$ is taken as a variable. So the rate of growth of employment in the foodgrains producing sector may be taken as a proportion of that of the total population, $\hat{N}^a{}_t = \gamma\hat{N}$, where γ is the elasticity of employment in the foodgrains sector with respect to the total population N_t. Under a process of industrialization in an underdeveloped labour surplus economy, it is likely that $\gamma < 1$. So the rate of growth of output in the foodgrains sector in (9) may be expressed as,

$$g_a = \xi_a.\gamma.\hat{N}_t \qquad \text{......(11)}$$

Let the production function in the nonfoodgrains sector be expressed as $Q_t = F(K^b_t, N^b_t, t)$ where Q_t is the output, K^b_t is the capital and N^b_t the quantity of labour in that sector. Let g_b be the rate of growth of output and ξ_b be the ratio of the relative change in output of that sector to the relative change in employment in that sector. So, $n = \hat{N}^b_t$ may be expressed as,

$$n = \frac{g_b}{\xi_b} \qquad \text{......(12)}$$

Henceforth, ξ_b will be designated as the elasticity of output with respect to employment in the manufacturing sector under given factor proportions. Incorporating the relationships in (9) and (12) into (7), the rate of change in the price of foodgrains would be as follows.

$$\hat{p}^a = \frac{\frac{g_b}{\xi_b} - \xi_a \gamma \hat{N}}{\eta_d + \eta_s} \qquad \text{......(13)}$$

Under steady state growth $\hat{p}^a = 0$. The condition of steady state growth, which is a situation of proportional growth, can be satisfied under the conditions of constant returns to scale in every sector. In the absence of technological change ξ_a and ξ_n will be respectively equal to 1. Labour will be proportionately distributed between the two sectors, so γ will also be equal to 1. All these together yields the familiar condition of the steady state growth $\hat{g}_b = \hat{N}$ from (13) and $\hat{g}_a = \hat{N}$ from (11). Derivation of the condition of steady state growth for a structural macroeconomic model like the one of Kalecki does not have any significance. A study of the effects of changes in the productivities of labour and that of the allocation of labour between the two sectors would be much more useful for a developing economy. Thus for a given $\hat{N}$ as g_b decreases the rate of growth of effective demand decreases and the price level of foodgrains would be dampened. With rising ξ_a or ξ_b or both $\hat{p}^a$ tends to fall. In order to maintain the price level of foodgrains or even to generate a small rise in it the government would have to increase procurement of foodgrains in situations of rising productivities in the two sectors. This amounts to an increase in government expenditure. So as productivities of labour in the various sectors rise government expenditure also rises.

IV

Let the market in the manufacturing sector be assumed to be oligopolistic. Here the competitors are assumed to determine the prices of their products on the basis of conjectures about the price behaviour of the rival firms.[7] Let us further assume that a limited number of firms are producing and supplying heterogeneous products. These products, although heterogeneous, have a certain degree of substitutability and are competitive in demand. Let the total number of firms be s. Let $D_i(p_1, \ldots, p_s)$ be the quantity demanded of the product of firm i, and it depends on the prices of the whole range of products, p_i, i =1, … ,s, produced and sold in the manufacturing sector, $\frac{\partial D_i}{\partial p_j} \geq 0$ for $j \neq i$ and $\frac{\partial D_i}{\partial p_j} < 0$. Let $C_i(Q_i)$ be the total total cost of production and Q_i be the amount of output supplied by the firm i. Marginal cost $\frac{\partial C_i}{\partial Q_i}$ is positive and increasing. But one thing to be considered here is that over the long period appropriate organizational and technological changes are made in order to neutralize the effect of rising marginal cost. Unless this was possible per unit cost of production would rise indefinitely with growth of output of the manufacturing sector. Such an indefinitely rising phenomenon of cost of manufacturing would halt the process of growth in the sector. So as a more plausible case the marginal cost curve is assumed to shift continuously to the right with time.

An oligopolistic firm under conjectural variation of price of product seeks to maximize profit. The profit function of a firm is given below.

$$\pi_i = p_i Q_i(p_1, \ldots, p_s) - C_i(Q_i(p_1, \ldots p_s))$$

The condition of maximum profit of the respective firms obtained by differentiating π_is with respect to the respective p_is and equating them to zero are as follows:

$$(p_1 - \frac{\partial C_1}{\partial Q_1})(\frac{\partial Q_1}{\partial p_1} + \frac{\partial Q_1}{\partial p_2} \cdot \frac{\partial p_2}{\partial p_1} + \ldots + \frac{\partial Q_1}{\partial p_s} \cdot \frac{\partial p_s}{\partial p_1}) + Q_1(p_1, \ldots, p_s) = 0$$

$$\ldots \quad \ldots \quad \ldots \quad \ldots \quad \ldots \quad \ldots \quad \ldots$$

$$(p_s - \frac{\partial C_s}{\partial Q_s})(\frac{\partial Q_s}{\partial p_1} \cdot \frac{\partial p_1}{\partial p_s} + \frac{\partial Q_s}{\partial p_s} \cdot \frac{\partial p_2}{\partial p_s} + \ldots + \frac{\partial Q_s}{\partial p_s}) + Q_s(p_1, \ldots, p_s) = 0$$

In equilibrium, $Q_i = D_i$ for any i, so the typical form of the first order condition for profit maximization would be,

$$(p_i - \frac{\partial C_i}{\partial Q_i})(\frac{\partial Q_i}{\partial p_i} + \sum_{\substack{i=I \\ i \neq j}}^{s} \frac{\partial Q_i}{\partial p_j} \cdot \frac{\partial p_j}{\partial p_i}) + Q_i(p_1, \ldots, p_s) = 0$$

These s number of equations give solutions for the s number of equilibrium prices for as many commodities. If $\frac{\partial C_i}{\partial D_i}$ remain given in the long run, the solutions of the prices p_is for i = 1, ... s are homo geneous of degree zero in demand D_is. The marginal cost $\frac{\partial C_i}{\partial D_i}$ can be taken as given in the long run for the reasons given above. Here the degree of monopoly for any firm producing a product k is,

$$\frac{p_k}{\partial C_k/\partial D_k} = I - \frac{D_K}{\partial C_k/\partial D_k \left(\sum_{j=1}^{s} \frac{\partial D_K}{\partial p_j} \cdot \frac{\partial p_j}{\partial p_k} \right)}$$

Let the marginal cost of a firm, which is an incremental on the prime cost be proportional to the cost of labour. If $w^m{}_b$ is the money wage rate in the manufacturing sector and λ_k is the factor that combines the weights of labour and raw materials required per unit of output, degree of monopoly, $\frac{p_k}{\partial C_k/\partial D_k} = \frac{p_k}{\lambda_k w_b} = (1 + \mu_k)$. In equilibrium p_ks are homogeneous of degree zero in D_ks, $\frac{\partial C_k}{\partial D_k}$ being given, degree of monopoly $(1+\mu_k)$ can be taken as given. Let us assume a degree of monopoly μ for the entire manufacturing sector. This is based on very common assumptions about aggregation of the manufacturing sector. Let the price per unit of the aggregated product of the manufacturing sector be p^b, and money wage rate in that sector be $w^m{}_b$ and λ is the general weight of labour and raw materials in the total cost. Following the above arguments the price equation of the manufacturing sector can be taken as follows.

$$p^b = (1 + \mu)\lambda w^m{}_b \qquad ......(14)$$

If the entire manufacturing sector is taken as an organized sector, labourers in this sector are to be assumed as organized under trade unions. The organized labour is assumed to protect its real wage against inflation. In the following, two alternative assumptions are made about determination of money wage by collective bargaining. In one case we assume that the money wage rate is adjusted to the price of foodgrains. Thus,

$$w^m{}_b = \beta p^a \qquad ......(15)$$

Substituting (15) into (14), the rate of change of price level of the manufactured goods will have an expression as follows.

$$\hat{p}^b = \hat{p}^a \text{ and } \frac{p^b}{p^a} = (1+\mu)\lambda\beta$$

Alternatively if we assume that money wage is adjusted to a weighted aggregate of prices of foodgrains and manufactured goods, the expressions for of money wage rate, w^m_b, and price level, p, will be as follows.

$$w^m_b = \beta p, \; p = (p^a)^{\alpha} (p^b)^{(1-\alpha)} \quad \text{.....(16)}$$

Here α and $(1 - \alpha)$ are the weights in a multiplicative formula of index number. In such a case the relationship between p^b and p^a as derived from (14) and (16) will be as given below.

$$\frac{p^b}{p^a} = [(1 + \mu)\lambda\beta]^{1/\alpha} \quad \text{.......(17)}$$

In the sketch of a model for growth with stability developed by Kalecki the analysis was carried out in terms of two basic equations. These were as follows. If the rate of increase of demand for foodgrains is c_n, rate of growth of population is q and the rate of growth of national income is r, and e is the income elasticity of demand for foodgrains, for price stability in the foodgrains market the following relationship should be satisfied.

$$c_n = q + e(r - q), \; e < 1 \quad \text{......(18)}$$

Here, supply is taken to be forthcoming to match this growth in demand and stability in the price level is satisfied as a consequence. This particular equation can be derived as a special case of equation (2). If we start from equation (2), the equation of aggregate demand for foodgrains, and replace the real wage w_b by per capita real income, y, we get,

$$D^a_t = (AN_0(e)^{nt}(p^a)^{-nd}(y)^{vd}$$

Taking logarithmic derivative of the above with respect of time we get,

$$\hat{D}^a_t = n - \eta_d \hat{p}^a + {}^{vd}\hat{y}$$

Under stable prices, $\hat{p}^a = 0$. So the above expression becomes, $\hat{D}^a_t = n + {}^{vd}\hat{y}$. If Y is national income then, $y = \frac{Y}{N}$ and $\hat{y} = g - n$. So the expression for the rate of growth of demand for foodgrains becomes,

$$\hat{D}^a_t = n + v_d (g - n) \quad \text{......(19)}$$

This is exactly the equation, in terms of a different set of symbols in Kalecki, shown as equation (18) above. The other basic equation of Kalecki, $c = r_0 + c_0 (r - c_0)$, is a relationship between rate of growth of consumption c and the rate of growth of national income r, with respect to a pair of initial values.

The idea of growth of foodgrains as taken by Kalecki represents a special case of the model developed under Section I of this chapter. In Kalecki no price response of the marketable surplus function was assumed and the exogenously given rate of growth of output of foodgrains was required to match the growth in demand. In that case, the supply function of marketable surplus of foodgrains in equation (5), $S^a_t = [h(p^a_t)^{\eta s}]. H(e)^{mt}$ would reduce to $S^a_t = h. H(e)^{mt}$ for $\eta_s = 0$. The behaviour of supply response is absent in Kalecki. Kalecki stated "c_n (here taken as the rate of growth of output of foodgrains– m) is directly affected by the institutional barriers to the development of agriculture."[8]

Kalecki took c_n as the rate of increase of demand for necessities. But by necessities he particularly meant 'staple food', the production of which is limited by feudal landlordship and domination of peasants by merchants and moneylenders.

In an elaboration of the analysis of Kalecki, E.V.K. FitzGerald also took the rate of growth of 'industrial employment' in place of the rate of growth of population.[9] In equation (23) in the approach of FitzGerald, for given relative prices of foodgrains and the manufactured consumer goods, described as 'non-necessities', the corresponding relationship was as follows.

$$\alpha_1 = \alpha' - (1 - \alpha)\beta \qquad \text{......(20)}$$

α_1 = Rate of growth of output of foodgrains, α' = warranted industrial growth, and β rate of growth of productivity of labour in the sector of 'non-necessities'. Thus, if $\alpha' - \beta$ is taken as the rate of growth of employment in the sector of 'non-necessities', the above expression of FitzGerald can be reformulated as,

$$\alpha_1 = (\alpha' - \beta) + \alpha. [\alpha' - (\alpha' - \beta)]$$

But in this presentation α is the weight of the deflator $p = (p^a)\alpha (p^b)^{(1-\alpha)}$ as in (16) above. According to the formulation of Kalecki e is income elasticity of demand for foodgrains and not the share of foodgrains in total consumption expenditure. But in FitzGerald 'α' which he took in place of 'e' is the weight of foodgrains in the consumption expenditure and it does not stand for the elasticity of the formula of Kalecki.

Kalecki had presented a simple model in terms of the rates of growth of the foodgrains and that of the entire economy, in order to demonstrate the effect of disproportionality in the rates of growth on the distribution of income. Here the limit of the rate of growth at stable prices is determined by the rate of growth of the 'staple food' item. A higher rate of growth of the economy than what is warranted by the rate of growth of 'staple food' would lead to rise in the prices of 'staple food'. Kalecki in his analysis of economic growth of a developing country was mainly interested in the effect of rate of growth of national income on the price of the 'staple food' and consequently on the distribution of income.

In Kalecki it is not the rate of growth as such but the relative rates of growth between the 'staple food' and the rest of the economy which is the matter of concern. In the present article, according to equation (13), $\hat{p} > 0$ if $g_b/g_a > \xi_b$. So the crucial parameter in this analysis is the elasticity of output with respect to employment in the manufacturing sector. Following the specification of a labour surplus economy as given in the beginning of this chapter the effect of a situation like $g_b/g_a > \xi_b$ on the distribution of income can be demonstrated very easily.

Let us consider the distribution of income between labourers in the informal sector, labourers in the organized sector and the rest of the population who do not earn their income from labour. The third group can be treated as surplus earners and may comprise of the industrial capitalists, big landowners and the financiers. The labourers in the organized sector are also assumed to realize and protect a share in the surplus through their power of collective bargaining. In such a situation, with the help of the identity of total income and its shares a direct relation between $\hat{p}^a$ and the income of the pure surplus earners can be demonstrated as follows. Let W_a be the total money wage of labourers in the informal sector, W_b be the total money income consisting of pure wage and share of surplus of the labourers in the organized sector and S_R be the nominal income of the pure surplus earners. If Y is the national income in money terms then the income distribution identity can be written as,

$$Y \equiv W_a + W_b + S_R \qquad \text{......(21)}$$

Let the national income in real terms, that is at constant prices be $\overline{Y} = \frac{Y}{p}$. Then the above identity can be rewritten as,

$$\overline{Y} \equiv \frac{W_a}{p} + \frac{W_b}{p} + \frac{S_R}{p} \qquad \text{......(22)}$$

In the discussion of distribution of income the sectors are being divided into informal and organized. Agriculture as well as portions of manufacturing, trade, transport and services together constitute the informal sector. As a simplification that is being made in this article foodgrains production and a part of manufacturing is taken to constitute the informal sector. The organized sector here is being distinguished from the informal sector by the power of the labourers of the former to protect their income by collective bargaining. As has been indicated already, the labourers in the organized sector might be earning under their income designated as wage a share in the surplus. Thus collective bargaining in this case is a means to protect the per capita earning in real terms of the employees consisting of wage proper and surplus in the organized sector. If there is any labour organization in the informal sector it may at most get a protection of their money wage due to the common phenomenon of downward inflexibility of the money wage rate. The total population of the labourers and their dependents, under given uniform dependency ratio, be divided between the informal and the organized sectors in the proportions k and (1-k). Nonwage income or surplus is assumed to arise in both the foodgrains and manufacturing sectors.

The identity (22) is manipulated below to show that even if relative prices p^a/p^b remains unchanged, but $g_b / g_a > \xi_b$ and p^a rises, the share of surplus in national income will rise at the cost of the share of wage income in the informal sector. In his formulation of the problem of Kalecki, Fitz Gerald derived a relationship between the rates of growth of demand for foodgrains α_1, that of national income α' and the population growth $(\alpha' - \beta)$ as follows:

$$\alpha_1 = (\alpha' - \beta) + \alpha \, . \, [\alpha' - (\alpha' - \beta)]$$

He took it to be the same as the relationship between the rate of growth of foodgrains, c_n, rate of growth of national income r and the rate of growth of population q of Kalecki given below.

$$c_n = q + e\,(r - q)$$

But actually these two expressions have a fundamental difference in the completely different connotations of α and e. There is greater difference in the analytical implications of these two equations. The equation of FitzGerald holds under given relative prices of the foodgrains and the manufactured goods. But the relationship of Kalecki holds only as long as the price level of foodgrains remains given. Thus, even under given relative prices the equation of Kalecki will be violated under rising prices of foodgrains. The principal purpose of the model of Kalecki was to show the effect of rise in price of foodgrains on the distribution of income. The conclusion of Kalecki about the effect of rise in price of foodgrains on the distribution of income is derived in the following analysis.

$$\overline{Y} \equiv \frac{W_a}{p^a} \cdot \frac{p^a}{p} + \frac{W_b}{p} + \frac{S_R}{p}$$

$$\equiv \frac{1}{p^a}\left(\frac{w_a}{k.\,N_0(e)^{nt}}\right).k.\,N_0(e)^{nt}.\;\frac{p^a}{p} + \left(\frac{W_b}{p(1\text{-}k).N_0(e)^{nt}}\right).(1\text{-}k)N_0(e)^{nt} + \frac{S_R}{p}$$

$N_t = N_0(e)^{nt}$ is the total population. The portion of population dependent on wage income in the informal sector is $k.\,N_0(e)^{nt}$. The portion of population dependant on the employees remuneration in the organized sector is $(1 - k)N_0(e)^{nt}$.

Thus $w^m{}_a = \left(\frac{w_a}{k.\,N_0(e)^{nt}}\right)$ is the money wage per capita in the informal sector.

$\beta = w_b = \left(\frac{W_b}{p(1\text{-}k)N_0(e)^{nt}}\right)$ is the remuneration per capita in the organized sector in real terms. $\frac{p^b}{p^a} = [(1 + \mu)\lambda\beta]^{1/}\alpha$ is the given ratio of prices according to equation (17). Substituting these expressions in the above identity, it becomes,

$$\overline{Y} \equiv \frac{w^m{}_a}{p^a}\left(\frac{p^a}{p}\right).k.N_0(e)^{nt} + w_b\,(1\text{-}k)N_0(e)^{nt} + \frac{S_R}{p}$$

Taking the derivative of above with respect to time at a given general price level, we get the following expressions.

$$g \equiv \frac{1}{\overline{Y}} \cdot \frac{d\overline{Y}}{dt}$$

$$=\frac{1}{\overline{Y}}\left(W_a{}^m.\frac{p^a}{p}\right)\frac{1}{p^a}.\,k\,.\,N_0(e)^{nt}.\left[n-\frac{1}{p^a}.\frac{dp^a}{dt}\right]+\frac{W_b}{\overline{Y}}.\,n(1-k)N_0(e)^{nt}+\frac{d\left(\frac{S_R}{p}\right)}{dt}.\frac{1}{\overline{Y}}$$

$$g\equiv\frac{W_a}{Y}(n-\hat{p}^a)+n(1-k)\frac{W_b}{X}+\left(\frac{\hat{S}_R}{p}\right).\left(\frac{S_R}{Y}\right) \qquad \text{......(23)}$$

Here, $x=\dfrac{\overline{Y}}{N_0(e)^{nt}}$, that is per capita income in real terms in the economy. The identity (23) shows that for any g the rate of increase of surplus in real terms rises with p^a. In a growing economy the rate of increase of surplus in real terms is always positive. But this rate of increase of surplus will be higher at the expense of the share of labourers in the informal sector under rising prices of foodgrains.

If a high rate of growth of the manufacturing sector was sought as a matter of policy by the state and $g_b > \xi_b.g_a$ is sought as an outcome of deliberate decision making, $\hat{p}^a > 0$ is an expected consequence. In this case $\left(\dfrac{\hat{S}_R}{p}\right)$ will rise. But the surplus earners might fritter away the additional surplus on luxuries. In such a situation in order to sustain the higher rate of growth which was planned by the state, Kalecki recommended mobilization of larger investible resources through taxation of the additional surplus.

V

In this article the basic condition for achieving growth with stability in a labour surplus economy as propounded by Kalecki has been rigorously derived from an analytical model. Similar exercise was done by FitzGerald earlier. But the conclusion of FitzGerald did not conform to the conclusion of Kalecki. Moreover Kalecki was mainly interested in demonstrating the effect of a growth without balance in the supply of foodgrains, on the distribution of income. Disproportionately high rate of growth than what is warranted by the supply of foodgrians would lead to rise in nonwage income. Kalecki would admit such a situation as a temporary measure if the additional nonwage income could be channelized into investment. These aspects of Kalecki's theory of growth of a labour surplus developing economy have been derived from a set of more detailed analytical assumptions in this article. In course of detail analytical formulation of the theory of Kalecki in this article the additional information that has been gained is a relationship between the rates of growth in the foodgrains sector g_a and the nonfoodgrains sector g_b and the elasticity of output with respect to employment in the nonfoodgrains sector ξ_b. A high rate of growth of g_b would lead to rise in p^a and increase in the share of nonwage income. Such a high rate of growth, on the other hand, can be sustained through larger investment mobilized out of the additional nonwage income.

REFERENCES

1. Kalecki, M. (1976) — *Essays on Developing Economics,* Harvester Press, Brighton. (This is a collection of essays published since the midfifties)
2. Eswaran, Mukesh and Ashok Kotwal (1992) — "Why Might Poverty be Impervious to Industrial Progress ?", in Kaushik Basu and Pulin Nayak edited *Development Policy and Economic Theory,* Oxford University Press, Delhi.
3. Bose, Amitava (1989) — "Short Period Equilibrium in a Less Developed Economy" in Mihir Rakshit edited *Studies in the Macroeconomics of Developing Countries,* Oxford University Press, Delhi.
4. Gupta, Anupam and Amita Majumdar (1994) — "Effect of Tax on Price Level in a Two-Sector Macroeconomic Framework", in *State Bank of India Monthly Review,* Bombay, December. (Contains statistically significant results in favour of the hypotheses that the foodgrains market is competitive and dominated by a strong political lobby in India).
5. Break, G.F. (1974) — "The Incidence and Economic Effects of Taxation" in the Volume of A. Blinder and others. *The Economics of Public Finance,* Brookings Institution, Washington D.C.
6. Basu, Kaushik (1984) — *The Less Developed Economy,* Oxford University Press, Delhi, Chapter 3, Section 2..
7. Varian, Hal R. (1984) — *Microeconomic Analysis,* W.W. Norton and Company, New York, Second Edition, Chapter 2, Section 2.10.
8. Kalecki, M. — *op. cit.,* p. 104.
9. FitzGerald, E.V.K. (1988) — "Kalecki on Planned Growth in the Mixed Economy", *Development and Change,* Vol. 19, pp. 33-52.

3

Inclusive Growth and Employment: On the Approach to the Eleventh Five Year Plan

DURGADAS ROY

Introduction

"Given the Sheer Magnitude to workers currently tied to land, as compared to those in the organized sector, this issue could really dwarf the ones usually raised in discussions regarding labour market flexibility, (p. 59, Approach Paper to the 11th Five Year Plan, Planning Commission) .... While employment growth has grown faster than before, with the demographic dynamics and high labour force participation also went up marginally.. slowing down of the growth in agriculture could be one of the main reasons for the growth in unemployment rate (p. 14, paragraph 1.46, Economic Survey 2006-07).

.... Putting more people in productive and sustainable job Lies at the heart of "Inclusive Growth." But such success, primarily will depend on the success in achieving and maintaining high growth (p. 15, paragraph 1.56, Economic Survey, 2006-07).

The importance of employment creation in the present set up in India can be seen in the very formation of the UPA Government, while the promise of "National Employment Guarantee" became the kingpin of the programme. At the start of the economic reforms, the strategy was that since the controlled market economy had restricted normal investment, growth potential had not been realized fully and building a modern, export-oriented, globally-competitive economy would bring in the best of employment opportunities for every one.

But the fact is that the growth potential has not brought with it the fruits of enhanced earning for a large number of people, in particular, the rural folk. Employment opportunities have come, but for a few. After more than a decade of reforms, 2006-07 Economic Survey on Employment says – "In what follows, we will review the employment trends in the last two decades and bring out some of the challenges for the recent policy initiatives on employment" (Economic Survey, p. 111).

The impressive economic growth and the economic reforms and the policies of the last two decades being vigorously followed also lead many to fear that the high growth might be exclusionary in nature and be characterized by 'jobless growth' : That the growth of the Indian economy has been 'exclusive and there is a need to make it 'inclusive' is, in fact, long felt (e.g. K.N. Raj in Mody 2006). The Planning Commission has also realized that economic growth has failed to be sufficiently inclusive, particularly after the mid-1990s. The Planning Commission has noted in the Approach to the Eleventh Five-Year Plan, "While the performance reflects the strength of the economy in many areas, it is also true that large parts of our population are still to experience a decisive improvement in their standard of living. .... Far two many people still lack access to basic services such as health, education, clean drinking water and sanitation facilities without which they can not be empowered to claim their share in the benefits of growth. These problems are more severe in some states than in others, and in general they are especially severe in rural areas". (The Planning Commission 2006, p. 1).

Eleventh Plan

'Inclusive Growth' has become the new 'mantra' of development. After pursuing a consistent policy of vigorous growth ever since the economic reforms of 1990s in the country, as it was believed that "there cannot be 'inclusive growth' without growth itself (Ministry of Finance 2007). Thus India has adopted as recommended by the World Bank, (2006) a development strategy of inclusive growth and set "faster and more inclusive growth" as the focus of Eleventh Five Year Plan (2007-12). The World Bank has pointed out that inclusive growth (2006) "the only sure means for converting the deeply ingrained regional imbalances, inequities and for consolidating economic gains," as inclusive growth is the growth "with emphasis not only on the distribution of income and economic gains but also on the security, vulnerability, empowerment, and sense of full participation that people may enjoy in social life."

The Planning Commission are aiming at faster growth against a background of exceptionally strong performances. The average growth rate in the last few years of the 10th plan is about 8 per cent and the planners are aiming at a gradual acceleration from current level of 8 per cent around 10 per cent at the end of the 11th plan in 2011-12. In the words of Planners, "The Indian Economy has demonstrated that rapid growth is possible in an environment of highly plurastic and vigorously participative democracy." This is not to say that the tradition to 10 per cent growth is an assured outcome. It is feasible but will happen only if we can address some critical constraints.

A process of inclusive growth would imply one where in the distribution of income moves in favour of the poor as a part and parcel of the growth process itself. And, in the Indian social context, inclusiveness in the economic sense has to be accompanied by socio-political processes and simultaneously systematically break the social-political processes and simultaneously systematically break the social barriers of discrimination based on caste, gender, religion and ethnicity. If this is what is meant by inclusive growth, the notwithstanding the high rates of economic growth of the last three years, the UPA Government has failed to deliver despite the presence of favourable conditions.

According to the Report Card, one of the "key components of our strategy of "inclusive growth" is providing a unique social safety net in the shape of the "National Rural Employment Guarantee Programme." But in the Union Budget for 2007-08, the expenditure provision for rural employment has been increased only marginally relative to the decisions to extend the coverage of the rural employment guarantee scheme for 200 to 330 districts. And, in the 200 districts covered in 2006-07, there is little evidence of any close monitoring of the scheme in terms of outcome. Over the last two decades of 1983-94 and 1993-2004, the overall employment growth declined from 2.01 per cent to 1.84 per cent. National Rural Employment Guarantee Programme launched in September 2005 is perhaps the most talked about national level employment generation programme. So far the response to this programme has been mixed with varied experiences of the states in terms of its performances—

for instance, Registration Percentage of 'eligible' households vary from 14.1 per cent in Bihar to 100 per cent in Shivpuri (M.P.). In a recent survey it was found that close to 80 per cent of the rural household were not aware of the fact that after getting the Job Card, one had to apply for getting wage employment. Less than 50 per cent of elected representatives of Panchayats, on an average, have received any input on their roles in implementation of NREGA.

The National Rural Employment Guarantee Scheme has so far posed no problem for the budget. Its allocation is only marginally higher than what was spent in the past by the Government on various rural employment programmes. It is a demand-driven scheme and it has fallen far short of meeting demand in some states. The fund utilization ratio also varies widely across states. The NREGP was enacted in 2005 to provide a minimum guaranteed wage employment of 100 days in every financial year to rural household with unemployed adult members prepared to do unskilled manual work. In the past, public employment programme in India targeted at the poor are generally identified with poverty alleviation. But the NREGA goes beyond poverty alleviation and recognizes employment as a legal right. The NREGP is also listed in the Approach Paper by The Planning Commission as one of the strategies for creating employment. NEGP, as a programme for income support, is, also seen as a mechanism for channelising resources for development of land and water and promoting rural connectivity in conjunction with 'Bharat Nirman', the Backward Region Great Fund and various other infrastructure -oriented projects. The premise is that the projects are to be selected by the panchayats so that they are relevant to the needs of the community. The experience with this programme so far is not commendable. What follows is an evaluation of the scheme based on the report of the grassroots organization.

NREGA

However, it is to be said that the existing institutional arrangement in poor states is not good enough to implement the NREGA in an effective way. It needs to be mentioned that the data provided in the latest report on NREGA published by the ministry of rural development also indicate that the fund utilization ration remains as low as 51 per cent even after the completion of one full year of operation of NREGA. Maharashtra, Gujarat, Punjab, Haryana, Karnataka and Orissa have not yet provided work to more than one-third of the registered households under the scheme. The national average, till October has been pathetic at just over 40. The Scheme's performance has been better in poorer states, than rich states like Punjab which has fallen behind after making an impressive start in 2007.

The NREGA provides for enhancement of livelihood security in rural areas of the country by providing at least 100 days of guaranteed wage employment every year to each household. In 2006-07, about 3.7 crore families (job cards) benefited from the scheme in 200 districts. In 2007 (by November 2007), the scheme covered 5.5 crore households covering 330 districts. In 2006-07, only about 1.83 crore households got employment. Although the programme is not confined to BPL familes, the experience in almost all districts/states is that most BPL families have been able to demand employment under NREGA. At the national level, the demand for employment is about 157 per cent of the number of rural BPL households. It is near 100 per cent or more than that in most of the states. This shows that the programme has reached out to the most needy households in the states where employment demand as a percentage is more than rural BPL households.

Table–1

UPA'S Pet Scheme to Create Employment in Rural Areas Shows Mixed Results: Assets Created Under NREGS : 2007-08

Type of Work	*Works Undertaken*	*Works Completed*	*Ongoing Works*	*Benefit Created (in Lakh)*
Water conservation and water harvesting (CUMT)	347515	94907	252608	960.88
Flood control and protection (KM)	29509	11984	17525	4.49
Micro irrigation works (KM)	57557	14366	43191	0.29
Provision of irrigation facility in land owned by SC/ST (hec)	161508	38355	123153	0.4
Renovation of traditional water bodies (CUMT)	97760	28565	69195	784.7
Land development (hec)	175790	50482	125308	6.65
Drought proofing (hec)	113294	31453	81841	5.55
Rural connectivity (KM)	206398	80472	125926	2.72
Any other activity	41799	20940	20859	

One of the most important features of the growth in employment in the recent decade is the growth of subsidiary status of workers and fall in number of formal full-time workers. There has been growth of regular salaried workers in subsidiary states (subsidiary status workers are non-workers or unemployed engaged in an economic activity for part of the year) in urban areas for both men and women. Now, what has been nature of labour absorption within principal status employment across social groups and educational levels?

Results from the NSSO 55th employment round, 1994-2000, and 61st round, 2004-05, suggest that in spite of the closing of gender gap in literacy, the gains of employment between men and women are strikingly unequal. The results of the NSSO's 61st round large scale quinquential survey on employment and unemployment conduct during 2004-05 throws a lot of light on the heated debate on 'jobless growth' under reforms. The survey results show the annual growth rate of employment, which had declined from 2.1 per cent during 1983-94 to 1.6 per cent during 1993-2000, went up to 2.5 per cent during 1999-2005. While employment has grown faster than before, with the demographic dynamics and higher labour force participation, rate of unemployment (as measured by 'usual principal status') also went up marginally from 2.8 per cent to 3.1 per cent during 1999-2000 to 2004-05. While detailed analysis of the results of the survey is yet to be carried out, slowing down of the growth of agriculture could be one of the main reasons for the growth in the unemployment rate. Furthermore, the worrisome marginal decline in employment in the organized sector between 1994 and 2004, according to the Annual Survey of industry data, has raised some disturbing issues about optimal regulation and incentives.

Employment Pattern

Viewed over the long-term, employment growth slowed slightly in 1993-2004, compared to 1983-93; the slowdown is quite marked in rural India. Employment has grown in urban areas over the last decade, but the nature of this growth and the quality of employment generating need probing. There has been substantial increase in self-employment, much of which is poorly remunerated and for the first time in recent decade in India, there has been decline in the real wage rates of regular salaried workers and urban casual workers.

Further, from the NSSO's 55th round, it can be shown that within the illiterate, 53 per cent self-employed amongst STs are women.

Amongst the self-employed the other groups like SCs, OBCs and others, women are between 42 to 47 per cent. The situation changes drastically, even for middle level education. Self-employed women are as low as 15 to 23 per cent across all social groups. Only 9 to 16 per cent of women have regular salaried jobs level of education across various social groups. And again, on the type of employment across social groups, the employment story is once again not very encouraging. The future of employment in the coming year is seen by the government sectorally in labour intensive manufacturing (food processing, textiles, tourism, hotels, catering, entertainment and construction) and in self-employment programmes. What can we say about the potential of employment in manufacturing? And which policy instruments will turn the manufacturing sector towards 'labour intensive manufacturing? (Ref. 'Citizen's Report on Governance and Development 2007)'. See the Tables.

Table-2

Percentage Distribution of Femal Workers by Social Group and Education Level 2004-05

	ST	*SC*	*OBC*	*Others*	*Total*
ILLITERATE					
Self employed	53.31	42.04	47.54	41.90	46.36
Regular salaried	40.50	43.54	35.67	30.70	37.35
Casual labour	49.58	43.86	47.33	35.35	44.94
Total	**51.21**	**43.18**	**46.95**	**38.99**	**45.32**
BELOW PRIMARY					
Self employed	28.07	14.42	21.46	22.56	21.54
Regular salaried	20.18	19.97	22.87	21.14	21.43
Casual labour	22.61	21.09	24.85	15.87	21.90
Total	**25.36**	**18.57**	**22.73**	**20.71**	**21.66**
PRIMARY					
Self employed	24.87	16.43	21.71	20.63	20.96
Regular salaried	20.88	18.89	13.83	10.07	14.13
Casual labour	24.95	15.01	21.65	15.49	18.84
Total	**24.63**	**16.14**	**20.80**	**17.98**	**19.42**
MIDDLE					
Self employed	23.31	14.92	15.31	16.56	16.25

Contd.

	ST	*SC*	*OBC*	*Others*	*Total*
Regular salaried	16.17	11.11	11.56	09.07	10.79
Casual labour	20.72	12.89	15.68	11.90	14.49
Total	**21.69**	**13.29**	**14.82**	**14.45**	**14.88**
SECONDARY					
Self employed	18.40	09.72	12.61	10.13	11.46
Regular salaried	14.78	13.18	13.48	13.36	13.56
Casual labour	13.73	11.76	11.56	10.41	11.48
Total	**16.75**	**11.43**	**12.75**	**11.07**	**12.02**
HIGHER SECONDARY					
Self employed	15.49	12.76	09.89	08.31	09.49
Regular salaried	17.11	19.23	17.12	18.03	17.80
Casual labour	18.97	10.59	07.41	07.23	09.42
Total	**16.78**	**14.93**	**12.53**	**12.35**	**12.88**
GRADUATE & ABOVE					
Self employed	06.82	09.66	06.29	08.09	07.63
Regular salaried	20.34	15.39	20.08	22.65	21.32
Casual labour	23.81	05.90	04.64	06.49	06.18
Total	**15.41**	**12.75**	**13.53**	**16.31**	**15.24**
ALL					
Self employed	40.61	27.74	28.97	21.07	27.46
Regular salaried	23.40	21.47	18.47	17.77	18.93
Casual labour	40.38	31.59	33.58	23.51	32.28
Total	**39.27**	**28.81**	**28.87**	**20.71**	**27.60**

Source: NSSO 61st Round data, 2004-05.

The above analysis will clearly show that the existing institutional arrangement in poorer states is not good enough to implement the NREGA in an effective way. It should be mentioned here already mentioned in earlier para that the data provided in the latest Report on NREGA published by the ministry of rural development also indicate that the fund utilization ration remains as low as 51 per cent even after the completion of one full year of operation of NREGA. The utilization ratio is also low in poorer states. There is an urgent need for both vertical and horizontal coordination across levels of governments within the states. It is also true that Gram Sabha can play an effective role in the planning, monitoring and also supervision of projects. In many states panchayats

Table-3
Employment and Output Growth in Organized Manufacturing Sector

States	Pre-reform		Post-reform	
	Employment	*Output*	*Employment*	*Output*
Andhra Pradesh	1.25	09.58	00.84	8.21
Madhya Pradesh	1.65	10.65	00.15	7.96
Karnataka	0.73	08.65	03.14	9.26
Haryana	2.15	09.40	04.14	11.94
Gujarat	–0.96	05.93	01.94	11.38
Bihar	0.15	05.70	–2.58	03.84
Assam	0.06	11.21	–0.62	06.32
Tamil Nadu	1.64	07.13	01.97	07.86
Rajasthan	2.33	10.41	01.95	08.93
Punjab	4.27	10.00	01.34	06.07
Orissa	1.40	10.17	–6.06	02.97
Maharashtra	–1.37	06.73	01.64	08.03
West Bengal	–3.46	01.98	–1.65	04.44
Uttar Pradesh	0.15	11.16	–1.63	05.93
Kerala	–1.83	04.97	01.37	09.86
All India	–0.01	07.35	01.11	08.30

Source: Pankaj Vashist, Organized Manufacturing Sector in India: An Inter State Analysis, Un-published M. Phil dissertation, Centre for the Study of Regional Development, JNU, 2006.

do not have the necessary capacity to manage the scheme and capacity building ought to take placed at the panchayat level. There should also be an oversight mechanism to guard against the possibility of the intention of the NREGA scheme being frustrated through 'elite capture' by Panchayats whether by the ruling party cadres or through domination of caste-based politics.

The distribution of the benefits of accelerated over-all growth has been palpably uneven. Inter-class, inter-sectoral and inter-regional disparities have widened; several segments of the socially, especially peasants, and under pri-village social groups feel that they have not benefited much even in absolute terms. There is widespread and growing resentment among these groups at attempts to change policies – subsidies, affirmative action, privatization of health and education and even anti-poverty programmes – to their disadvantages and to promote policies – notably fiscal concessions, special economic zones, forcible acquisition of farm land and land in tribal areas - favouring the emerging new elite. The spread of the Naxalite movement in the tribal belt, large number of farmers' suicides, violent agitations over land acquisitions for Special Economic Zones (SEZs), intensified conflicts over access to land and use of natural resources and the growing confrontation over caste/community reservations in education and jobs are all manifestations of increasing disfunctions in society. The political class is eager to please the new elite in the belief that it will sustain the momentum of high growth and that fast growth will dissolve tensions by bringing prosperity to all classes and regions. However, this has not happened and there is a good reason to be spectical if it will happen in the future.

'Citizens' Report on Governance and Development 2007' – *Social Watch India* has judiciously summarized the NREGP in this way :

'TRENDS IN EMPLOYMENT over the last two decades of 1983-94 and 1993-2005'.

1. The overall employment growth declined from 2.01 per cent to 1.84 per cent.
2. The growth in employment of males is faster in both decades – interestingly though the male employment growth has declined from 2.19 to 1.87 per cent.
3. The female employment growth has infact increased from 1.84 to 1.78 per cent per annum over all. The female employment growth has increased in rural areas (1.3 to 1.55%). While in urban areas, it has declined from 3.36 per cent annum to 3.08 per cent.
4. In urban areas, the employment growth of males has been faster in 1993-2005.
5. Men are growing faster in urban jobs and females are getting more into rural occupations with employment growth much faster in urban areas compared to rural employment.
6. Urban job growth is being maintained at 3 per cent in the two sub periods with rural employment declined from 1.72 per cent to 1.46 per cent per annum between 1983-94 and 1993-2005.

7. Women are getting a proportionately larger share of employment in the now-a-days receding segment of the economy (Report, pp. 64-65).

The future of employment in the coming years is seen by the government sectorally in labour intensive manufacturing (food processing, textiles, tourism, catering, entertainment and construction) and in self-employment programmes. What can you say about the potential of employment in manufacturing ? And which policy instruments will turn the manufacturing sector towards labour intensive manufacturing? What the Approach Paper says about the labour intensive manufacturing is in the following.

Table–4

Employment and Output Growth Inorganized Manufacturing Sector

	Pre-reform		*Post-reform*	
States	*Employment*	*Output*	*Employment*	*Output*
Andhra Pradesh	1.25	09.58	00.84	8.21
Madhya Pradesh	1.65	10.65	00.15	7.96
Karnataka	0.73	08.65	03.14	9.26
Haryana	2.15	09.40	04.14	11.94
Gujarat	–0.96	05.93	01.94	11.38
Bihar	0.15	05.70	–2.58	03.84
Assam	0.06	11.21	–0.62	06.32
Tamil Nadu	1.64	07.13	01.97	07.86
Rajasthan	2.33	10.41	01.95	08.93
Punjab	4.27	10.00	01.34	06.07
Orissa	1.40	10.17	–6.06	02.97
Maharashtra	–1.37	06.73	01.64	08.03
West Bengal	–3.46	01.98	–1.65	04.44
Uttar Pradesh	0.15	11.16	–1.63	05.93
Kerala	–1.83	04.97	01.37	09.86
All India	–0.01	07.35	01.11	08.30

Source: Centre for the Study of Regional Development—Pankaj Vashist, JNU, Delhi.

"Labour intensive mass manufacturing based on relatively lower skill levels provides in opportunity to expand employment in the industrial sector. Confederation has been exceptionally well in industrial sector ..... A Key issue in this context is the need for greater flexibility in some of the labour laws. In particular, there is need to consider appropriate amendments in Section V-B of the Industrial Disputes Act, 1947, to facilitate Exit and Contract labour (Abolition and Regulation Act) to give to the industry the flexibility necessary to compete in international markets." (Report, pp. 65-66).

Citizens' Report further says, 'Overall the strategy of high growth of employment has not been accompanied by high growth of employment. The existing strategy to bring about more 'inclusive growth' does not have much potential to deliver what is being promised. Even though the idea of 'employment guarantee' is a laudable objective in an age and there when the focus in most countries is to kinds of state guarantees, except guarantees on behalf of investors to lenders, the programme is experiencing many challenges that need to be addressed even before the minimalist objectives of this programme can be met. NREGP is more of an income support programme which is intended to help people face the current drought of work and is not instrument for generating employment in the medium to long run.

Review

One major lacunae of the NREGP so far is the complete disconnection between rural infrastructure plans and the NREGP related creation of infrastructure. Some times the question arises, what does NREGP mean for employment? In the past without the NREGA, the government had allocated a higher amount of resources in terms of proportion of GDP for rural employment creation in India. Moreover, in terms of the share of the Central Government Budget, the NREGP scheme has not made much of a difference to governmental expenditure on rural employment programmes. Furthermore, NREG scheme has not been able to provide the employment that would have expected in poor states that has largely to do with implementation and funding.

Inclusive growth is the new clarion call in the Indian political scenario. As more and more people want to participate in India's growth story, the young and restless in rural Bharat want to be part of prosperous India, living as they are, a life diametrically opposite, so, the importance of 'aam aadmi' and his well-being are pre-occupying the corridors of political minds. Many new populist schemes including 'inclusive growth' were initiated, but unfortunately corruption at most levels in the administrative pyramid have seen slippages in the percolation of funds. The Comptroller and Auditor General (CAG) slammed the government's flagship rural employment guarantee scheme. The CAG's six month audit of NREGS has left the political class and the nation as a whole in shock. The reality check conducted in 513 Gram Panchayats in 68 districts across 26 states left behind an interesting statistics that only 3.2 per cent of the registered households could benefit by securing 100 days of employment in year between February 2006 and March 2007. Siphoning off money through fraudulent cards was a common complaint. First Information Reports have now been filled in Madhubani, Bihar, Dhar, M.P. and Chamba, H.P. against those accused of corruption. And this is not all. Ingenious human minds have wrecked havoc on other schemes like Sampoorna Gramin Bazar Yojana, Indira Awas Yojana, Swarnajayanti Gram Swrojgar Yojana and Pradhan Mantri Gram Sadak Yojana. Corruption and inefficiencies have been part and parcel of these schemes.

West Bengal

Coming to West Bengal this tragic episode had brought into fore the fact that the poor in West Bengal in distant corners of the country accepted and internationalized this programme as in other sectors of India as their own. They were demanding, like the demonstrators in Dinhata in Coochbehar, its proper and effective administration which would give them a slightly better income and security of the poor and destitute households. Obviously, such a demand would be treated as inimical to the interests of the 'kulak' lobby which was eager to get cheap labour for maximizing profit. Here we are referring particularly to Dinhata in Coochbehar where many lives were lost for a totally legal demand. Dr. Santosh Merhotra, Advisor (RD), Planning Commission, made a composite comparative table giving statewise prevailing market rates of wages, the NREGA wage and employment provided in percentage.

The table makes a dismal and despairing reading, West Bengal ranks fourth from the bottom in implementing the NREGA. Even states like Chhattisgarh (44.6%), Jharkhand (32.6%) and Uttarakhand (27.4%) are better performers. It is why behind Tamil Nadu (61.1 %). Maharashtra (55.9%), Rajasthan (52.5%) and Punjab (41.7%). West Bengal's performance deteriorated from 14.3 per cent in 2006-07 to 11.8 per cent in 2007-08

Table–5
Wage-Rates in Rural India and NREGA Wage Rates and Numbar of Person Days

States	*Average Daily Wages Rates in Agricultural Occupations in Rural India, 2004-05 (Rs.)*		*NREGA Wage Rates (Rs.)*	*Employment Provided Number of Person Days per Household*	
	Men	*Women*		*2006-07*	*2007-08*
Andhra Pradesh	36.61	27.83	80.00	31.40	27.80
Arunachal Pradesh	–	–	66.00	26.80	00.00
Assam	30.23	15.52	66.00	72.30	23.50
Bihar	45.06	26.24	77.00	35.30	18.30
Gujarat	55.48	30.14	50.00	44.40	31.60
Haryana	57.83	23.35	99.21	47.50	35.70
Himachal Pradesh	12.95	–	75.00	47.10	25.30
Jammu & Kashmir	31.82	–	70.00	26.60	20.20
Karnataka	49.00	27.85	74.00	40.70	41.20
Kerala	55.89	27.99	125.00	20.70	21.00
Madhya Pradesh	40.61	26.54	67.00	68.80	42.60
Maharashtra	52.97	31.90	69.00	41.20	55.90
Manipur	38.66	19.79	81.40	100.00	11.00
Meghalaya	21.44	09.77	70.00	02.50	33.60
Mizoram	–	–	91.00	15.40	41.90
Nagaland	–	–	100.00	46.90	04.90
Orissa	44.86	14.02	70.00	57.30	34.90
Punjab	32.01	–	94.48	49.20	41.70
Rajasthan	44.16	09.45	73.00	84.90	52.50
Sikkim	–	–	85.00	58.90	06.40
Tamil Nadu	60.97	31.23	80.00	26.70	61.10
Tripura	38.18	00.00	60.00	67.40	21.40
Uttar Pradesh	47.49	26.09	100.00	31.90	14.90
West Bengal	44.58	32.35	70.00	14.30	11.80

Contd...

States	*Average Daily Wages Rates in Agricultural Occupations in Rural India, 2004-05 (Rs.)*		*NREGA Wage Rates (Rs.)*	*Employment Provided Number of Person Days per Household*	
	Men	*Women*		*2006-07*	*2007-08*
Chattisgarh	–	–	66.70	55.70	44.60
Jharkhand	–	–	76.68	37.30	32.60
Uttarakhand	–	–	73.00	30.20	27.40
All India	61.23	44.59	–	–	–

Prepared by Santosh Merhotra, Planning Commission of India.

(December). There is a degree of consistency in its non-performance. The ruling class is now dominated by the middle and upper peasantry in the rural areas. It is not in their class interest to implement the NREGA properly which would push up wages from Rs. 44.58 (per male worker) and Rs. 32.35 per female worker to anywhere near Rs. 70 per day which would drastically reduce the profit margin for them.

Against this backdrop, the Planning Commission has done a commendable job by pointing out that a GDP growth rate of round 8.5 per cent is feasible considering the recent performance of the economy as well as its potential. Equally persuasive is its argument that such a growth is necessary to generate the resources for Investment as well as the demand for achieving 'inclusive growth'. For example, agricultural growth of 4 per cent and the high growth of rural non-farm enterprises require massive public investments in rural infrastructure and this high rural growth can be sustained only if adequate demand is generated in the economy through higher GDP growth.

While aiming at faster growth, the 'Approach Paper' also emphases the need for making growth more inclusive and recognizes that this is in many ways more difficult. Inclusiveness may at first glance appear to be only a restatement of distributional objectives which have always been part of planning, most notably a commitment to reducing poverty. Poverty reduction is indeed important, but the concept of 'inclusiveness' goes beyond the narrow objective of poverty reduction. It encompasses a much broader approach to distributional objectives, Distributional objectives are not viewed as an 'add on' to a dominantly growth-oriented strategy. Rather 'inclusiveness' is an integral part of the growth strategy and indeed the structure of growth sought to be achieved is one which is most likely to achieve inclusiveness.

Conclusion

The overall strategy of high growth has not been accompanied by high growth of employment. It can be concluded that the existing strategy to bring about more 'inclusive growth' does not have much potential to deliver what is being promised. NREGP is more of an income-support programme which is indeed intended to help people face the current drought of work and is not an instrument of generating employment in the medium of long run.

REFERENCES

Approach Paper to the Eleventh Five Year Plan; Towards Faster and More Inclusive Growth: The Planning Commission, 2007-2012.

Approach Paper to the Eleventh Five Year Plan – A Spectical Note – D.K. Nashane Economic and Political Weekly: July 22-28, 2006, pp. 3141-3143.

Citizen's Report on Governance and Development 2007 – Social Watch, India.

Dreze, Jean (2004): 'Employment as a Social Responsibility' – The Hindu, 2004.

Dreze, Jean and Amartya Sen (1989): Hunger and Public Action: OUP, Oxford.

Gaiha, Raghav (1997) : 'Rural Public Works and the Poor : The Case of The Employment Guarantee Scheme in India in S., Polachek (ed.): Research in Labour Economics, JAI Press, Connecticut.

Jeemol, Onni, G. Raveendran – 'Growth of Employment (1993-94) to (2004-05) – 'Illusion of Inclusiveness ? EPW, January 20, 2007 (pp. 196-199).

Employment and Unemployment Situation in India 2004-05; NSS 61st Round, Report No. 515-16 (September-October, 2006) – Government of India.

Mody, Ashok (ed.) 2006: 'Inclusive Growth: K.N. Raj on Economic Development' Orient Longman, Hyderabad.

Pinaki Chakravarty: 'Implementation of Employment Guarantee : A Preliminary Appraisal' – EPW, February. 17, 2007, pp. 548-551.

K. Sundaram: 'Employment and Poverty in India, 2000-05', EPW, July 28-August 3, 2007, pp. 3121-3131.

'Employment and Poverty in 1990s. Further results from NSS 55th Round Employment - Unemployment Survey, 1999-2000.

The Economist (2005a) 'Guaranteed to Disappointment : Employing the Indian Poor' – The Economist, 374, January 1, p. 28.

Ravallion, M. and G. Datt (1999); 'When is Growth Pro-Poor? : Evidence from the Diverse Experience of Indian States' – World Bank, Washington DC.

Rinku Murgai, Martin Ravallion – Employment Guarantee in Rural India: What would it cost and How much would it reduce poverty, EPW, July 30 – August 5, 2005 (pp. 3450-3455).

4

Growth and Stability

AMALESH BANERJEE

Contemporary growth theories have opened up different dimensions of growth strategies which the developing and developed countries are pursuing. While endogenous growth model emphasize on intensive cultivation of domestic skill and knowledge for adopting innovation and attaining higher production the open economy model lend support to international cooperation and multilateral trade for rapid growth and development in a neoliberal framework. In an endogenous framework inclusive growth strategy seeks to strike a balance between supply and demand in the over all sectors of the economy in which agriculture, industry and services sectors open the opportunity of income and employment generation. External trade and multinational led capital flow and production structure are the characteristics of exogenous growth pattern. The latter growth strategy remind us the vicissitudes of South-East Asian countries in recent times. As the endogenous growth theories emphasize on human capital development, this is a long-term process heavily loaded with high growth rate of population.

In the early stage of Indian economic development a state of Harrodiam capital - intensive strategy was adopted with the avowed objective of building capital base for rapid development. Over decades the building blocks of heavy and manufacturing industries have been built - up which are now the propelling force of growth. On the other hand, human capital and infrastructure received unequal importance which acted as an inbuilt drag in India economic growth process. At this stage globalization of India economy began as a part of economic reform. The endogenous strategy has yielded place to neo – liberal open economic strategy. Indian economic growth received new impetus under this new strategy of globalization. The experience of tiger countries imparted lessons for India, she followed somewhat cautious approach in liberalizing and globalizing her economy.

Here also the sustainability of the present high rate (9.4%) of growth depends on inclusive programme which again embraces the skill formation, infrastructure development and poverty eradication. The Eleventh Five Year Plan therefore attempts to combine both the endogenous and exogenous strategy. Innovation, infrastructure development and poverty eradication are the key components of the present strategy of India economic growth. It is an inclusive development strategy which emphasizes in lagging regions and social groups through intervention programme.

In this chapter we first explore the relative advantage of exogenous and endogenous techniques in the Section II. India's experience of inclusive growth since reform process started is discussed in the Section III. In the Section IV prospects of India's globalization strategy as a device of rapid growth is examined. Section V deals with the current stabilization policy Section VI draws the conclusion.

II

Endogenous Vs. Exogenous

Endogenous growth implies investment in physical capital so that productivity of human capital can be enhanced. Accumulation of knowledge following greater emphasis on R & D is the fundamental basis of growth. Accumulation of knowledge, as such itself is of no importance unless that knowledge, the abstract idea, is implemented by labour force. Hence acquiring the knowledge by labour force and endogenizing those new technology by new knowledge is the fundamental dynamics of endogenous growth model. With higher skill and productivity the capital and labour will acquire surplus. The savings thus earned can be devoted to consumption leading to higher aggregate demand. It thus means replacement of endogenous technology by endogenous human capital.

Rebelo provided alternative approaches to modelling human capital accumulation. Uzawa 1965 and Lucas (1988) models contain households optimization problem. Endogenous models thus have an important distributive angle so that households can ensure optimum utility. Broadly a high proportion of human capital relative to physical will accelerate growth and vice versa. Education expenditure in developing human capital is paying, as because it enhances human quality and productivity.

Endogenous models assume productivity gain at an wide scale because process of spill over of knowledge over the economy brings about a wave of high rate. As the level of output, technology and capital stock increase these offer a sustained level of growth. However, there are humps and troughs in the process. When A.K. technology reflects positive long run per capita growth, it faces no problem. But broder definition of capital embracing human capital and knowledge may have a long run troughs or traps. There may be rise of growth rate along with languishing unemployment. Poverty trap is a transitional phenomenon under this situation. If the economy can spread over or diffuse the newly acquired knowledge across – sectors of the economy then swampy traps in certain areas may be eliminated and the economy again attains the even level of growth throughout and overtime.

Endogenous model thus puts important responsibility on the government or the country to follow social development policy consistent with sectoral needs. Output will increase as more resources are devoted to education, health care, training, research development. The workers' existing stock of knowledge and the addition to that stock with the learning experience on the job, together gives the pool of that capital stock which augments further production.

One simple implication of this growth experience is that savings of the economy is pre-eminence. Economic growth depends positively on the rate of growth of savings. Higher savings stimulates higher investment in physical capital which has positive leverage effect on human capital. This is a departure from earlier growth models which conceptualized long-term growth independent of savings rate.

Application of exogenous parameters is another device of development. External factor like technology is the dominant factor both in Harrod and Solow models. Similarly labour force is another crucial external factor to determine the rate of growth. Externally determined innovation and technology and the independent growth of labour force are the prime mover of growth in this formulation. Arrow has a complete theory of technical progress. However, the concept of 'learning by doing' has endogenizested both the innovation and technical progress and reduced the whole set of labour and capital productivity as endogenized variables. Thus what joined in production, labour force and technology, as the external factors become internal overtime and determine the rate of growth of the economy.

In the neo-classical growth model steady growth is generated by certain rate of growth of accumulation equal to the growth of labour force. However, then technical progress, embodied or disembodied, enters into the process of production and effect production differently according to the 'neutrality' character of the technical progress. Harrod's stady growth rate of full – employment is not affected by inclusion of Harrod – neutral technical progress when such technical charges are inducted at a constant proportional rate. Neo-classical balanced – growth path is not equally effected by inclusion of lobour augmenting technical progress. A vintage model with technical progress displays the importance of technology in growth process.

In our modern global economic set-up international trade and capital flow have become a strong exogenous force to growth of a country. Contribution of foreign trade, capital and technology, can broaden the canvas of the real growth models. This open economy exogenous forces enhance the production potential of the economy and strengthen the process of sustainable growth. Contemporary liberal trade and capital market relations are under the guidance of globalization programme. Exogenous forces of economic growth under this perspective are export surplus, capital flow and transfer of technology. The perspective of economic reform encourages economic growth through exogenous forces. It is an extension of the original closed economy formate. This open economy competitive strategy has been adopted in some countries of Asian and Latin America in order to attain rapid growth. However, some of these countries experienced revulsion and eruptions. We shall see in the next section how India has enmeshed the endogenity and exogenity together so as to attain growth with stability.

III

India's Growth Experience

India's growth experience over last two decades is unique in terms of several indicators. Before 1990-91 India's rate of growth was on average 5.8 per cent between 1980-90; but after 1990 the rate of growth hovered around 8-9 per cent. The latest is 9.4 per cent by the first quarter of 2007. Thus the rate has now crossed over the so - called 'Hindu rate' to high rate of growth of 9 per cent and above. The current upswing of Indian economy has come to stay for come time as the economic fundamentals are now strong, and the pro-active policy of the Government is likely to give good.

The present growth of Indian economy has some past behaviour pattern and some future prospects. In the past, during the early phase of planning, India followed rapid industrialization programme under the government controlled public sector. However, the growth rate was sluggish during this phase and this has come to be treated as 'Hindu rate' of growth. In later period, in eighties and early nineties the economy experienced impressive growth over 5 per cent. Since reform process started in nineties, growth rate of India economy recorded high rate and reached to 9.4 per cent in 2007. It is expected that during Eleventh Five Year Plan the growth rate will be strong 10 per cent.

Over this period of transition there has been significant changes in India economy. It is not globalization alone which is a recent phenomenon, there were some other fundamental changes which have brought about rapid growth of India economy. Indian economy has now completed a crucial phase of structural shift. Agriculture which was the mainstay of the economy in the early phase of our planning has now receded to the third position after services, and industry in respect of their contribution to the G.D.P. Agriculture now contributes 19.5 per cent of G.D.P. but supports 60 per cent of our population. The industrial sector now contributes 19.6 per cent and services contribute 61.9 per cent in 2007. The contribution of agriculture, industry and services to G.D.P. or average between 2000- 01 and 2006-07 were 21.4, 19.6 and 59.0. The average G.D.P. growth over this period was 6.9 per cent. Indian economy is now practically led by services and manufacturing sector.

In the industrial sector manufacturing, with 93.3 per cent weightage, has higher rate of growth. In the use–based industries capital goods give the lead which is followed by intermediate goods and consumer goods. The simple message of this growth pattern after the reform process started is that, Indian economy is being led by leading manufacturing and services sectors and is being supported by investment in capital goods and consumption of intermediate and consumer goods sector. Various kinds of high-tech service consumption and investment in those are the prime mover of the economy. However, this archaic growth has serious implications for equity and social justice.

With 2.5 per cent average growth rate between 2000-01 to 2006 -07 and supporting 60 per cent of population, agriculture has to bear the burden of unemployment. The gap between employment growth rate economic growth rate is widening : it is a high growth process with thinner employment opportunity. Since investment in agricultural sector is weak the multiplier effect is poor in terms of employment and income.

The investment pattern has shifted to the high growth machinery and infrastructure from the primary sector. It is estimated that with expected 9 per cent growth rate during the Eleventh Five Year Plan, the savings rate will be 34.7 per cent of G.D.P. and investment rate would be 37.5 of G.D.P. by closing year of the Plan 2011-12.

Indian economy thus crossed over from the Ricardian economy to a high growth economy with Harrodian technological adoption and high consumption propagation. Obviously the scenario has a risk of imbalance to which Indian economy is now heading for. The suppressed inflation with occasional spurts has become a constant risk to which the Reserve Bank of India has kept sharp attention. There is hardly any chance of balanced growth.

The liberalized financial sector has now an important role in propelling the growth. With burgeoning liquidity in the kity of the banking sector, the investment channels have become wider and the new areas, like housing, real estates are getting higher share of credit from banks. Capital market movement of fund makes occasional spurts and the sensex is rapidly galloping. The RBI finds itself in a tight position in order to maintain the stability consistent with growth.

Again we face the old question of unbalanced growth. Will the unbalanced growth, now we are following with the support of multinational capital, be inclusive of all section of the population, particularly labour force. Since a major segment of labour force in agriculture and small enterprises will remain outside this income flow from high-tech investment, Harrodian disproportionality and Solovian capital-labour disproportionality emerges in the same plane and instability is an inevitable outcome.

IV

Growth by Globalization

Liberalization of Indian economy has a number of positive and negative contents. The export earnings, capital inflow and technology transfer and imports are the positive aspects which are expected to increase both the demand-supply aspects. On the negative fronts are the factors like capital flight, dumping, oil crisis. At the current phase of globalization of Indian economy, exports-imports markets and foreign exchange rules, have been liberalized. As an, outcome India's exports increased and foreign exchange reserves have increased. What have been the impact on the growth of Indian economy ? Even with W.T.O. bounds, India has gained from trade liberalization.

India's share in World export of agricultural products in 1990 was 0.8 and rose to 1.2 in 2000 and 1.2 in 2005. Over the same period manufactured export increased from 0.3 to 1.1 of World export. The significant aspect of export growth was the growth of merchandise which is due to favourable commodity composition, favourable market distribution and positive competitiveness effect. India's share in World export of goods and services was 4.21 per cent during 1960-69 and rose to 17-19 per cent during 2002-06. The recent growth of export has been mainly due to positive competitiveness.

The other aspects of globalization strategy were the increase in foreign exchange reserve. Although partly with the contribution of NRI, foreign exchange reserve has reached to a record height of US $ 165.3 billion at the end of September 2006 and US $ 180.0 billion on February 2, 2007. Foreign Exchange reserves thus provided an import cover of about 11 months at the stage.

Globalization has improved India's Foreign Direct Investment, Liberalization of foreign investment regulation has encouraged a considerable foreign direct investment in Indian economy. FDI inflows was (net) $ 4.7 billion in 2001-02. FDI inflows were mainly in the form of equity.

India has carefully liberalized her current and capital accounts. While current account convertibility has come into operation the move towards further capital account convertibility is on and good economic fundamentals have encouraged the confidence. India has learned from South-East Asian turmoil and hence gradually opening her external accounts.

Globalization strategy has another aspects of trade agreements. Besides SAARC India has made agreement of free trade with number of countries. Agreements with Japan, Thailand and China, Singapore and Thailand are significant.

The globalization policy has benefited India in the field of oil and power agreements with some Asian countries. The global strategy of collaboration and cooperation in respect of money important commodities will surely yield benefit for India.

The open economy strategy of growth has yielded benefits. India's capital out-flow is another significant development. Indian corporates are taking part in the development in foreign countries. With the liberalization of the economy Indian firms are increasingly taking part in the global scene. Leading Indian service industries taking part in global scene are pharmaceuticals and biotechnology, hotel and hospitality, automotives, software and IT services. With these expansion in the global field, India is gaining from that. Both exports and capital outflow will strengthen India's open economy growth strategy. Current effort of India to strengthen her Asian and African contacts and trade agreements is sure to enhance the enterprise of the ethnic Indians (like ethnic Chinese) to participate in India's growth process. India has a large body of diaspora who are already in line with our open economy strategy.

In the post-reform stage India is increasingly exploiting this open economy strategy of collaboration and growth.

Endogenous growth strategy emphasized on human capital and international of knowledge. The concept of innovation and technology adaptation are enmeshed in learning by doing process. India at the early phase of planning followed inward looking capital intensive strategy of growth. However, the experience of low growth performance persisted over long period until economic process began to change in 1980.

The exogenous technique of liberalization and globalization begin to yield some good results, Growth rate of India economy has increased from low 'Hindu rate' to high-tech and multinational led high rate of growth. The Eleventh Five Year Plan envisages inclusive growth. The current problem of high-tech growth can be managed with diffusion of learning of skill and improvement of human quality. This strategy of endogenous growth technique will overcome the supply side problems. Along with that the policy mix of globalization will enhance export earning and broaden Indian trading base among Asian and African countries. Increased foreign exchange reserve and increased inflow of foreign direct investment will contribute to the rapid growth of Indian economy.

Current policy of the Government to strengthen the economic relation with the Asian and African countries will enhance India's economic growth.

V

The Fallout

In fallout of the current high-tech strategy of growth is reflected in various social indices. The constraints of open economic strategy such as inflation, capital market instability and exchange rate variation are to be contained by careful monetary policy and cautious approach to capital market flexibility. India is now following a mix of endogenous and exogenous strategy instead of only closed economic policy of earlier period and the complete open door policy of neo-liberal globalization.

The fallout of current high growth strategy appear in three fronts. The primary sector drag is paralyzing, agricultural is not responding to high growth stimulus. Food crisis and farms' suicide is an endemic feature. Along with that poverty and unemployment are equally having grinding effect on the people, rural and urban together. Rural per capita caloric intake has declined in many states from the level of 1972-73 to that of 2001-05 (Table-5). From 2000-01 to 2006-07 the average annual growth rate of agriculture was only 2.5 per cent (Table-1). Percentage of population poor and vulnerable only slightly declined from 81.8 in 1993-94 to 76.3 in 2004-05. Again in terms of work force majority of the unorganized work force are in SC/ST and OBC group. Thus there is a clear division of the society in terms of riches and occupation. Economic growth has to benefit the under privileged occupation and social groups. Planning has to be devised in order to include the people of these occupation and social groups in the production process which enhances growth.

VI

Stability

The open and imbalanced growth process of Indian economy has now brought in its tail serious instability. Inflation has taken strong footing. Exchange rate has also become volatile. The financial market has also become sensitive.

India's wholesale price index rose an annual 7.83 per cent in the work ended May 3, its-highest since November 2004. While international factors like oil price hike and high commodity price in international market are there, the domestic factors like declining production of agriculture are more important. Rise of CRR and other monetary measures that the RBI has taken are all aimed at management of liquidity. These go hardly deep into the production level. The liquidity control measure of the Central Bank is partly frustrated by capital inflow. With the Federal Reserve reducing the rate step by step the inflow of capital increases in the domestic market. Hence the monetary measures made only marginal effect on the inflation process. The important aspect is that monetary mechanism has not been effective in reducing inflation.

The main hurdle is the market structure. In the guise of liberalization monopolists have been given free access to the retail market. They hoard the main products making the retail markets to dry. The monopoly market is killing the common men's market. The free market in thus killing retail and common men's market.

All the propaganda that inflation favours the growth is only buffetting the monopoly game. The government only meekly calling upon the hoarders to honestly reduce the price which is against the market ethics. To maintain the stability while pursuing growth, the government has to play an activist role.

The policy mechanism has to be adopted in order to augment production and activate the market channel and delivery system. Secondly the administrative measures have to be effective in order to discourage the cornering and hoarding.

VII

Conclusion

Present Indian growth strategy combines surge in domestic manufacturing and service on the own hand and on the other, export and inflow of foreign investment (FDI). Foreign Institutional Investment (FII) is also making a good headway resulting in instability in the capital market.

However there are two sets of constraints. First set is the social divide and employment gap and persistence of poverty. The second set of problems consists of inflation, exchange rate volatility and uncertain capital flow.

Current government monetary policy is engaged in the liquidity management government intervention programme is to provide incentive to farmers and manufactures for higher production.

However to attain sustained growth government has to accommodate the external oil shocks and inflation as the correlation between inflation and GDP is low (Table 7).

Table–1
Growth Rates of Real G.D.P. and Sectoral Share

Sector	*2000-01 to 2006-07 (average)*	*2004-05*	*2005-06*	*2006-07*
Agriculture and allied activities	2.5 (21.4)	0.0 (20.2)	6.0 (19.7)	2.7 (18.5)
Industry	7.6 (19.6)	8.4 (19.6)	8.0 (19.4)	12.2 (19.6)
Mining and querrying	4.5	7.5	3.6	4.5
Manufacturing	7.5	8.7	9.1	11.3
Electricity, gas and water supply	4.5	7.5	5.3	7.7
Services	8.6 (59.0)	10.0 (60.7)	10.3 (60.9)	11.0 (61.9)
Trade, Hotel, Transport communication	10.3	10.9	10.4	13.0
Finance, insurance, real estate and business services	8.0	8.7	10.9	11.1
Community, social and personal services	6.0	7.9	7.7	7.8
Construction	9.7	14.1	14.2	9.4
Real G.D.P. at factor cost	6.9	7.5	9.0	9.2

Note: Figures in parentheses denote share in G.D.P.

Source: Annual Policy Statement 2006-07, R.B.I., R.B.I. Bulletin, May 2007.

Table-2

Decadal Growth Rates of G.D.P. and Per Capita Income

Decades	*Growth Rates (%)*		
	G.D.P.	*Population*	*Per Capita Income*
1920-1947	1.18	1.20	0.03
1950-1960	3.91	1.96	1.95
1960-1970	3.70	2.22	1.48
1970-1980	3.08	2.20	0.88
1980-1990	5.38	2.14	3.24
1990-2000	5.58	1.93	3.65
2000-2005	5.99	1.70	4.29

Source: Arjun Sen Gupta – "India's Common People", E.P.W., March 15, 2008.

Table-3*(a)*

Industry

Annual Growth Rate of Industrial Production in Major Sectors of Industry.
(Based on the Index of Industrial Production)
Base = 1993-94 = 100 per cent

	Mining and Quarrying	*Manufacturing*	*Electricity*	*Overall*
Weights	10.47	79.36	10.17	100.00
1995-96	9.7	14.1	8.1	13.0
1996-97	1.9	7.3	4.0	6.1
1997-98	6.9	6.7	6.6	6.7
1998-99	–0.8	4.4	6.5	4.1
1999-00	1.0	7.1	7.3	6.7
2000-01	2.8	5.3	4.0	5.0
2002-03	5.8	6.0	3.2	5.7
2003-04	5.2	7.4	5.1	7.0
2004-05	4.4	9.2	5.2	8.4
2005-06	1.0	9.1	5.2	8.2
2006-07	3.8	11.5	7.3	10.6

Source: Economic Survey 2006-07.

Table–3(*b*)

Growth Rates of Industrial Production by Used-based Classification

Base: 1993-94 = 100 per cent

Sector	*Weight*	*2000-01*	*2001-02*	*2002-03*	*2003-04*	*2004-05*	*2005-06*
Basic goods	35.5	3.7	2.6	4.9	5.4	5.5	6.7
Capital goods	9.3	1.8	–3.4	10.5	13.6	13.9	15.8
Intermediate goods	26.5	4.7	1.5	3.9	6.4	6.1	2.5
Consumer goods	28.7	8.0	6.0	7.1	7.1	11.7	12.0
Of which Durables	5.4	14.5	11.5	–6.3	11.6	14.4	15.3
Non-durables	23.3	5.8	4.1	12.0	5.8	10.4	11.0
IIP (Index of Industrial Production)	100	5.0	2.7	5.7	7.0	8.4	8.2

Table–4

Rural Per Capita Calorie Intake Per Day

States	*1972-73*	*2004-05*
Tamil Nadu	1,955	1,842
Karnataka	2,202	1,845
Gujarat	2,142	1,923
Madhya Pradesh	2,423	1,929
Maharashtra	1,895	1,933 +
Andhra Pradesh	2,103	1,995 –
Kerala	1,559	2,014 +
Orissa	1,995	2,023 +
Bihar	2,225	2,049
Assam	2,074	2,067
West Bengal	1,921	2,070 +
Rajasthan	2,730	2,180
Uttar Pradesh	2,575	2,200
Haryana	3,215	2,226
Punjab	3,493	2,240

Based on NSS 27th and 61st Round, reported in Economic Times, May 21, 2008.

Except West Bengal, Orissa, Kerala and Maharashtra all other states experienced reduction of calorie intake after 32 year in 61st round of NSS (in 2004-05).

Table–5
Percentage Distribution of Population and Unorganized Works—by Poverty Status and Social Group (2004-05)

Poverty Status	*Population*					*Unorganized Works*
	Total	*SC/ST*	*OBC*	*Muslim*	*Others*	
Extremely poor	6.4 (6.5)	10.9 (11.4)	5.1 (5.2)	8.2 (8.2)	2.1 (1.6)	5.8
Poor	15.4 (15.5)	21.5 (21.8)	25.1 (15.3)	15.2 (19.9)	6.4 (6.1)	15.0
Marginal	19.0 (17.9)	22.4 (21.2)	20.4 (19.6)	22.3 (19.9)	11.1 (10.3)	19.6
Vulnerable	36.0 (35.5)	33.0 (32.7)	39.2 (38.2)	34.8 (34.8)	35.3 (35.3)	38.4
Middle class	19.3 (20.3)	11.2 (11.6)	17.8 (18.9)	13.3 (14.7)	34.2 (35.7)	18.7
High income	4.0 (4.4)	1.0 (1.3)	2.4 (3.0)	2.2 (2.5)	11.0 (11.3)	2.7
Extremely poor and poor (1+2)	21.8 (22.0)	32.4 (33.3)	20.3 (20.4)	27.4 (28.1)	8.5 (7.7)	20.8
Marginal and vulnerable (3+4)	55.0 (53.3)	55.4 (53.8)	59.6 (57.8)	57.1 (54.7)	46.3 (45.4)	57.9
Poor and vulnerable (7+8)	76.7 (75.3)	87.8 (87.1)	79.9 (78.2)	84.5 (82.4)	54.8 (53.1)	78.7
Middle and high income (5+6)	23.3 (24.7)	12.2 (12.9)	20.2 (21.8)	15.5 (17.2)	45.2 (47.0)	21.3
All	100 (100)	100 (100)	100 (100)	100 (100)	100 (100)	100

Figure in brackets is based on detailed consumer expenditure.

Source: Sengupta A. : India's Common People', E.P.W. March 15, 2008.

Table–6
Distribution of Population by Poverty Status

	1993-94		*1999-2000*		*2004-05*	
	Million	*P.C.*	*Million*	*P.C.*	*Million*	*P.C.*
Extremely poor	102.6	11.5	87.4	8.7	69.7	6.4
Poor	171.6	19.2	174.1	17.3	167.3	15.4
Marginal	168.2	18.8	200.2	19.9	207.1	19.0

Contd.

	1993-94		*1999-2000*		*2004-05*	
	Million	*P.C.*	*Million*	*P.C.*	*Million*	*P.C.*
Vulnerable	289.5	32.4	349.0	34.8	392.0	36.0
Middle income	138.5	15.5	167.3	16.7	209.8	19.3
High income	23.9	2.7	26.1	2.6	43.7	4.0
Extremely poor and poor (1+2)	274.2	30.7	261.6	26.1	237.0	21.8
Marginal and vulnerable (3+4)	457.7	51.2	549.2	54.7	599.1	55.0
Poor and vulnerable (7+8)	731.9	81.8	810.7	80.7	836.1	76.7
Middle and high income (5+6)	162.4	18.7	193.4	19.3	253.5	23.3
All	894.4	100.0	1004.1	100.0	1089.6	100.0

Source: Sengupta A., 'India's Common People', E.P.W. March 15, 2008.

Table–7
GDP Growth Rate and Inflation Rate

	GDP Growth	*Inflation Rate*
1993-94	5.7	8.4
1994-95	6.4	12.5
1995-96	7.3	8.1
1996-97	8.0	4.6
1997-98	4.3	4.4
1998-99	6.7	5.9
1999-00	6.4	3.3
2000-01	4.4	7.2
2001-02	5.8	3.6
2002-03	3.8	3.5
2003-04	8.5	5.4
2004-05	7.5	6.5
2005-06	9.0	4.4
2006-07	9.4	5.4

Note: GDP is on the basis of 1999-00 prices and inflation rate is on the basis of 1993-94 = 100.

REFERENCES

Acharya, Sankar, (2006) Economic Growth : Some Reflection Economic and Political Weekly, November 4.

Bhattacharya B.B. and S. Kar, (2007) Macro-economic Reforms, Growth and Stability, Oxford.

Chandra Sekhar, C.P., (2006) The Demographic Dividend and Young India's Economic Future. Economic and Political Weekly, December 9.

Chakraborty, S., (1987) Development Planning, Oxford University Press, New York.

Fulvio Caste Macci, (2006) A Critical Realist Interpretation of Evolutionary Growth Theorising, Cambridge Journal of Economic, Vol. 30, November 06.

Government of India, (2007) Economic Survey 2005-06.

Himanshu, (2007) 'Recent Trends in Poverty and Inequality. Some Preliminary Results'. Economic and Political Weekly, February 10.

Kalecki. M., (1954) Theory of Economic Dynamics, George Allan and Unwin, London.

Kaldor, N. and A.J. Mirless, (1962) A New Model of Economic Growth, Review of Economic Studies Reprinted Amartya Sen (ed.) Growth Economics, Penguin (1970).

Patnaik, P., (2007) 'A Model of Growth of the Contemporary Indian Economy' Economic and Political Weekly, June 2.

Purfiled, C. and Schiff, J., (2006) India Goes Global: Its Expanding Role in the World Economy, Washington, IMF.

Rakshit, M.K., (1991) Trade, Mercantile Capital and Economic Development, Orient Longman Ltd., Hyderabad.

Rebelo, S., (1991) 'Long-run Policy Analysis and Long-run Growth' Journal of Political Economy, 99.

Sen, Amartya, (1990) Growth Economics, Penguin, Delhi.

Reserve Bank of India, (2005) 'Report on Currency and Finance 2004', R.B.I., Bombay.

Reddy Y.V., (2007) Role of Monetary Policy in Attaining Growth with Stability: 'The Indian Experience', R.B.I. Bulletin, May.

Reserve Bank of India, (2007) 'Report of the Working Group on Savings for Eleventh Five Year Plan (2007-08 to 2011-12). Reserve Bank of India, Bulletin, May.

Sengupta, A. (2008) India's Common People, E.P.W., March 15-21.

5

Fallacy of Inclusive Growth

RABIN MUKHERJEE

Economic development is the process of a society's activity in which the national income of a particular country increases over a long period of time. This definition of growth is generally expressed in monetary unit for common understanding. But this is a view from an apparently simplistic notion of the capitalist society, which has restrictions and suffers from limitation and superficiality. Economic development is primarily concerned with interaction with nature.

Basic Premise

The nature is the coherent whole of the objects and society is based on the nature's existence, extension and evolution over a long period of time. Devoid of the bounty of nature's material products as free gifts, the idea of production and human organization's sustenance and economic development falls through. Without nature's endowment it becomes absurd and meaningless. Man himself is a part of nature and cannot produce anything in isolation from nature. Production in the society is actually based on shaping, combining and fabricating the elements and products of nature with labour power in an organized and systematic manner. Materially, the premises of production and growth ultimately to the nature.

Nature created its products on its own in long historical process and through its own evolution, and man appeared in differentiation[1] of nature's objective realm. But, nature is some what restrained there, for it did not create commodity, money and market, which are made by man in his practical life over the years. So, being apart from nature, it is partial, arbitrary, and wrong on the part of man to recognize market as the only indicator, and supreme in economic development and ideal governor of 'inclusive growth' in the society. Apart from economies, there are politics, sociology, law ethics and philosophical issues that are deeply involved and inherent in the subject. Nature being secular, did not produce and conserve the material products for the exclusive right and ownership of any group, fraction or class in the human society. It produced and conserved those as free gift, common for all members of the mankind. Why man as a social being but struggling as wage labour should be deprived of equal right or share of the gifts of nature? Man has long been interacting with nature with his own labour for his subsistence and development of progeny. Nature did not discriminate any section of mankind and here lies the very deep-rooted fact and embeded rationale of economics, politics and philosophy of inclusive growth. Rationality must be the key to inclusive growth for the society.

It becomes self-evident that nature is the basic and primary and labour theory of value in production measured in terms of labour hours actually performed and incorporated in the products forms the broad base and corner stone of economic development and social progress over time. Though commodity, money and market have been gradually formed, evolved and integrated with it in the much later period of commodity production, they do not disclose, rather hide the hard reality of human labour as the real motive force of the development of production and civilization. Price in the market is the relative value to measure and express the quantity of output in an economy during a particular period of time and bears the value or quantity of labour incorporated in the product of economic activity in the given period. What lies veiled behind the market price is the human labour materialized and congealed in the process of production and creation of useful effects in the circulation of the product. The idea of necessity works as the assertive force at large in the society and the demand and supply interact and actually play their roles in the market.

Inclusive growth in the strict theoretical sense absorbs both labour congealed and its relative value as market price of the product in the context of the gain, satisfaction and full realization of the entire value of the product for labour. It cannot remain confined to the expression of mere market price paid to the labourer, where labour is converted into a commodity, in the large-scale commodity production under capitalism.

The entity of market is partial and anarchic. It fleeces and shades labour, and shrouds the real value of labour. The mode and process of production under modern capitalism characterized with monopoly severely wrenches and exploits labour power and is constantly geared upto crush labour by realizing surplus value more than ever, with advanced technology but under certain objective reality of limits and variations, over time. The operation of the law of value, generation of surplus value and distribution of the product immanent in the mode of production continue to be holy and absolute in the capitalist mode of production to maintain labour at a subsistence level. Here lies the theism of market and falsity of equity in the bourgeois mode of production that actually thwarts and vitiates inclusive growth only to ensure reaping surplus value and protect the acquisition of wealth and property, and domination of the owners of the means of production in the society.

Private property, commodity production, wage labour and market work as the basic pre-requisites for the capitalist rendezvous and operate in unison to generate surplus value continually and develop productive forces in the society. They are the hallmarks of the capitalist society. It has reached the most coercive, acquisitive and violent position in the present condition of the monopoly capitalism characterized with imperialist domination and its market design ushered in since the 1990s through the pervasive action of liberalization, privatization and globalization. All work under the severe pressure of the ever growing and momentous technological developments and productive forces in the world economy.

In the circuit of commodity production and circulation or exchange, there lies a contradiction, and to resolve it, money and credit in the generic term, finance capital increasingly performs the work of motor mechanism in the world market system. The commodity bears its characteristics both in its use value and exchange value. In the process of exchange value and use value, it is mediated, but with a certain friction. The commodity contains value in terms of congealed labour which is measured in the average market price. While the market price of a commodity is realized and is finally used either for subjective or objective consumption, it turns into the glaring reality that many goods are sold above their values and a large number are sold below their values. But surplus value or profit is realized at different points of exchange emanting through the process of production congealing the value of labour. The whole process deprives the latter. He gets the average subsistence value and never gets the full value of his labour. The surplus value is appropriated by the capitalists and landlords arbitrarily through the mechanism of the market system.

Labour, the original source of value, has turned into a mere commodity in the capitalist system. It is only partially paid in wages and remains unpaid more than ever with the advancement of technology resulting in more exploitation and displacement of labour in the factory sector. The entire unpaid labour, its surplus value, is grabbed by the capitalist, landlord and trading classes in the society. The production becomes social but distribution of product remains private and dominated by the capitalists landlords and traders being the owners of the means of production. The array in the market is thus coercive and arbitrary and this entire process has divided the people more violently over the years. It has become of more acquisitive and perverse character with the ossification and domination of finance capital in the present times. The nexus intensely works at large to assure generation of more surplus value and its transfer in favour of the capitalist, landlord and parasite classes. The condition and basic pre-requisite of social production for inclusive growth is thus thwarted and marred by internal rigidities and external shock waves like liberalization, privatization and globalization in the realm of international finance capital which is but a collasal sum transformed or metamorphosis of surplus value in the long past years. The actuality in the international economy, in essence, can be stressed in the design and operation system of the monopoly (manufacturing and industrial) and finance capital (Banks and other financial organizations). There is nevertheless a contradiction in the approach, interaction, manoeuvring, appropriation of surplus value and metamorphosis between them. They struggle for realizing surplus value and to acquire and hoard financial assets of different categories in the world economy with the ultimate motive of making profit. As early as 1865, Marx observed "The *will* of the capitalist is certainly to take as much as possible. What we have to do is not to talk about his *will*, but to enquire into his *power*, the *limits of that power* and the *character of those limits*."[2] There has been much elapse of time and the capitalist class never cease to take as much as possible by exploiting human labour. Its consequence has been that, in the present day world monopoly capitalism dominates at large.

A Great Division

The number of people with $ 1 million or more in investable assets increased by 3 per cent in 2001 over 2000 to 7.1 million, according to the world wealth Report from Merill Lynch and Cap Gemini Ernst Young. It provides with the useful data on the ownership, gains and losses of property in the form of financial assets in the world economy. The millionaires in that year held $ 26200 billion between them, up from $ 25500 billion at the end of 2000, also a 3 per cent gain. The data concretize the physical existence and power or strength of the international bourgeoisie in the present time of globalization.

European and North Americans still dominate the Group but Latin American and Asian high-net worth invertors posted the largest gains in 2001, thanks to their large bond and cash positions. "Going into this we thought that we would see much smaller growth and may be even a decline in wealth and numbers, but high-net-worth investors tend to save especially in recessionary times", said Alvi Albuaf, director of global securities industry consulting for Cap Gemini Ernst and Young. The growth of 2000-2001 in high net worth wealth pales in comparison with the 18 per cent achieved in 1999 and 6 per cent logged in 2000. Albuaf and his colleagues expected that the millionaires 'assets would grow at an average annual rate of 5 per cent until 2006, despite a stagnant economy. That brought total high net worth wealth to $ 38500 billion. John Morris, a Merryl Lynch, Vice-President said, "In these difficult times, the high net worthy have not been greedy." They have been looking for sound, cautious allocation, that includes fixed income securities as well as physical assets, such as property, and alternative investments, such as hedge funds.

Latin Americans have long favoured dollar denominated bonds, which helped them to boost their assets by 8 per cent in 2001. They accounted $ 3406 billion or 13 per cent share of the world's high net-worth wealth. Asia's wealthy investors prospered despite problems in Japan. This was due to high savings rates and selected investments in Asia's emerging market stocks. Their assets increased 7.1 per cent and accounted for nearly $ 6288 billion or 24 per cent of the world's high-net-worth wealth. Nearby 2 per cent of the total ($ 26200 billion) or $ 520 billion was held by others excluding Europe and North America.

North America maintained second place in wealth concentration with $ 7600 billion (29%) but investors saw their assets rise by only 1.7 per cent, less than the rate of inflation.

Europe and North America's millionaires together held 61 per cent of the world's high-net-worth wealth according to the World Wealth Report released by Merril Lynch and Cap Gemini Ernst and Young in June 2002. In North America inheritances accounted for 5 to 15 per cent of high-net-worth wealth, compared with 15 to 25 per cent in Europe. Europe's wealthy are slightly older at 59 to 62 years on average, compared with 55 to 57 in the US, and the European group was more heavily dominated by men. North American millionaires defined as those with $ 1 million or more investable assets, had a domestic bias, investing only 6.4 per cent of their portfolios internationally, compared with 29.8 per cent invested internationally, compared with 29.8 per cent invested internationally by the Europeans.

The monopoly capitalist classes – the masters of finance capital, in North American, Europe and Asia-Pacific region-at present control 90 per cent of the world's wealth and the population of the poor countries with the vast majority of world population have only 10 per cent of the world's wealth according to a recent report of the university of the United Nations in 2005.

This shows the long-term un-directional trend and movement in commodity production and growth of profit and consequently rapid and phenomenal accumulation, centralization and concentration of capital under monopoly capitalism over time and more especially since the 1990s through 2003. This development can be related with and objectively followed from the date of the inflows of foreign direct investment and cross border mergers and amalgamations in the world economy. During 1988-93, the inflow of foreign direct investment[3] in the world economy was $ 190.6 billion, which rose to $ 331.8 billion in 1995 as average $ 544 billion in 1995-99. Of this total inflow investment the developed countries hosted $ 140.1 billion in 1988-93 but it rose to $ 364 billion or 67 per cent on the average in 1996-99. Developing countries hosted $ 46.96 billion on the average in 1988-93 but witnessed a phenomenal increase to $ 164.5 billion on the average in 1995-99.

The value of cross border mergers and amalgamations of business in the world economy amounted to $ 150.6 billion in 1990 and $ 143.2 billion and more than 95 per cent was accounted for by the developed countries, and the developing countries shared $ 7 billion or less than 5 per cent in 1990. The value of cross border mergers and amalgamation in 1995 was $ 186.6 billion in 1995 but on the average sharply increased to $ 518 billion during 1997-99.

The most important and crucial fact that can be witnessed from the data is that the value of cross border merger and amalgamation rapidly increased during 1990-2000 the first decade of so-called globalization. Compared to 1990, it grew 7.57 times in the world economy in 2000. In the developed and developing countries it increased 7.6 and 6.7 times respectively. But after 2000, the value of mergers and amalgamations witnessed a drastic fall to $ 594 billion in 2001, $ 369.8 billion in 2002 and further fell to $ 297 billion in 2003. This amount for the world economy was only 26 per cent in 2003 compared with 2000. For the developed countries it fell to 23.4 per cent and to 64 per cent in the developing countries.

From the trends of foreign direct investment and cross border merger and amalgamations, it can be followed at large that there lies a very continuous high positive correlation between the rise and fall in their values from 1990 through 2003. It confirms that the intensity of economic activity worldwide is strongly influenced, manoeuvred and increasingly more dominated by the operations of the monopoly and finance capital which have become more perverse and dominant to annex market, grab agricultural land, fleece the people and subjugate nations in the last fifteen years of economic development in the world. Its design and strategy is to foist its own laws more aggressively to exploit nations' resource, undermine home market and cause displacement of labour on a much wider scale than ever.

The rule of monopoly annexes, gags, coaxes for capitalizing everything in the home market and abroad. Its production causes instability, functionalists and vicissitudes in the market. It greatly reduces purchasing power of the masses and causes mass poverty by shading labour in the factory and other sectors, employing higher technology and by dispossessing the peasants of their land—their meager means of production and subsistence.

Energy supply has been a crucial factor on which the world monopoly capital greatly depends on foreign countries. While the law of diminishing return on capital, strong economic rigidity in production, and strong resistance also are growing in the major oil producing countries which raised the price of oil to a new high of $ 90 a barrel in December, 2007. The USA being the largest country of monopoly capitalism now import about two-thirds of its oil and the proportion keeps rising as the US citizens burn as much gasoline over the years. Its dependency on oil import in the context of the US military intervention in the middle-east and nationalist resistance movements there will further increase in future. Last year's US domestic production of 1.86 million[4] barrels of crude oil was the nation's lowest since 1949 and production, at best will level off in 2007. Texas remains the country's biggest oil producer, representing 20 per cent of national output, but production has been declining steadily from 444 million barrels in 2000 to 397 million barrels in 2006. Spending on exploration and development in the United States has tripled in recent years, to $ 90 billion a year, according to Gohn S. Herold, an energy consulting firm. High in the Coloado Rockies, long deserted towns are coming back to life amid a drilling surge. This measure would not be enough to stop the decline of U.S. production and it would be forced to control and exploit more national resources of other countries for its sustenance and growth.

To ensure energy supply and build up a higher quantity of strategic reserve of oil the US Government has lunched war against Iraq and Afghanistan for establishing command over rich oil bearing territories of the world.

Monopoly Capitalism

The law of diminishing returns in production and falling rate of profit operates at large in the home countries of the large multinationals and world economy, as well. During 1990-2001, the first decade of privatization and liberalization under the flagship of globalization, while index numbers of agricultural production[6] for the world witnessed a marginal annual compound growth rate of 0.6 per cent and US recorded 0.5 per cent, they fell in most of the developed capitalist countries. In Canada, it annually decreased 0.1. In Australia 0.6, France 0.3, UK 1.0, Germany 0.9, Japan 1.2, South Africa 0.9, Israel 2.6 per cent. Structure of production showed that in GDP of 2002 agriculture contributed 2 per cent in USA, 3 per cent in Italy. France 3 per cent, Japan 1 per cent and Germany 1 per cent. In these countries the average annual rate of growth of value addition in agriculture was much less than that of industry and services. In Japan, its growth average in 1990-02 actually showed a decline of 2.9 per cent against rise of 4.2 per cent in the service sector for the same period. The acute imbalance in the structure of production resulted in the lop-sided growth and they constantly interact with each other overtime. This pattern of production and development with arbitrary exchange of commodities in the operation of world economy created enormous amount of hot money and banking capital inevitably in further strengthening the position of international finance capital leading to the inflow of large foreign direct investment and supporting cross border merger and amalgamation of business at large. For instance, foreign direct and protfolio investment in India surged to $ 28.7 billion from 2001-02 to 2003-04. The capitalist mode of production constantly narrows its social base, vitiates civil society, has brought in systematic coercion and anarchy in the society and violently divided the people between the rich and poor worldwide. World has economically developed on an enormous scale but the profile of human poverty has reached an abysmal stage with the increasing exploitation of wage labour. The accompanied data in the table confirm and expose the glaring reality in different countries of the world.

Inclusive growth denotes imparting the material benefit for widened labour and common welfare of the society. It means just and adequate distribution of the product in favour of the labour and masses of the people for social justice. Does its pre-condition and pre-requisite actually exist in the countries of the world?

The above conditions and facts uncontroversly substantiate and warrant the existence and operation of the vile law of value and exploitation of man by man, grabbing surplus value and depriving the labour and masses of the people only to enrich a minority rich section of the society with the writ of the market god. This is the result of the ossified rule of monopoly and finance capital.

Historical developments definitely confirm that monopoly capitalism is opposed anachronistic to human development and progress of the society since it grows with severe exploitation of labour and ever growing poverty of the masses of the people.

In the 1980s and 1990s, the largest 350 ml multinational corporation had higher trade concentration among themselves, which was 40 per cent of the trade of corporations own countries of origin. More than one-third of the US trade takes place between the US based multinational corporations and their overseas agents and collaborators. In the similar way, the shares for the "Japanese multinationals" exports and imports were 25 and 33 per cent respectively.

The relations and connections of the multinational corporations have developed to such characteristic form and penetrating character and manner that they have succeeded to change the traditional nature of state in different countries on the world. Monopoly capitalism and state have been aligned and enmeshed in an integrated whole. Jan Nipars Black, who worked on the alliance between the multinational corporations and states, observes that, at present, the major function of the state has been to give priority to the protection and safety of multinational corporation.

This practice has become common in developed countries like USA and Canada, as well as the countries of the third world. Urshula Franklin, a reputed environment scientist has commented that we are engaged in such an economic warfare where the state, in the interests of the multinational corporation, has declared man and nature as the enemy. She said that, the physique of state, protecting the investment and profit of the multinational corporation has been exposed to be ugly and nakedly aggressive. John Momarty, Philosopher and a Champion of Environment Movement, point out that the multinational corporations have such world-wide networks of legal armour that those function as immense safeguard for their protection. Whatever offence the multinational corporations do against any person, society and natural environment, they do not face any difficult to get relief and reprieve.

It clearly shows that the conditions of competition, free trade, and equitable distribution of the product do not actually prevail in the economy. Those have been subdue and reversed by the monopoly. Basis and existing conditions grew and evalued over times, and they systematically care and foster monopoly capital all round. It curbs and devours individuals right to get relief and rehabilitation, succour, initiative enterprise, and builds and ossified dictatorship of finance capital as necessity in the name of democracy. It is all about coercion and despotism crushing workers and peasants in the semblance of right, liberty and democracy.

Nearly two decades before, the UN sources reported that there were seven thousand multinational corporations operating in the world economy. Their number has increased to 37 thousand and their approved factor and agent institutions to 17 lakhs in 2005. Institute for Policy Research, Washington noted that the total annual sales of 200 giant multinational corporations were more than volume of sales in the economies of 182 countries out of 191 countries in the world. From this, the vast area of operation and might of the multinational corporations with awesome productive forces can be followed at large.

Out of the private sector's total resources in the world, the Multinational Corporations Control one-third, 70 per cent of the world trade, greater share of the international transactions and advanced technology. Their sphere of business has expanded more than ever as 500 multinational corporations control 70 per cent of world trade. The invisible hand of market and free trade is thus dominated and actually controlled by the monopoly organizations of the multinational corporations and their close associates and collaborators.

One estimate of a financial journal in 2000 estimated that the largest multinational corporation was Exxon Mobil of USA. The annual gross income of this giant was more than the total revenue of 22 nation states. The second was General Motors. The sales of Ford Motors exceeded annual revenue of Norway of Thai Government. The top 200 Multinational Corporations sales grew 160 per cent in 1983-97 and their total profit grew 224 per cent in the same period. But world economic growth in the same time increased 144 per cent.

Gross border merger and amalgamation constantly intensifies the process of centralization and concentration of production and conditions the high tension monopolistic contention and rivalry among them. The Lion and Share of the oil production and refining system in the world is accounted for by Exxon-Mobil and British Petroleum Ameco. The firest and paper industry is dominated by International, Georgia Pacific, Kimberly Clark and Warner Hourse and Walmart command world-wide of sale of goods in the retail market. Nestle and Unilever dominate in the food processing market in the world economy.

Inclusive Growth: Character and Limits

India is a part, appendage of the mammoth network and domain of the world-wide monopoly capitalism. The condition of rational and inclusive growth of the economy simply does not exist at all as finance capital dominates everything and does not allow freedom in the production system. The free development of the means of production has become a mirage, countries of Europe passed through along bitter struggle against the church and feudal absolutism, organized class war and revolution to establish rights of man and civil society, yet, with the growth and expansion of colonialism and capitalism, and its transformation into monopoly and finance capital, it inevitably turned into imperialism for its growth and sustenance by exploiting overseas countries and nations, India has not gone through a protracted struggle against idealist religious philosophy and its supporting internal feudal and foreign imperialist forces. For this major reason, the face of economic development has been partial, sketchy and more biased, and some what imposed by exogenous forces over the years, rather than getting more support strength and nourishment from the domestic and endogenous forces.

Table–1
Profile of Human Poverty

	Share of Income Consumption		*Percentage of Population*			
	Richest 20%	*Poorest 20%*	*In Poverty* (PPP $1 a Day)*	*Below Poverty Line +*	*Not Likely to Survive upto 40 Years*	*Adult Illiteracy Rate ++*
	1990-02		*1990-02*	*1990-01*	*2000-05*	*2002*
India	42	9	35	29	15	39
Jamaica	46	7	<2	19	05	12
Brazil	64	2	08	17	12	14
Zimbabwe	56	5	36	35	75	10
Mexico	59	3	10	10	08	10
Nigeria	56	4	70	34	35	33
Nicaragua	60	4	45	48	10	23
Zambia	57	3	64	73	70	20
Malaysia	54	4	<2	16	04	11
Philippines	52	5	15	37	07	07
Kenya	51	6	23	52	50	16

Contd...

	Share of Income Consumption		*Percentage of Population*			
	Richest 20%	*Poorest 20%*	*In Poverty* (PPP $1 a Day)*	*Below Poverty Line +*	*Not Likely to Survive upto 40 Years*	*Adult Illiteracy Rate ++*
	1990-02		*1990-02*	*1990-01*	*2000-05*	*2002*
Thailand	50	6	<2	13	10	07
China	50	5	17	4.6	07	09
Indonesia	43	8	08	27	11	12
Vietnam	45	8	18	51	11	10
Bangladesh	41	9	36	50	17	59
Sri Lanka	43	8	07	25	05	08
Pakistan	42	9	13	33	18	59
Egypt	44	9	03	17	09	44

Note: Based on Human Development Report, 2004, UNDP.

* Based on consumption expenditure of $1 (PPP) a day per person. See Glossary on Purchasing Power Parity (PPP).

+ Refers to the poverty line determined by national authorities and is based on population-weighted sub-group estimates from household surveys.

++ Defined as the proportion of the population age, 15 years and older, who usually cannot read and write.

Source: Statistical outline of India 2004-05, Tata Services Limited, Mumbai, p. 278.

Economic development under the rule of Finance Capital has progressed to a considerable extent but the worst features of the primitive and medieval society like caste and tribe, religious and ethnic characteristics and psyche still prodominate and largely influence the polity that interacts with the state and parliamentary system grafted by the British colonialism. The substantial latter part being altogether different from the rich urban Ango-saxon India actually belongs to the Bharat. The growing dichotomy and varied social stratification being real and obnoxious, can hardly be emphasized. Economic development in India has taken place in such a pace and fashion that it has largely led to the very high concentration and centralization of wealth in a very minority section of the people over the years. Forbes magazine, reports that India's 40 richest list had $ 351 billion in 2007. It says "In aggregate, their wealth surged to $ 351 billion a bit more than double of last year's $ 170 billion, making India's 40 by for the wealthiest such group in all of Asia." This four richest India's are worth" are astonishing $ 180 billion", Forbes said, attributing surge in wealth to a booming stock market.

More than six lakhs millionaries[8] are concentrated in just ten cities of India, with the National Capital accounting for the maximum number of them, a recent survey says. The country's financial centre, Mumbai has over one lakh household earning more than Rs. 10 lakh per year, data compiled by Indians Analyties' Housing skyline of India 2007-08 shows. The four richest Indians are worth astonishing $ 180 billion" Forbes said, attributing the surge to a booking stock market charged with the operations of the Foreign Financial Institutions. Top ten richest Indian's assets are follows: Lakshmi Mittal $ 51 billion, Mukesh Ambani $ 49 billion, Azim Premji $ 14.8 billion, Sunil Mittal $ 12.5 billion, Shashi and Ravi Ruia $ 12 billion, Ramesh Chandra $ 11.6 billion, Kumar Birla $ 11 billion and Tulsi Tani $ 10 billion in 2007. It can be accounted for and stressed that the surge in their wealth owes to a booming stock market where the Foreign Financial Institutions play a major and very powerful role. Participatory Note is a kind of instrument issued by the Foreign Financial Institutions to enable foreign investors trade in stocks without disclosing their identity. Out of a total inflow of $ 176 billion dollars by the Foreign Financial Institutions as much as $ 88 billion was accounted for participatory note through August, 2007. Long ago N.A. Palkivala noted jurist and lawyer expressed concern on the dubious character of the Foreign Financial Institutions. S.S. Tarapore, Chairman Capital Account convertibility Committee 2006, said 'FIIs should be prohibited from investing fresh money raised through participatory notes. Joseph Stiglitz recently observed, "When there is chaos, wall street makes more money."

This has been the consequence of planned development in India. The Deputy Chairman of the Planning Commission Montek Singh Alhualia, however, glidly preaches that the 11th plan aims" not only at faster economic growth but also inclusive growth so that fruits of development reach the aam admi."[9] The plan has placed special emphasis on infrastructure – both urban and rural. "Many people think of infrastructure as relevant only for economic growth;

(but) it is also relevant for inclusiveness," he said in an interview. This is not a new approach. It was profounded and practices by the British Colonial Rule in India while building railways, mines, telegraph and telephone network. That did not prevent in any way colonial exploitation and impoverishment of the country. Further, development like laying water pipe line and road building have had a reverse impact in the market system though both are in the infrastructure. For instance, pipeline may bring water to the village while the road helps the urban businessmen to extract and command over local resources and labour and that enrich them faster through unequal exchange over the years. It actually goes against the interests of the aam admi. Development of infrastructure has never satisfies the interests of the toiling people or aam admi in the free market capitalism. According to official data, the National Rural Employment Guarantee Act was employing nearly three million workers on an average day in 2006-07 (when the Act was in force in 200 districts). As the act is extended to the whole of rural India, this could rise to 10 million or so the largest public works programme ever. CAG report shows that less than three per cent of registered beneficiaries got the promised 100 days of employment a year.

While the act presents new challenges "there is a risk that it night boomerang unless adequate preparations are made to face them." Employment still quite limited in NREGA provides some facility for political mobilization and reform but "It is a telling commentary on the state of Indian democracy that, with few exceptions, political parties across the spectrum have so far failed to seize this opportunity."[10]

One report says that in Rajasthan and Madhya Pradesh as much as 30-60 per cent of the NREGA fund was misappropriated and went through the leakages. Rajasthan's failure to implement is at the root of stout resistance to the exercise at the level of the local authorities. West Bengal follows the same way as barely 7.54 per cent of the funds were spent under NREGA, 66.36 per cent Sawayamjayanti Gram Swarojgar Yojana, 58.13 per cent under the Swampuran Gramean Rojgar Yojana and 53.24 per cent under the Indira Awas Yojana funds spill over from one year to the next and the stipulation of 100 day's work a year remains overwhelmingly unfulfilled despite administration's stress on job and employment. 'Inclusive growth' has become a fad in the highest echelon of the Union Government. The President says[11] agriculture growth is key to inclusive growth and agriculture has to remain in the center-stage of economic thinking making it attractive and rewarding. On the contrary, it applies the atrocious policy of acquiring rich fertile agricultural land from the peasants to establish hundreds of Special Economic Zones to placate foreign monopoly concerns and their Indian collaborators. It affects peasants interest and sends anominous message. It creates an all round bad social atmosphere that only subverts the base of agriculture, thwart the incentive and psychology of the producers and peasants, and saps their initiative and enterprise for agriculture. It is bound to be more counter-productive as the Union Commerce Ministry seeks to lift[12] any cap on the area of Special Economic Zones which would be nothing but foreign imperialist enclaves in the Indian soil from where international monopoly organizations, employing cheap Indian labour would be free to operate against their adversaries in the international economy and spread their tentacles more in India. The Commerce Minister thinks Indian economy will attract more global investments, even benefiting from the US slowdown and says that the country should not get "psyched" by the bubble burst in the USA. The market sources to the contrary, claimed that at least four major Indian Banks, State Bank of India, ICICI Bank, Bank of Baroda and Bank of India should collectively have about US dollar 4 billion exposure to sub-prime housing mortgage crisis in USA, while Citi Bank tops the list with $ 18 billion. Indian Economy, records a high growth rate while the Reserve Bank's expert group is finalizing its report on the issue of reviving 114000 units in the small and medium sector which had become sick during the period of globalization. The Union Government had de-reserved 500 items from the small scale industrial sector during 2005-07.

Giving the keynote address at the fifth awards function of the ICRA Mutual Fund, C. Rangarajan, Chief Government Economist expressed concern over the limited reach of mutual funds in the rural areas. 'And according to Invest India Economic Foundation survey there are around 34 million people with potential and capacity to invest in mutual funds," he pointed out, adding that 57 per cent of such people live in rural areas. He says that the expansion of the mutual fund industry is 'critical' on account of the major role the government is expecting it to play in garnering the huge resources, required for developing India's infrastructure which he pointed out "is currently the single biggest long-term constraint on sustaining high growth rates of 9-10 per cent." In sum, the infrastructure development would be held as ransom of the stock exchange and goaded with the market operations of the coercive big Foreign Bank and Financial Institutions. But what he did not disclose is that market factors conspired to rob more than Rs. 6 lakh crore wealth in a single trading session of the Mumbai Stock Exchange on 21.1.2008. Shares crashed following a panic that stripped stock exchange across the world. While numerous investors incurred bad incurred huge loss, big financial institutions made little loss. This high lights all round domination of finance capital and its consequence in the society.

The emerging socio-economic factors and circumstances in general suggest that globalization would reduce nation states' sovereignty though they would not disappear in the future. The nature of the nation state is undergoing changes dramatically due to globalization. "It is reducing the sovereignty of the nation with respect to global events which we need collaboration and transnational institutions to deal with."[13] "Globalization also has a pushdown effects which promotes local autonomy and local cultural difference. This has a double impact. On the one hand, it creates somewhat noxious forms of the local nationalism. On the other hand, it also opens new opportunities for civic participation and it is not accidental that there is a renewal of participatory democracy around the world, partly a result of globalization itself but partly a result of things."[14] In India, Nehru's daughter, after the Emergency, personalized congress as her own family affair and anointed sons to succeed, "Years of living by sycophancy had rendered congress worse"[15] than any other monolithic party.

The responsible leaders convey their rather dim view of current corps of politicians in the country. Speaking at the Fourth International Conference on federalism participated by more than 1000 delegates from over 30 countries, Prime Minister Manmohan Singh's speech was a reflection nearer home though he was addressing an international audience. By way of allusion to the current state of rather uneasy coalition exercise, he said narrow political considerations, based on regional or sections loyalties and ideologies, could distort national vision and sense of collective purpose.

He spoke of pulls and pressures[16] and various challenges on account of river water sharing, natural resources and fiscal federalism in a country like India while igniting a debate on single party rule as against a multi-party regime. In a world of multi-ethnic, multi-cultural, plural societies, Dr. Singh observed, federal political systems faced new political challenges. He stressed on the problem of managing a difficult coalition set-up in the period of competitive market economy where large international monopoly organizations struggled for their interests.

Dr. A.P.J. Abdul Kalam, former President of India there pointed out that the India's core competence was its over one billion people of multi-ethnic, multi-religions and multi-linguistic background "enjoying the fruits of a democratic dispensation."[17] He said India needed quality leadership and asked the states in the Indian "Union to share their infrastructure and knowledge to reduce disparities among them." "We are a democratic billion people who need quality leadership, he observed. The succeed, be noted, leaders require a shared vision for the nation with an ability to take real time decisions to travel along an un-explored path and nobility in management. "Working together is the need of the hour. The nation can work together on common issues for achieving sustainable growth." India is a country of diverse agro-climatic zones, each offering its own unique resources to be tapped according to its natural resources so that the economic benefits "flow to the local population" in adequate measure, regional aspirations can be ignored at federalism's own peril. For, lop-sided economic development, he added, could spell the death of federalism.

Monopoly capitalism and inclusive growth are opposed and antithetical to each other. It can be added to the above view that, in India, there is rigidity even in the internal migration of labour. A conference of Sikh scholars strongly opposed the influx of labourers from other states into Punjab saying it had "Complicated" the situation in the start "The mass ingress of over 20 lakh immigrants from Uttar Pradesh, Bihar, Madhya Pradesh, Orissa and other states have created many problems,"[18] they said at a two-day seminar." On changing demography of Punjab." But what must not be forgotten that the migrating labourers sufficiently contributed to added value to the state's domestic product continually over the years. Further, nature, time and process of economic development draws different ethnic groups and communities nearer.

One of the major lacunas of India's development strategy is that while it thrives on highly skilled services and it had neglected[19] mass education and health services. India's elite educational institutions stand like isolated ivory towers amidst encircling large poverty, illiteracy and backwardness. Rural India is completely neglected in health, nutrition and other elements of human necessities. The number of universities and colleges are also very small. For more than one billion population 400 universities and 16000 colleges are too few. According to the latest statistics, only about 8 per cent of youth manage to get admitted in colleges and universities. Most children drop out of school for a variety of reasons, mainly for poverty and parents' unwillingness to get their children educated due to socio-cultural backwardness.

The state funding of education as a proportion to GDP in India is one of the lowest among the emerging economies. The quality of education has gone down drastically in most state universities. Most of the teachers do not have the sense of obligation and commitment to their duties to their profession. The autonomy of the educational institutions has been on the wane[20] for a long period, and presently is at stake. A recently retired Education Secretary in the Central Government said in a talk given at the University of Bombay in early 2007, "Those of us who were involved in the field of liberalization know that the state was a predator. I believe that the state is somewhat predatory when it comes to education. It is a source of patronage, it is also a source of money,"[21] such observations are commonly made by senior civil servants in the capital, though not often in print or in public. There is growing concern in the country over the erosion of autonomy in the institutions of science and scholarship. Their freedom to make rules for their own internal governance has become restricted, and they have been made to fall in line with rules made by external agencies, when they find it hard to comply with rules in whose making they had no part, financial and other sanctions are applied against them. A shift from the public to the private sector brings new networks of patronage into operation without destroying the past ones; businessmen and company managers are no less skilled in the art of patronage obviously to their interests and profitability in business.

The direct aim and interest of the dominating classes, viz. capitalists and landlords in the capitalist society is profit[22] at the expense of the vast majority or oppressed people in the society. This can be broadly followed and illustrated well from the date of the financial performance of the Indian Corporate Sector representing

1286 companies in the more recent years. The operating profit of the Indian Corporate Sector increased from Rs. 53443 crores to Rs. 64767 crores during 2002-03 and 2003-04 or an increase of 21.2 per cent. Interest payment in the same period decreased from Rs. 16394 crores to Rs. 13736 crores or by 16.2 per cent. Their profit before tax rose from Rs. 28802 crores to Rs. 44036 crores, while profit after tax grew from Rs. 22229 crores to Rs. 34666 crores. Profits before tax and after tax during the intervening period grew 52.9 and 55.9 per cent respectively. Operating margin, gross margin and interest cover as proportion of sales and interest respectively also considerably increased. Earlier, data for very big 805 Public Limited Companies including Banks showed that during 1998-99 and 1999-2000 gross profits increased from Rs. 226160 crores to Rs. 257811 crores or by 14 per cent profit before tax also grew 15.4 per cent.

The key profitability ratios of the Indian Corporate Sector representing 2031 companies showed that gross profit to sales increased from 9.8 per cent during 2000-01 to 10.3 per cent in 2002-03, along with this, ratios for the other indicators showed remarkable improvement. The cost structure for same 1286 companies showed that the share of raw materials. Stores etc. as a percentage of sale relatively decreased from 58 per cent in 2000-01 to 55.9 per cent in 2002-03, while the share of wages and salaries witnessed a little rise from 5.9 per cent to 6.6 per cent. Operating profit as a percentage of sales for 805 companies during 1994-95 and 1999-2000 decreased from 9.6 per cent to 8.3 per cent, but in the later period, operating profit as a percentage of sales for 2031 companies showed an increase from 9.8 in 2000-01 to 10.3 per cent in 2002-03. Operating profit as percentage of total invested capital for 805 companies declined from 15.4 per cent in 1994-95 to 11.1 per cent in 1999-2000 while operating profit as percentage of sales for 1286 companies a steadily improved 3.6 per cent in 2000-2001 to 4.3 per cent and 5.4 per cent in 2001-02 and 2002-03 respectively.

Further, gross profit after adjusting depreciation for 2730 public limited companies[23] surveyed by the Reserve Bank of India amounting to Rs. 32042, 45596 and 61217 crores in 2003-04, 2004-05 and 2005-06 respectively. Making provisions for high salaries bonus and other allowances for the executive staff, the date show that the rate of labourer exploitation in the companies can be estimated at 100, 125 and 138 per cent respectively in 2003-04, 2004-05. The rate of labourer exploitation would be higher if the allowances for the executive staff are excluded or reduced.

It becomes evident that some companies earn more and make handsome profit, some others earn modest, while many earn only small profit or even make loss over the years. But in the whole production system the laws of value and generation of surplus value works at large. And for this sole cause and inherent contradiction there is friction, fluctuation and vicissitudes in the capitalist production. Wages and salaries in 805 corporations remained at 5.1 to 5.4 per cent of the total sales during 1994-95 and 1999-2000. It showed a little upward trend for 2031 companies when it moved from 5.9 per cent in 2000-01, to 6.5 per cent in 2001-02, and 6.6 per cent in 2002-03, but in these years in was nearer to the share of expenditure for power and fuel consumed, but for the 805 companies in the earlier period it was lower than the latter.

Clearly, wild and anarchic market operation, capitalist interceptions for reaping levy at different points, large scale mechanization of production, private appropriation, monopoly business and its associated coercion and overall, contradiction in the mode of production-all grow and manifest to thwart and further narrow the social base of monopoly capitalism at large, end their long-term complicated process undermine the scope for real inclusive development in the international economy and different countries of the world.

In India, the socio-economic lack-up little support the conditions of inclusive growth and does not warrant welfare for the vast majority of the people. Inclusive growth, as espolized by the major parties in India actually covers up the very inequities growth and continual arbitrary distribution of the social product in favour of the large interest groups. Developments show that the idea of inclusive growth is only a figure of speech of the Indian ruling elite-actually, a misnomer. The table showing the continuous decline of employment in the organized sphere of the factory sector employment confirms this fact at large. Service sector utilizing professionally qualified manpower, such as finance, banking, software media, entertainment etc. are recording fastest growth, where there is not yet any sign of diminishing returns.

Manufacturing growth on an average has been lower than services. Again within manufacturing sector, large-scale industries using higher technology and more technical labours are having faster growth than small and medium industries employing modest technology and more unskilled labours. During the last three decades, services GDP in India increased at an average of nearly 10 per cent a year. But in spite of slow growth of agriculture, which is now virtually stagnant at less than two per cent growth bulk of the population (70%) depending on agriculture lives in the village areas.

Agriculture with less than one-fifth share in GDP continues to provide employment to nearby 60 of labour force in the country. Further with the land in the private and unorganized sector, 57 per cent of the agricultural credit is supplied by the financial institutions and 43 per cent of it is still controlled by the village money lenders who charge interest rate of at least 20-25 per cent a year. The influence and score of the semi-fendal system, with scattered individual form of ownership and cultivation of land continues and proliferates to support and sustain backward mode of production and its social formation.

All these associated with the caste, ethnic group and religious factors of discrimination and exclusion aggravates the existing social set-up and leads to its manifestation which exacerbates the tendency of exclusion and more deprivation of labourers in the Indian society. The problem has become so acute, deep and manifest that according to the Government over 1,12,000 peasants committed suicide[24] in India in 1993 through 2006 because of debt bondage and poverty. But this is gross underestimate.

The depletion of the natural resource base in India is a very real problem which, if unattended, would seriously limit the ability to raise agricultural growth in the near future. Growth of agricultural GDP slowed down from 3.5 per cent per annum during the period from 1981-82 to 1996-97 to less than 2 per cent per annum in the period from 1997-98 to 2001-02.

The yields in agriculture have reached a plateau and have been stagnating for some time. Rice yield stagnated very much all through the 1990s and increase in wheat yield also slowed down in the 1990, and after some improvement towards the end of the decade, has been declining since 2000-01. The planning commission has reported that the scope for yield increase in many crops in many parts of the country using existing technology and better cultivation practices is a high as 60-100 per cent. This is obviously a capital intensive practice. On the contrary, in a recent NSS survey, it was found that 49 per cent of the farmers indicated that they want to leave farming.

The share of agriculture in GDP has declined to 22 per cent but it still provides the major source of subsistence and substances for over 50 per cent of the Indian population. Their welfare and country's food security is naturally dependant on agriculture, but agriculture sector could not keep pace with the relatively higher growth in India in the past decade of globalization, although its resurgence is viewed very crucial for achieving the important objective of inclusiveness of overall growth process. According to a paper done by Debroy and Bhandari (2007), as part of Tea Lease Labour Report, inequality in India has grown more especially since the late 1990s. It has become more intense in urban India than the rural. A recent World Bank Report shows that the wage differential between primary-educated workers and those beyond have sharply increased, in India, from the 1990s onward and 'liberalization has increased the return on skills'. This can be illustrated with the data on growing inequality among the people in the more recent period.

Table–2

Inequality (Gini Co-efficient) Among the Indians

Sector	*1983*	*1993-94*	*2004-05*
Rural	0.298	0.286	0.305
Urban	0.330	0.334	0.375

* Ginie co-efficient is used to measure inequality, where 0 means complete equality and 1 means complete inequality.

Source: World Bank.

Alongside, the current account balance as a share of India's gross domestic product in 2006-07 witnessed a negative of 2 per cent. Short-term debt turned out 7.7 per cent of the external debt. Total debt service as ratio of gross national income turned out 4.6 per cent. Domestic and foreign companies' borrowings aborad in 2007 amounted to $ 25 billion.

The government and its major ruling party however, is never tired of speaking of 'inclusive growth'. Inclusive growth, as it conceives, is but idealization and theorization of the development under the domination of foreign monopoly capitalism of the developed capital exporting countries and their Indian agents, factors, associates and collaborators – the array of Indian Compradors at the service of the international monopolies and finance capital. The development is the inclusive growth to the interest and privileges for domination of the Indian Comprador bourgeoisies and their imperialist masters. Globalization is synonymous of the imperialist domination in the Indian soil and political subjugation of the country. This "inclusive growth" is the innc ,ation of the theoreticians of the Indian Compradors and their principal foreign imperialist bourgeoisie. It draws near and unites them to confuse, exploit and oppress the masses of the people.

All this is patently against labour and stands solely to protect the vile interest and design of the capitalist and landlord classes at large. It is biased, arbitrary, anti-labour and anti-welfare and against humanism. Its design is to cover up the operation of the law of surplus value generation in the process of production and cross amarchic private distribution of the product in the society. Actually it is not the inclusive growth but a distortion and opposite to it. It is a part of the disinformation always circulated by the international capital to maintain its own writ in the system. For instance, the inequality of the content of the Indo-US joint statement[25] 2 March, 2006 is quite pertinent and revealing at large "Endorsing the efforts of the US-INDIA Trade Policy Forum to reduce barriers to trade and investment with the goal of doubling bilateral trade in three years. 'Advance mutually beneficial bilateral trade and investment flows by holding a high level public-private investment summit in 2006, continuing efforts to facilitate and promote foreign direct investment and eliminate impediments to it, and enhancing bilateral consultations on various issues in including tariff and non-tariff barriers to trade in goods, and services, and preventing the illicit use of the financial system, "Expand cooperation in agriculture, endorsing and agreed work plan to promote bilateral trade in agriculture through agreements."

Welcome the participation of India in the ITER initiative on fusion energy as an important step towards the common goal of full unclear energy cooperation. "Work together to promote innovation, creativity and technological advancement by providing a vibrant intellectual property rights regime, and to cooperate in the field of intellectual property rights to include capacity building activities, human resource development and public awareness programmes, take measures for "Deepening democracy, meeting international challenges."

The present day rule of monopoly capitalism is very coercive and atrocious, and annex every thin for its all pervasive domination. Such acquisitive society's ruling elite that striving to acquire meagre property of the millions of persons can little support or help inclusive growth. Predatory role of monopoly capitalism is anachronism, an antithesis to the idea of just and equitable growth for the real welfare of the vast majority of people in the society. During capital's surging period. Marx said in 1850s that under capitalism scientific and technological progress created a situation in which all "our inventions and progress seem to result in endowing material forces with intellectual life and in stultifying human life into a material force."[26] A hundred years after Marx and Engels, Gabriel Mercel virtually repeated their words but imparted an extraordinary historical meaning to them. He maintains that "More mankind secures domination over nature the more will individual man become the slave of that conquest."

Conclusion

It follows that man's triumph over nature spells this defeat in social plane, that this is a pyrrhic victory bringing incalculable suffering to mankind. Productive forces develop under scientific and technological progress, but invariably brings with it real social problems like the distribution and utilization of the productive forces, the intelligent and rational utilization of natural weather and the ways and means of preventing the pollution of air and water by the industrial waste of mammoth industrial units.

Marx and Engels exposed that in bourgeois society alienation (as the domination of people by the results of their own activity) was all out and total, it left an indelible imprint on the life and work of each individual, irrespective of the class to which the belonged. As distinct from idealists, they proved that in this system of total alienation the different classes nonetheless occupy different positions. They explained this key truth, which is one of the major points of Marxist, revolutionary—critical, real humanism, as follows: "The properties class sand the class of the proletariat present the same human alienation. But the former class finds in this self-alienation its confirmation and its good, its own power: it has in it a semblance of human existence. The class of the proletarist feels annihilated on its self-alienation; it sees in its own powerlessness and the reality of an inhuman existence."[27]

Wage labour does not create any bit of property for the labourer. It creates capital i.e. that kind of property which exploits wage labour. Thus, when material forces with some fringes of the railways etc. were trusted upon India in the nineteenth century, by the English bourgeoisie, Marx unequivocally observed in 1853, stressing that "All the English bourgeoisie may be forced to do will neither emancipate nor materially mend the social condition of the mass of the people, depending not only on the development of productive powers, but on their appropriation by the people.

"The Indians will not reap the fruits of the new elements of society scattered among them by the British bourgeoisie, till in Great Britain itself the new ruling classes shall have been supplanted by the industrial proletarial or till the Hindus (Indian people) themselves shall have grown strong enough to throw off the English Yoke altogether."[28] What is the rationale of "industrialization" and "development" at the command of imperialism and finance capital in India to-day? What halo is there to the working class for higher rate of growth which trickles down most on the owners of the means of production and masters of the international capital?

Stressing on the abolishing the previous mode of production and appropriation generally. Marx and Engels, refuted the bourgeois allegation of abolishing the property of the petty artisan and of the small peasant. As they declared in the Communist Manifesto, "Hard won, self-earned property : Do you mean the property of the petty artisan and of the small peasant, a form of property that preceded the bourgeois form? There is no need to abolish that; the development of industry has to a great extent already destroyed it, and is still destroying it daily."[29] Engels reiterated the same view and stand and asked for support to the small peasants' rights and interests, in his peasant question in France and Germany.

It becomes clear that the founders of scientific socialism do not at all idealise forcible occupation, usurpation and abolishing of small arisan and small peasant. The parliamentary and government "Left" along with the rightist parties, disregard the view and blatantly violates the basic postlilate of socialism and bow before the penetrating international monopoly capitalism in order to serve imperialism, i.e., moribund capitalism in a dastardly manner.

What is the motive, import and significance of forcibly acquiring small peasants' land for establishing special economic zones, chemical hub, big luxurious residential complex and malls in India in the 21st century? It cannot be except to the interest and profit-domination of the Indian and foreign monopoly capitalists at the cost of sterilization of the labour and abolition of their meager landed property. All this greatly undermines and vitiates the basis and condition of inclusive growth, leading to more pauferiazation of the masses of people, opening the home market to the predatory foreign monopoly capitalism for fleecing the labour more and reducing the country merely into a colony. The rightist and the "left" governments follow the same cause to appease and serve the international finance capital by ruthlessly suppressing the workers and peasants of the country.

Social structure of the ourgeisie society and impact of monopoly capital's rule is not at all conductive and the frontiers of inclusive growth are greatly shrinking in India and many other countries. But one can at least see partially see existing pre-requisite and technical conditions of inclusive (labour widening) growth in the countries like Russia and China which had undergone rapid and revolutionary transformation in the past and labour became aware and conscious of its rights and responsibilities. Demographically, Russia needs labour migrants, while agrarian regions on Central Asia are so much populated that inability of find employment elsewhere would social tension and lead to an undesirable political results. Russia is working to regain its own good relation and influence in the former Soviet Republics. Three issues – the transport system, the openness of markets and labour migration are also linked with Russia's security interests. Russia wants Central Asian States to have stable and secular political regimes. China basically holds the same idea and had signed economic, political, military and cultural treaty with Russia in 2000.

The idea and some scope for movement towards inclusive growth can be generally followed in the provisions of Russian constitution of 1993. It declares[30] :

The Russian Federation shall protect the work and health of the people, establish a guaranteed minimum wage, provide state support for family, motherhood, fatherhood and childhood and also for disabled and elderly citizens, develop a system of social services and establish government pensions, benefits and other social security guarantees (Art. 7:2). The land and other natural resources shall be used and protected in the Russian Federation as the basis of the life and activity of the people living on their respective territories (Art. 9:1).

The land and other natural resources may be private, state, municipal and other forms of ownership (Art. 9:2).

China, following the same principle, rules out the possibility of land privatization, saying that government ownership of land is enshrined in the constitution and has been a key factor in the country's advancement in development. Land ownership was determined by China's constitution rather than Central Government Policy, Director of the Central Leading Group for Rural Work, Chen Xiwen, told the press on 30.01.2007 in Beijing, when asked whether China would allow privatization of land. He said the Government would continue land utilization reform to control illegal sale of farmland and protect peasants' interests.

China is facing problems in handling the issue of rural land and rights. With peasants increasingly being evicted from their homes to make way for roads, factories, malls and residential areas, premier. We Jiabliao warned in 2006 that illegal seizures of land without compensation and resettlement were a key source of instability in rural areas. "It is sparking mass incidents in the countryside," Mr. Wen said, adding that "We absolutely cannot commit a historic error regarding land problems." The Chineese Government issued a notice in 2006 on strengthening Land Control, through which the Government tightened controls over transforming farmlands to urban construction uses.

Mr. Chen Xiwen, Director, Central Leading Group acknowledged that land confiscation is the most frequent subject of petitions made by Chinese peasants, with complaints about village finances and environment pollution coming next. He told Government officials that they "should not turn a deaf wear to farmers' requests."

The land question was reviewed and it was reiterated and further stressed in 2007 by the Chinese state. As Mao-Siwel, council General of China in Calcutta, said that the land is owned by the State in China and the administration always holds discussions with peasants' bodies when farm land is required to be acquired for industrial purposes. In China farmers collectively use land and as such for any industrial units to be set up on farms land the collective body of farmers is taken into confidence.

Russia has taken certain important measures to check offensive of the foreign multinational corporations and their predatory campaign design in the name of democracy. Its foreign debt has substantially decreased with large export surplus and the higher growth rate of the economy. China's development also generally follows the same trend. Alongside people's movements for right and entitlement in the two countries are growing on for years. For insurance, protests in China rose from 10000 in 1994 to 74000 in 2004 and some 3.67 million people took active part. But, Cuba's rich experience in socialist construction, and some genuine reform measures taken against imperialist capital by the popularly elected left Governments in a few Latin American countries are encouraging and noteworthy, showing a solver line of social advancement at the present time.

Economic development under monopoly and finance capital can not ever conceive of and never ensures inclusive growth. Its direct aim and sole motive is maximum profit. Property exists as the product of the confrontation between capital and labour. It stands for severe exploitation and displacement of labour, anarchy, naked aggression and tramping upon human rights, and independence and sovereignty of nations. Factory sector of the Indian economy witnessed a great fall in employment from 10 million 32 in 1998 to 5.9 million of by 40 per cent in 2001-02. The contention of the international bourgeoisie and comprador ruling classes of India is to denude the country of its precious natural resources and early expulsion of the labourers not only from the productive system but also from the world. Like the bailiffs of the East India Company they are expropriating thousands of small peasants of their meager agricultural land in the name of industrialization, pushing them before the deep gorge of annihilation. This is the actual result of the rule of monopoly capitalism in the present world of the twenty-first century. Inevitably, the distribution of the product between the capitalist and labourer glaringly comes to the fore of the world economy facing crisis with its ever narrowing social base. Inclusive growth under such a condition has been conspicuously absent, a falsehood, and great mirage in the world's coercive market economy, and more particularly, in the traditionally backward and semi-colonial countries like India.

It reveals that distribution is the product of the mode of production and intense class struggle and scientific socialism have no substitute for that can only bring in and warrant inclusive growth for commonwealth of society. Objectively, the trend of the development in the world economy is moving in that direction, though subjective forces for transformations are not so strong enough at present. But nevertheless, it is becoming and growing over time.

NOTES AND REFERENCES

1. Frederick Engelas, The Part Played by Labour in the transition from Ape to Man, Foreign Languages Press, Peaksing, 1975, pp. 1-18. Engels observes, "Man, too, arises by differentiation, Not only individually, by development from a single egg-cell to the most complicated organism that nature produces but also historically. When the differentiation of hand from foot and erect gait were finally established after thousands of years of struggle, man became distinct from the ape, and the basis was laid for the development of articulate speech and the tremendous progress of the brain that has since made the gulf between man and ape unbridgeable" (citation from Engels' introduction to his Dialectics of Nature).
2. Karl Marx, Wages, Price and Profit, Foreign Languages Press, Peking 1975, p. 6, p. 6. (Italics in the original).
3. The Statement, Kolkata, 20 June 2002 (Supplement section); Statistical Outline of India 2000-01, 2004-05. Tata Services Limited, Bombay House, Mumbai, pp. 254-255 and pp. 264-65.
4. Clifford Krauss, Tapped out, but Hopeful, The Indian Express, Lucknow, 5 November 2007, p. 12.
5. The Statesman, Kolkata—14, November 2007, p. 2.
6. The Indian Express, Kolkata, 7 February, 2008 p. 6.
7. Kalantar (Bengali), Kolkata, 28 and 29, November 2007 p. 4 (Art by Sunil Mitra).
8. The Statesman, Kolkata, 16 and 25 November 2007, p. 8 and p. 13; India Today, New Delhi, 5 November, 2007, pp. 27-28; and The Statesman, 3 November, 2007, Kolkata, p. 17.
9. "Citation" in Bharat Jhunjhunwala, Flip Side of Growth. The Statesman, Kolkata, 2 February 2008, p. 6.
10. Aruna Roy, Geon Drze and Nikhil Dey, Finish the job, Hindusthan Times, Kolkata, 1 February 2008, p. 6. The Statesman.
11. Indian Express, Kolkata, 7 February, 2008, p. 1.
12. The Statesman, Kolkata, 7 and 8 February, 2008, p. 8.
13. Antony Giddens, D.T. Lakdwala Lecture, The Times of India, New Delhi, 31 October, 2007, p. 14.
14. *Ibid.*

15. Meghnad Desai, It's a Family Affair, The Times of India, New Delhi, 31 October, 2007, p. 14.
16. The Statesman, Kolkata, 12 November 2007, p. 5.
17. *Ibid.*
18. *Ibid.*
19. B.B. Bhattacharya, Educational Skill Formation and India's Economic Development, Presidential Address to the Conference of the Indian Economic Association, Srinagar, 2007.
20. Andre Beteille, Autonomy is at Staake, The Times of India, Lucknow, 1 November 2007, p. 12.
21. *Ibid.*
22. Statistical outline of India 2000-01 and 2004-05. Tata Services Limited, Bombay House, Mumbai, pp. 98-99 and pp. 102-105.
23. Reserve Bank of India Bulletin, November 2007, Mumbai , p. 1005.
24. Sukhadeo Thorat, on Economic Exclusion and Inclusive Policy SNDT University, Mumbai 2007 and Y.V. Krishna Rao. The State of Indian Agriculture: A Reality Check, The New Age, New Delhi 16-22 September 2007, p. 5. Dr. Ishar Judge Ahkuwatia, Presidential Address at the 67th conference of the Indian Society of Agricultural, Economics Lucknow, December 2007, pp. 2-4.
25. Cf. Hindustan Times, Kolkata, 3 March 2006, p. 2.
26. The People's Paper No. 207, London 19 April, 1956; Gabriel March Les homes contre L'humain, Paris, 1951, p. 46, see Karl Marx and Modern Philosophy, Progress Publishers, Moscow, 1968.
27. Karl Marx and Frederick Engels, The Holy Family or Critique of Critical Critique, Foreign Languages Publishing House, 1956, p. 51 (Italics in the original).
28. Karl Marx and Frederick Engels, Manifesto of the Communist Party, Progress Publishers, Moscow, 1967, p. 63; The future of Results of the British Rule in India, On Colonialism, Foreign Languages Publishing House, 1956, p. 80.
29. Karl Marx and Frederick Engels, Manifesto of the Communist Party, Progress Publishers, Moscow, 1967, p. 58 and p. 63.
30. M.V. Pylee (ed.), Constitutions of the World, Universal Law Publishing Company Pvt. Ltd. Delhi, 2000, p. 1184; Yevgeny Khozokin, Central Asia, The Statesman, Kolkata, 6 December 2004, p. 8.
31. The Statesman Kolkata, 31 January 2007 and 22 November 2007, p. 6 and p. 5. People's Daily (Peking) reported that from 1986 to 2004 Arbitration network had to handle over 1.07 million.
32. Statistical Outline of India 2000-01 and 2004-05, Tata Services Abstract 2003, Central Statistical Organization, Government of India, New Delhi, 2004, p. 298.

6

Globalization and Pace of Economic Growth in India

MITHILESH KUMAR SINHA

Introduction

India today is rated as the third largest economy in the world. The Indian economy's strength is now being recognised world over. Only the US and Chinese economies are larger than ours. In terms of Gross Domestic Product (GDP) growth rates India is one of the fastest growing economies in the world. India has displaced the US as the second most favoured destination for foreign direct investment in the world after China.

The economic reforms in India that began in the early '90s fundamentally altered the nature of our engagement with the world. Globalization got a new meaning and the wave of economic liberalization changed the way big and small nations started perceiving India. Very few would have imagined a decade ago that companies from Indian IT, pharma and auto sectors will make such significant in roads into international markets and gain global recognition. This is reality now and India is moving at an accelerated pace into this horizon of potential (Singh: 2007).

The object of this chapter is to assess the performance of the Indian economy during the globalization era. In doing so, it seeks to focus on economic growth. The chapter is organised as follows. In the first brief section, I deal with GDP perspective of global economy. Section II outlines historical perspective of growth in India. Section III provide an assessment of economic growth in India since 2001. Section IV discusses the concerns and issues with concluding observations.

I

GDP Perspective of Global Economy

The world economy is headed for a slow down – this the prediction that many market experts are making. The US seems to be headed for a recession, China is prone to a hard landing, while some other emerging markets, too, look vulnerable. Risk appetite for emerging market equities is on the decline and India is showing early signs of a growth scare. Asian Development Bank (ADB) forecasts developing Asian economies to grow by 7.6 per cent in 2007, contracting from the 8.3 per cent growth in 2006. The International Monetary Fund (IMF) expects most economies, except Japan and the UK, to slow down in 2007, but it expects advanced economies to recover in 2008.

The consensus, at present, seems to indicate that the US economy is needed for a slowdown. The economy is moving from 'high growth, low inflation to low growth, high inflation'.

The research undertaken by the Princeton Economic Institute provides more insights. It states that the beginning of the end starts when you witness a top everywhere and then, confusing signs or uncertainty or reduced risk appetite becomes visible. At present, low cost money followed by high inflation M&A activity, mind-boggling bonuses, accelerating FII inflows, increase in hedge funds and their assets under management, private equity deals, and high appreciation in asset markets are some factors. All these are cooling off from their recent highs. We are currently in confusing times. The Dow Theory has the same story to tell about the US market and it could have lessons for other markets too. The theory suggests that there are three clear trends and currently, the market is in trend 3. This is a trend where prices drop significantly, reverse sharply and then continue moving down. This indicates that each trend has three stages – distribution, big move and despair (Table 1).

The post-1950 growth experience of developing countries has been much more varied. Persistence of good growth over decades has been rare (Easterly *et al.,* 1993). Individual countries have experience of big changes in growth (Hansmann *et al.,* 2005 a). There has been enormous variability in growth rates across countries, upwards of 5 per cent a year between fast and slow growers in any given decade (World Bank: 2005).

Very few developing countries have sustained decent per capita growth for two decades or more. Specifically, out of 117 developing countries with population over half a million, only 12 countries achieved per capita growth of more than 3 per cent per year in 1980-2002, with at least 2 per cent growth in each decade of the 1980s and 1990s. These 12 countries were: China (8.2), Vietnam (4.6), South Korea (6.1), Chile (3.3), Mauritius (4.4), Malaysia (3.4), India (3.6), Thailand (4.6), Bhutan (4.3), Sri Lanka (3.1), Botswana (4.7), and Indonesia (3.5). (The number falls to nine if we specify a minimum population of 3 million). Nine of these 12 countries are in Asia and fortunately, they include the three most populous: China, India and Indonesia (Table-2).

Table–1
Gross Domestic Product Growth Estimates (in per cent)

Countries and World	*2001*	*2002*	*2003*	*2004*	*2005*	*2006*	*2007 E*	*2008 E*
World	2.5	3.1	4.0	5.3	4.9	5.4	4.9	4.9
United States	0.8	1.6	2.5	3.9	3.2	3.3	2.2	2.8
Euro Area	1.9	0.9	0.8	2.0	1.4	2.6	2.3	2.3
United Kingdom	2.4	2.1	2.7	3.3	1.9	2.7	2.9	2.7
Japan	0.2	0.3	1.4	2.7	1.9	2.2	2.3	1.9
Korea	3.8	7.0	3.1	4.7	4.2	5.0	4.4	4.4
China	8.3	9.1	10.0	10.1	10.4	10.7	10.0	9.5
India	4.1	4.3	7.3	7.8	9.2	9.2	8.4	7.8
Advanced Economies	1.2	1.6	1.9	3.3	2.5	3.1	2.5	2.7
Other Advanced Economies	1.7	3.2	2.4	4.1	3.2	3.6	3.3	3.4
Other Emerging Market and Developing Countries	4.3	5.0	6.7	7.7	7.5	7.9	7.5	7.1

Source: World Economic Outlook 2007, IMF. E = Estimated.

II

Historical Perspective of Indian Growth

The economic historian Angus Maddison has estimated that in 1700 AD, towards the end of the Mughal Empire. India's GDP was not

Table-2
Good Growth Performers of Recent Decades Average Annual Per Capita Growth (per cent)

Country	*1980-2002*	*1990s*	*1980s*	*Population in 2000 (Million)*
China	8.2	8.6	7.7	12.62
Vietnam	4.6	5.7	1.9	78.00
South Korea	6.1	5.0	7.4	47.00
Chile	3.3	4.3	2.1	15.00
Mauritius	4.4	4.1	4.9	1.00
Malaysia	3.4	3.7	3.1	23.00
India	3.6	3.6	3.6	10.16
Thailand	4.6	3.4	6.0	6.10
Bhutan	4.3	3.4	5.4	1.00
Sri Lanka	3.1	3.1	3.1	18.00
Botswana	4.7	2.7	7.2	2.00
Indonesia	3.5	2.6	4.4	20.60

Source: World Bank (2005).

only higher than that of China, but that of western Europe combined. In terms of productivity and technology, however, it had already begun to fall behind Europe. Roughly at par in 1000 AD, per capita GDP in India and China had fallen to roughly half of the average European level by 1700. It was this growing gap between Europe and the rest of the world that fuelled European expansion to other parts of the globe.

Overall, per capita income growth under British India was stagnant or very low. Imported manufactures, the decimation of one of the most opulent ruling classes in the world, and the westernization of the new elites, destroyed the demand for Indian booming artisan industry. Unemployment rose, especially underemployment, since much of the traditional industry, such as spinning of cloth yarn, was a widespread household activity that supplemented rural (agricultural) incomes (Sheel: 2007).

With the onset of the industrial revolution, India's artisan industry was doomed to decline anyway, just as in England. The attempt to protect traditional industry in post-Independence India failed because both demand and productivity patterns have vastly changed. The lack of protection to modern infant industries is the more credible criticism of imperial rule.

However, by the end of British Rule in India's modern textile industry was giving Manchester a run for its money and India's per capita industrial output was higher than any other Asian country with the exception of Japan. More than half of Indian exports were manufactures. It was the protective shroud descending on Indian industry following independence that destroyed the competitiveness of this infant industry.

While foreign conquerors such as Mahmud Ghaznavi and Nadir Shah carried off wealth accumulated over centuries in lightening forays through India's vulnerable north western passes, the British were unique in their sustained leaching of the country's wealth for over two centuries. However, unlike their predecessors who used this wealth for war of self-aggrandisement, personal luxury and building great moments of no benefit to the common man, the British also used this wealth to put in place great public works that transformed India. All weather roads, railways, canals, telegraphs, the Suez Canal, combined with the long peace of Pox Britannica, gradually put an end to periodic famines and stimulated agricultural expansion from the 1870s through close market.

The impact of public works was to slightly increase per capita income, which had largely stagnated or declined since Robert Clive's conquest of Bengal in 1757. According to Maddison's estimates, per capita income in British India rose by approximately 1 per cent per annum between 1885 and 1910, by which time the impact of developmental works was exhausted. While there was on average a marginal decline in the per capita growth rate thereafter, it is nevertheless intriguing that per capita income growth during the high noon of India's post-Independence command-and-control autarchy was not appreciably higher than that between 1885 and 1910, as the Table 3 indicates. It was the loosening of controls and opening up the economy from the eighties that accelerated growth.

III

Some Facts About Growth of India (1991-2000)

- Between 1981-82 and 1990-91, the growth rate of economy was 5.6 per cent per annum. The year 1991-92 was an exceptionally bad year. If we leave out 1991-92, between

Table-3
Average Annual Real GDP Growth Per Capita (in per cent)

Decades	*Average Annual Real GDP Growth Per Capita in %*	
1885-90	1.00	
1891-00	0.60	1885-1910=1.07
1901-10	1.60	
1911-20	-0.70	
1921-30	1.40	1911-1950=-0.20
1931-40	-0.5	
1941-50	-1.00	
1951-60	2.04	
1961-70	1.54	1951-1980=1.48
1971-80	0.87	
1981-90	3.50	
1991-00	3.60	1981-2000=3.55
2000+	5.60	5.60

Source: Pre 1950 data: Angus Maddison.

1992-93 and 2000-01 the average annual growth rate comes to 6.3 per cent. Even if we include 1991-92 the annual growth rate in the Nineties will be 5.7 per cent (Rangarajan: 2001-02).

- It is interesting to note that between 1992-93 and 1999-2000 there was only one year in which the growth rate was less than 5 per cent. The coefficient of the variation of growth rate in the nineties is distinctly lower than in the eighties (Ibid).
- Between 1992-93 and 2000-01 the industrial growth rate was 6.6 per cent per annum and the growth rate in services was 7.9 per cent.
- The gross domestic savings rate of the economy on an average during the period 1992-93 to 1999-2000 has remained at 23.1 per cent of GDP.
- Inflation rate as measured by the Wholesale Price Index though high in the early Nineties started declining from 1995-96 and the average inflation rate has arrived five per cent since then.

- The current account deficit after reaching the high around one per cent of the GDP in the last few years. With the current account deficit remaining low and with continued capital inflows. It has been possible to add to the foreign exchange reserves. These reserves have increased from $ 5.8 billion in 1990-91 to $ 38.0 billion by March, 2000. They have subsquently increased by $ 6 billion.
- The macroeconomic indicators do show a distinct improvement in the performance as compared with the previous periods.
- However, even in relation to the growth rate a disturbing trend is that there has been a dinstinct slowing since 1997-98. While the growth rate between 1992-93 and 1996-97 was 6.5 per cent, in the subsequent four years the growth rate has been 5.8 per cent. (for details of all see Table 4).

Facts About Growth of India (2000-01 to 2005-06)

- Between 2000-01 and 2005-06, the average annual growth rate comes 6.5. Between 2000-01 and 2005-06 there were two years i.e. 2000-01 and 2002-03 in which the growth rate was less than 5 per cent. The Central Statistical Organization's advance estimates of national income for 2006-07, which place Gross Domestic Product (GDP) growth at 9.2 per cent surpass all earlier official and independent forecasts. With the CSO revising upwards its quick estimate for 2005-06, India's record, according to the official statistics, over the past three years have been extremely impressive—GDP annual growth of 8.5 per cent, 7.5 per cent and now 9.2 per cent. Only China has done better than India during this period. It is apparent that India has broken through the relative stagnation of the late 1990s and the early years of the current decade.
- A notable feature of the current phase is the sharp rise in the rate of investment in the economy. Investment, the general being a forward looking variable, reflects a high degree of business optimism. The revival in Gross Domestic Product Formation (GDCF) that commenced in 2002-03 has been followed by a sharp rise in the rate of investment in the economy for four cosecutive years. The earlier estimates of GDCF for 2004-05 of 30.1 per cent released by CSO in their advance estimates, now stand upgrade to 31.5 per cent in

Table–4

Selected Macroeconomic Indicators of India, 1990-91 to 1999-2000

Item	*1990-91*	*1991-92*	*1992-93*	*1993-94*	*1994-95*	*1995-96*	*1996-97*	*1997-98*	*1998-99*	*1999-2000*	*Average 1990-2000*	*Average 1992-2000*
GDPFC (1993-94=100) (Growth Rate)	5.3	1.5	4.5	6.0	7.0	7.3	7.5	5.0	6.8	6.4	5.7	6.3
Rate of GDCF at constant Price	25.9	21.7	22.3	22.3	26.0	26.8	24.5	25.0	23.0	23.3	24.1	24.2
Gross Domestic Saving Rateat Current Prices (%)	24.3	22.9	22	22.7	24.8	25.1	23.2	23.5	22.0	22.3	23.3	23.2
Industrial Production (Growth Rate)	8.2	0.6	2.3	6.0	8.9	13.1	6.1	6.6	3.8	8.1	6.4	6.9
Agricultural Production (Growth Rate)	3.8	-2.0	4.2	3.8	5.0	-2.7	9.3	-6.1	7.8	-0.7	2.2	2.6
Foodgrains Production (Growth Rate)	3.3	-4.2	4.7	4.1	3.9	-6.3	10.1	-3.2	5.8	2.6	2.1	2.7
WPI (1993-94=100) Rate of Increase	10.3	13.7	10.1	8.4	12.5	8.1	4.6	4.4	5.9	3.3	8.1	7.2

Contd...

Item	*1990-91*	*1991-92*	*1992-93*	*1993-94*	*1994-95*	*1995-96*	*1996-97*	*1997-98*	*1998-99*	*1999-2000*	*Average 1990-02*	*Average 1992-02*
CPI (Industrial Workers) Rate of Increase	11.6	13.5	9.6	7.5	10.1	10.2	9.4	6.8	13.1	3.4	9.5	8.8
Exports (US $ Million) (Growth Rate)	9.2	-1.5	3.8	20	18.4	20.8	5.3	4.6	-5.1	13.2	8.9	10.1
Imports (US $ Million) (Growth Rate)	13.5	19.4	12.7	6.5	22.9	28.0	6.7	6.0	2.2	11.4	12.9	12.1
Foreign Exchange Reserves (US $ Million)	5834	9220	9832	19254	25186	21687	26423	29367	32490	38036	–	–
Current A/C Deficit (as % of GDP)	-3.1	-0.3	-1.7	-0.4	-1.0	-1.7	-1.2	-1.4	-1.0	-0.9	-1.3	-1.2
Foreign Investment (as % of GDP)	0	0.1	0.2	1.5	1.5	1.4	1.6	1.3	0.6	1.2	0.9	1.2
US $ Exchange Rate	17.9	24.5	30.7	31.4	31.4	33.5	35.5	37.2	42.1	43.3	–	–

Source: Handbook of Statistics on Indian Economy, 2000. Reserve Bank of India, Mumbai.

the quick estimates. The rate of GDCF for 2005-06 as per the quick estimates released by CSO is 33.8 per cent. This sharp increase in the investment rate has sustained the industrial performance and reinforces the outlook for growth.

- The increasing trend in gross domestic savings as a proportion of GDP observed since 2001-02 has continued with the savings ratio rising from 26.4 per cent in 2002-03 to 29.7 per cent in 2003-04, 31.1 per cent in 2004-05 and 32.4 per cent in 2005-06. The rise in the savings rate of 2005-06 was contributed by two of its three components: private corporate and the household sector, which as proportion of GDP, increased by 1 percentage point and 0.7 percentage point respectively. The third component, namely public savings declined by 0.4 percentage points and made a negative contribution to the overall savings rate. However, redeeming feature of recent years is that the savings of the public sector which had been negative until 2002-03, was positive for the third successive year in 2005-06. A dramatic element in the savings profile of the Indian economy has been the sharp rise in the savings rate of the private corporate sector for four years in a row.
- Growth of industrial sector from a low of 2.7 per cent in 2001- 02, revived to 7.1 per cent and 7.4 per cent in 2002-03 and 2003-04 respectively and after accelerating to over 9.5 per cent in the next two years, touched 10.0 per cent in 2006-07.
- After an annual average of 3 per cent in the first five years of the new millennium starting 2001-02 growth of agriculture at only 2.7 per cent in 2006-07, on a base of 6 per cent growth in the previous year, is a cause of concern. Low investment, imbalance in fertiliser use, low seeds replacement rate, a distorted incentive system and low post-harvest value addition continued to be a drag on the sector's performance.
- Inflation rate as measured by the Wholesale Price Index though low in the years of 2001-02 and 2002-03 started increasing from 2003-04 and again decline in 2005-06 Q. and the average inflation rate has been around 5 per cent since then.
- The current account deficit after reaching the high of 2.3 per cent of GDP in 2003-04 has been steadily declining in 2004-05 and 2005-06 and it has reached at negative point.

- With the current account deficit remaining low and with continued capital inflows, it has been possible to add to the foreign exchange reserves. These reserves have increased from $ 4.5 billion in 2000-01 to $ 28.1 billion in 2004-05 and it has declined in 2005-06 (Table-5).

Table–5

Selected Macroeconomic Indicators of India (2000-01 to 2006-07)

Item	*2000-01*	*2001-02*	*2002-03*	*2003-04*	*2004-05*	*2005-06*	*Average 2000-06*
GDPFC (1999-00=100) (Growth Rate)	4.4	5.8	3.8	8.5	7.5	9.0 Q	6.5
Rate of GDCF at Constant Prices (%)	24.0	22.9	25.2	28.0	31.5	33.8	27.57
Gross Domestic Savings Rate at Current Prices (%)	23.4	23.5	26.4	29.7	31.1	32.4	27.75
Industrial Production (Growth Rate)	5.0	2.7	5.7	7.0	8.4	8.2	6.17
Agricultural Production (Growth Rate)	–5.4	7.9	–15.9	20.3	–1	6.0	1.98
Foodgrains Production (Growth Rate)	–	8.2	–17.9	22.1	–6.9	5.1P	2.12
WPI (1999-00) (Rate of Increase)	–	3.6	3.4	5.5	6.5	4.4	4.68
CPI (Industrial Workers) (Rate of Increase)	–	5.1	3.8	3.7	3.6	4.7	4.18
Exports (US $ Million) (Growth of Rate)	21.1	–1.6	20.3	21.1	30.8	23.4	19.18
Imports (US $ Million) (Growth Rate)	4.6	1.7	19.4	27.3	42.7	33.8	21.58

Contd...

Item	*2000-01*	*2001-02*	*2002-03*	*2003-04*	*2004-05*	*2005-06*	*Average 2000-06*
Foreign Exchange Reserves (US $ Million)	4494	11503	20835	35556	28126	9535	-
Current A/C Deficit (as % of GDP)	−0.6	0.7	1.3	2.3	−0.4	−1.1	0.37
Foreign Investment (as % of GDP)	-	-	-	-	-	-	-
US $ Exchange Rate	45.68	47.69	48.4	45.95	44.93	44.27	-

Source: Economic Survey 2005-06, 2006-07 GoI.

In brief, we can say that during 2000-01 to 2005-06, vigorous growth with strong macroeconomic fundamentals have characterized developments in the Indian economy. However, there are some genuine concerns on the inflation front. Growth of 9 per cent and 9.2 per cent in 2005-06 and 2006-07, respectively, by most accounts, surpassed expectations. While the up-and-down pattern in agriculture continued with growth estimated at 6 per cent and 2.7 per cent in the two recent years, and services maintained its vigorous growth performance, there were distinct signs of sustained improvements in the industrial front.

In brief, the overall macroeconomic fundamentals are robust, particularly with tangible progress towards fiscal consolidation and a strong balance of payment's position with an upsurge in investment, the outlook is distinctly upbeat.

IV

Concerns and Issues

A major criticism of the liberalisation process is that the higher growth rate achieved has made no dent on poverty and unemployment. Based on the National Sample Survey data on consumption expenditure, over years certain methodologies have been evolved to estimate the number of people below poverty line. Estimates of the percentage of the people below poverty line based on various NSS rounds show that the combined rural and urban poverty ratio came down from 44.48 per cent in 1983 to 38.86 per cent in 1987-88 and further to 35.07 per cent in 1993-94. The poverty ratio in 1999-2000 was 26.10 per cent.

Based on the data on NSSO's 61st round large scale sample survey on household consumer expenditure for the year 2004-05, it may be concluded that the incidence of poverty came down to about 22 per cent in 2004-05 from a level of 26.1 per cent in 1999-2000 in terms of the mixed recall period.

The results of the NSSO's 61st round large-scale quinquennial survey on employment and unemployment conducted during 2004-05 throws a lot of light on the heated debate on jobless growth under reforms. The survey results show how the annual growth rate of employment, which had declined from 2.1 per cent during 1983-1994 to 1.6 per cent during 1993-2000 went up to 2.5 per cent during 1999-05.While employment has grown faster than before, with the demographic dynamics and higher labour force participation, rate of unemployment (as measured by 'usual principal status') also went up marginally from 2.8 per cent to 3.1 per cent during 1999-2000 to 2004-05.

The economy appears to have decidedly 'taken off' and moved from a phase of moderate growth to a new phase of high growth. Achieving the necessary escape velocity to move from tepid growth into a sustained high-growth trajectory requires careful consideration of two issues and three priorities. The two issues are: The sustainability of high growth with moderate inflation; and the inclusive nature of such high growth. The three priorities are: Rising to the challenge of maintaining and managing high growth; bolstering the twin-pillars of growth, namely fiscal prudence and high investment; and improving the effectiveness of government intervention in critical areas such as education, health and support for the needy.

On the first issue of sustainability of high growth without running into high inflation, various indicators suggest that the current growth phase is sustainable.

First, higher growth together with the demographic dividend (from a growing proportion of the population in the working age group) is likely to lead to a rise in the savings rate to finance more and more investment. There is already evidence of this virtuous and mutually reinforcing growth-savings-growth cycle in the recently released savings and investment figures for 2005-06.

Second, efficiency improvements in the economy since 1999-2000 reinforce the confidence in the high-growth phase. The ratio of net capital stock to gross value added in the economy, according to the National Account Statistics, went down from 2.78 to 2.6 between 1999-2000 and 2004-05. While the ratio increased to 2.66 in 2004-05, the rise was primarily due to a corresponding rise in the ratio of net capital stock to value added in agriculture. There is an encouraging and almost steady decline in the ratio of net capital stock to value added in industry.

Third, it is not only the sustained increase in savings and investment, availability of labour at reasonable wage rates, and efficiency increases, but also the opening up of new avenues in services, beyond the already well-known IT and ITES, that bolster confidence in the new high-growth phase. For example, in a remarkable transition, the tourism industry has displayed buoyant double-digit annual growth rates in each of the last three years. Tourism contributes over 10 per cent of global GDP and its potential in India, given the country's enormous natural, human and technological resources, is well-recognised. The sector, through its backward and forward linkages, can stimulate many others, particularly hotels, restaurants, and handicrafts. While a recent study by National Council of Applied Economic Research estimates tourism's contribution towards GDP (both direct and indirect) in India at only 5.90 per cent, India has already emerged as among the fastest growing tourist destinations in the world. Given its bio-diversity, variety of unique destinations and naturals locals. India can transform itself into a 365 days a year destination with increased emphasis on new products like medical tourism, and marketing India as a destinaton for Meetings/Incentives/Conventions and Exhibitions (MICE).

Fourth, concerns have been expressed about whether the country is growing beyond its growth potential thereby straining its labour force and capital stock, and hence engendering inflationary instabilities. In India, with unemployment, both open and disguised, concerns about over-heating are connected more with capacity utilization and skill shortages. Rapid growth in capacity addition through investments can avert the problem of capacity constraints.

Another indicator of over-heating namely, merchandise import growth, also appears to be within reasonable limits.

Fifth, infrastructure, that constrained for years the growth performance of the economy, appears to be improving. There are signs of tangible progress in areas such as power, roads, ports, and airports. Following the road shows abroad for attracting global financial capital, the setting up of a US $ 5 billion fund to finance Indian Infrastructure on February 15, 2007 by four major financial institutions (Citygroup, Blackstone, Infrastructure Development and Finance Corporation and India Infrastructure Finance Company), is an encouraging development.

The second issue is about the nature of this high growth in terms of inclusiveness. Putting more people in productive and sustainable jobs lies at the heart of inclusive growth. But such success, primarily, will depend on the success in achieving and maintaining high growth. There can not be inclusive growth without growth itself. The experience of East Asia clearly reveals how high growth can eliminate poverty and transform a developing country into a developed one.

The results of the latest NSSO's 61st round clearly show how the annual growth rate of employment has not only accelerated from 1.6 per cent during 1993-2000 to 2.5 per cent during 1999-2005, but crossed the 2.1 per cent rate recorded during 1983-94. Unemployment has gone up not because of high growth, but because growth was not high enough. It is important to avoid the misconception that inclusive growth, by necessity, will have to be low growth.

The inclusive nature of the growth itself will be conditioned by the progress that is made in the areas of education, health and physical infrastructure. A young girl, when denied the benefit of education, often grows up to be excluded from participating in the growth process. Similarly, villagers are literally left behind in the growth process, when their village does not have the benefit of connectivity, be it roads, electricity, or communication.

Among the priorities, first is rising to the challenge of maintaining and managing high growth. Phase-transition invariably throws up new problems and challenges. It is necessary to make the required adjustments in mindsets, economic behaviour, and policy making. There is no scope for uneasiness or nervousness about high growth.

In the latter half of the 20th century, the East Asian 'miracle' has been followed by even more rapid growth in China in more recent times. Fostering the momentum of growth in India continues to be a top priority.

The second priority is bolstering the twin pillars of high growth, namely, fiscal prudence and high investment. The growth resurgence observed in the economy is not an accident but the result of sound policies and several reform measures. The experience of the past few years has clearly demonstrated the benefits of fiscal prudence along the, FRBMA lines. Reforms, along with the high growth, have brought about a surge in investment in the past few years. While accelerating growth and the demographic dividend will continue to boost savings and investment, simultaneously, policies have to be designed in a flexible manner to enhance investments in the economy to lay a robust foundation for growth. There is need for investment, both public and private, domestic and foreign. But is important to resist the temptation of fiscal profligacy in the anxiety to enhance public investment.

The third priority is improving the effectiveness of Government intervention in critical areas especially in the social sector. The goal of inclusive growth can be achieved only through effective government intervention in the areas of education, health and support to the needy. Value for every tax rupee spent has to be ensured by emphasising the outcomes and avoiding any wastage or leakages in the delivery mechanism of public goods and services. Appropriate design of programmes and placing effective monitors over the programmes are critical in this regard.

Conclusion

In conclusion we can say that the macro-story is unambiguously brighter. The economy may have hit a sweet spot, a 'virtuous cycle' where higher growth leads to more saving leading to higher growth. According to the recent Goldman Sachs BRIC Report. India is expected to resume their 1700/AD status as the biggest economy in the world by 2050 AD, just behind the US Parity in per capita GDP— the position that prevailed in 1000 AD is still a long way off, however, with India's per capita income at just 10 per cent of Western European levels at the turn of the millennium.

REFERENCES

Easterly, William, Michael Kremer, Lant Pritchett and Lawrence Summers (1993): "Good Policy or Good Luck? Country Growth Performance and Temporary Shocks," Journal of Monetary Economics, December, 32, pp. 459-83.

Hansmann, Ricardo, Lant Pritchett and Dani Rodrik (2005 a): "Growth Accelerations," Journal of Economic Growth, 10 (4), December, pp. 303-29.

Rangarajan, C. (2001-02): "Economic Reforms: An Assessment," The Indian Economic Journal, Vol. 49, No. 1, July-September, p. 16.

Ibid.

Sheel, Alok (2007): "Putting Indian Growth in Perspective," The Economic Times, Kolkata, March 20.

Singh, Malvinder Mohan (2007): "Globalization, the Unstoppable Wave," The Economic Times, January 8, p. 13.

World Bank (2005): "Economic Growth in the 1990s: Learning from a Decade of Reform" Washington.

Report/Survey/Handbook.

Economic Survey 2005-06, 2006-07, GoI.

Handbook of Statistics on Indian Economy, 2000, Reserve Bank of India, Mumbai.

Pre 1950 data, Angus Maddison.

World Economic Outlook 2007, IMF.

7

Dynamics of Higher Education for Tribal Population and Economic Growth

AMALESH BANERJEE

Introduction

In the education field, India has reached a stage of take-off phase. It is now the task of reducing the double gaps: the gap between the literacy and illiteracy and backwardness on the one hand, and knowledge gap between the high level of scientific and technological knowledge attained by a small section of population and the vast section of populace, who do not have access to that store of knowledge. Dualism in knowledge and dualism in the economy both are widening to the detriment of social welfare. Exploration of knowledge and the application of those innovations at the production level are the important structural adaptations which the administration has to ensure in the interest of high growth and employment. Extensive cost-effective education programme will make it possible to diffuse the knowledge to the grassroot level and benefit the people from the revolutionary changes in knowledge. This chapter first makes a brief reference to the knowledge innovation and economic progress at the macro level in the Section II. India's education and population structure are disussed in Section III. The mechanism of diffusion of higher knowledge are treated in the Section IV. The prospects of application of knowledge in agriculture and industry and the potentiality of employment expansion through learning-by-doing are also assessed in the Section V. Education policy and employment are treated in the Section VI. Conclusions are in the Section VII.

II

Knowledge Innovation and Growth

Modern economic growth has two important base level conditions. First is the knowledge-based innovation and technological diffusion at firm level resulting in augmenting growth. The second source of growth is the development of human resources through improvement of social sector activities including education and health etc. While higher education including latest technological innovation can go for adaptation and diffusion at the firm level the human development in general raises the productivity of labour and the quality of products. Both the levels of education are complementary to each other. Technical education produces innovation. In the endogenous model this knowledge spills over to other firms and hence, as Schumpeter thought, a cluster of innovation come into being. Hence higher education in science and technology generators the extensive possibility of development. A corollary of this process in the learning – by doing process in which knowledge finally rolls over to number of firms and helping higher and higher production in the trail.

But it is possible with larger investment. Their must be extensive investment, private or public, to encourage this dynamic process of knowledge spill over and higher production. The knowledge expansion therefore implies technical progress and the larger the technical progress the larger is the potentiality of growth. Under the present state of globalization the growth strategy is couched in terms of high technical expansion – export promotion and growth. This strategy has worked considerable in our economy without significant expansion of employment. In the Eleventh Plan draft an alternative inclusive growth strategy has been accepted. Under this strategy the emphasis on Small Mechanical Enterprises (SME) on the one hand and the extension of micro finance, a La, Mohammad Yunus have become the prime mover of growth and employment generation as well as poverty alleviation. This strategy has a great potentiality of generations of higher technology are successfully adoption to the SME. If we consider higher education and technology knowledge as the social pool of knowledge of the industrial art and the rate of technical progress as the rate at which this stock of knowledge is increasing then two things become important. First, is the task to enhance the pool of high-technical knowledge and second is the art transmission of that knowledge to the different level of production activities. Hicks and Kald have made important classification of technology utilization. Technology is often capital and labour saving. This is for further research which will adopt the technology at the production level. India has attained a high pool of technical knowledge which have become a remarkable achievements. Now it is the task of endogenizing the technical knowledge (progress) by successive application at production level and to attain the productivity growth. To understand this process and to recommend the process for that we are to know first, in the next section, the knowledge (education structure) in India and its limitation and then to examine in the Section IV the state of diffusion of technical knowledge in different sectors and to the tribals.

III

Education and Knowledge Structure

Indias has made impressive record in the field of higher education. It is reported that between 1997-98 to 2003-04 student enrolment in higher education has increase significantly. Against this the 55th round NSS also recorded that there were inequalities in enrolment across various groups and castes particularly among the SC/ST.

If we analyse the system of acquiring knowledge in our country it appears that only a handful of our young generation receive that opportunity. On average around thirty per cent of our population is illiterate and another ten/fifteen per cent leave the school at quite an early age. This implies that not more than ten per cent of student force has access to higher education. Besides cost, caste, infrastructure and poverty, there are many of reasons which impede the access of limited students to the even limited citadel of higher education institutions. A vast section of SC/ST population virtually remain outside this relm of high knowledge.

Higher technical and scientific institutions are beyond the reach of poorer segment of population. IITs, IIMs Research Laboratories and other specialized scientific institutions are only for well-off section of population. The reasons are that students of poorer section of population particularly SC/ST or do not possess requisite quality of their teaching background. As such those communities who live on those backward regions do not get enrolment in those high-tech enterprises.

The entire rural education system of our country is dismal. Apart from the critical primary education, the school and college level educational institutions are awfully inadequate, inefficient and insufficient. Hence knowledge creation process in laboratories and technical institutions in most of the rural education set up of the country is far from satisfactory. Under this condition of knowledge infrastructure the development of knowledge society and human resource development will be hardly satisfactory. Our status in this respect in the world is insignificant. Although about fifty per cent of our population is women, about fifty per cent of women are in darkness of illiteracy. Throughout the world, women literacy above 15 years of age is 73 per cent in our country this rate is only 44.4 per cent. Even Sri Lanka has much better record, 94.5 per cent. It is recorded that there are still about 45 districts in the country where women literacy is less than 30 per cent.

Against this perspective the Central Government has formed a National Knowledge Commission in order to hasten the emergence of knowledge society. The Commission has envisaged a number of recommendations for continuous implementation. The knowledge society includes both farmers and non-farmers. Knowledge is not only the adoption of a machine designed or borrowed/imported from abroad. It is a composition of ideas for creativity which develops from habitual acquaintance with traditional and non-traditional skill. In this knowledge process both rural and urban education system have to develop an array of activities which spurts ideas and creativity and which generates ideas for up-gradation of existing knowledge. National knowledge commission as well as the National Commission of Farmers (NCF) both ultimately hinge on this education system for generation of knowledge stage by stage resulting in higher level of human and physical capital formation and growth.

IV

Recommendations for Access to Higher Education

- *(a)* The first essential task of the knowledge society is to ensure facilities of basic education for all, with special care for all girl child and SC/ST population who are traditionally neglected.
- *(b)* Cluster of institutions have to be built for learning.
- *(c)* Panchayat level committees have to be formed for proper implementation of universal literacy programme and resume the access to higher education for SC/ST.
- *(d)* Special camps have to be organized for imparting for vocation

training of groups of turn in computer and various other operational implements.

(e) Formation of self-help groups in dissemination of knowledge and setting up knowledge-based activities with necessary institutional financial support have to be implemented throughout the country, particularly among the backward communities.

Once the base level education become stronger the higher knowledge based education has to be evenly spread. We have a tendency to concentrate universities at the big cities. But the backward regions should have greater necessity because universities have the responsibilities in imparting technical knowledge.

(f) The present tendency of privatization of education is detrimental to the rapid growth of knowledge society. This is because the tendency of globalization has the result of inroad of multinationals in higher education which is by nature exclusive and leave out the poor people and poor regions because cost is a deterrent.

(g) Research and development are the key functions of higher education. At present we have a very low allocation for R&D which is much lower than many advanced countries. Extensive research can develop innovation which result clustered development of industries. This process of industrial growth can fit well with end genous growth process initiated by solo and other celebrated economists who contributed to the emergence of New Growth Theory.

(h) Modern information technological knowledge is location non-specific in character and can be imparted throughout rural and urban set up with the support of limited infrastructural facilities. It has brought about a revolutionary change in different fields. Our higher education system can thus be made accebel to the remote corner of the country and to the marginalised section of the community as well without much effort. Universal tel-education delivery system can virtually convert the wise region in a class room. The Distant Education Programme can thus be, if properly worked out in a net-work, an effective means of reaching out to the end line of social and economic bounds, to the backward regions and backward class.

(i) Massive expenditure on R&D is a major step to make access to the world of knowledge for the distant people. Both the government and MNCs are making extensive investment in research and development sector. But this is still not sufficient compared to other advanced countries. Indian advance in modern information industry is remarkable but access to those by the weaker segment of students is hardly possible. A complete overhauling of our education curriculum and the infrastructure of the institutions are urgent for these modern knowledge to be disseminated to the larger segment of students. India has world famous science and technology institutions. With 400 state-run labs, 380 universities and 2900 research centres, India provide a strong infrastructure for advancement of science and technology. She produces 2 lakhs engineers and 3 lakhs graduates and P-6 students annually. To transmit the benefits of these research down to the grassroot level for augmenting production at farm and factories it requires a special structure of learning by doing programme. Let us now see how their learning by doing mechanism makes possible access to knowledge for the under-privileged regions and casts in agriculture and industry. Special network of institutions of higher education has to be set up for SC/ST, not for crème layer alone.

V

Learning by Doing—At Farm Level

Access to scientific knowledge particularly in farming technology has made progress in different parts of the country Farm level training of the peasant and the extensive experiment in the demonstration farming has widely benefited the large segments of farmers in our country. The green revolution has brought to the farmers a lot but now the second green revolution requires learning in an extensive way to raise productivity and to diversify the farm output. Extensive training and work at different stages will raise productivity. Farm research in genetically modified seeds in an important advance. Extension of scientific education to the SC/ST will intensify this process. Inclusive higher education will strengthen the higher rate of economic growth.

Learning by Doing – At Industry Level

Learning by doing is vastly practiced in the IT sector. IT sector has made extensive progress in our country and ordinary IT firms and manufacturing units may secure as the training sport for the unlettered workers. CSIR with its network of 38 laboratories and collaboration with 35 countries provide a tremendous support to the young entrepreneurs.

One important channel for dissemination of IT technology at the production level is the setting up of a cluster of small manufacturing enterprises. Small scale industries serve as the learning stage for the enterprising youths. Modern technology has to be fitted even at the small production units. This will not only serve as the learning stage but will also open the employment opportunity. IT innovation and the cluster network in Bangalore and Hyderabad provide a good example of learning and development. The innovation clusters in a series of laboratories doing IT, Bio-technology cluster, electronics and aeronautics works in Bangalore and Hyderabad are stong pull of knowledge spill over. Practically these industrial research centres have become attraction for new industrialization in Asian and European Countries.

VI

Education Policy and Employment

For economic progress education policy has to be oriented with industrial advance. Investment in education and research has to be oriented with production and job requirements. A large segment of our unemployed people are in the rural sector. Hence educational advance must equip the rural unemployed and should help reorient rural production base so that unemployed are absorbed in upgraded traditional activities as well as in new lines of manufacturing at non-farm level. The policy has to be designed to include the SC/ST people particularly.

We have at present two pieces of documents pertaining to education before us. The Approach Paper of the Eleventh Plan and the Model Right to Education Bill of 2006. The Approach Paper envisages steps towards 'Faster and More Inclusive Growth.' It calls for a more market-oriented system which only the richer and corporate entities will avail of.

The Model Bill 2006 should mould the higher education and endozenising the trend. At present a host of our talented students are going abroad. Having attained skill and qualification they serve other countries. In the USA at present of the foreign students as major segment is Indian. The country is being deprived of the services of those talents.

Our present Approach Paper on education makes provision for special treatment of girl education by setting up. National Programme for Education of Girls at Elementary Level (NPEGELY). It also envisages subsidized private schools that will earn profit. Thus the Approach Paper hinges at commercialization of higher level education which will be beyond the reach of poor people.

The education policy must also address the Indian knowledge capital play. At the present stage China has become the leading high-tech manufactured country and India has become a leading IT services export hub. Since major US firms spent hudge amount on R&D and make trade on knowledge generation and export, third world countries are spending only poultry amount on R&D. Many of our IT firms are foreign origin and many products of these firms are expatriated in foreign countries for trade. This type of high-tech employment generation is neither for growth of domestic output nor for sustained employment propagation. Higher education policy of the Government must address this problem of facile growth and elitist education expansion.

VII

Conclusion

Entire education system in our country is in a mismatch. While around forty per cent of population is virtually illiterate, the top level limited education centres are beyond the reach of common men and SC/ST. Most of our high level education centres and universities are ill-equipped and inefficient. Hence the products of those institutions are not sufficiently capable of technical employment.

Education system has to be not only inclusive for all section of learners irrespective of cast, creed and gender, it must also be job-oriented. Hence knowledge generation and innovation must be production-oriented. Modern endogenous economic growth theory is based on human resource development and knowledge generation.

Discrimination of higher education to the farms factories and unreached tribals is possible by extensive research for adaptation. Green revolution and manufacturing revolution which is now in the offing requires setting up of extensive training at different levels so that knowledge can be widely applied at the production level. Our education policy must aim at extensive investment in R&D so that generation of innovation and application of those at the farm and industry level is possible. Public and private collaboration is necessary in this area.

India has become the hub of IT services export while China has become the hub of high-tech manufacturing exports. Our education policy must aim at controlling the higher education such that our Intellectual Property Rights (IPR) are not exploited by foreign firms for the benefit of multinational corporations. Education policy must walk on two legs. On the one hand the policy should be for inclusion of all children in the knowledge process even at the elementary level, on the other hand, the higher education should be cost-effective and accessible to all. Cluster of education institutions should be set up in all corners of the country for all sections of communities. Along with that higher education must generate output and employment at different levels. The process of learning by doing at farm and factories is relevant. Small manufacturing enterprises are effective mechanism for knowledge transmission, output and employment generation.

REFERENCES

Government of India, (2006) Economic Survey, 2005-06.

Reserve Bank of India, (2006) Annual Report 2006, Bombay.

Romer, David (1996) Advanced Macro-economics McGraw-Hill Companies, Singapore.

Yojana February (2006) Parameters of Knowledge Society Summery of President Dr. Abdual Kalam's Convocation address at Maulana Azad National Urdu University, Hyderabad.

8

Eleventh Five Year Plan for Economic Development of Bihar

BIRENDRA KUMAR JHA

Introduction

Bihar is a demographically sick and economically, politically as well as socially bleak state. It enjoys the unenviable distinction of occupying the lowest rung of the ladder among states. With respect to the level of economic development, both in terms of per capita consumption expenditure and per capita income the state has the lowest figures among the major Indian states. According to the special report of the World Bank the growth of Bihar's economy from 1990 to 1995 has been zero and from 1995 to 2005 the growth rate has been 3.8 per cent and this is lowest in India. The debt liabilities of the state in 1995 come to 30 per cent of the G.S.D.P. and in 2000 it shot up to 42 per cent and in 2005 it soared to 61 per cent of the G.D.P. The liabilities of Bihar are Rs. 30,000 crores and the assets are Rs. 20,000 crores. It means that there are more liabilities than asset. It a child is born in Bihar he/she finds that there is a debt of Rs. 4200 on each head (Ugra Mohan Jha, 2006). A natural question arises: Why Bihar has been sloping downward rather than moving upward? Its socio-economic situation was not so depressing as it has reached today. It registered an annual growth rate of 3.95 per cent as compared to the all India growth rate of 3.30 per cent in 1950s. In terms of key indicators of development, Bihar was fifth from the top; it is now the lowest (Prasad, 1999) in the post reform period. During the 10th Five Year Plan, Bihar's economy grew at a rate that was marginally higher than its growth rate in the 9th Five Year Plan period. However, the state's average annual growth rate i.e. 4.01 per cent has been low compared to an average growth rate of 7 per cent for the Indian economy during the 10th Five Year Plan. Thus, it is needless to say that lower growth rate of a state like Bihar creates hurdle in achieving higher growth rate for the country as a whole in double digit even after adopting the model of development under the aegis of liberalization, privatization and globalization. In the process of economic development for the country as a whole, the populous state like Bihar deserves priority— Although Bihar is a state of India, it has its own importance from demographic point of view. The state is the third largest state in respect of size of population and even many countries of the world have less population than that of Bihar. There is utmost need for a productive utilization of human resources for economic development of the state. But our experience of post-reform period in this respect is somewhat different.

It is useful to underline what Adam Smith (1976) had said, "No society can surely be flourishing and happy of which by far the greater part of numbers are poor and miserable" and Bihar is a tragic paradox of starvation, poverty and backwardness amidst nature's bounties and blessings. Even in the post reform period the state continues to be saddled with 425.6 lakh persons below the poverty line, which exceed that of any other state in the country next only to that of Uttar Pradesh and this may be due to widening economic inequality and limited scope for employment opportunities. Despite of running flow of plan after plan programmes or policies the state is facing these problems. The model or say strategy for economic development adopted during post reform period has generated the problem of economic insecurity because this is but mal-development, which has led to the displacement of lakhs and lakhs of people from their land and all possible sources of livelihood. Destroying the vast sections of the agrarian masses, displacing millions from permanent employment and generating in its place thousands of temporary and contract jobs for a pittance, it has driven the bulk of the middle classes to destitution while accommodating a small section into the elite club resulting in widening inequality. It is well known that inequality, poverty and unemployment are interlinked and none of these can be eradicated separately. As early as in 1929, Jawaharlal Nehru has said, If we are to eradicate poverty, we must first do away with this widespread unemployment" (Nehru, 1977). It is needless to say that unemployment always retards economic development and unfortunately, the present employment situation of Bihar is far from satisfactory. An analysis of the NSSO data on employment-unemployment reveals that unemployment in the state has increased from 6.34 per cent in 1993-94 to 7.32 per cent in 1999-2000. Then estimated number of unemployed persons (by current daily status) in the state in 1999-2000 is found of the order of 23.97 lakh of which 20.33 lakh persons belonging to rural areas, constituting 84.81 per cent of the total unemployment. Thus, problems like poverty, unemployment and inequality have remained untracked in the post reform period and these recreating constraints in the way of economic development of the state.

Economic Growth

For economic development, a series of five year plans have been adopted and it was hoped that these plans would be proved instrumental in lifting the economy from poverty to prosperity from wise spread want to broad based welfare, encompassing the achievement of a definite and marked improvement in the levels of living of the mass of population, through an increase in aggregate as well as per capita output and improvement in distribution of the national income, viz., through a reduction in the inequalities of income wealth and opportunity together with an increase of income and improvement of employment. But bitter experiences from planned economy we got up to now. Controls and regulations that have been piling up, are blocking initiative, encouraging corruption, reducing efficiency and causing misallocation of resources. Corruption has gone to the extent that our Late Prime Minister Rajiv Gandhi has to accept the fact that 85 per cent of the development expenditure goes down the drain because it is pocketed by those who are the incharge of the implementation of developmental plans. No doubt, corruption is found on all India's level but Bihar is on forefront. In Bihar there are records in works like earthwork and digging that 100 per cent allotted amount is drained away and the purpose of the project is hijacked. If such a state of affair continues, economic development becomes a mirage. And ultimately, all these have brought our economy on the drink of total collapse of international confidence in the fiscal and economic system, creating scenario in which adoption of the New Economic Policy (NEP) has become an absolute necessity. In the last decade of the past century India embarked on the process of new economic reforms, whith an emphasis on Liberalization, Privatization and Globalization (LPG) and thus, bringing Indian economy into the mainstream of the world economic order. Although reforms in its mild form had begun early in the 1980s, it was only from 1991 that reforms were implemented in its full form. And this policy has kindled new hopes and aspirations in the minds of policy makers of the problem-ridden developing or say undeveloped economy as the NEP has been deemed as a panacea for all economic ills. The neo-liberal policies for globalization have given a further boost to the sector-wise uneven capitalist development which restricts the potential growth of a developing economy. Since the adoption of the NEP we have succeeded in toning up our economic growth rate which has much slower than what would have been ideally required for creating new job opportunities in the country as whole and Bihar in particular. Even the Finance Minister of NDA, Yashwant Sinha was not unaware of the fact that 'Growth is not just an end in itself'. He appeared to be more optimistic when he stated in his budget speech 2000-01 that "It is the critical vehicle for increasing employment and raising the living standards of our people, especially of the poorest. Sustained, broad-based growth, combined with all our programmes for accelerating rural development, building roads, promoting housing, boosting knowledge-based industries and enhancing the quality of human resources, will impart a strong impetus to employment expansion. There can be no better cure for poverty than this in the country" (Sinha Yashwant 2000-01). But the real picture is not so rosy. Increased competition amongst the domestic industrial units and with units outside the country forced a restructuring of many units, which invariably involved labour restructuring with shrinkage in employment. The ILO-ARTEP workshop in 1991 summarized the global experience of the adjustment programme on the labour market as follows, "Except in few countries, real wages fell, and the labour market conditions started to deteriorate. Although open unemployment fell in many instances jobs landed to become more precarious and the urban informal sector proliferated. Living conditions in general worsened" (ILO-ARTEP, 1991). And thus, the NEP could not answer to the challenges faced by Bihar in particular and India in general. On the contrary, inter-state and inter-regional disparities are particularly evident after introduction of economic reforms and in the post reform period underdeveloped like Bihar region has been badly and adversely affected. A scenario created in the post reform period in which the poor become poorer and the rich richer. Above all our neo-liberal policies for globalization pose certain limitations and suspicions as the developed countries from time to time adopt such tactics which prove detrimental to its success, and the developing countries like India find it difficult to stand with the developed countries which like to give little to the developing countries but try to get more from them for which they go to any possible extent.

Bihar: Then and Now

Presently, the most economically bleak state-Bihar has glorious past and promising future. The regional disparities were not as pronounced as it is today. The regional disparities that existed then were mainly on account of differences in the natural endowment. The gap between rich and poor regions began to widen due to mercantile business and merchant capital. (Pradhan H. Prasad, 1987). And unfortunately, planning in our country seems to have increased the existing regional disparities among states instead of reducing it and if such problem of regional disparities in development are serious for the country, it is indeed more so for a region like. Bihar, which has constantly been at the lower end of this disparity. Bhagwati and Chakravarty have rightly commented, "It is interesting to note that while Indian planning models have been fairly sophisticated in relation to interetemporal phasing and perspective planning, there has been no comparable extension of analysis to questions of spatial planning" (Bhagwati and Chakravarty, 1969). Perhaps, behind devoiding any regional consideration, the argument of Lefeber may be, "It is paradoxical but inevitable fact that in order to accelerate the future development of retarded regions, the growth of industrially more advanced areas must be encouraged. If the latter is shifted by insufficient investment, the overall capacity to save will be diminished and the advancement or retarded areas will be retarded even longer." (Lefeber, 1961). Arguing alike, Rosenstein-Rodan also was in favour of disregarding the specific problems of backward regions because "efficient resources allocation requires an uneven growth of country or region. The economic radiation effects into the hinterland will absorb an inflow of labour and thereby reduce the proverty of emigration areas" (Rosenstein-Rodan, 1963) but as years passed by, the inter-state disparities in our country actually increased because expected spread effects of development of the already developed regions were not to be operative. In such a scenario it is not surprising that Bihar remained at the worst end of growing economic polarization in the Indian economy but more surprising fact in that even after considering the regional-balanced economic development desirability, problems of the state became worse in the post reform period, instead of being reduced.

In the pre-idependence period Bihar, being part of the former Bengal presidency during the colonial period, was subjected to maximum exploitation and in fact, Bihar's fate was finally sealed for nearly two centuries. The historical process, which brought about development of certain regions also resulted in underdevelopment of others. When industrial revolution was sweeping in England there was systematic and widespread de-industrialization in India, particularly in regions like Bihar. It is needless to say that the colonial state adopted policies inimical of the economic development of any region of the country and international trade become an instrument of exploitation and underdevelopment. "Colonialism in India encompassed by the twin notions of unequal exchange and internal disarticulation of the economy and the articulation of its different disarticulated parts through the world market and imperialist hegemony with the metropolitan economy. This feature took the form of a structure of production whereby India specialized in the production of raw materials and food stuffs and Britain in manufactured food thereby Britain produced high technology, high productivity, high wage and high capital intensive goods while India produced low technology, low productivity, low wage and labour intensive gods" (Bipin Chandra, 1992). Bihar experienced this disastrous impact. Surprisingly as well as ironically, we appear to be not conscious for taking a lesson from the past and "still many shout from the house tops that the policy changes adopted in India since August 1991 is indicative of better days ahead... It was the middle of the twentieth century which witnessed the transformation of colonies and semi-colonies into neo-colonial states and the imperial nations into neo-imperial ones. This transformation was not an indication that colonial exploitation was not needed for the survival of capitalism but that the imperialist nations have evolved a mechanism where in the militancy occupation of territories was not essential for regional exploitation" (Pradhan H. Prasad, 2000).

In the post-independence we find that Bihar enjoyed the reputation of being one of the best administered states in 1950s and as I have been already mentioned, it registered an annual compound growth rate of key indicators of development the state was sixth or seventh from the top but the decline began from the beginning of 1960s and the set-back suffered in the 1960s continued to affect the overall processes of growth in the 1970s, although the growth rate picked up in the seventies reaching 2.99 per cent, while compared to the sixties, but the state continued to lag-behind the all India growth rate of 3.50 per cent. The state is not only the least developed but the distance between it and the most developed states is also widening. In the period from 1961-62 to 1965-66, the average per capita SDP was Rs. 221 for Bihar and Rs. 401 for Maharashtra. It is noteworthy that in the early 1960s the per capita GSDP of the richer states like Punjab, Maharashtra and Gujarat was, on an average about 80 per cent higher than the average per capita SDP of the bottom four states viz., Bihar, Uttar Pradesh, Orissa and Madhya Pradesh. This disparity increased to 125 per cent by the early 1970s; was contained at a little over 100 per cent during the 1980s and escalated steeply to 200 per cent towards the end of the 1990s. The most worrisome is the fact that states whose per capita GSDP is below the national average, account for over 60 per cent of the country's population and as high as 75 per cent of the country's population below the poverty line (C.H. Hanumantha Rao, 2005). The state of Bihar typifies a sort of reverse journey in economic development. The irony of development is that the planning commission by the end of the last century has identified 100 most backward districts of which 38 districts belong to the state of Bihar. About 39 per cent people are landless in Bihar in 2004 as against 26 per cent in 1951. It is not the proof of pauperization which is the logical conclusion of crippled and retrogressive economy? The interstate disparities in the growth of GSDP have increased in the post-economic reform period beginning from the early nineties when compared to the eighties. In general, the richer states have grown faster than the poorer states and for this one of the most responsible factors may be a faster growth in population experienced in the poorer states. No doubt, the planning process, by helping the backward regions, made an effort to reduce regional disparities, but the forces of liberalization, privatization and globalization strengthened investment in forward states much more than backward states resulting in widening regional disparities. For instance, the average growth rate of net state domestic product of forward states like Punjab, Maharashtra, Haryana, Gujarat, West Bengal, Karnataka, Kerala, Tamil Nadu and Andhra Pradesh at constant prices (1993-94) was 5.6 per cent per annum while that of the backward states was only 1.7 per cent annum during 1990-91 to 2002-03. The backward states like Uttar Pradesh, Madhya Pradesh and Bihar having very large population recorded very low percentage of NSDP i.e., 2.1, 0.4 and 0.7 respectively during 12 years from 1990-91 to 2002-03 while during the same period recorded percentages of NSDP for West Bengal, Karnataka and Gujarat was 6.8, 6.6 and 6.3 respectively. In the pre-reform period during 1980-91 NSDP in forward states indicated an annual average growth rate of 5.2 per cent that was less than that of the figure of the post reform period. In 2002-03 Bihar was at the bottom on the basis of per capita income where as Maharashtra was at the top.

Table–1

Statewise Net Domestic Product at Constant Prices 1993-94

Forward States	*Annual Average Growth Rate (1990-91 to 2002-03)*
Punjab	3.9
Maharashtra	5.6
Haryana	4.8
Gujarat	6.3
West Bengal	6.8
Karnataka	6.6
Kerala	5.4
Tamil Nadu	5.2
Andhra Pradesh	5.1
Sub-total	5.6
Backward States	
Madhya Pradesh	0.4
Assam	2.6
Uttar Pradesh	2.1
Rajasthan	3.5
Orissa	4.1
Bihar	0.7
Sub-total	1.7
All India	5.4

Source: Ministry of Finance, Indian Public Finance in Statistics (2004-05).

Per Capita Income

As per capita income is the most important measure of the level of development, the following Table-2 presents the per capita income gap between the erstwhile Bihar and India for half a century and between the present Bihar and India for 1994, 2001 and 2004.

Table–2
Trend of Per Capita Income Gap

Year	*Erstwhile Bihar/India (%)*
1951	59.7
1961	66.1
1971	62.6
1981	54.8
1986	57.6
1991	53.0
1996	37.6
2000	44.5
	Income Gap, Present Bihar/India
1994	38.01
2001	36.19
2004	30.66

Source: Based on Publications of Ashok Mathur (1993, 1994 and 2002).

As per Planning and Development Department, Bihar per capita income of Bihar has increased from Rs. 3334 in 1993-94 to Rs. 6739 in 2005-06 at current prices but on constant prices per capita income has increased from Rs. 3334 in 1993-94 to Rs. 4013 in 2005-06. Hereby it is noteworthy that inter-disparities in per capita GSDP have increased significantly in the post reform period but the corresponding disparity in Human Development Index (HDI) has declined because investment requirements in primary education and primary healthcare are not as heavy as in the capital-intensive physical infrastructure. As a result the coefficient of variation in HDI declined from 22.6 in 1981 to 19.0 in 1991 and 16.3 in 2001 (Hanumantha Rao, 2005). But very slow rise in public expenditure in these sectors in the poorer states in the post reform period results in the smaller decline in regional disparities in HDI and since human development has a positive impact of GDP growth, lack of due priority to this sector in the poorer states like Bihar in the post reform period is not less responsible for the rise in regional disparities in per capita GSDP. Bihar, Madhya Pradesh, Orissa and Uttar Pradesh, which have had lower per capita income, can be said to form the poorer category of states.

The trend in the growth rate of Bihar's GSDP during the 10th Plan has been volatile, mainly because of the dominance of the agricultural sector in the state's economy. The following table shows the trend of Bihar's GSDP.

Table-3
Trends in Bihar's GSDP (9th and 10th Plans)

Year	*Annual Average Growth Rate Constant Price (1993-94%)*	*Year*	*Annual Average Growth Rate Constant Price (1993-94%)*
1997-98	3.25	2002-03	5.25
1998-99	4.10	2003-04	3.73
1999-00	4.03	2004-05	4.46
2000-01	6.09	2005-06	3.92
2001-02	4.02		

Source: GOB, Planning and Development Department, Patna 2006.

Sectoral Growth

If in India, a location of industry was to be determined from the Waberian concept, then Bihar would have witnessed giant stride to industrialization as the state, contributing about 41 per cent of total mineral production, ranked first on the mineral map of India. But it never completed the process of transition, although it was one of the first states where the process of transformation of potential resources into real resources was initiated, whereas many states starting later with much lesser resources, are much ahead the road to industrialization now, the Bihar has failed to develop a group of industrialists with a vision of Tatas and Birala, who could have mopped up surplus and ploughed back for the regional industrialization. But this was undivided Bihar, Bifurcation of the state in 2000 has changed the picture and now, the creation of Jharkhand robbed the state of accesses of minerals while transferring the dominant portion of its industrial base to the newly created state. And the fact remains that Bihar which was once recognized as the Rule of India has been suddenly transformed into a predominantly agricultural and rural region. Agriculture, contributing 35 per cent to state GDP as employing 77 per cent of the workforce has become more dominant in Bihar's economy and lack of opportunities in industries, poor rural-urban growth linkages and underdeveloped infrastructure has contributed to continued dominance of agriculture. It is noteworthy that in addition to the rate of economy growth it is the regional and sectoral composition of growth that affects the national rate of reduction in poverty, unemployment and inequality. If economic growth of a nation bypasses poor regions, growth may lead to rising inequality, unemployment as well as poverty and *vice versa*. Unfortunately, our experience of the post reform period indiscates lack of due priority for regional equality and Bihar is the victim of such policy. Although agriculture in the post independence period recorded impressive strides, the agricultural growth rate of Bihar remained considerably short of the need of the economy. It is but true that the strategy which has come to be known as green revolution or new technology has been successful in limited pockets like Punjab, Haryana, Uttar Pradesh, coastal Andhra etc. but at the same time this new technology has further widened disparity between various regions as well as various classes in the country. Its fruits have been cornered by a few selected states and Bihar was left behind to reap the fruits. No doubt, the cause of regional disparity in agricultural development and of backwardness of agricultural in the state are believed to be deep rooted in the historical fact of protracted colonial dominance and in mechanism of imperial exploitation which affect differently the various segments and regions of the Indian economy. Taking together 22 per cent of the gross investment outlays in irrigation, road and power, during 1860-1947 against only 3 per cent of the gross investment outlay during the same period cannot be considered a less responsible factor. Ironically, we remain failure in taking lesson from the pre-independence period and more or less we are on the same track till the recent past. No doubt, bifurcation of the state has left the economy of Bihar hopeless and helpless but out state is endowed with rich fertile soil, aboundant water resources, favourable climate and what not needed for making our state prosperous and fully developed through agricultural growth. It is heartening to take down that in the 1980s, Bihar's agricultural growth rate of 4.6 per cent was above the national average. But this plummeted between 1991-92 and 1995-96 to 2 per cent and revived somewhat in recent years. There is no denying the fact that the future of Bihar obviously belongs to agriculture and agricultural productivity in the state remains below its potential and so if Bihar is to achieve yields tomorrow, comparable to those achieved in Punjab today a great deal of investment particularly in infrastructure is highly required. But unfortunately enough, at the national level public investment in agriculture declined from 1.6 per cent of GDP in 1993-94 to 1.3 per cent in 1999-2000 recording a decline from Rs. 4467 to Rs. 4112 during this period. Similar course is found in Bihar state owing to fiscal constraint plan expenditure in agriculture has been declining over the past few years. The plan expenditure in agriculture and allied activities has declined from Rs. 87.65 crore per annum during 1980-90 to Rs. 23.73 crore per annum during 1991-2000 (Singh Raghubansh, 2002). There is no need for going far from reality that the state is a predominantly agrarian with a small manufacturing base, although the share of agriculture has declined to an extent while the share of industry has remained more or less stagnant and services sector has increased its share from 415 to nearly 50 per cent of GSDP. The share of agriculture and allied sectors have been declining from 58.77 per cent in 1980-81 to 50.6 per cent in 1990-91 and further to 44 per cent in 2000-01 which is still higher than the average contribution of agricultural at the national level i.e., 27 per cent in 2000-01. It is well known that 40 per cent of land was transferred to Jharkhand while 75 per cent of population remained with Bihar, leading to an increase in population density in the latter. As per Bihar, approach to 11th Five Year Plan in the year 2004-05 the contribution of agriculture, industry and service sectors in GSDP in 1993-94 prices will 40, 12 and 46 per cent respectively as against 20, 27 and 53 per cent respectively at 1999-2000 prices for the country as a whole.

Although fairly good trend growth rate figures by themselves can have little meaning for the poorer segments of the population, yet the desirability for good trend growth rate in comparison to a low growth rate cannot be denied and so it would be meaningful to take a look at the sectoral and sub sectoral growth rates.

"It simply is not possible to have the fruits of a modern agriculture and the abundance of modern industry without making large investments in human beings" (Schultz, 1967). It was the contribution of Schultz (1961) who coined the term human capital which focused on the fact that labour itself performed not only one but two functions. One of these provided the usually recognized role of supplying physical labour. But with the progress of knowledge, it is the second role of production and enhancing its productivity through application of knowledge and skills in the

Table–4
Trend Growth Rates of Aggregate and Sectoral GSDP of Bihar and India (1994-2000)

Industry	*Total Growth Rate*	
	Bihar	*India*
Agriculture	2.19	2.21
Sub-total of Primary	2.58	2.48
Manufacturing	4.46	6.15
Sub-total of Secondary	7.70	6.14
Transport, Storage and Communication	7.32	10.01
Sub-total of Tertiary	7.59	8.19
State Domestic Product	5.34	6.03

Source: Sharma and Mathur 2007.

process of production (Mathur A. and Mamgain R.P., 2004). And so in the process of economic growth of any region human capital need not be ignored. Despite meager resources, Japan, South Korea and Taiwan had attained high rate economic growth on the basis of their sound human capital base. The World Bank evidences indicated that as much as 64 per cent of growth is explained by human capital alone while the shares of physical and natural/ resource are much lower recording 16 per cent and 20 per cent respectively. Denison (1967) estimated that 40 per cent growth in real national income during the period 1948-63 in the United State could be attributed to improvements in human capital. The National Human Development Report 2001 released by the Planning Commission shows that Bihar hangs at the 15th position in 1981, 1991 and 2001 in HDI ranking whereas Kerala maintains its ranking of 1st during the same period followed by Punjab. The HDI for Bihar has improved from 0.237 in 1981 to 0.348 in 1991 and further to 0.367 in 2001 but there is no change in its ranking. Disparity in this regard is vividly visible when one comes to know that Kerala remains at the top with an index of 0.638 an increase from 0.500 in 1981. In an interview to Business line, the World Bank's Director, Human Development, South Asia Range Mr. Julian Schweitzer once said, you can't have human development without sustainable economic growth. You can't have sustainable economic growth without human development. The two are absolutely linked together and Bihar appears to a best example. In the year 1950-51 Bihar's per capita income was the lowest in the country and even today it is the lowest likewise its lowest ranking in HDI. Prof. P.N. Singh in his Presidential address in the 8th annual conference of BEA quoted Prof. Bahala who says that Bihar is the only state whose per capita income is declining year after year. Of course, for this low human capital formation is not less responsible.

Infrastructure hurdles inhibit growth and development in all the sectors of the state and Bihar witnesses are extremely dismal infrastructure state. If the state has to be dragged out from acute stagnation and abject poverty, the development of infrastructure is sin-qua-non. It is needless to say that along with a host of factors responsible for the backwardness of the state, low development and availability of necessary infrastructure of both types economic and social, is one of prime reasons Prof. Raj Krishna has suggested that policy-makers can break the vicious circle in the backward regions only with a deliberate and massive investments push of same magnitude as the luckier regions received in the past (Raj Krishna, 1981). Infrastructure through its backward and forward linkage initiates, sustains and accelerates growth process. It goes without saying that any viable strategy for accelerated growth in Bihar must pay much greater attention to raising agricultural productivity levels which can be possible only through enhancing infrastructure facilities in the firm of irrigation, flood control, drainage, water management, power research, extension, input supply, credit, transport, marking, procession etc. which widen the scope for technological application in this sector.

Ground Reality

A right kind of vision and mission is must for economic development of any state or a nation. If Punjab and Haryana are number one states, credit goes to good government led by Pratap Singh Kairo and Banshilal. But what would be, when the Chief of Government has no vision and no pious mission except to safe his chair at the cost of Punjab interest? This is really a tragedy; what has happened in Bihar in the recent past. What kind of outcome in the state can be expected when a Chief Minister of that very state had to go to jail for corruption charges? What kind of economic development can be expected when bureaucratic and political system are badly exposed to corruption and the law and order machine has completely collapsed and jungle raj has established?

Of course, Bihar has become the grazing ground for criminals, extortionists and extremists. In such a scenario it is but natural for business and industrial establishments to move from this state and there is no question for new investment to take place because security of capital is mist for attracting new investment. Who is going to risk capital investment in a state where life is not secured, what to talk of capital's security? The only industry where is flourishing in the state is Kidnapping industry and Rangdari and Firauti taxes have become natural phenomena. The nexus between criminal gangs, mafias, police, bureaucracy and politicians is complete in this state. A rather smooth system is functioning under the government of the Dons of different crime syndicates (Sinha Ajit Kumar 1997). There is no surprise in such circumstance when one comes to know the fact that more than 100 representatives have been elected to assembly and parliament having serious criminal backgrounds. The United Nation's Human Development Report 2002 concludes that good governance and leads to decline of human development. India Today's annual ranking of 20 states on governance published in September 2006 it is found that Tamil Nadu emerges a clear winner with a decent head start over its closest competitor, Madhya Pradesh where as Bihar is at the bottom except Assam. Corruption is the most endemic and entrenched manifestation of poor governance, so much so that it has almost become an accepted reality and a way of life (Myrdal Gunnar, 1970). But with a new government a new hope growth up.

Bihar During the 11th Five Year Plan

Considering Bihar's past predominance and unsatisfactory progress, the state needs a really ambitious blue print of social and economic development to generate the need mass enthusiasm which will unit all its people to mobilize the vast human resources of state, and in particular the energies of its youth, for a frontal attack on mass poverty. Bihar needs a new vision of a prosperous Bihar and a new will to realize this vision so as to overcome the visible collapse in the morale of Bihar's elite and its apparent loss of faith in the states future (Singh Manmohan, 1997). It is heartening to take down that the 11th five year plan provides Bihar with a unique opportunity to restructure policies to achieve a new vision of growth that will be much more broad based and inclusive. In the 11th plan four rates of growth of SDP at 7 per cent, 8.5 per cent, 9 per cent and 10 per cent for the state have been assumed for which varying average rates of investment are required. Bihar's average rate of investment was an abysmally low at 15 per cent of GSDP from 1999-2000 to 2003-04 while for the country this was around 27 per cent but for acceleration from 7 per cent growth to 10 per cent will require an increase in the total investment from 19.72 per cent to 24.52 per cent.

Table-5
Alternative Investment Scenario for the 11th Plan

Target rate of growth	7%	8.5%	9%	10%
Average investment rate	19.72%	23.65%	24.95%	27.52%
Public investment rate	6.90%	8.25%	8.73%	9.63%
Private investment rate	12.82%	15.37%	16.22%	17.89%

Source: GOB Planning and Development Department, Patna.

These different growth scenarios give to alternative estimates of GSDP.

Table-6
Project GSDP at Alternative Growth Rates

Year	*7% Growth Rate*	*8.5% Growth Rate*	*9% Growth Rate*	*10% Growth Rate*
2007-08	70784	71776	72107	72769
2008-09	75739	77877	78597	80046
2009-10	81041	84497	85671	88050
2010-11	86714	91679	93381	96856
2011-12	92784	99472	101785	106541

Source: GOB, Planning and Development Department, Patna.

These different growth scenario also give rise to alternative estimate of outlays for the plan period.

Rate of Growth	*Public*	*Private*	*Total Rs. Crores*
7%	46600	86551	133151
8.5%	58310	108283	166593
9%	62353	115804	178159
10%	70680	131267	201937

Source: GOB, Planning and Development Department Patna.

For achieving projected growth rate projected outlay for the plan period has been estimated and currently 59 per cent private investment of total investment needs to be received in the upward direction and 65 per cent share of private sector in total investment for the 11th plan has been estimated. The global meet for resurgent Bihar in the third week during 19-21, 2007 was really a right step to invite private investors living inside or outside of the state because success for achieving target in success in attracting a large share of private investment and foreign direct investment that can be brought about through infrastructure development and maintain law and order situation in the state. And it is a good sing that public sector outlays in the 11th plan is proposed to be just double the actual expending of the 10th plan and about 18 to 20 per cent of the total outlay to be allotted to power sector, about 15 per cent to irrigation and flood control and about 23 per cent to transport and communication. Role of social infrastructure in the economic growth has also been realized and due priority has been given to this sector at the time of allocation of public outlay.

Feasibility of Projected Growth Rate

Undoubtedly, the approach to the 11th five year is very optimistic and it should be so. But a natural question arise regarding feasibility of different projected growth rate. The 9th five year plan recorded 5.5 per cent growth rate whereas it was 7 per cent for the 10th plan. For Bihar 8.5 per cent growth rate in the 11th five year plan has been considered feasible for which the sectoral growth rates have been projected at 5 per cent for agriculture, 11 per cent for industry and 10 per cent for service. Now the question arise as to whether this sector wise project growth rates consistence with 8.5 per cent growth rates are feasible. For answering this question we need to peruse the sector wise growth rates in the past. Agriculture has shown a decelerating trend after the 1990s recording negative growth rate in the 9th plan where as it was less than 1 per cent in the 10th plan. Reasons behind such deceleration in this sector were supply side constraints like irrigation, power supply, seeds, fertilizer etc.

Naturally, for achieving 5 per cent growth rate in agriculture such supply side constants need to be eliminated but this is not enough. Adequate demand for agricultural products needs to be created through increasing real income of the rural and urban poor and setting up agro-based industries. Besides these, security of tenure of small, marginal farmers and landless laborers needs to be granted. The projected growth rate of 11 per cent for industry may be feasible only through proper infrastructure development which is highly desirable for attracting investors in the private sector along with normal law and order situation for the state it is heartening to take down that the present government has taken positive step in this direction. It tries to improve governance through increased transparency, instituting the right to information and more intensive use of information technology to increase the participation of citizens and non-governmental organizations in developmental programmes with a view to arousing confidence in government. The present government has taken the issue of improving law order situated on the priority basis. Recent initiatives in institutional and policy reforms are yielding results, with private capital beginning to enter Bihar. During 1994-2006 the trend rate of growth of industry has been of the order of 5.26 per cent. The trend rate of growth for service sector has been of the order of around 6 per cent and projected 10 per cent growth rate appears to be feasible for services, which will get an automatic boost with proper emphasis on the agricultural and the industry. Hereby it is noteworthy that the planning commission's project for agriculture and industry are 7 per cent and 8 per cent respectively.

Promoting Inclusive Growth Rate

Our experiences of post reform period are of jobless economic growth and so the 11th five year plan aims at avoiding and period of jobless growth and fostering policies, which will increase growth and also create avenues for meaningful employment for the young demographic profile of Bihar. In the 11th five year plan the objective of inclusive growth will require sufficient number of jobs to be created and it has been estimated that 57.78 per cent lakhs job opportunities in both rural and urban areas need to be created to clear the backlog and to absorb the new entrants in the plan period. But the planning commission has estimated that 49.37 per cent additional jobs are likely to be created in the plan period and thus, at the end of the 11th plan around 8.41 lakh have no job. It has been planned to simplify labour laws so as to bring in flexibility in their applications for improving competitiveness of manufacturing sector, and policies relating to labour employment are desired to focus on ensuring minimum wages, reduction of disguised unemployment, absolution of child labour. Elimination of gender inequality and upgrading skills through periodic training, among other things, social security and measures for labour. The target for the 11th plan is to raise real wage rate of unskilled workers by 20 per cent and reduction of head count ration of consumption poverty by 13.1 per cent points for 41.5 in 2004-05 to 28.4 in 2011-12. Raising the percentage of women and children to 33 per cent beneficiaries in all governmental schemes reduction in anemia among woman and girls by 50 per cent from 63.4 to 31.7, reduction in malnutrition among children of age group 0.3 to half its present level from 54.4 to 27.2 and reduction in IMR from 61 per cent at present to 29 per cent as well as MMR from 371 per lakh at present to 123 per lakh are the monitorable socio-economic targests for the 11th plan. Porgramme will be formulated for social, educational and economic rehabilitation of children and woman in need and distress. Schemes will be drawn up for social and economic rehabilitation of old age persons and for protection, prevention as well as rehabilitation of victims/survivors of trafficking of children and women. The plan pupose to set up institutes that focus on skill building and at least one residential high school in each district for boys and girls belonging to the SC, ST and OBC communities. Provisions for creating a cell for the eradication of beggary and rehabilitation to sex workers are also included in the socio-economic targets of the 11th plan. For widow the plan has to institute a scheme to provide residential facilities and for woman and children development it has to establish a state resource centre. All the disabled persons will be provided identity cards and free travel concessions in state owned transport corporation buses. Keeping in view the constitutional obligation and the need for optimum opportunity to the children and youth in the state, the policy decisions are specifically aimed at rate bringing teacher pupil ratio to the national norm of 1:40, increasing literacy rate for persons of age 7 + from 46.96 per cent in 2001 to 64.04 per cent 1011-12, reducing dropout rate elementary school from 78.03 per cent in 2003-04 to 27.85 per cent in 2011-12 and lowering gender gap in literacy to be growth oriented plan with human face based on our past experiences of the post reform period in which removing the shortcoming of LPG strategy for economic development of a nation or a region has been into consideration.

Concluding Remark

The bifurcation of the state in 2000 had an impact on the structure of Bihar's economy but whatever it got in its share in enough for becoming the engine to propel India's economic growth in the 11th five year plan. By the end of the 11th plan, Bihar is believed to redress its development deficits and join the national mainstream of the fast growing states. Nothing is impossible and it is never too late. If Japan can build ship building industry without resources and the

U.K. Government can feed its population without agricultural base, is it not surprising that Bihar with sound agricultural base and human resources is almost at the lowest rung to the developmental ladder? A review of East Asian Economic growth experiences clearly indicate the catalytic role of agriculture in generating economic growth and reducing poverty in countries like Taiwan, South Korea, China, Thailand and Malaysia, then, why is in Bihar. Economic development of any nation or any region ultimately depends on production and productivity. This combination and co-ordination is ensured by the only active agent of production, say human resources which account for the pace and direction of economic growth and its quantum. Fortunately, Bihar is in a demographic gift phase as reflected in rising working age population to total population ratio. It is heartening to take down that "among the Asian countries, India is an demographic gift phase.... This ratio has already begun to decline for China, Korea and Japan. India's ratio is projected to begin to decline around 2030 and the decline will be gradual. Even in 2050 India will still have the highest share of working age to total population (Mukul G. Asher, 2006). Even after bifurcation, Bihar is the third populous state of India. When a state of the demographic size of Bihar does so, no constraint, not even the lack of mineral resources can hold up the economic growth. But human resource needs to be endowed with moral force, national character and commitment like Japanese. The key challenge for the government is to make the state free from corruption on all levels and to create a scenario favourable for economic development. We have to face problems, which become worse in the post reform period. Of course, the strategies of development that we have followed so far have given us at best only moderate successes, and none has helped so far to address the fundamentals problems of poverty, unemployment, inequality and so on. And at this juncture there is need to think over in this direction. It is heartening to take down that our Hon'ble President of the Nation Kalam invoked 10 commandments with a view to put the state on the path of overall development while setting up of the road map for the development.

Undoubtedly, we can succeed in achiveing our projected economic growth in the 11th five-year plan and overall development through accepting honesty the vision and mission given by our Hou'ble President for Bihar. If India is to be developed, Bihar must be developed.

REFERENCES

Gunnar Myrdal (1970) The 'Soft State' in the Challenge of World Poverty a Penguin, p. 287.

Singh Manmohan (1997) Bihar's Revival EAB, p. 2.

Sinha Ajit Kumar (1997) Bihar's Revival EAB, p. 86.

Chandra Bipin (1992) The Colonial Legacy in Bimal Jalan (ed.). The Indian Economy Problems and Prospects, Viking New Delhi. p. 4.

Bhagwati and Chakravarty (1969) Contribution to the Indian Economic Analysis: A Survey American Economic Review, Vol. IX, No. 4, Part 2.

Lefeir L. (1961) Regional Allocation of Resources in India in Perspective of Development 1961-76 from Planning Commission G.O.I. New Delhi, p. 27.

Rosenstein Rodan (1963) Reflections on Regional Development Centre for International Studies MIT Cambridge Massachusetts (Mimco), p. 9.

Prasad Pradhan H. (2000) India Dilemma of Development Meeta Krishna Pub., pp. 203-204.

Matur Ashok and Rajendra P. Mamgain (2004) Human Capital Stocks, Their Level of Utilization and Economic Development in I.J.L.E., Vol. 47, No. 4.

Singh P.N. (2004) Management Challenges of Bihar's Economy Presidential Address in the 8th EAB.

Raj Krishna (1981) The Centre and The Periphery Interstate Disparities in Economic Development Social Action, Vol. 31, No. 1, p. 9.

Schultz, T.W. (1967) Investment in Human Capital in Principles of Economic Development (ed.) by S. Chandrashakar, Charles W. Haltman, D.S. Health and Company Boston, p. 178.

Jha Ugra Mohan (2006) Economic Development of Bihar Need for New Strategy Presidential Address EAB.

Singh Ragubansh (2002) Presidential Address EAB.

Pandit Nehru (1977) Selected Words of Nehru Orient Longman, Vol. 3.

Sharma Alakh N. and Ashok Mathur (2007) Towards Transforming Bihar: Challenges an Opportunities in Global Meet for Resurgent Bihar.

Bihar: Approach to 11th Five Year Plan Vision for Accelerated Inclusive Growth, Govt. of Bihar, Planning and Development Department, Patna.

Prasad, Jagdish (1999) Agricultural Development and Rural Poverty: A Study with Reference to Bihar, in the Bihar Journal of Agricultural Marketing, Vol. 7, No. 2.

Mukul G. Asher (2006) India's Rising Role in Asia A memorial lecture in the 89th Annual Conf. IEA.

Hanumantha Rao C.H. (2005) Growing Regional Disparities in Development in India Post Reform Experience and Challenges Ahead Memorial Lecture the 88th Annual Conf. IEA.

Adam Smith (1776) An Enquiry into the Nature and Causes of the Wealth of Nations 6th E. Cannan Edition, New York.

Part–II : EMPLOYMENT AND EMPOWERMENT

9

Agrarian Distress and Farmers' Suicide

RAKESH A. JOSHI

Introduction

Agricultural sector is the backbone of Indian economy. It occupies a prominent place in the Indian Economy. It supports about 70 per cent of the total population in providing jobs. The contribution of Indian Agricultural Sector to Gross Domestic Products is 28 per cent. And it also supports India's exports to a large extent. Even then, agriculture is a way of life rather than a commercial occupation. In a predominantly agriculture based economy like India, where approximately 70 per cent of the total population lives in rural area and nearly 28 per cent of the total national income is generated in the agricultural sector – agricultural and rural development is a must for the sound economy of the country. A majority of the population connected with agricultural sector lives under the problems of poverty, unemployment and low standard of living. Therefore, after independence, the ultimate objectives of all planned development efforts are for the well-being of the masses and since the very beginning of economic planning (1950), agricultural and rural development has been the main concern of our country. Development is no longer identified with a mere increase in national income or even per capita national income. But, the increased income should be so distributed as to result in a significant diminution of inequalities of income and wealth. The abolition of absolute poverty with minimum level of employment or remuneration to all, who seek employment, should be arranged. Public distribution of goods and services at lower rates in agricultural sector – is also a step for development, as it increases welfare. Development is also expected to include the areas of health, education, roads, water, electricity and cultural values. By all these aspects, the standards of living improve. Development should be described as 'Sarvodaya', or promoting the welfare of each individual. In our country, still 32 per cent of population is living below the poverty line, of which more than 80 per cent are estimated to be living in rural areas and connected with agricultural sector. Emphasizing and successfully implementing rural development programmes can mitigate backwardness of the agricultural sector, unemployment and mass poverty. A special favour towards agricultural and rural development in our future economic plans is essential.

In this chapter, I have described the reasons for Agrarian Distress and Farmers' Suicides in India and some suggestions to improve these unwanted events.

Reasons for Agrarian Distress

According to Dr. Vandana Shiva (Renowned agronomist and social activist), "There is a genuine crisis in Indian Agriculture, subsidies and selective promotions of some sectors have benefited only a few rich farmers. Free trade or globalization is a two way trend, while Indian exports in the years of liberalization have made no great strides, infact only declined, and the entry of multinationals in the seeds, chemical fertilizers and pesticides sector has hit the Indian Farmers hard."

The main reasons for agrarian distress in India are as under:

1. ***Too Much Dependent on Nature***

Comparing with other occupations, agriculture is more dependent on nature. Approximately 66 per cent of the cultivated land is non-irrigated, major portion of the cultivated land is depended on rain and the rain is quite irregular in our country. Because of uncertain nature and agriculture is too much dependent on it, we find large ups and downs in our country's national income, trade, employment opportunities and overall prosperity.

2. ***Predominance of Small Cultivators***

According to the All India Report on Agricultural Census (1970-71), 70 per cent of the land holding come into the category of marginal and small land holdings. This is due to the population pressure resulting in fragmentation and sub-division. So many farmers are not even owners of the land. Thus, neither there is any motivation nor resources to invest for better farming. Small cultivators are not in a position to use modern technology, as it is very costly.

3. *Low Productivity*

Productivity in agriculture can be measured through output per hectare of land. Comparing Indian Agriculture with that in other countries, we find that productivity is distinctly low in India. Trends in productivity reveal that the annual rate of growth of agricultural productivity 1950-51 to 2003-04 has been as low as 1.6 per cent. Social economic, technical and social factors are responsible for it.

4. *Inadequate Non-farm Services*

Many non-farm services in India like credit and marketing, electricity, transportation are either non-existent or if available, these are quite costly. A lot of farmers depend upon the village moneylender and they have to pay very high rate of interest, high to the extent that once a farmer borrows, he is bound to lose his land and become a landless labourer. Similarly, due to scarcity of electricity, farmers are not in a position to water their farms from wells. Similarly, due to lack of storage facilities and transportation facilities, the farmers have to sell their produce at very low rates in local markets. Such types of inadequate non-farm services are responsible in keeping Indian agriculture backward.

5. *Farmers' Suicides*

Agrarian distress has led the farmers to suicides in rural areas. Agrarian distress is very common in the times of droughts and other natural calamities. Such types of sad events are taking place in Andhra Pradesh, Karnataka, and Maharashtra. It is very surprising, that in Punjab (a successful state in agricultural sphere) also more than 10000 farmers have committed suicides.

Farmers' suicides are a sad commentary on the impact of liberalization policies that made agriculture unremunerative. Neither the ruling party nor the opposition parties are prepared to confront the reality and address the issues squarely.

Of course, so many problems are involved-ranging from the severe unrelenting non-stop drought conditions, ever-rising infrastructural and input costs, crashing prices for outputs, high rates of interests for loans, extra-economic coercion by moneylenders, etc. in the sad events of farmers' suicides.

6. *Surprising Report on Farmers' Suicides*

The Karnataka State Government formed a committee chaired by Mr. G.K. Veeresh to get deep information about these sad and unwanted events. Veeresh Committee was proud for having adopted a 'Psycho-economic' approach, only to conclude that the suicide was a personal choice of individuals.

The committee found the highest probability of causes of suicide as 'alcohol-related problems', followed by indebtedness, chronic illness, family disorders, and family responsibilities. For them, crop failure and price crash did not appear to be major probable causes. The committee's brilliance was revealed in its suggestion for not paying any compensation in order to prevent suicides.

Suggestions for Improvement

1. According to noted agricultural economist V.S. Vyas, "There is an urgent need for reducing the interest burden on agricultural credit to ease agrarian distress; which is leading to suicides by farmers and starvation deaths in rural areas.
2. The Formal Rural Financial Institutions (Nationalised Banks and Co-operative Banks) are not keeping pace with expenditure on inputs, thereby forcing the farmers to take credit from private moneylenders. These private moneylenders are charging very high rates of interests for loans. There should be a legal ceiling on the high rates of interest.
3. There is a need for increase in irrigation facilities. These will be quite useful even in the scarcity of rain.
4. The cent per cent electrification all over the country is essential to support agricultural production.
5. The construction regarding irrigation facilities, transportation facilities, electrification, etc. can create many job opportunities in rural areas that may be useful in reducing agrarian distress.
6. Indian agriculture has to be modernized and diversified with scientific approaches.

7. The productivity of the land and the crop should be improved with introduction of drip irrigation system.
8. The farmers should be provided adequate information regarding exports of agricultural products.
9. The farmers should be given proper guidance for planning their cultivation and marketing programmes.
10. A separate institution should be set up for the supply of all essential inputs to agriculture at cheaper rates.
11. Some religious leaders and social activists should convince the people to quit the habit of alcohol and drugs.
12. The unemployed mass from the rural areas should be shifted to the industrial and service sector existing in the urban areas.

The Central as well as State Governments should take such type of steps. With government's proactive role towards the agricultural sector, agrarian distress can be reduced. *"Feel Good Factor" should be seen in every village of India.* The parliamentary election results and some legislative assembly results of year 2004 have proved that the political leaders should not neglect agrarian needs.

REFERENCES

Alagh Y.K., "Indian Development Planning and Policy," Vikas Publishing House, Delhi.

Agrawal A.N., "Indian Economy – Problems of Development and Planning," Wishwa Prakashan, New Delhi, 2000.

Kamta Prasad, "Farmers' Participation in Irrigation Management in India" – Status, Impact and Determinants, Uppal Publishing House, New Delhi, 2001.

Datt Rudar and K.P.M. Sundaram "Indian Economy," S. Chand and Co. Ltd., New Delhi, 2005.

Vasavi A.R., Harbingers of Rain, Land and Life in South India, OUP, New Delhi, 1999.

Jain Mahesh K. "Agricultural Productivity and Co-operative Credit," Shree Publishers and Distributers, Delhi 2004.

10

Employment Generation: Case of Jharkhand

ASHOK KUMAR MAJI

Introduction

Today the biggest crime against society is to overlook the unemployment and poverty. The growing unemployment in the country in general and Jharkhand State in particular, even after massive investment in industrial and agricultural development causes concern. This point out the failure of the plans and Planning strategy. The largest and everlasting problem the country faces today is unemployment (including under-employment) and poverty. To my mind, the main reasons for our failure on the employment generation front may be the refusal to accept the futility and unusefullness of large industries as an instrument for providing sizeable employment opportunities. The expansion of capital intensive technique and development of growth polls further aggravated the problem of unemployment and increased social tension and social injustice. Even after several years of development, efforts and massive investment, more than 70 per cent of the people still live in absolute poverty. There has been a record increase in gaps between rural and urban economy. The gap of income and output in rural and urban sectors of economy has widened considerable at present.

The past experience shows that our strategy based on capital intensive technique has miserably failed to solve the problem of growing unemployment. The unemployment and poverty constitute the crux of the problems confronting the government. The government with, the help of Planning Commission is busy in devising such a strategy, which may suit the capital scarce and labour surplus economy, such as ours. While evolving employment oriented strategy of development, due regard is to be given to the nature of rural and agricultural economy, distribution of population between rural and urban sectors, regional imbalances and availability of indigenous technique. Due regard should also be given to the existence of seven lakh villages inhabited by 80 per cent poor people, waiting for centuries in anticipation of a better life. The new strategy should aim at the reduction in the vast disparities in income and wages within rural and urban life.

The new development strategy is so devised as to provide jobs for 100 million unemployed and underemployed in the shortest time. With massive labour force and acute scarcity of capital and lack of modern technique small-scale, village and cottage industries can play a decisive role in realising the objectives of maximising production of consumer goods, optimum utilisation of human and material resources scattered in the countryside, prevention of monopoly concentration of economic power, speedy development of employment-oriented industries and to make the industry respond to social needs. We have to find out such a production technique by which, with a low capital investment, we can generate employment opportunities, especially in rural areas where more than 56 crores of people reside. Development of these industries will also help us in reducing the regional imbalance and would promote the 'reverse flow' process of population (from urban to rural areas) for employment and for better economic life. This would also provide 'forward and backward linkage' for agriculture industry and would make more effective the 'Spread Effect' of development. Establishment of small-scale, village and cottage industries would remove disparities in our social and economic structure by providing rural population a higher purchasing power, leading to a better standard of living.

Economics of Small Units and Employment Generation

Now we are in a position to discuss the economics of small-scale and village industries and their suitability in the present economic situation. Suitability of these units may be strongly recommended on the following grounds:

Labour Intensive Technique

Development of small sector in India is the only wayout to save the serious problem of unemployment and underemployment, specially, to solve the problem of rural unemployment and educated unemployment, both overt and disguised. These industries not only make less demand on scarce capital resources but also create much larger opportunities for employment including self-employment. There is a great variation between investment and employment ratio, as well as in the ratio of value added to the investments in large and small sectors. According to various estimations for creating one job in organised sector investment ranging from Rs. 50,000 to Rs. 150,000 as against that of Rs. 3000 to 4000 in small-scale industries is required. In case of cottage industries an investment around Rs. 1,000 for gainful work generation would suffice. Similarly, ratio between investment and production is much higher in small-sector than the large sector. Emphasising the role of the industries, Late Dr. Gadgil urged that rural industrialisation be major economic and social objective of the planned economic development. Thus, it seems that the target of creating 100 million jobs during the next 10 years can only be achieved through rural industrialisation.

Local Base

A country like ours cannot afford industrialisation based on imported technology and other inputs specially when we are short of foreign exchange. We need low cost economy. This can be possible only by optimum use of indigenous resources and techniques. Available raw material in rural areas provides the most important base for rural industrialisation. There are hundreds of items which can be produced in rural and small-scale industries more economically than in large sector, which mostly depends on drawing men and material from the rural sector. This would save rural economy from disaster and would encourage reverse flow of population and ease the strain on urban economy.

Regional Development

Development of large sector not only failed to provide jobs but have also created problems of centralisation leading to urbanisation. This unbalanced growth generated a wide gap in rural and urban economy, almost ruining our village economy. The development of backward regions is of uppermost importance to remove regional development disparities. This is not possible with large sector establishment of small-scale and village industries in rural areas can only remove the existing regional imbalances. The development of village industries with indigenous technique and resources would infuse confidence in our present generation and to some extent put a check on braindrain. During the last five decades an adequate rural infrastructure for development has been developed which would facilitate the development of small sector industries in backward regions.

Indigenous Technique

Small sector industries can easily be established with indigenous techniques. This will take science and technology to countryside, where the benefits of industrialisation have not reached a desired level. Adoption of science and technology in agriculture would serve three purposes. Firstly, it would increase agricultural productivity. Secondly, it would reduce manpower currently employed in agriculture. And lastly, it would create on a very large-scale new non-farm employment labour force in rural areas absorbing to a large extent skilled and semi-skilled unemployed labour force.

Poverty Removal Scheme

Removal of poverty so programmed in our plans cannot be achieved through creating high technical jobs in capital intensive industries or by creating unproductive employment, which has a multiplier effect of unemployment. There is a need of providing rural population a higher purchasing power, leading to better standard of living. This would remove disparities in our social and economic structure. Creating productive employment through small sectors would trigger off a chain reaction in social and economic development and enlarge the indigenous market for goods produced in the country which in turn, would further stimulate industrial and agricultural activities. Thus, long-term benefits of trade and industry lie in the overall prosperity of the rural masses.

Decentralised Planning

Planning has failed to mobilise man and material from the countryside for active participation in our development process. To reverse the process of plan formation is not questionable laying the foundation of an agro-industrial economy through small-scale, village and cottage industries alone can solve the problem of unemployment and eradicate poverty. This could be built through decentralised planning. This could provide planning cells at the region, block and village levels to draw up schemes of village development with active participation and involvement of the people in self-development schemes is an essential precondition for the growth and success of democracy in the country.

Local Marketing

Forward linkage for industrial growth is an essential condition for secular growth and development. Production under large sector finds it difficult to get indigenous market for its produce, as the masses live in the remote areas and require simple and low cost goods to cater to their daily needs.

Thus, in short, the development of small-scale, village and cottage industry sector as an alternative strategy of employment-oriented development can no more be undermined. If the democracy is to be saved rural development cannot be treated as a second grade objective. Now, I like to briefly analyse the role of small-scale industries in the Indian economy.

The small-scale industries in their varied aspects have been regarded as 'an integral and continuing element' both in the economic structure and in the scheme of national planning of India. Their development has been from the very beginning one of the key programme under the Five-Year Plans. The small-scale industries are of diverse types. Their common features are their urban or semi-urban location and use of machines, power and modern techniques. They are run by small entrepreneurs or by self-supporting workers, and sometimes by cooperatives. Some industries, e.g., those manufacturing bicycle parts or sewing machine parts, may be ancillary to the large industries but, as a rule, they are not linked to them by any well-established sub-contracting system and are mere suppliers of products against occasional orders. Another significant feature is that several small-scale industries are of more recent origin and have an organisation in which the middleman has a less prominent role to play than in the older industries. They employ a higher level of technique that demands a higher level of training. They can be located in planned manner.

The role of small-scale industries needs a brief explanation. The reasons behind developing the small-scale industries are fuller use of local resources like capital and skills which may otherwise remain inadequately mobilised, meeting a significant part of the increased demand for consumer goods and simple producer goods forming a vital link between agriculture and large-scale industry, that is, to bring about integration of the development of the small-scale industries with the rural economy and the large-scale industry, providing expanding opportunities for employment both in the rural and the urban areas at a relatively capital cost, ensuring more equitable distribution of the national income. One of the objectives of the small-scale industry programme is the promotion of decentralisation and dispersal of industry in the rural areas and small towns in order to extend work opportunities, raise income and standard of living, and to bring about a more balanced and integrated rural economy. The guiding principle is that in each branch of industry a comprehensive view of the requirements of the community, the contribution which the small-scale industries can make in relation to the large-scale industries and the extent to which the processes and stages of production can be decentralised is to be taken. Another objective is to promote agro-based industries. The next area is to promote the development of the small-scale industries as ancillaries to the large-scale ones. The final objective is to organise industrial co-operatives of the small-scale industrialists with state participation.

What Should be the New Plan ?

Now, the question arises, if the development of small-scale, village and cottage industries is taken as an alternative strategy of development, then how to plan for a success? The following are the suggestions for employment-oriented development of small sectors during the eleventh plan.

Reservation of Items

To makes the small sector more successful the first step is to save small sector from competition with the large sector. This can only be done by reservation of items for production in small-scale sector. Items so selected should be those for which there is a rising effective demand at home. Government should freeze the production of such reserved items, in the large sector, production of items consumed by the countryside population be assigned to this sector and an exhaustive list of such items be prepared by the experts.

Marketing Assistance

One of the major and difficult problems currently faced by small units may be marketing their finished products. The small producers with limited resources may find it difficult to complete with organised sector. Thus, Government should provide assured market to them. In government sectors consumption of these items should be made compulsory. Co-operative marketing should be encouraged. Every possible effort should be made to promote the consumption of labour intensive items.

Low Cost Economy

To make the small sector responsive to social needs, adequate assistance should be provided for reducing cost to bring down the prices. The small sector would meet the social needs it produces goods and services required by the masses, modern agriculture and construction activities in sufficient quantities and at cheaper rates. This objective can be achieved by assuring adequate raw materials, cheap and financial assistance as basic inputs.

Development of Agro-Industry

Ours is the rural agriculturally dominated economy spread over seven lakhs villages, we should develop agro-industries which can be started with local talent, resources and in the villages. These industries cater for demand and posses forward and backward linkage in the country. Moreover, these industries could be labour intensive.

Finance

Funding of these industries is another problem. For financing this sector the help of the banks may be sought. Banks have very ambitious plan for industrial development and are busy in mobilising rural resources. If they take up financing the small industries in rural areas, mobilisation of rural resources may be quite effective for mopping up the rural saving rural adventure scheme be popularised.

Planning from Below

In order to make success of the new strategy of development, we have to reverse the process of centralised planning to decentralised planning. District level planning bodies be formed. The village nucleus massive thrust be laid on the development of small scale, village and cottage industries. The plan should serve as mode for every economic region and district in the country covering handloom, sericulture rural industries projects and rural artisans programmes.

Thus, to conclude the restructuring of Indian economy be carried out with rural industrial development basis small-scale, village and cottage industries be developed for creating productive jobs.

Policy Instruments Common Production Programme

Let us now turn to the policy instruments proposed to be adopted for the achievement of the above mentioned goals. On the eve of the First Plan the policy instruments were largely confined to such activities as provision of power or distribution of controlled materials. There had been hardly any considered and coordinated programme of development and technical improvement. The most salient feature of the policy in the First Plan was "The enunciation of the common production programme." This "programme" was, in fact, an expression of the desirability of considering, while formulating the programme for development of different branches of industry, the respective contributions which the large and the small units could make towards the aggregate requirements of the community and the measures to be adopted successively to enable the small-scale producers to fulfil the targets fixed for them. This programme was but a part of the totality of action to be taken for the development of the small-scale industries. It was intended mainly to afford time and opportunity to the small, decentralised sector to gain necessary strength to develop on its own. Two important aspects of the programme were :

1. Provision of a degree of preference of assurance of a market for the small unit; and
2. Provision of positive assistance so that the role of subsides, sales rebate and sheltered markets could be reduced substantially. To facilitate the realisation of the first part of the programme two steps were taken :
   (a) The spheres of production of the large and the small branches were clearly earmarked. Reservation or demarcation of the spheres of production was through to be specially helpful for the small-scale units;
   (b) Capacity of the large-scale industries was not to be allowed to expand after a certain level; and

Access or excuse on the products of the large-scale industries was levied. The objects of this levy are; first, to raise funds for improving the efficiency and organisation of the small-scale units; second, to reduce the difference in the cost of production and to provide for a limited price differential in favour of the small units; and third, to take away a portion of the additional profits accuring to the large units in consequence of a limit on the expansion of capacity or production.

In attempting to evaluate the impact of the different planned measures it can be said with a degree of confidence that whereas the growth of the small-scale industries during 1931-51 had been an unplanned process, their growth since 1951 has been remarkable in all aspects, i.e., production, number of units, employment provided, value of output, growth of entrepreneurship, changed composition of the small sector, and so forth. The growth of an energetic class of small entrepreneurs has been yet another remarkable result. A part for quantitative growth, there has been material improvement in the quality of the products of the numerous small-scale industries. This was evidenced by the increased variety of items produced according to the standard and specifications prescribed by the defense services and the railways. A number of small-scale units supplied parts and components to the large-scale industries engaged in the manufacture of machine tools, bicycles, automobiles, electronics etc. The product of some of these industries were exported. Production of a number of new items, parts and components requiring high degree of technology and precision was successfully undertaken in the small-scale sector. Some of them replaced imports. Large numbers of small establishments have been set up in the manufacture of dye-stuffs and plastic goods. In this manner the structure of industry has undergone an appreciable change. This is an event of far-reaching significance.

Jharkhand Today

In this part of this chapter, a case study of Jharkhand, which is a unique case of growing unemployment and poverty amidst plenty, will be discussed. A case for achieving twin objectives-removal of poverty and unemployment through small sector will be made out.

Jharkhand State was carved out of the State of Bihar and was organised on 1st November, 2000. This State as 28th State of India came into existence on 15th November, 2000. Total area of Jharkhand stands at 79,714 square kilometers :

(a) Urban area covers 1838 square kms and *(b)* Rural area covers 77,876 sq.kms. Jharkhand State accounts for almost 2.42 per cent of the total area of the country and it holds 15th position in the country from the point of view of total area. According to 2001 Census, total population of Jharkhand goes upto 2,69,09,428 (male population-1,30,48,151 and female population-1,3048,151) Urban population is 22.25 per cent and rural population is 77.75 per cent of the total

population of State. From the point of view of population, Jharkhand is the 13th State of India. Villages in Jharkhand are predominantly inhabited by agriculturists, 84 per cent people live in 32,615 remote village. Of the total population, scheduled castes (22 in number) have reached the figure of 25,82,252 (male numbering 13,47,254 and female numbering 12,41,998). Of the total population of Jharkhand the scheduled tribes (30 in number) have gone up to 60,44,010 (male numbering 30,59,715 and female number 29,82,295). In this way of the total population about 27.67 per cent of it comprises scheduled tribes. More than 74 per cent comprises scheduled castes, scheduled tribes and backward classes. Poverty amidst plenty—A Cruel Paradox—as the facts speak of, Jharkhand is richly endowed in natural resources and possesses rich and inexhaustible development potential, but unfortunately, it has remained a pocket of backwardness in the vast landscape in the developing economy of the country. Jharkhand stands much below the average level of development of the country. The State is blessed with lush green vegetation and dense forests and mineral wealth, providing basic raw material for innumerable small sector industries. It is endowed with rich minerals like coal, iron ore, manganese or limestone, copper, gold, uranium, thorium, fire clay, kayonite, dolomite, earth, clay, asbestos etc. In the field of agriculture, Jharkhand is backward and undeveloped. Irrigation is available to only 8 per cent of the cultivable land. However, agriculture is the main source of livelihood of the three-fourth of population of Jharkhand.

On the other hand, as pointed out earlier, Jharkhand is one of the backward States in the country, with the vast development potentials its masses suffer from abject poverty and unemployment.

Tribal and Rural Economy

Agriculture is the backbone of the state's economy and it is a predominantly agricultural state and 84 per cent of the working population living in villages is engaged in agriculture and allied industry, which speaks for itself of the rural economy of the State. Moreover, 27.67 per cent of the total population belongs to tribals and scheduled castes, scheduled tribes and backward classes taken together, about 74 per cent of the population earn their livelihood wholly from agriculture and forests. Forests provide direct and indirect jobs for millions of tribals and backward class people to earn their livelihood.

Employment Generation Through Small Industries

In the first part of this chapter importance of small industries for employment generation has been emphatically made out. In Jharkhand, there is special need for creating employment in tribal areas. For development of tribal areas, the forest-based industries have a special place and ample scope for employment generation. It is an established fact that in comparison with large-scale industries, small-scale industries have low capital employment ratio (K) specially in Jharkhand.

Forest Based Industries

Alongwith rural unemployment the pressure of educated unemployment is also increasing in the State. Therefore, there is need for creasing self-employment opportunities in rural areas. For the forest-based industries offer the best opportunities in the State. There is scope for starting these industries in the minimum of time since the State possesses an inexhaustible forest wealth.

The following forest-based industries in small sector may be started or expanded for rural employment generation in the State:

Silk Industry

More than 50 per cent of raw materials of tassar silk of the whole country is found in Jharkhand. Main producing regions of tassar silk cover Chaibasa, Tatanagar, Raj Kharsanwa, Hatgamaria, Daltonganj, Govindpur, Hazaribag, Giridih, Lohardagga and Dumka. 40 per cent of raw silk of Jharkhand are produced in Singhbhum, 25 per cent Dumka and 13 per cent in Hazaribag. Thus, silk industry in small sector is a great source of employment of job-seekers, both literate and illiterate.

Tobacco Industry

Adivasis manufacture bidis from locally found tobacco and Singhbhum tops the list in flourishing tobacco industry. Bidis are manufactured from tendu leaves and tobacco. Local people in Dumka are also engaged in this industry. Bidi industry has an ample scope for development. A mass of women folk in rural and urban areas are engaged in this industry. This industry may provide large employment.

Match Industry

On forest-based industry match industry is very prominent. In Kodarma area of Jharkhand several match industries have sprung up and they are source of employment of landless labourers.

Wood-based Industries

There is an ample scope for developing wood-based industries in the State. Jharkhand is rich in the best type of industrial woods like teak, haldoo, sal etc. They may provide base for furniture building material and industry. There is vast scope for expansion of fuel industries by using inferior quality wood. This may provide employment to lakhs of tribals. The forest may also provide base for cart-making plywood, machines, agricultural, implements, toys, wall plates, poles and sleepers, etc. Timber-based industries for producing usable material for sugar mills, oil mills, rice-pounders, boats etc. Match industry is another industry which may be developed in the State. Various other consumers articles like walking sticks, combs, lentpeds, cots and sports items may also be added in the list of these industries.

Bamboo-based Industries

Bamboo and grass are another forest produce in the State, which may provide base for many important products like pulpand paper. These can be easily developed in small sector.

Tanning Industries

Forests in Jharkhand are rich in tanning material, which have not only domestic market but are also in demand in foreign countries. Harra, flower of Dhawai and Babool bark are the basic raw materials for these industries. These may also be used as raw material for dying industries. Picking up of these materials is generally done by tribals. If developed scientifically, it may provide jobs for lakhs of people in rural areas.

Other Industries

There is a vast scope for various small and village industries based on forest products. They may be mentioned as gum industry, Resino industry, Katha Industry etc. These industries require small capital and local technique and unskilled workers, which are in abundance in Jharkhand. Scope for other small-scale industries, besides the forest based industries as mentioned above, there is also possibility to develop the following industries in small, cottage and village sector.

Soap Industry

This industry may be developed in the form of foam and cottage industry, which requires simple technique, locally available material and little of the finance. It has local market also.

Engineering Industry

In Jharkhand, small and marginal farmers are engaged in agricultural work. For scientific development of agriculture and small industries, simple tools and implements may be required in a large quantity. Therefore, there is a vast scope of development of agro-engineering industries. It may also have potential market.

Dairy Product Industries

Jharkhand has large number of live stock population and some of its area is rich in dairy and dairy product based industries like cattle feed, fodder etc., which have abundant employment and development opportunities.

Oil Industry

Another industry which has scope for development in this state is the oil industry. Mustard can be purchased from other states and oil industry can function opening employment scope for unskilled labour.

Handloom Industry

In Jharkhand handloom industry is encouraged and assisted by Khadi and Gram Udyog Sector. Ranchi, Daltonganj and Hazaribag are key centres for handloom industry. Scope of employment of surplus manpower in this industry is also bright.

Miscellaneous Industries

The possibilities for development of various other small and village industries exist in Jharkhand. An intensive survey is needed for repairing and exhaustive list of such employment—oriented industries.

Conclusion

Jharkhand possesses immense possibilities for starting labour oriented small sector industries. The future of development and eradication of poverty lies in expansion of small scale, village and cottage industries sector in Jharkhand.

11

Employment Generation and Inclusive Growth

MANOJ KUMAR SINGH

I

Introduction

Jobless growth has become the lament of our times. In an age when economic growth in India and China is making the rest of the world seen with envy, the government of our country is keen to distance itself from some of the most exciting development-particularly in the service sector-because growth is taking place with apparently too few additional jobs created. Unemployment is said to be multiplying in the countryside as agriculture stagnates. Arjun Sen Gupta's National Commission on Unorganised Enterprise has reportedly calculated that over 800 million Indian live on less than Rs. 20 a day and nearly 400 million workers (86% of the labour force) work under "utterly deplorable conditions" and have "extremely few livelihood options."

The approach chapter of 11th plan talks of inclusive growth with 9 per cent growth of GDP though without any clear targets for employment growth while recent over all employment, growth is a positive feature. There are a number of aspects of current growth that are worrisome, besides the sharp growth of unemployed.

This chapter is organized as follows. The 2nd Section presents and discusses the estimates of population and work force over the period 1983-2005 as backdrop to more detailed analysis of the changes in size and structure of work force between 2000 and 2005. The 3rd Section deals with unorganized sector employment "residual estimates." The Section IV analysis the status of growth in low paid jobs. The Section V contains concluding remarks and suggestions for policy makers to expedite the generation of employment.

II

Population, Worker Population Ratio and Workforce Growth

Estimate of population, separately for rural males, rural females, urban males and urban females, for (the mid-point) of the surveys years, provide the starting point for estimating the size of the work force by gender and rural urban location.

Table 1 provides the estimates of all-India population for the four surveys years (January-December) 1983, and (July-June) 1993-94, 1999-2000 and 2004-05. For the first three time points, the segment-wise population totals are based on inter-censual interpolations based on the 1981, 1991, and the 2001 population censuses. The estimates for 2004-05 are based on population projections for India and states, 2001-06 prepared by the technical group on population projections constituted by the National Commission on population, May 2006 [ORG and CCI 2006).

As can be readily seen, in all the four population segments, there has been a significant slowdown in the rate of grown of population in the first quinquennium of the 21st century from a little under 2 per cent per annum between 1994 and 2000 to a little under 1.7 per cent per annum nevertheless. India's population has growth by close to 88 million between 2000 and 2005. In a recent paper [Sundaram 2007] we had drawn attention to the fact that the segment specific overall worker population ratios are nothing but weighted averages of age-specific WPRs with the share of each age group in population total as per the survey; providing the weights. It was shown that using the survey based age-distribution results in a sharp-slowdown in the growth of prime age (15-59) population from 274 per cent per annum between 1983 and 1994 to 1.93 PcPa between 1994 and 2000. In the context of the observed slowdown in the rate of growth of total population over the same period, equally problematic is the acceleration albeit small in the rate of growth of population in the 0.9 age group raising doubts about the order of decline in the share of 0.9 age group between 1983 and 1993-94.

Table-1

All India Population by Gender and Rural Urban Location 1983-2004-05 (All India Population) ('0005')

Population Segment	*1983 (1.7.83)*	*1993-94 (1.1.94)*	*1999-2000 (1.1.2000)*	*2004-05 (1.1.05)*	*Rates of Growth (% Per Annum)*		
					1983-1994	*1994-2000*	*2000-2005*
Rural males	281,288	339,642	374,432	400,865	1.81	1.64	1.37
Rural females	266,637	319,411	353,785	379,102	1.73	1.72	1.39
Rural persons	547,925	659,053	728,217	779,967	1.77	1.68	1.38
Urban males	91,217	124,031	145,878	164,732	2.97	2.74	2.46
Urban females	80,445	111,104	131,244	148,332	3.12	2.82	2.48
Urban persons	171,662	235,136	277,122	313,064	3.04	2.78	2.47
Total (R+U) males	372,505	463,673	520,310	565,597	2.11	1.94	1.68
Total (R+U) females	347,082	430,515	485,029	527,434	2.07	2.01	1.69
Total (R+U) persons	719,587	984,188	1005,339	1093,031	2.09	1.97	1.69

Note: Segment wise population in totals for 1983, 1993-94 and 1999-2000 are based on inter-censal interpolations of total population, share of urban area in total population and the share of females in rural and urban area based on the 1981, 1991 and 2001 census. The estimates for 2004-05 are based on interpolation of the total and urban population as on October 1, 2004 and March 1, 2005 as per population projections for India and states, 2001-2026 [ORG and CCI, 2006].

Taking care of the concerns about age misreporting in the population census by using "smoothed" age-distribution for the censuses, Table 2 presents the survey-based age-distribution and the census-based age-distribution for 1981, 1991 and 2001. This brings out the nature of the differences in the two age-distributions; especially for 1983 where the survey based share of 0-9 is higher for rural males and urban males and for 1993-94 relative to the 1991 census where the survey-based age-shares in this and the next age-groups are substantially lower for females.

Table–2
Survey and Census-based Age Distribution of All India Population by Gender and Rural-Urban Location 1981-2004-05
Per 1000 Distribution of Population by Rural Age-Groups

	Survey-based				*Census-based (Smoothed)*			
Age Group	*1983*	*1993-94*	*1999-2000*	*2004-05*	*1981*	*1991*	*2001*	*2005*
PANEL A : RURAL MALES								
0-9	284	261	255	238	278	268	255	237
10-14	136	120	128	127	127	121	122	118
15-29	244	158	250	253	250	259	261	272
30-59	270	294	296	311	280	289	295	302
60+	66	68	71	71	65	63	67	71
All age	1000	1000	1000	1000	1000	1000	1000	1000
PANEL B : RURAL MALES								
0-9	275	254	248	230	280	269	252	231
10-14	121	107	117	113	122	115	116	115
15-29	255	266	258	258	256	265	261	264
30-59	280	304	304	324	284	289	298	311
60+	68	69	73	75	58	63	73	79
All age	1000	1000	1000	1000	1000	1000	1000	1000
PANEL C : URBAN MALES								
0-9	241	218	202	183	280	225	196	177
10-14	125	115	116	113	104	113	110	100
15-29	294	292	291	258	298	292	296	303
30-59	287	321	331	324	300	317	336	153
60+	52	55	59	75	48	53	62	67
All age	1000	1000	1000	1000	1000	1000	1000	1000

Contd.

	Survey-based				Census-based (Smoothed)			
Age Group	*1983*	*1993-94*	*1999-2000*	*2004-05*	*1981*	*1991*	*2001*	*2005*
PANEL D : URBAN FEMALES								
0-9	249	216	201	179	256	236	199	177
10-14	122	114	114	108	112	115	109	98
15-29	291	291	287	283	295	297	293	303
30-59	275	314	327	154	275	295	328	347
60+	63	65	71	76	52	57	71	75
All age	1000	1000	1000	1000	1000	1000	1000	1000

Note: Starting with the more detailed (by 5 year age group) age-distributions, the census ages-distribution for 1981, 1991 and 2001 has been smoothed using the smoothing procedure spilt out in the report of technical group on population projections (pp. 3-4), for 2005, the age-distribution has been computed by the author by interpolation of age-sex-location-specific population for January 1, 2005 from population projections by age-sex and location for April 1, 2002 and April 1, 2007.

Table 2 also presents for 2004-05 a comparison of the survey based age-distribution with our estimate based on interpolations of projected population for April 1, 2002 and 2007.

For rural and urban females, the age distributions are fairly well matched. For rural males the age-share in the 0-9 and 60+ age group are well matched but the projections based age distribution shows a higher share for the 15-29 age group with lower share for both the 10-14 and the 30-59 age group.

For urban males, the projections-based distribution show smaller share for the 0-9 and 10-14 age groups and fractionally higher share for the 15-29 and the 30-59 age groups. As we shall see presently, the projection based age-distribution yield a some-what higher overall WPRs for males in both rural and urban areas of the country and slightly lower WPR for rural females. Given that our estimates of age distributions for 2004-05 are based on projections rather than a census count for 2004-05 we accept the survey based age-distributions for 2004-05.

In Table 3, we present the age specific WPRs on the usual status for the four population segments for 1983, 1993-94, 1999-2000 and

2004-05 to see the changes between 2000 and 2005, which is what we will focus on against the backdrop of trends since 1983.

Table–3
All India Age-Specific Usual Status Worker-Population Ratios by Gender and Rural Urban Location 1983-2004-05
Per 1000 Worker-Population Ratios

	Rural Males				*Rural Females*			
Group	*1983*	*1993-94*	*1999-00*	*2004-05*	*1983*	*1993-94*	*1999-2000*	*2004-05*
PANEL A : RURAL MALES								
0-9	13	6	4	2	13	7	4	2
10-14	203	138	91	68	240	141	96	74
15-19	666	578	503	497	452	364	304	319
20-24	897	859	844	849	488	456	410	410
25-29	968	958	950	966	557	525	491	513
30-44	985	986	982	984	614	598	572	614
45-59	955	968	958	962	552	543	518	569
60+	670	695	625	644	232	242	218	253
All ages (1)	547	553	531	546	340	328	299	327
All ages (2)	558	454	535	555	341	319	297	322
PANEL B : URBAN AREAS								
	Urban Males				*Urban Females*			
0-9	3	3	2	1	3	2	1	2
10-14	113	66	49	48	70	45	36	33
15-19	414	356	314	335	155	123	105	128
20-24	727	674	658	684	182	180	155	201
25-29	921	904	883	909	229	224	194	229
30-44	975	975	969	975	291	205	266	310
45-59	926	935	921	923	276	283	250	252
60+	505	442	402	366	140	113	94	100
All ages (1)	512	521	518	549	151	155	133	166
All ages (2)	525	517	528	558	150	149	140	167

Notes: Estimate of overall (all ages) WPRs is row 9 represents the weighted average of age specific WPRs with survey-based age-shares as weights while those in row 10 have the census-based age shares as weights.

For rural males, the changes in age-specific WPRs are either small or broadly in live with the trends since 1983—except for the rise in WPR in the 25-29 age group.

For urban males, the sizeable increase in WPRs in the 15-19; 20-24, 25-29 age-groups do appear to be out of line with the trends since 1983.

The increase in WPRs females—the four cases identified above-pale into insignificance compared to the big jumps in the age-specific WPRs for females. For rural females we have a 22 points (per 1000) rise in the 25-29 age group, a 42 point rise in the 30-44 age group and a whopping 51 point rise in the 45-59 age group.

In the 25-29 age-group; the 22 point rise in WPR on UPSS is made up of a 6 point decline on the principal status and 28 point rise on the subsidiary status. The increase in the VPSS WPR for rural females in the 30-44 age group is made up of a 15 point rise on the principal status and a 27 point rise on the subsidiary status. While in the 45-59 age-groups, the rise in the UPSS WPR overwhelmingly reflects a rise in WPR on the principal status. In all the three age-groups, the WPRs on the subsidiary status are still below the levels in 1993-94 and, there is no a prior basis for not accepting the increase in WPRs on the principal status.

For urban females the increase in WPRs are significant in the 15-19 and the 20-24 age 0 groups and are snot out of sync with the trends since 1983. In the 30-44 age group, three, fourth of the rise in the UPSS WPR reflects a rise in WPR on the principal status and the underlying WPR on the subsidiary status, while being higher than the 1999-2000 level, are still lower than the level for 1993-94.

In row 9 of Table 3, we present the overall (all age) WPRs with the survey-based age shares providing the weight to derive the weighted-average of age-specific WPRs; while row 10 reports the overall WPRs when the census-based age shares are used to weight the age specific WPRs from the respective surveys.

In deriving our estimates of usual work force, for reasons already discussed, for 1983, 1993-2004 and 1999-2000 we combine the segment specific population totals (Table-I) with the overall WPRs given in row 10 to derive our workforce estimates for 2004-05).

III

Employment : Organized and Unorganized

Given the unskilled profile of the poor, they are likely to be employed in blue-collar activities as against white-collar ones. Since the unorganized sector holds out more employment opportunities of the blue-collar variety, it may be of interest to compare the employment growth in the organized sector with that in the organized sector (Table-4).

Table-4
Employment Growth in Organized and Unorganized Sectors, (per cent)

Activity	*1999-2000*	*Per Annum Growth During 1994-2000*			*1993-94*
	Share in Employment	*Organi-zed*	*Unor-ganized*	*Overall*	*Overall*
Agriculture	56.7	1.00	0.30	0.02	2.23
Mining and quarrying	0.67	1.30	2.40	1.91	3.68
Manufacturing	12.11	0.87	2.58	2.58	2.26
Electricity, gas and water supply	0.34	0.51	5.85	5.21	5.31
Construction	4.44	0.69	5.85	5.21	4.18
Trade hotel and restaurants	11.15	1.43	5.79	5.72	4.18
Transport, storage and communication	4.05	0.21	7.50	5.53	3.35
Finance, insurance real estate, and business services	1.38	1.27	8.30	5.40	4.60
Community, social and personal services	9.16	0.8	3.56	2.08	3.85
All sectors	100	0.56	1.12	1.07	2.67

Note: DGE & T, Derived from NSSO' Employment as per CDS measure.
Source: Planning Commission (2001 b, 2002).

While employment growth slowed down at the aggregate level to 1.07 per cent in 1999-2000 from 2.67 per cent in 1993-94, it stands higher at 1.12 per cent for the unorganized sector as compared to 0.56 per cent for the organized sector as compared to 0.56 per cent for the organized segment in 1999-2000. At the sectoral level unorganized employment growth has been higher in the majority of activities which together account for around 90 per cent of total employment. Only in the activities, viz., "mining and quarrying", "electricity, gas and water supply" and "community, social and personal services," has unorganized employment growth been lower than organized employment growth. While overall unorganised employment growth slowed down in 1999-2000 over 1993-94, the sectoral pattern of employment growth in the unorganized *viz-a-viz* organized sector, as emergent in 1999-2000, cloud be a factor contributing to the declining poverty ratio.

National Sample Survey (NSS) results show an increase in unemployment throughout the 1990s mirroring the set-back in poverty reduction (Table-5).

Table-5
Growth and Employment—Some Indicators
(Growth Rates in Per cent Per Annum)

	1993-94 to 1999-00	*1999-00 to 2004-05*	*1993-94 to 2004-03*
Agricultural self employment	0.53	2.89	1.01
Agricultural wage management	1.06	3.18	0.89
Total agricultural employment	0.03	0.85	0.40
Agricultural GDP	2.88	1.76	2.37
Non-agricultural self employment	2.34	5.72	3.86
Non-agricultural wage employment	2.68	3.79	3.18
Rural non-agricultural employment	2.26	5.27	3.52
Urban non-agricultural employment	3.13	4.08	3.46
Secondary sector employment	2.91	4.64	3.70
Tertiary sector employment	2.27	4.67	3.35
Total non-agricultural employment	2.53	4.66	3.49
Non-agricultural GDP	8.11	7.22	7.71
Total employment	1.02	2.85	1.85

Table 5, summaries some of the results on growth and employment.

Table 5, present growth rates of employment days non-farm workers and wages of rural male casual workers for major states from the NSS employment-unemployment surveys." For the working population as a whole, daily status unemployment increased from 6.1 per cent in 1993-94 to 7.3 per cent in 1999-2000 to 8.3 per cent in 2004-05, and was higher in 2004-05 than 1993-94 in all states except West Bengal, Assam and Gujarat. More importantly daily status unemployment among agricultural labour households increased from 9.5 per cent in 1993-94, 12.3 per cent in 1999-2000 and further to 15.3 per cent in 2004-05. Yet, importantly, the surveys also suggest that the growth rate of employment, at 2.85 per cent per annum, outpaced, population growth rate between 1999-2000 and 2004-05, after having been much less than population growth, at only 1.02 per cent per annum, between 1993-2004 and 1999-2000. Closer inspection of the data suggests that most of this increase in employment during 1999-2005 was in the form of self employed with days of wage labour actually declining. But, nonetheless, one possible reason why poverty reduction during 1999-2005 after a sharp increase during 1999-2005 compared to 1993-2000. For example, the share of carnal labourers in general actually declined during 1993-2000 and also rural non-agricultural employment registered a sharp increase from 1999-2000 onwards, following almost complete stagnancy earlier in the 1990s.

Table–6
Growth Rate of Unemployment, Non-farms Workers and Wages by States, (in per cent Per Annum)

State	*Unemployment*		*Non-farm Worker*		*Rural Male Real Wage*	
	1993-00	*1999-05*	*1993-00*	*1999-05*	*1993-00*	*1999-05*
Andhra Pradesh	4.9	8.2	0.7	7.1	4.3	1.5
Assam	0.4	0.8	9.9	–0.1	2.4	3.5
Bihar	4.6	1.5	5.1	7.7	5.1	3.4
Gujarat	–0.8	–1.4	0.6	4.5	3.4	1.1
Haryana	–5.2	12.2	1.8	8.6	2.8	0.8
Karnataka	–0.3	13.3	–0.4	3.8	3.8	0.8
Kerala	9.6	6.2	4.3	3.1	5.5	3.6
Madhya Pradesh	7.5	13.7	3.7	7.8	0.9	3.4
Maharashtra	8.0	10.9	0.0	5.5	3.1	–0.5
Rajasthan	17.8	12.8	1.7	7.1	3.4	0.6
Orissa	1.1	10.9	2.0	11.1	1.7	5.9
Punjab	7.6	25.7	4.4	6.7	0.2	0.0
Tamil Nadu	0.6	2.3	–0.3	1.1	6.5	0.0
Uttar Pradesh	3.2	4.3	3.7	7.4	2.9	1.5
West Bengal	13.0	–6.5	–1.0	4.3	2.8	0.2

Table-6, shows that, although casual real wages decelerated between 1999-2000 and 2004-05 for all India, these increased at more than 3 per cent per annum in Assam, Bihar, Madhya Pradesh and Orissa, and in fact accelerated in most of these poor states. Wages are an important indicators, it is useful to look at some of the non income indicators. On this, the preliminary results are available from the National Family Health Survey (NFHS)-3 of 2005-06" the previous two surveys in this regard were NFHS-1 and NFHS-2. That is, these three surveys are roughly co-terminus with the NSS thick round surveys Table 6.

IV

Growth in Low Paid Jobs

In order to further understand the nature of this employment, we disaggregate the participation rates by levels of education. Among men, while the increase in participation occurred at all education levels, for women it has been mainly for workers below the middle school level (Table 7). Graduate women showed an increase in participation in the latest period, but not over the longer term since 1993-94. The increase in participation of women mainly at lower levels of education implies that their access to employment is either in self-employment or at the bottom of the hierarchy in wage salaried employment. Therefore, the rosy picture of growth of regular employment for women is to be weighted against their employment in low paid jobs, often in subsidy capacity, in the service sector, either in school and hospitals or as domestic help in households. The consequences for returns to employment are obvious. The increase in participation observed in 2004-05 for those with graduate education and above for men and women in only with respect to 1999-2000 and not above the level in 1993-94. Over the long-term, therefore, the perspective is not very encouraging in terms of the nature of employment.

The phenomenon of growth of poor earning jobs urban areas in regular salaried employment further evidenced by the level of average real wage earnings. For the first time in decades, the average daily real earning of regular workers was seen decline in 2004-05 (Table 8). These was true of urban and rural men and women in non-agricultural activities. The nature of the growth of urban jobs for women remains a question. In facts, in urban areas the casual workers also showed a decline in real wages for the first time, though at a lower rate than the regular workers casual workers in rural areas were able to more or less maintain their already very low real daily earnings.

Table–7
Workforce Participation Rates by Level of Education by Usual Status for Age 15+
(As a Percentage of Population in Respective Education Levels)

	1993-94	*1999-00*	*2004-05*	*1993-94*	*1999-00*	*2004-05*
	Rural Female			*Urban Female*		
Not literate	54.0	51.3	55.0	33.0	27.1	30.4
Literate primary	41.6	40.3	44.9	20.3	17.7	23.4
Middle	29.0	29.0	37.1	13.1	12.9	16.1
Secondary	25.8	25.7	30.5	13.4	12.4	12.3
Higher secondary	23.4	20.6	25.2	14.7	12.4	12.9
Diploma/certificate			52.3			48.6
Graduate and above	36.6	31.0	34.5	30.1	273	29.0
All	48.6	45.2	48.5	22.3	19.7	22.7
	1993-94	*1999-00*	*2004-05*	*1993-94*	*1999-00*	*2004-05*
	Rural Male			*Urban Male*		
Not literate	91.8	89.5	89.2	87.0	83.9	83.1
Literate primary	90.9	88.0	89.5	85.0	83.0	85.5
Middle	77.0	76.8	80.2	72.3	73.2	76.0
Secondary	72.8	73.7	73.2	67.7	66.8	67.3
Higher secondary	68.6	71.3	70.9	60.7	60.8	60.8
Diploma/certificate			82.1	60.7		79.8
Graduate and above	83.4	83.6	85.1	81.8	80.6	79.5
All	86.4	84.1	84.6	76.8	75.2	79.3

Source: Statement 5,5, Employment—Unemployment survey 61st round, 2004-05, Report No. 515, National Sample Survey Organisation, 2006.

The NSS does not collect data on incomes of the self-employed. However with the phenomenon of growing self-employment it is necessary to reconsider this issue. As a first and rather poor effort the NSS did, in its 61st round; collect information on perception of the self-employed with regard to their earnings. Interesting results

Table-8
Average Real Daily Wage Earnings of Regular and Casual Workers: All India: 15 to 50 Years (in Rs/day at 1993-94 Prices)

	1983	*1987-1988*	*1993-1994*	*1999-2000*	*2004-2005*	*1983*	*1987-1988*	*1993-1994*	*1999-2000*	*2004-2005*
REGULAR SALARIED WORKERS										
	Rural Male					*Rural Female*				
Agriculture	17.3	26.1	27.5	44.2	41.1	21.9	19.0	22.8	31.0	31.5
Non-agri-culture	45.5	62.4	66.5	90.8	88.2	26.8	46.4	40.6	91.3	51.6
All	37.0	53.9	58.5	80.2	83.8	25.0	38.5	34.9	71.8	49.4
REGULAR SALARIED WORKERS										
	Urban Male					*Urban Female*				
Agriculture	30.6	47.6	51.4	92.9	52.1	23.8	32.9	46.7	38.9	39.6
Non-agri-culture	58.3	72.5	79.2	106.5	101.4	43.0	60.1	62.7	97.3	76.5
All	57.7	72.3	78.1	102.3	101.0	42.2	60.1	62.3	84.6	76.1
CASUAL WORKERS										
	Rural Male					*Rural Female*				
Agriculture	16.6	20.1	21.6	25.5	27.8	11.3	13.3	15.1	18.1	19.3
Non-agri-culture	24.1	28.1	30.1	37.5	39.5	11.8	16.3	17.46	23.5	25.8
All	18.7	20.3	23.7	28.6	31.1	11.3	13.8	15.33	18.5	20.2
CASUAL WORKERS										
	Urban Male					*Urban Female*				
Agriculture	20.8	22.6	25.5	30.0	28.1	12.2	13.2	16.5	19.4	17.2
Non-agri-culture	27.6	30.9	33.8	39.3	38.2	13.1	16.7	19.5	24.7	23.7
All	26.5	29.4	32.4	38.1	37.3	12.9	15.5	18.5	23.0	21.8

Note: Real wages are computed at 1993-94 prices.
Source: Employment and unemployment surveys. National sample organization various rounds.

emerged, with only a little over 50 per cent of the rural and nearly 60 per cent of the urban self-employed reporting that their employment was remunerative (Table 9).

Table–9
Percentage of Self Employed Persons Reporting their Earning from Self-employment as Remunerative and Distribution by Amount Regarded as Remunerative

		Percent Finding Amount of Earnings (Rs.) Remunerative					
	Percent Finding Self-employment Remunerative	*0-1000*	*1001-1500*	*1501-2000*	*2001-2500*	*250/-3000*	*>3000*
Rural Male	51.1	12.9	17.5	16.5	11.4	12.9	27.3
Rural Female	51.4	34.2	23.5	15.4	8.9	7.2	9.9
Rural Persons	51.2	21.2	19.7	16.0	10.5	10.7	20.5
Urban Male	60.9	4.9	8.2	9.9	7.2	12.2	56.5
Urban Female	50.9	32.8	20.2	12.6	7.7	8.1	18.3
Urban Persons	58.6	10.4	10.6	10.4	7.4	11.5	48.9

Note: Self-employment by usual status (Principal plus subsidiary).
Source: Statement 5, 12, Survey of Employment and Unemployment, Report 515, Part, NSSO, September 2006.

Worse still, about 40 per cent of the self-employed in rural areas felt that their income of less than Rs. 1500 per month was remunerative enough (Chandrasekhar and Ghosh 2006b). About 30 per cent of the urban self-employed felt that less than Rs. 2000 per month was remunerative employment. The minimal income on which the self-employed survive and their low levels of expectation come out starkly even using this crude indicator of income. We would however, plead for better accounting of self-employed incomes in the next NSS employment and unemployment survey to be able to understand better the economic status of their growing group of workers.

Interesting insights can be gained into the nature of work by analyzing the location of work of the workers. A conventional place of work is an enterprise such as the factory, offices or any institution. It was observed that in 2004-05 about 40 per cent of the urban workers did not have such a conventional designed place of work (Table-10). The difference was more striking by gender, nearly half (47%) the men and 70 per cent of the women did not have such designated places of work.

Table-10
Place of Work of Non-agricultural Workers Aged 15-64 Years by Usual Status (Principal Plus Subsidiary) 1999-2000 and 2004-05 (in per cent)

Location of Work	*Rural*		*Urban*	
	1999-2000	*2004-2005*	*1999-2000*	*2004-2005*
No fixed place	17.8	9.3	10.5	3.9
Own dwelling	20.2	29.8	13.5	13.9
Own enterprise	13.9	14.7	20.9	18.3
Employer's dwell	3.4	3.0	5.2	5.3
Employer's enterprise	26.2	22.3	31.6	41.2
Street	2.2	5.7	3.9	7.4
Construction sites	10.0	11.0	7.7	6.6
Others	6.2	4.2	6.7	3.2
Total	100.0	100.0	100.0	100.0
Location of Work	*Male*		*Female*	
	1999-2000	*2004-2005*	*1999-2000*	*2004-2005*
No fixed place	13.8	83	11.2	3.2
Own dwelling	11.1	12.3	35.5	51.3
Own enterprise	17.7	18.5	8.4	10.7
Employer's dwell	3.1	3.0	7.5	6.7
Employer's enterprise	35.9	35.0	26.3	18.9
Street	2.9	7.7	2.1	2.9
Construction sites	9.0	11.0	5.1	4.0
Others	6.4	4.2	3.8	2.4
Total	100.0	100.0	100.0	100.0

Source: Survey of Employment and Unemployment, Report 460, Part I, Table 8, July 2001, NSSO; Prime Minister's High Level Committee Report on Social, Economic and Educational Status of Muslim Community of India, Table 5.7 and 5, 8, November 2006.

V

In a growth accounting framework, production in generally attributed to three sources "Capital, Labour and Total Factor Productivity (TFP). The relationship between growth in GDP and employment is generally characterized by a summary statistic, viz. elasticity of employment with respect to GDP. Normally, an increase in output is associated with an increase in labour use or employment, implying a positive elasticity of employment. However, employment elasticities may be very low in sectors with large underemployment, which means there is considerable room for output expansion without any corresponding increase in employment. Employment elasticity is typically expected to be less than unity since productivity per person employed is likely to increase over time with productivity growth being an important determinate of wage rate as also the quality of employment, high employment elasticities are not necessarily the best way of achieving employment objectives, decline in employment clasticity can even be welcome for sectors where productivity per person is very low. Ideally, what is a level of GDP growth that sufficiently high to allow for an increase in employment as also productivity in order to ensure rising real wages and growth of income per person employed (Planning Commission 2001). Employment elasticity of the economy (as per the UPSS measures), which was at 0.53 during the period 1977-78 to 1983 declined to 0.41 from 1983 to 1993-94. Thus, while employment elasticity has been declining over the years, the decline has been particularly sharp in the 1990's, giving rise to the phenomenon of jobless growth.

At the sectoral levels employment elasticities declined for seven out of nine sectors. While the employment elasticity for construction was sustained as per the UPSS measure of employment, it declined as per the CDS measure. Similarly, the employment elasticity for "financing, insurance, real estate and business services" increased as per the CDS measure, it declined as per the UPSS measure. However, as per both the measures, the employment elasticity increased for "Transport, storage and communication" over the period. Much of the decline in aggregate employment elasticity was due to agriculture and "Community, social and personnel services," which together account for nearly 70 per cent of total employment. For the first time, the number of persons employed in agriculture turned out largely static over this period, perhaps reflecting the reduction in underemployed with the salutary impact on the poverty ratio."

The euphoria with which the growth of the economy, measured in term of GDP growth, and the high salary packages received by the media, hides the truth on employment. If the growth of the economy is to be inclusive, the majority of the workforce; who do not seem to be peeping the benefits of GDP acceleration, will have to be brought into the growth process. However, this can only happen if there is ample recognition of this fact. If we do wish to understand the nature of this growth, we first need to refine our statistics fail to capture the diversity of the labour force, and certain new and growing statistics fail to capture the diversity of the labour force, and certain new and growing form of work such as homework, the levels of incomes obtained by the workers in different segments and the lack of social security benefits accruing to them. We appeal to the Statistical Commission of India to prepare more inclusive statistics of the work-force before we can expect the Planning Commission to promote inclusive growth.

NOTES

These projections were carried out the P.N. Mari Bhat, needless to say, the responsibility for the interpolation based estimates of age distributions for January 1, 2005 rest solely with author.

If we had gone with projections–based age distributions the estimated workforce would be higher by 3.5 million, which at 0.76 per cent of the estimates based on the survey–based age distributions, is quite small.

The WPR in the 60+ age group for 1999-2000 is perhaps too low and the 2004-05 figure more in line with the trends since 1983.

Unemployment growth rates one growth rate of unemployment person days. Non-farm worker growth rate is by usual status.

NFHS-3 results reported here are taken from the fact-sheet for various states available at www.nfhsindia.org key results for 22 states are available on the website.

The various alternative interpretations of the emerging episode are best described in Planning Commission (2002). "The decline is largely due to changes in intra - sectoral composition within this sector when most of the labour intensive sub-sectors grew comparatively slower, along with some significant - mechanization in other sub-sectors. This decline might also be reflecting some reduction in under employment in the agriculture sector, when there is a shift of labour from agriculture to non–farm rural activities and migration to urban areas."

REFERENCES

Chandrasekhar, CP and Jayati Ghosh, (2006); Employment Growth; The Latest Trends, Macroscan: An Alternative Economics; webecentre; November 17, www.macroscan.org.

HANDA, SANJAY K. and Ray, Partha, (2006) "Employment and Poverty in

India During the 1990 S, Is there a Diverging Trend" Economic and Political Weekly, July 8, 2006, pp. 3019-3020.

ORG and CCI (2006) "Report of the Technical Group on Population Projection Constituted by the National Commission on Population," 2006.

Planning Commission (2001); Report of the Task Force on Employment Opportunities, Chairman Montek S. Ahluwalia, GOI; New Delhi.

Sundaram, K. (2007): "Growth of Work Opportunities in India, 1983-99 to 2000" in A. Vaidanathan and K.L. Krishna (eds.), Institutions and Markets in India's Development, Essays for K.N. Raj Oxford University Press; New Delhi.

Sundaram, K. (2007), "Employment and Poverty in India, 2000-2005" Economic and Political Weekly July 28-2007, pp. 3122-3123.

Unni, Jeemol and Raveendram, G. (2007) "Growth of Employment (1993-94 to 2004-05): Illusion of Inclusiveness." Economic and Political Weekly, January 20, 2007, pp. 198-199.

12

Rural Non-Farm Employment and Economic Development: A Case Study of West Bengal

KUNTAL CHAKRABORTY

I

Introduction

Employment generation in any country depends to a great extent on the level of development. In India during the past three decades production has increased in all the sectors of the economy, but employment in adequate number has not been generated. Hence economic growth by itself does not solve the problem of unemployment and poverty.

With the adoption of neo-liberal economic policies in India over the past one and half decade the government's obsession with the high rate of economic growth has made it completely oblivious of possible conflict between economic growth and employment. So economic growth in recent years is not 'job-oriented'.

The 61st Round, (2004-05) of NSS data on Employment-Unemployment shows that with the increased workforce, the number of unemployed persons grew substantially during 1993-94 to 1999-2000. The overall growth in employment declined from 2.01 per cent per annum during 1983 to 1993-94 to 0.98 per cent per annum during the period 1993-94 to 2004-05.The employment situation in rural area is so far worse. The growth rate of employment in rural sector declined form 1.72 per cent per annum during 1993-94 to 2004-05.

Employment generation is one of the most significant issues. In terms of living conditions, in West Bengal now a day, enough jobs are not created for working people willing to work. The rate of employment generation in terms of aggregate main work has been lower than the rate of expansion of population and substantially lower than the rate of income growth. As a result the pattern of job creation has shifted towards more casual, marginal, part-time and insecure contracts or self employment or what has come to be known as informal unorganized activities.

Most of the poverty-stricken people belong to identifiable poor social groups e.g., SC/ST/Muslim etc. For various reasons sociological and economically week people are under the intense poverty conditions. Through planned economic activities and cluster of work development programme. These people can be absorbed in employment arena. Only when some kind of minimal employment and income generation opportunities are open to them they will be able to come up and respond to different kinds of incentives programme.

So employment generation programme of old and new types of activities has to be adopted at the village level. Inclusiveness begins at this stage and step by step these programmes will gather momentum. Poor people will get employment, and productivity will increase. Output will be generated at low cost. This will enable the poor people to live in dignity and will be able to come up in the ladder of higher and higher level of income.

There are two sides of this particular issue: the contribution of the agriculture to the GDP. When the contribution of the agriculture to the GDP increases there is a likelihood of increase in non-farm employment in the rural sector. On the other hand even though the contribution of the agriculture to the GDP remain stagnant, as it is now, the non-farm employment and income is likely to increase if the productivity of non-farm labour force can be raised with the adoption of new technique of production and improvement of the quality of the product. The primary objective is to see the improvement of income and employment opportunities in non-farm sector, in which ever way it is possible. The absence of both push and pull factors only result in persistence of poverty among rural non-farm sector. We primarily pay attention to the rural informal sector which is a little different from the urban informal sector.

The present analysis mainly focuses on the available employment opportunities in the rural area of West Bengal during the post reform period. The diversification of employment opportunities from the agriculture to non-farm informal sector can improve the living condition of such rural asset less labour force. It is of special interest to examine whether the rural non-farm sector has the potential to absorb the diversified labour force from the agriculture and non-agricultural sectors and can reduce the income inequalities of such labour forces.

Data and Methodology

The brand available National Sample Survey data partly assist in articulating this proposition. We shall see that NSSO data over a certain period indicate a broad trend line on income and employment of the non-farm labour force. However, this is substantiated by limited sample study of the selected area of our study. To compute the actual availability of work in agriculture and non-agriculture sector in a highly seasonal economy in rural West Bengal, we use available Census data.

II

Informal Sector and Non-Farm Activities

Informal/unorganized sector is defined as residual of organized sector employing ten or more workers and unorganized sector as residual. As this definition is not very satisfactory the commission (ICLS 1993) listed some characteristics to identify the informal sector. These characteristics are mainly low level organization, casual labour relation, small owned accounting family, own enterprise or micro enterprise, ownership of fixed and other asset by self, involvement of family worker, easy entry and exit, free mobility, use of indigenous resources and technology, absence of fixed working hours, unregistered and ported work, lack of employment social securities, use of labour intensive technology etc. As such the unorganized sector is not independent or exclusive. This is dependent on organized/formal sector and rest of the economy shows variety of linkages such as raw material, capital, market facility etc.

For analytical purpose it is important to define the meaning of non-farm activity. Here the term non-farm means non-agricultural activity. It includes cattle farming, forestry, fishing, mining and quarrying, small scale manufacturing industries, manufacturing of tobacco, wood products, transport, trade and various type of services in rural and semi urban areas. Labour force engaged in the said activities is termed as non-agricultural labour force. We can make a tentative list of non-farm activities on the basis of the following industries: *(a)* Knowledge base industries. Such as modern printing and communication industries at village level. *(b)* Modern processing industries e.g., food processing and other processing industry. *(c)* Transformation of traditional village industries e.g., sericulture, handloom, dairying etc. The non-farm activity provide employment to the asset less labour force throughout the year and supplementary employment to small and marginal farm household during off-farm session.

Composition of Informal Workforce

The informal sector (on the basis of workers approach) broadly compressed of two types of workers: non-wage or self-employed and wage earner. The non-wage component takes into account workers of household enterprises, employer or unpaid family labour. All these three categories can jointly be termed as self-employed. Regular salaried or wage earning workers in the informal sector are the wage component of the informal workforce.

From the 55th and 61st round of NSS data it is clear that unorganized sector is largely a self-employed sector. About 60 per cent of the total workforces in this sector are self-employed and remaining 4 per cent are mainly regular and casual worker. Casual workers account for 21 per cent of the total unorganized workers. The concentration of informal work activity is higher in rural sector than in the urban sector.

The above composition clearly reveals that informal sector consists mainly of workers with non-contract job, having non-formal employer-employee relationship and no social security benefits.

The rural urban difference shows that rural males are much more likely to be own account workers. On the other hand urban workers are much more salaried workers. In case of females, rural female workers are unpaid family workers but urban female workers are much more likely to be own account workers.

The Problems of Informal Sector

Informal/unorganised sector constitute a major section of workers (82.6%). The workers in the unorganised sector are not satisfied with their present work status and therefore seek additional work for various reasons. One of the main reason is low income in casual non-farm work irrespective of sex and caste i.e., insecurity of work, lack of social security and low wage rate are some of the reason that forced them to find alternative job.

Although economic growth rate at state and all India level is attractive, poverty intensity is also very high among the rural non-farm workers. As there is no formal job contract in the unorganised sector the wage rate is not attractive in such sector and the standard of living is very low, especially in the rural area.

In India the average daily wage of the casual workers in the informal sector is Rs. 60.8. The daily wages of rural unorganised workers are comparatively low than that of urban workers. The daily wages of rural male worker is 1.7 times higher than that of the female worker.

Table–1
Average Daily Wages (in Rs.) of Casual Workers in the Informal Non-farm Sector. Industry and Location, 1999/00

Sectors	*Rural*		*Person*
	Male	*Female*	
Mining and Quarrying	67.6	38.4	61.9
Manufacturing	56.1	36.3	51.9
Construction	66.5	48.4	64.9
Trade, hotel and restaurant	53.7	40.8	53.1
Transport	72.7	86.6	72.8
Community, social and personal services	77.5	29.5	59.7
Total	64.2	38.4	60.5

Source: NLI Research Studies Series No. 1056/2004.

The above table shows that in rural areas the wage gap between male and female workers is highest in community social welfare services and lowest in informal services. The rural women workers suffers from a huge discrimination in wage compare to male workers. This discrimination also varies across the social group. Women workers belonging to SC/ST/Muslim category in the unorganised sector suffer much and poverty intensity among of this people is also very high.

The wage differential in the sector such as community social personal services, trade, hotels and restaurants, manufacturing (which accounts for 60% of the informal sector workers) is very high.

This wage rate is lower compared to all India average. The low wage rate of the rural unorganised sector is mainly due to the fact that the rural informal workers are not organized.

The available data on trade union shows that registered trade union exist only in formal/organized sector. There is no such registered trade union in the informal sector. Informal activities are basically localized activity with small number of workers in the unit. Any dispute regarding labour or wage is solved by mutual bargaining. As a result the level of exploitation is very high in the unorganized sector. Until initiatives are taken to organize the informal workers, the work condition of such labour force shall not be improved.

Another problem of the unorganised sector is that there is no prudential benefit in terms of insurance, provident fund, pension, gratuity, healthcare, maternity benefit etc. With the changing pattern of employment rural non-farm activity has the potential to reduce income inequalities of such labour force. As the workers in the informal sector are not organized they fail to extract the said prudential benefits from the work.

There has been a continuous struggle of the organized labour force under different trade union organizations to attain their rights for higher wage and welfare in West Bengal. The Government of West Bengal has recently taken an important step towards amelioration of distress of unorganised labour force. The Government has introduced a provident fund-cum-welfare scheme for unorganised labour force. Arjun Sengupta committee has made some important recommendations in this respect.

III

All India Picture of Rural Non-Farm Labour Force

It is evident from the 61st round NSS data that non-farm activity at the rural area has the potentiality to absorb the labour force migrated from the agricultural sector. The non-farm sector at rural area is the fastest growing sector in West Bengal during the era of post liberalization compare to other major states like Punjab, Gujarat, M.P., U.P. etc.

In the post reform period the occupational diversification in the rural India has taken place. The poor agricultural labours without land acquisition are forced to migrate into non-farm activity for their livelihood. With a high rate of GDP growth and low rate of employment generation of agriculture sector in the rural area are forced the labour force to move into the non-farm rural sector.

In terms of employment opportunities, the rural non-farm sector has been identified as one of the potential area. Non-farm sector in rural area can absorb labour force uprooted from agriculture sector. Rural non-farm sector can reduce the rural unemployment and poverty in the developing countries like India.

In case of women the number of agricultural labour force has declined sharply. At the same time the importance of informal activity has increased significantly. This is the most important change of employment structure out side the agriculture in West Bengal. NSS data shows in 2001 the proportion of cultivators is only one fourth of the rural work force in West Bengal. Most of the district of West Bengal has experienced a general shift of labour force from agriculture to non-farm activity.

IV

Rural Non-Farm Activity in West Bengal

Across the social category the unemployment rate and work participation ratios are changing sharply. It is evident from the 61st survey of NSS data that the concentration of poverty in the rural West Bengal is high among those people who are primarily related with non-farm activity. It is also evident that work participation in the unorganized sector is highest among schedule caste male and lowest among general caste female in rural areas. The work participation rates for schedule tribe women are significantly high in rural areas of West Bengal compare to all India standards.

In rural India the non-farm activity plays a major role in a large number of sates during post liberalization period. All fifteen major states in India experiences a high rate of concentration of non-farm employment with respect to total employment during 2004-05. Kerala experience 62.9 per cent, Haryana 50.6 per cent, Punjab 45.2 per cent, Tamil Nadu 41.4 per cent and West Bengal 36.2 per cent non-farm employment out of total employment. The rate of growth of non-farm employment in rural sector is highest in Kerala (48.3%) and then West Bengal (41.3%) on the basis of NSS 61st survey 2004-05 (US+PS+SS).

This chapter makes an attempt to get a closer look of district wise changes in rural employment according to Census 2001 in the post liberalization period.

Table–2
Work Participation in Rural West Bengal Per cent of Total Workers (Main+Marginal)

District	*Cultivators*		*Agricultural Labours*		*Non-agricultural Workers*	
	1991	*2001*	*1991*	*2001*	*1991*	*2001*
Darjeeling	33.5	20.6	16	14.4	50.5	65
Jalpaiguri	33.3	23.6	19.5	20.4	47.2	56
Koch Behar	51.8	40.4	28.2	31.8	20	27.8
Uttar Dinajpur	42.9	38	38.6	43.7	18.5	18.3
Dakshin Dinajpur	46.4	34.3	33.4	40	20.2	25.7
Malda	35.6	21.9	36.7	32.5	27.7	45.6
Murshidabad	33.9	21.3	34.6	32.3	31.5	46.4
Birbhum	36.5	24.9	40.7	39.7	22.8	35.4
Bardhaman	30.1	20.4	36.9	41.9	33	37.7
Nadia	36.3	24.7	33.1	29.1	30.6	46.2
North 24 Parganas	34.2	21	32.4	28.5	33.4	50.5
Hugli	29.2	20.9	36.5	34.1	34.3	45
Bankura	43.2	32.6	36.5	37.1	20.3	30.3
Purulia	52.2	33.3	30.7	38.4	17.1	28.3
Medinipur	47.4	30.4	26.1	33.9	26.5	35.7
Haora	21.6	9.9	27.7	19.6	50.7	70.5
South 24 Parganas	33.1	18.8	33	30.4	33.9	50.8
WEST BENGAL	38.4	25.4	32.3	33	29.3	41.6

Source: Census of India 2001.

It is evident from the table that non-farm activity is almost double than farm employment in Darjeeling, Jalpaiguri and Haora. More than half of the total work forces are engaged in non-farm activity in Darjeeling, Jalpaiguri, North 24 Parganas, Haora and South 24 Parganas. The rate of increase of non-farm activity in rural Bengal is more than 12 per cent during last decade.

The diversification of employment from agriculture to non-farm sector is not uniformly high across all the district of West Bengal. Uttar Dinajpur, Dakshin Dinajpur, Purulia and Bankura are the district where non-farm activity is 30 per cent or less. These four districts are considered as backward district. Not only suburban district like Haora, Darjeeling registered a high percentage of non-farm workers but district like North 24 Parganas, South 24 Parganas, Nadia, Murshidabad where agricultural activity is very high has also registered a high percentage of non-farm employment opportunities.

The sectoral composition of rural non-farm employment shows that wholesale and retail trade, manufacturing and service sector are the prime sector to absorb the diversified asset less labour force during post reform period.

V

Conclusion

In India the rural non-farm employment has increased rapidly during 1999-2000 to 2004-05. The picture of West Bengal is also same. The wholesale and retail trades are the prime sector where concentration of non-farm activity is very high. Again study shows that concentration of non-farm activity is very high across the poor and backward section of population of West Bengal. As the skill and technical knowledge of such labour force is almost nil, their wage structure is also very low.

Another reason for such low wage structure of the non-farm labour is due to the fact that they are unorganised. So it is quite impossible for them to extract better wage package. As a result they can not come across the poverty trap. The efficiency and technical knowledge of such rural unorganised labour force can be increased with the help of some special training programme and we can include them into the usual growth pattern of the economy.

Initiative should be taken at Government level. The NGOs can take an important role into local areas by arranging special training programme at block and village level. The roles of SHGs are also very important in this respect to reduce the problem of poverty through microfinance facility at the village level. Through SHG programme many of the informal sector activity and the labour force engaged in them may be stylysed and step by step they can catch up with the changing market structure and pattern of occupation. If the microfinance facility is properly chanalised by the institutions it can bring about a substantial transformation of the rural economy. Specially microfinance support can transform the type of activity of the informal sector.

Informal sectors work force are mainly landless labour. They are not organized. Wage rate in this sector is determined by mutual bargaining and there may be the possibility of losing the job. Therefore the labour must be organized. Organized labour both male and female in the unorganised sector can extract better work opportunities and prudential benefits like provident fund, gratuity, medical benefit, insurance claim etc. social security measures are very important from the point of view of landless unorganised labour force. Initiative must be taken by the Government as well as private welfare societies like NGOs. Several recommendations have been made by Arjun Sengupta Committee in this respect.

The Government of West Bengal has recently taken an important step towards amelioration of distress of unorganised labour force. The Government of West Bengal has recently introduced a provident fund-cum-welfare scheme for the unorganised labour force.

REFERENCES

Banerjee Abhijit, Bardhan Pranab, Basu Kaushik (2002): 'Strategy for Economic Reforms in West Bengal.'

Banerjee Nirmala (1985): 'Women Workers in the Unorganised Sector.' Sangam Book Delhi.

Basak Uma, Bhattacharya Sudipto, Sinha Sucharita (2005): 'Study of Tribal Women in Unorganised Labour Force.'

Bhowmik S.K. (2007): 'Growth and Composition of Rural non-farm Employment in India in the Era of Economic Reforms.' — The Indian Economic Journal, Vol. 55, No. 3.

Bhalla, Sheila (2003): Analysing the unorganized non-farm sector in India. Issues of methodology and main findings of a recent report of Planning Commission. Special lecture delivered at V.V. Giri National Labour Institute, Noida.

Bose A.N.: 'Calcutta and the Rural Bengal: Small Scale Sector Symbiosis.' Minerva Publishing.

Cadha G.K. (2002): 'Non-agricultural Employment in Rural Area.' — Evidence at Disaggregated Level.

Daniel Coppard (2007): 'The Rural Non-farm Economy in India a Review of Literature.' NRI Report No. 2662.

Government of India (2001): 'Census.'

Government of West Bengal (2004): 'Human Development Report.'

Haggblade, Hazel, and Reardon (2007): 'Transforming the Rural Non-farm Economy Opportunities and Threat in the Developing World.' Johns Hopkins University Press.

Sengupta (2008): 'India's Common People' – EPW March 15.

Sengupta (2001): Reforms Equity and IMF' – Har Anand Publication New Delhi.

V. Mahajan and A. Sinha (1997): 'Forgotten Sector' – Oxford and IBH Publishers Pvt. Ltd. Delhi.

World Development Report 2008.

Part–III : MICROCREDIT AND FINANCIAL INCLUSION

13

Swarnajayanti Gram Swarozgar Yojana in Jammu & Kashmir

SANKAR CHATTERJEE

After independence of India, country had many problems, inter alia, of which include, poverty particularly rural poverty. Although Government of India and provincial governments time to time initiated measures to tackle the issue of poverty but all these were ad hoc in nature.

The poverty alleviation measures were systematically initiated from late 70s in India. The statistics show that percentage of persons living below the poverty line in India was 54.88 in 1973-74 with absolute number of 321.3 million. Against this backdrop, poverty ratio in rural India was 56.44 per cent (261.2 million). The figures naturally caused worry to Government of India as many countries in the world did not have population which India had poor population. Most of the poor in India were in absolute poverty, even getting two square meals a days was a problem for the poor. In view of this, poverty alleviation measures were initiated by the Government of India including rural India in late 70s. These inter alia, include Integrated Rural Development Programme (IRDP), Training of Rural Youth for Self-employment (TRYSEM) and Improved Toolkits for Rural Artisans (SITRA). Million Wells Scheme (MWS), Development of Women and Children in Rural Areas (DWCRA) etc. However these programmes could not make much dent to eradicate proverty from rural India as focus of the programme was on individual person. As a result in 1999, 1st April, a new programme has been introduced in India under the caption of Swarnajayanti Gram Swarojgar Yojana, popularly known as SGSY (henceforth SGSY will only be used). The basic approached of the programme is on social mobilization of the rural poor. It focuses on organizing the rural poor at grassroot level through the process of social mobilization. SGSY is a massive self-employment programme for poverty alleviation presently going on in rural India. It is massive in the sense that in the initial year i.e., in 1999-2000, availability of fund under SGSY was Rs. 1961.97 crore which over a period of time increased several fold. The cumulative figure shows, total available fund was Rs. 11308.86 crore up to July 2006. (National Conference of PDs, 2006). SGSY is implemented by mobilizing poor under Self-Help Groups (SHGs). The data on self-help groups reveal that in the year 1999-2000 number of self-help groups formed was 292426 which increased to 2437913 up to 9th February, 2007 (cumulative figure). As result of implementation of SGSY, lakh of unemployed rural youths have been benefited by getting employment opportunities as is evident from the Annual Report of the Ministry of Rural Development (2006-07), Government of India. The Report also reveals that more than 74 lakh youth have got employment through SGSY, since inception to December 2006. To get an idea about the programme content of SGSY some salient features are presented here (*Source:* SGSY Guidelines, Ministry of Rural Development, Government of India, New Delhi, 2003).

Salient Features of SGSY

The beneficiaries of SGSY are known as Swarozgaris. SGSY lays emphasis on the group approach under which rural poor are organized into Self-Help Groups. However individually swarozgaris may also be assisted, but focus is on group approach. The groups that are formed with thrift and credit have demonstrated that poor can secure greater access to credit and other support services for enhancing their income levels.

Strategy

SGSY has been conceived as a holistic programme of self-employment. It covers all aspects of self-employment of the rural poor namely, organization of the poor into Self-Help Groups and their capacity building, training, selection of key activities and planning of activity clusters, infrastructure build up, technology and marketing support.

Social Mobilization

A major focus of SGSY is its emphasis on the social mobilization of the poor. The programme focuses on organization of the poor at grassroots level through a process of social mobilization for poverty eradication. Social mobilization enables the poor to build their own SHGs in which they fully and directly participate and take decisions on all issues that will help them in coming above the poverty line. A self-help group may consist of 10-20 persons belonging to families (BPL) and a person should not be a member of more than one group. In case of minor irrigation schemes and in case of disabled persons, this number may be a minimum of five (5). According to guidelines, 50 per cent of self-help groups in each block should be exclusively of women.

The members of self-help groups have to save regularly and convert their savings into a Common Fund known as the Group Corpus. The fund is used among the members through borrowing, which is known as internal lending.

The Group Corpus is supplemented with Revolving Fund sanctioned as Cash Credit Limit by the Banks. The Group has to take up economic activity of their choice for income generation.

Activity Clusters—Planning and Selection

The SGSY emphasizes assistance to the Swarozgaris only for those activities, which have been identified and selected as key activity in terms of their economic viability in the area. Each block has to concentrate on 4-5 key activities based on local resources, occupational skills of the people and availability of markets so that the Swarozgaris can draw sustainable income from their investments. The SGSY adopts a project approach for each key activity and project reports are to be prepared in respect of each identified key activity. The banks and other financial institutions have to be closely associated and involved in preparing these project reports.

Target Group

Families below the poverty line constitute the target group of SGSY. Within the target group, special safeguards have been provided to vulnerable sections, by way of reserving 50 per cent benefits to Scheduled Castes/Scheduled Tribes, 40 per cent for women and 3 per cent for disabled persons.

Financial Assistance

Assistance under the SGSY to individual Swarozgaris or self-help groups in given in the form of subsidy by the government and credit by the banks. Credit is the critical component of SGSY, subsidy being a minor and enabling element. Accordingly, SGSY envisages greater involvement of the banks. They are to be closely involved in the planning and preparation of project reports, identification of activity clusters, infrastructure planning as well as capacity building and choice of activity of the SHGs, selection of individual Swarozgaris, pre-credit activities and post-credit monitoring including loan recovery.

SGSY also seeks to promote multiple credits rather than a one-time credit 'injection'. Subsidy under the SGSY to individuals is uniform at 30 per cent of the project cost subject to a maximum of Rs. 7,500. In respect of Scheduled Castes and Scheduled Tribes, the subsidy is 50 per cent of the project cost, subject to a maximum of Rs. 10,000. For groups of Swarozgaris, the subsidy is 50 per cent of the cost of the project, subject to a ceiling of Rs. 1.25 lakh. There is no monetary limit on subsidy for irrigation projects. Subsidy is back ended i.e., it is released as part of the loan to be adjusted against last installment on satisfactory utilization of the loan for the project. No interest is charged on the subsidy amount.

Marketing and Technology Support

SGSY attempts to ensure up gradation of technology in the identified key activity. The technology intervention seeks to add value to the local resources, including processing of the locally available materials from natural and other resources for the local and non-local market. SGSY also provides for promotion of marketing of goods through organization and participation in exhibitions/melas at District/State/National/International levels to sell goods produced by the Swarozgaris.

Implementing Agencies

SGSY is being implemented by the District Rural Development Agencies with the active involvement of Panchayati Raj Institutions, the banks, the Line Departments and the Non-Government Organizations.

Funding Pattern

SGSY is financed on 75:25 cost sharing basis between the Centre and the States. Some important points on SGSY are:

(i) Focus is on group (minimum 10 members); persons are assisted mainly after forming self-help groups.
(ii) Self-help groups are given projects for income generation activities.

(iii) Initially members of self-help groups have to save regularly and saving fund is used among the members as internal lending.

(iv) Performance of self-help groups is assessed by government officials and bankers after six months.

(v) A paltry sum of Rs. 25000 is given after final grading as Revolving Fund and Cash Credit Limit by the Government and Bank.

(vi) With Revolving Fund and Cash Credit Limit income generation activities are carried out.

Effectiveness of SGSY can thoroughly be understood after concurrent evaluation studies. But recent poverty data published by Government of India reveal that poverty ratio in percentage term has substantially declined. For example, in 1973-74, the percentages of Below Poverty Line (BPL) families in India as a whole and in Rural India were 54.88 and 56.44 respectively. The poverty data of 2004-05 (latest data) show the percentage of BPL families were 27.50 in India and 28.30 in rural areas of India. Coming down of rural poverty as well as poverty in India may be attributed to the fact that programmes like SGYS have done well. A few of the cases of self-help groups funded under SGSY are discussed here. These cases were studied by the author in different points of time *vis-à-vis* in different parts of India. Although the author studied many cases but 3 cases only presented here.

Cases of Self-Help Groups under SGSY:
A Case from Jammu and Kashmir

The State Jammu and Kashmir is located in the northern side of India. Its total geographical area is 222236 square kilometers with a total population of 10 million as per 2001 census. The State had high poverty ratio once upon a time. For example, the poverty data for 1973-74 reveal that 40.83 per cent of its total population was below the poverty line in 1973-74 with rural and urban percentages were 45.51 and 21.32 respectively. With the initiatives of poverty alleviation measures, inter alia of which include SGSY, poverty for the state has come down to 5.4 per cent with rural and urban percentage of 4.6 and 7.9 respectively. Naturally the credit goes to systematic effort to eradicate poverty from rural India. In spite of about 17 year's militancy in the State, with Government of India's effort *vis-à-vis* effort of Jammu and Kashmir Government, rural poverty has declined substantially in the State. The author recently (June 2007) have visited Jammu and Kashmir to get an idea about the implementation of SGSY in the State. As a part of the study Baramulla district of Jammu and Kashmir was visited. It was observed that officials were sincere to implement the rural development programmes. It has to be admitted that Secretary, Rural Development of Jammu and Kashmir Government, a Senior Government Officer, is dynamic person and taking care to implement the programmes.

The district Baramulla is having an area of 4588 square kilometers with 17 blocks and 646 inhabited villages. The author visited Tangmarg block of Baramulla district for studying the implementation of SGSY. As a part of the study Yembarzal self-help group of Mohim village was contacted. There are about 70 families in this village out which 35 are identified as Below Poverty Line (BPL) families. Again out of 35 BPL families only 10 families have come forward of form groups. Thus only two self-help groups have been formed in the village. Formation of groups is due to initiatives taken by the officials as no NGOs are coming forward to facilitate SGSY swarozgaris in the area, as reported. In the year 2001, (February) these 5 women members of Mohim village under the guidance of block officials self-help group under the umbrella of Yembarzal self-help group. As an initial step, the members of the group started savings at the rate of Rs. 50 per month per member. Finally with their savings, they opened a bank account in the month of September 2001 which is a precondition to get assistance under SGSY. In the meantime, after assessing the performance of SHG, First Grading took place in July 2003. The SHG was extended an amount of Rs. 25000 as assistance (Revolving Fund and Cash Credit Limit) (for the meaning please see later on in the note). With this amount, they extended their business. Since the members of the group were doing well so after Second Grading the group was extended a loan amount of Rs. 2 lakhs on 13 January 2005, with an annual rate of interest of 10.5 per cent. As a part of SGSY programme, once the loan amount is repaid, the group will be given Rs. 1.25 lakh as subsidy. This is known as bank-end subsidy which a group may get to a maximum extent of Rs. 1.25 lakh (out of total project cost). During the time of study, it was observed that the members of the self-help group repaid a sum of Rs. 83,000 to the bank. Their repayment has been going on as per schedule. It is heartening to mention that even after the repayment of bank loan each member of the group has been earning in between Rs. 4000 and Rs. 5000 per month. They were happy to inform that they were spending their earning on children education, good foods and clothes. All the members unanimously told that SGSY has greatly benefited them as earlier their income was uncertain *vis-à-vis* too meager to sustain their families. Now they have at least assured income as well as good enough to maintain their families. Earlier their husband's income was not sufficient to maintain families. To a query about their problems, members informed that bank rate of interest should be reduced. It is too high for them. For marketing of their produce, they suggested more number of fairs may be organized in other parts of the country.

SGSY: Two Cases from Uttar Pradesh

Uttar Pradesh, a province of India, is located in the central part of the country. Its population is about 160 million (2001 census) spread over to an area of 294411 square kilometers. As per the Government data, the state had 57.07 per cent of its population living Below the Poverty Line (BPL) in 1973-74 with rural poverty of 56.53 per cent and urban poverty of 60.09 per cent. Decline in the poverty ratio is observed in 2004-05 report (latest statistics published by the Government of India). The data show that percentage of population below the poverty line is 32.8 in the state. The percentages of rural and urban poverty are 33.4 and 30.6 respectively. This may be attributed to various poverty alleviation measures initiated by the Government of India. In this connection, two cases from Hamirpur district of Uttar Pradesh are presented here.

The district is having population of little more than 1 million presently. Total geographical area of the district is 4122 square kilometers. It is one of the backward districts of the state. Due to this reason, poverty ratio (42.64%) is comparatively high in the district. The cases of two self-help groups from Makrao village of Moudaha block of Hamirpur district are presented.

The study was conducted in 2004. It is pertinent to mention here that all the self-help groups in a village are given one name so that it is easier to identify the group. One name cannot be for two self-help groups in the same village. As per guidelines, besides government official, Non-Governmental Organizations should preferably by look after self-help groups. But our Jammu and Kashmir experience shows due to lack of participation of Non-Governmental Organizations (non-existence of NGOs in the area) only governmental officials have been looking after self-help groups. In the contrary, in case of Makrao village, situation is different Here, a Government of India's sponsored organization viz. Nehru Yuvak Kendra was looking after the self-help groups. For better identification of the groups. Nehru Yuvak Kendra simply gives the number. Two self-help groups, which were contacted for the study, are No. 16 and No. 91.

The self-help group No.16 consists of 11 male members belong to Scheduled Caste and Backward community. They formed self-help group in November 2002 and in September 2003 respectively. After First Grading the self-help group was given Rs. 25,000 as Cash Credit Limit and Revolving Fund. The Nehru Yuvak Kendra officials suggested them to start bulb-making unit (only outer part of small bulb used in marriages etc.), which they started. Each of the members was provided with a small bulb-producing machine costing Rs. 1100. As a part of raw materials glass pipes are used. Kerosene oil is used for operating of the machine. It means no electricity is required for the project. Before starting the unit, members were trained. During the course of visit it was observed that the members were producing bulbs but at slow space. The produce after certain quantity will be sold at Kanpur city, 70 kilometers away (a commercial city of India). According to members of the group marketing of the bulbs is not the problem. However to enhance their business they would like to have more money which they were expected after Second Grading.

The members of No. 9 self-help group were involved with leaf-plate making. The group formed in February 2003 consists of 11 women belonging to both Scheduled Caste and Backward Caste communities. The self-help group received Cash Credit Limit and Revolving Fund in November 2003 after First Grading. The group leader, although studied up to High School but not aware about grading system. Even the members of the self-help group were not acquainted with SGSY guidelines. They had poor ideas about Cash Credit Limit, Revolving Fund and loan for economic activities. It is due to Government Officials and Nehru Yuvak Kendra officials self-help group has been functioning.

The self-help group members themselves collect leaves for leaf-plate from the forest which is about 8 kilometers away. They pluck leaves from the trees around 150 numbers for whole year. For each free, the members pay in between Rs. 20 and Rs. 25 to the owner of the tree depending upon the availability of leaves in the trees. Locally the tree is known as 'Palas tree'. They themselves bring the leaves in the truck and make plates in their house. For marking purpose, they take to nearby (5 kilometers away) where most of their produce is sold. Sometimes middlemen also come to purchase their goods in the village itself. At the time of study, the members informed that they were earning in between Rs. 1,000 and Rs. 1,500 per month. They were in the opinion that if bank loan is provided after Second Grading they can extend their business in a large scale. It was observed that members were not clear ideas about SGSY.

Reduction in Rural Poverty in India: Focus on Recent Data

Altogether three cases were discussed to show the impact of SGSY. Besides these, the author studied many other self-help groups under SGSY in the states of Andhra Pradesh, Assam, Karnataka, Gujarat, Meghalaya, Uttar Pradesh, Tripura and West Bengal. And it was observed that many poor families were benefited under SGSY. As mentioned already lakh of rural youths have got employment under SGSY (more than 74 lakh). Reduction of rural poverty may also be attributed to implementation of SGSY and other poverty alleviation programmes going on in rural India. In this connection latest statistics on poverty, published by Government of India may be mentioned. Based on Uniform Recall Period, rural poverty in India was 37.3 per cent in 1993-94 which came down to 28.3 per cent in 2004-05. And based on Mixed Recall Period, percentage of people below poverty line in rural India was 27.1 in 1999-2000 which declined to 21.8 per cent in 2004-05. This comparative data whether based on Mixed Recall Period or Uniform Recall Period clearly reveal that poverty ratio has declined substantially. Even the state wise data reveal that from 1999-2000, rural poverty ratio for almost all the states have declined in 2004-05 (Table-1). This, inter alia, may be attributed to implementation of SGSY.

Conclusion

This study *vis-à-vis* recent poverty data reveal that poverty ratio in the country as well as in all the states and rural areas of India have declined substantially. For this, credit goes to poverty alleviation programme like SGSY initiated by the Government of India. SGSY has not only helped to alleviate poverty from rural India but simultaneously helped to generate employment opportunities also where lakh of unemployed youths have got employment.

Table–1
Percentage of Population Below Poverty Line in Rural India

States/U.T.	*1999-2000*	*2004-2005*	
		*Based on URP**	*Based on MRP***
Andhra Pradesh	11.05	11.20	7.50
Arunachal Pradesh	40.04	22.30	17.00
Assam	40.04	22.30	17.00
Bihar	44.30	42.10	32.90
Chattisgarh	–	40.80	31.20
Goa	1.35	5.40	1.90
Gujarat	13.17	19.10	13.90
Haryana	8.27	13.60	9.20
Himachal Pradesh	7.94	10.70	7.20
Jammu & Kashmir	3.97	4.60	2.70
Jharkhand	–	46.30	40.20
Karnataka	17.38	20.80	12.00
Kerala	9.38	13.20	9.60
Madhya Pradesh	37.8	36.90	29.80
Maharashtra	23.72	29.60	22.20
Manipur	40.04	22.30	17.00
Meghalaya	40.04	22.30	17.00
Mizoram	40.04	22.30	17.00
Nagaland	40.04	22.30	17.00
Orissa	48.01	46.80	39.80
Punjab	6.35	9.10	5.90
Rajasthan	13.74	18.70	14.30
Sikkim	40.04	22.30	17.00
Tamil Nadu	20.55	22.80	16.90
Tripura	40.04	22.30	17.00
Uttar Pradesh	31.72	33.40	25.30
Uttarakhand	–	40.80	31.70
West Bengal	31.85	28.60	24.20

Contd...

States/U.T.	1999-2000	2004-2005	
		Based on URP*	Based on MRP**
A & N Islands	20.55	22.90	16.90
Daman & Diu	1.35	5.40	1.90
D & N Haveli	17.57	39.80	36.80
Lakshadweep	9.38	13.30	9.60
Pondicherry	20.55	22.90	16.90
Total	27.09	28.30	21.80

*URP = Uniform Recall Period consumption in which the consumer expenditure data for all items are collected from 30-day recall period.

** MRP = Mixed Recall Period consumption in which the consumer expenditure data for five non-food items namely clothing, footwear, durable goods, education and institutional medical expenses are collected from 365-day recall period and consumption data from 365-day recall period and the consumption data for the remaining items are collected from 30-day recall period.

Source: Planning Commission, India.

NOTES

Cash Credit Limit (CCL): It is a sort of loan given to the self-help groups.

Grading: Grading is part of SGSY. In order to assess the performance of SGSY grading is taken up where government officials and bankers assess the performance of the self-help groups.

Revolving Fund: It is a sort of subsidy given to the self-help groups by the Government of India.

REFERENCES

Ministry of Rural Development, Government of India (2003), SGSY Guidelines, New Delhi.

Ministry of Rural Development, Government of India (2006-07), Annual Report.

Ministry of Rural Development, Government of India (2006), Back Ground Note on National Conference of Project Directors of District Rural Development Agencies.

Ojha R.K. (April 21, 2007)": Poverty Dynamics in Rural Uttar Pradesh", Economic and Political Weekly, Mumbai, India.

14

Women Empowerment through Micro Credit Intervention in Bodoland Economy

SUJATA BHADRA

Introduction

Inclusive growth is a common word in our present economic planning and has been considered to be the focal point of National Development Policy. The dimension of the new development strategies, the inclusive growth has the prime focus on women and inclusiveness of weaker social groups.

The Eleventh Five Years Plan has particularly stressed on formulating all economic activities particularly in rural areas so as to secure rapid and sustained growth in productivity and to expand levels of income and employment to transform these social groups.

From different studies it has now become evident that about 90 per cent workers are in the informal sector. A high proportion of rural informal workers are women and their work place is in the rural area. This proportion is increasing due to spillover of labour force from agriculture to informal sector, retrenched from urban mechanised activities. It has become evident that present nature of economic growth has reduced employment opportunities in general and still less to women.

NSS data (61st round, Employment and Unemployment data) indicates that poor and vulnerable section of population is mainly SC/ST and minorities and they constitute 75 per cent of population and 79 per cent of unorganized workforce. Around 50 per cent of these afflicted people are women. Hence, their work participation and income generation is the first step towards inclusive growth and economic progress.

Today, Bodoland has gained the recognition of autonomy and Bodoland Territorial Area District has been constituted. This gave an impetus to women activism in different fields irrespective of ethnic limitations. The women are assuming new roles in the socio-economic transformation of Bodoland. Over the last few decades, the work participation of women in the Bodoland area is under notable shift to new opportunities.

In Bodoland area, the implementation of government sponsored programmes for poverty alleviation by the rural development wings have been shown remarkable successes in enhancing economic participation through SHG programme. Infact, Swarnajayanti Gram Swarojgar Yojana (SGSY) is the mother unit of all poverty alleviation programmes subject to uplift the economic status of rural people through micro-credit intervention of bank loan and government subsidy by generating income-promoting options to the Below Poverty Line (BPL) populace.

In Assam, till the 2006-07, 131948 numbers of SHGs have been formed and 24250 numbers of SHGs have been provided bank loan with subsidy. During the year 2006-07,5837 nos. of SHGs and 1399 nos. of individual beneficiaries were assisted under the SGSY programme. A total number of 5837 SHGs, out of which 66188 nos. of families were assisted of which 16040 were ST families (Economic Survey of Assam, 2006-07).

The D.R.D.A. wise physical achievement under S.G.S.Y. in the year 2005-06 reveals that the total number of SHGs formed since 01-04-99 is 116437 and 2560 and during the current year the number of SHGs formed is 21066 and 212 for Assam and Kokrajhar district respectively.

At this backdrop, the present study examines the growth of economic activity in the informal sector through SHG formation and identify these unorganised poor women of the Bodo ethnic group and their SHGs, in Kokrajhar district of Bodoland location of Assam.

Objectives of the Study

The specific objectives of the study are to understand the dimension of new economic space of some tribal women in Kokrajhar district.

The sub- areas of the study constitutes:

1. To study the socio-economic condition of the sample women.
2. To assess the economic performances of the sample SHGs.

in terms of loan recovery, initial and cumulative asset position etc.

3. To put forward suggestion to build up an agenda to keep up growth momentum in Bodoland.
4. To evaluate a SWOT status of the sample SHGs.

Methodology

The study is based on both primary and secondary data. The primary data constitutes the investigation of 10-sample SHGs. 7 SHGs have been selected with the consultation of D.R.D.A. officials in Kokrajhar town, head quarters of B.T.A.D., in a SHGs exhibition sponsored by D.R.D.A. The rest 3 groups have been selected with the consultation of Assam Grameen Bikash Bank (A.G.B.B.) Manager, Serfanguri branch of Kokrajhar District. The survey was initiated from 1st July to 31st July, 2008.

The primary data collection constituted field visit, interview, focus group discussion and participant's observation.

As a part of the study, a total of 61(47%) numbers of women sample units comprising all the president and secretary of the entire sample SHGs had been interviewed with a designed schedule based on the objectives of the study. During field visit, almost all the members of each group participated with great enthusiasm and spirit. They consider this experience as the recognition of their hard work and aspirations with an expectation for financial help from reliable sources that can reach to them in relation to this project. This is first of its kind to them.

For secondary data, relevant documents have been used which are compiled in the list of references.

Data have been collected from the sample SHGs of heterogeneous character like socio-economic attributes of the sample tribal women, performances of the sample groups in terms of growth in an average understanding of nominal and physical assets etc.

An attempt has been made to evaluate the SWOT stature of the sample SHGs.

The article has been developed meticulously following the core and sub objectives of the research study and divided in sections.

The location and number of sample SHGs are purposively preferred on consideration of easy access to communication, time and cost.

Today, the SHG revolution in the Bodoland area is in boost but the performances and contribution of SHGs in the growth process of Bodoland economy need to be critically evaluated. Infact, this study can act as an evidence of the functioning and achievements of the SGSY Programme in B.T.A.D. of Assam. The socio-economic features especially the pulse of tribal life is very representative in all the rural vicinity of Bodoland area. Therefore, the study is highly relevant to the context of economic growth and development in gender perspective in the study area.

Analysis

Some of the key information of the sample SHGs have been projected in Table-I (APPENDIX).

The group activities confer a diverse category of works. The functioning of some of the crucial economic variables in relation to the production function of the production units of the sample SHGs reveal that though the initial investment is meagre, the operation of fixed and working capital in a certain time limit has rigorously ensured the production and marketing progression in terms of profitable returns. In this context, it is essential to understand the propagation of income of the SHGs in different phases so as to estimate the final return in relation to the investment.

Here, in the present study, time period has been appropriated differently for varied group activities. For piggery, the completion of crop cycle of working capital has been considered one year, for weaving, it is fortnightly, for sericulture, it is six monthly, for agriculture, it is six monthly at average.

The socio- economic attributes of the respondents highlight an approximate estimate of the livelihood situation of the tribal women in Bodoland area. Today, these women are thriving for a new opportunity with the existing resource base to the process of economic generation

Table–II contains the various paradigms of socio-economic indicators like age, education, civil status, religion, community information, economic status, household size, monthly income, decision-making process, father/husbands occupation, group member's occupation before joining the group, reasons for joining the SHGs etc. These findings are considered to be the most critical outcome of the research study.

The findings of Table-II (APPENDIX) are following:

Age: The maximum number of young participants of age group (25-35) years with frequency 75 (57%) has been witnessed. In 02 (1.5%) cases, very elderly tribal women of age group (55- 60) years have been observed to be a part of economic liberation in Bodoland economy.

Education: The level of education of the respondents reveals a very appalling picture. Attainment of higher education and their participation in SHGs is very scanty in the present study. The study confirms that as the level of education is towards the higher level, a deceleration of frequencies tends to set in.

In fact, the study findings in respect of educational status, it is conformable with the Census of India record, 2001 in the context of Kokrajhar District. The total ST literacy in Kokrajhar district was 46.60 (1991 Census) and 57.59 in 2001 Census while for ST female literacy it was only 34.6 in 1991 (Census).

The Civil status of the group members reveals that majority of them 89 (68%) are married following 33 (25%) of unmarried and 09 (7%) widow participants.

Religion: Amongst the 131 group members 128 (98%) follow Hinduism with 03 (2%) of Christianity.

Community Information: The main crux of the study is to be the economic emancipation of tribal women in the process of growth and productive employment; thereby limited its scope within the tribal population only.

Economic Status: Majority of the group members is poorest of the poor category of 57 (44%) numbers, 52 (40%) are very poor, following a very little number of non-poor 22 (16%) population.

Monthly Family Income: The range of monthly family income of the respondents is highly appalling. 52 (40%) of the families have an income range of Rs. (0-500) and 50 members (38%) have a monthly familial income ranges from Rs. (500-3000). Moreover, they have very little access to land and property possession.

In fact, there is a strong correlation between family size and monthly familial income. Big size family always exhausts the family income for food consumption, thereby denies other socio-economic well being at the familial level. Importantly, no sample family has been reported to their monthly familial income exceeds Rs.10000.00.

Household Size: It is a key indicator in respect of socio-economic development and livelihood condition of a particular group of population. The present study establishes higher frequencies towards the larger family size. Small family size has lesser number of frequencies.

There has been established a strong linkage amongst the variables like very poor asset holding, low monthly income, poverty, big family size, low education with significant number of dropouts and participation in the workforce comparatively at young age with very low return.

Decision-Making: Traditionally Bodo tribal women enjoy social progressiveness. They are an integral part of decision-making process in familial aspects. The present study confirms the hypothesis.

The study reflects the highest frequency of 116 (89%) for decision-making in the families both by male and females. In case of widow and few unmarried group members 15 (11%), enjoy decision-making liberty of their own.

Occupation of Father/Husband: The distribution of occupational status of the respondents father/husband shows that cultivation is the mainstay of life of 54 (44%) members. 37 (30%) numbers are in seasonal labourer/wage earner/petty trader category followed by 27 (22%) of service/businessmen.

Importantly, the services are mostly casual in nature and poor salaried. The business represents contract works especially in the field of construction and small trading with irregular and petty income.

The Previous Experience: Almost 72 (55%) members used to busy with household chores, 31 (24%) were casual/vendor as disguisedly employed. Hopefully, they are involved in income generating process and successfully operating their units.

Reasons for Joining the Group Activity

111 (85%) of respondents have joined the group for quest of better living. 13 (10%) respondents joined the group to get out of the cobweb of familial poverty. In 07 (5%) cases, motivation from NGO/Bank/ D.R.D.A. and fellow members acted as an effective ingredient to initiate SHG activities.

The Operational Mechanism of the SHGs

The sample SHGs are found to be efficient in functioning so as to generate income and productive employment. It has been studied that the entire sample SHGs charge 5 per cent rate of interest for internal lending. For outside borrower it is 10 per cent approximately.

All the groups are very selective in issuing loans to the outside borrower (Table-III).

In Table-III, the range of monthly incremental income has been presented. The average rate of incremental income has been estimated as Rs. 1453.00 (in approx), which is not meager.

Again, the uneven earnings from interest rate represent the unequal and inefficient functioning of some of the groups in the process of income generation.

Regarding the repayment period of loans, individual group has developed their own constitution according to their own convenience. Under this study, it varies from three months to three years.

The rate of recovery has been experienced to be very good like (90-100 %). In two cases, the rate of recovery has been observed to be (50-60%) and the reason has been found to be abject poverty.

Table-III has its high significance in revealing the facts of operational mechanism of the sample SHGs in attaining the economic sustenance. The sample groups have been successfully undertaken savings and credit operation from their own resources.

Table-III explains the estimated income growth in favour of the sample SHGs through the initial money asset. The cumulative asset (nominal + physical) possession of the sample group has been found satisfactory. All the sample SHGs have had the total initial savings at the time of group formation of Rs. 27,050.00 followed by a total cumulative asset of Rs. 24,75,000.00. The average time span covered of the sample groups is four (4) years at the average rate of interest of 5 per cent. Therefore, the income propagation through SHG activities by this critical mass from the remote bases of Bodoland economy deserves more attention and need based policy execution.

The functioning and better performances of the sample SHGs are due to the collective actions of all the members. It has been understood through survey study that the women members have developed remarkable self-confidence and capacity building. Today they have emerged as a collective force to open up new avenues for economic sustenance. The study has experienced the following outcomes that have been achieved by these women folk in the course of functioning and maintaining their respective groups.

(a) Genuine need and aspiration is the prime essence behind the formation of these SHGs.

(b) The sample groups have satisfied both the necessary and sufficient condition for active sustenance of six months.

(c) The functioning of these SHGs have been proved to be democratic and transparent.

(d) The group members are found to be rigid and concerned in maintaining group disciplines.

(e) The group members are concerned about the organizational strengthening, economic activities, internal loaning and different social and familial issues. The members are very selective in granting loans especially to the genuinely.

(f) They have considerably developed the skill of mutual help, promotion of thrift habits and successfully managing the SHG unit.

(g) The sample SHGs conduct regular group meeting in respective centres and the absentee has to pay a fine of Rs. 5-10 (for SHGs Daogafu, Laimwn, Maidangshri, Ranjali, Purnima, Bidinta). The frequency of group meeting has been found once or twice in a month. The attendance is found as high as 98 per cent.

(h) The group members have acquired a great deal of courage and self-confidence in dealing with the officials and organizations. The members became familiar with banking procedures and transactions. In Daogafhu, Laimwn, Ranjali SHGs, the elderly members are shouldering the main responsibilities of the group.

SWOT Stature

Based on the findings of the functioning of the sample SHGs, a SWOT evaluation has been constructed and presented below:

Strength

- Favourable group spirit and harmony.
- Traditional knowledge–the tribal legacy.
- Degree of awareness and information raising.
- Enable to recognize their capability to operate in clusters.

- Realisation of power in terms self-hood, self-esteem and freedom.
- Group discipline and collective action.
- Growth in savings and group assets.
- Social capital.
- Trust and confidence with the facilitators and bank linkage programmes.
- A reliable forum where the group members can critically assess their situations.

Weaknesse

- Illiteracy, inadequate information base.
- Lack of infrastructure.
- Insufficient access to credit and financial support.
- Lack of managerial skill.
- Unfavourable socio-politico and economic base.
- Low margin business.

Opportunities

- Evolves harmonious relation amongst group members.
- Favourable demand-supply relation in respect of production.
- Supportive relation with NGOs, administrative set ups, financial institutions etc.
- Traditional knowledge and exotic output.
- Group discipline and necessary action.
- High demand for the product.
- Scope for enhancing quality of life.
- Scope for attaining gender equity and gender equality.
- Avenues to build up more awareness, power and skill up gradation.
- Abundant natural resources.
- Innovativeness and adoption of new technology to reform traditional activities and production system.

Threat

- Abject poverty and denial of basic securities of life.
- Intervention of modern technology and tough market competition.
- Ineffective and irregular collective actions and responsibilities within the group.
- High cost of production.

- Inefficient group leadership and limited training for capacity building.
- Poor knowledge of accounts.
- Too much dependence on leadership and ineffective participation of some of the participants.

Suggestions and Conclusion

The micro credit intervention has been proved to be an effective instrument in alleviating poverty atleast group level. There are plenty of examples of role models of successful group entrepreneurship that lead to procure economic sustenance and social justice. In this context, reconstruction of socio-economic set up especially edcuation, health and empolyment, selective and innovative product, adequate marketing network, skill development training for both production and management unit, suitable informations about the government schemes etc. are the urgent need of the hour. In this respect, the B.T.A.D. Government has to deal with the rural development issues more rigorously especially for the tribal women development. The rural development strategies in B.T.A.D. need to tap policy opportunities. In fact, SHGs is one of the safest and cost effective routes of credit flow to support the socio-economically disadvantaged groups.

These above information draw the conclusion that the SHGs play a critical role in the economic development of any economy particularly in the traditional subsistence economy.

SHG formation has tremendously assisted the women to come out of social-domestic repression. Their attainment of income status enable them to have dignity and participation in the decision-making process.

REFERENCES

Banerjee Amalesh, 2008, "Women Emancipation and Development: N.E. Perspective" in Ray Ashok Kumar and Dutta Ray Basudev (eds. 2008), Women Emancipation Focus North East India, NEICSSR, OM Publications, New Delhi.

Bhadra Sujata, 2007, "Women Entrepreneurs in Rural Area: A Case Study of Tribal Women in Kokrajhar District", Bihar Economic Journal, Economic Association of Bihar, 10th Annual Conference, Patna, Bihar.

Bhadra Sujata, 2008, "Women Emancipation Through SHGs: The Case of Bodoland" in Ray Ashok Kumar and Dutta Ray Basudev (eds. 2008), Women Emancipation Focus North East India, NEICSSR, OM Publications, New Delhi.

Basic Statistics, NER, 2006, NEC, Shillong Meghalaya.

Economic Survey, Assam, 2007-08, Directorate of Economic and Statistics Dispur: Guwahati-06.

Employment, Productivity and Poverty Reduction, World Employment Report 2004-05, International Labour Office, Geneva.

Fact Sheet on Women in India, 2005, NIPCCD.

Gopalan Dr. Sarala, Towards Equality—The Unfinished Agenda, Status of Women in India 2001, The National Commission for Women, Government of India.

Kapila Uma (ed.) Indian Economy Since Independence, 2003, AF Publications, New Delhi.

Planning Commission (2006) Towards Faster and More Inclusive Growth: An Approach Paper to the 11th Five Year Plan, Government of India/ *www.planning* commission.nic.in

Statistical Hand Book, Assam, 2007, Directorate of Economics and Statistics, Government of India, Guwahati-06.

APPENDIX-I

Table-I. Basic Particulars of the Sample SHGs

Sl. No.	Name of the Group	Date of Formation	Number of Members	Monthly Contribution (in Rs.)	Facilitator	Group Activity	Economic Status	Linkage with
1.	Mukrang SHG (Rabha group)	05-10-2001	20	15	Anjali Sukhati SHG Foundation	Weaving	Poor: 10 Poorest of the poor: 04 Non-poor: 06	AGBB, Serfanguri Branch
2	Daogafu SHG (Bodo group)	18-05-2002	12	10	Own initiation	Piggery	Poor: 02 Poorest of the poor: 02 Non-poor: 08	AGBB, Serfanguri Branch
3.	Laimwan SHG (Bodo group)	04-04-2003	15	20	AGBB, Bhowraguri Branch	Weaving	Poor: 02 Poorest of the poor: 13	AGBB, Bhowraguri Branch
4.	Maidangshri SHG (Bodo group)	21-10-2003	20	50	Own initiation	Weaving	Poor: 03 Poorest of the poor: 15 Non-poor: 02	AGBB, Bhowraguri Branch
5.	Ranjali SHG (Bodo group)	02-06-2004	12	20	Own initiation	Weaving, Sericulture, Agriculture	Poorest of the poor: 12	AGBB, Serfanguri Branch
6.	Udangshree SHG (Bodo group)	09-06-2004	10	50	Anjali Sukhati SHG Foundation	Agriculture and allied activities	Poor: 05 Poorest of the poor: 05	SBI, Salakati Branch
7.	Laimwan Ishanshali SHG (Bodo group)	16-10-2004	10	25	Anjali Sukhati SHG Foundation	Weaving	Poorest of the poor: 10	AGBB, Kokrajhar Branch

Contd...

Sl. No.	Name of the Group	Date of Formation	Number of Members	Monthly Contribution (in Rs.)	Facilitator	Group Activity	Economic Status	Linkage with
8.	Maoriya SHG (Bodo group)	17-10-2004	12	50	Anjali Sukhati SHG Foundation	Sericulture	Poor: 12	SBI, Balagaon Branch
9.	Purnima SHG (Bodo group)	15-07-2005	10	15	Own initiation	Bee Rearing	Poor: 03 Poorest of the poor: 05 Non-poor: 02	AGBB, Kokrajhar Branch
10.	Bidinta SHG (Bodo group)	10-10-2005	10	50	Own initiation	Piggery	Poor: 06 Poorest of the poor: 01 Non-poor: 03	AGBB, Kokrajhar Branch
	Total		131					

Source: Field Study.

*AGBB: Assam Grameen Bikash Bank.

** SBI: State Bank of India.

***BPL: Below Poverty Line.

Table–II

Socio-Economic Characteristics of the Sample SHGs

Distribution of Age, Education, Civil Status, Religion, Social Status, Economic Background, Familial Income, Household Size, Decision-making Process, Father/Husband's occupation, previous experience of the group members and Reasons for joining the group etc.

Sl.No.	*Categories*	*Number of Units*	*Percentage*
1.	**Age:**		
	(a) 17-25	21	16
	(b) 25-35	75	57
	(c) 35-45	28	21
	(d) 45-55	05	04
	(e) 55-60	02	1.5
	Total	**131**	**100**
2.	**Education:**		
	(a) Illiterate	24	18
	(b) L.P. Level	26	20
	(c) M.E. Level	16	12
	(d) High School Level	49	37
	(e) Higher SecondaryLevel	14	11
	(f) Degree and above	02	1.5
	Total	**131**	**100**
3.	**Civil Status:**		
	(a) Married	89	68
	(b) Unmarried	25	25
	(c) Widow	07	07
	Total	**131**	**100**
4.	**Religion:**		
	(a) Hindu	128	98
	(b) Christian	03	02
	Total	**131**	**100**
5.	**Social Group:**		
	(a) Bodo tribe	111	85
	(b) Rabha tribe	20	15
	Total	**131**	**100**

Contd...

Sl.No.	*Categories*	*Number of Units*	*Percentage*
6.	**Economic Status:**		
	(a) Poor	52	40
	(b) Poorest to the poor	57	44
	(c) Non- poor	22	16
	Total	**131**	**100**
7.	**Household Size:**		
	02-03	11	08
	03-04	23	18.0
	04-05	42	32
	05-06	30	23
	06-07	10	07
	07-08	08	06
	08-09	05	04
	09-10	01	.75
	12-13	01	.75
	Total	**131**	**100**
8.	**Monthly Income:**		
	0-500	52	40
	500-1000	26	20
	1000-2000	12	09
	2000-3000	12	09
	3000-4000	06	4.5
	4000-5000	10	08
	5000-6000	06	4.5
	6000-7000	07	05
	Total	**131**	**100**
9.	**Decision-making Process:**		
	(a) Absolutely by Male	Nil	0
	(b) Absolutely by Female	11	11
	(c) Both Male and Female	116	89
	Total	**131**	**100**
10.	**Father/Husband's Occupation:**		
	(a) Service/Business #	27	22
	(b) Cultivator	54	44
	(c) Labour/Petty trader	37	30
	(d) Sick/unemployed	03	03
	Total	**122@**	**100**

Contd...

Sl.No.	Categories	Number of Units	Percentage
11.	**Group Members Occupation before Joining the SHGs:**		
	(a) Service	07	5.34
	(b) Labourer/petty trading	31	24
	(c) Weaving	21	16
	(d) Housewife	72	55
	Total	**131**	**100**
12.	**Reasons for Joining the SHGs Activities:**		
	(a) Familial poverty	13	10
	(b) For better living	111	85
	(c) Motivation by fellow members	07	05
	Total	**131**	**100**

Source: Field Study.

Services are mostly casual in nature/poor salaried.
@ 09 members of sample SHGs are widow and self-guardian.

Table-III

Operational Mechanism of the Sample SHGs

Distribution groups by Incremental income, Repayment period and Rate of recovery from individual loans.

Sl. No.	Name of the Sample SHGs	Monthly Incremental Income (in Rs.& in approx.)	For Individual Loan	
			Repayment Period	Percentage of Recovery
1.	Mukrang SHG (Rabha group)	4000.00	One year	(80-100)%
2.	Daogafu SHG (Bodo group)	2583.00	Two years	"
3.	Laimwan SHG (Bodo group)	3399.00	Three years	"
4.	Maidangshri SHG (Bodo group)	430.00	Six months	"
5.	Ranjali SHG (Bodo group)	2001.00	Three months	"
6.	Udangshree SHG (Bodo group)	417.00	Six months	"
7.	Laimwan Ishanshali SHG (Bodo group)	350.00	"	(40-60)%
8.	Maoriya SHG (Bodo group)	500.00	"	(80-100)%
9.	Purnima SHG (Bodo group)	350.00	"	(40-60)%
10.	Bidinta SHG (Bodo group)	500.00	One year	(80-100)%

Source: Field Study.

Table-IV
Distribution of Asset Holding Status and Bank Linkage Programme of the SHGs

Sl. No.	*Name of the Group*	*Asset Holding*		*Bank Linkage*	
		Initial Asset (Value in Terms of Rs.)	*Cumulative Asset (Value in Terms of in Rs.)*	*Name of the Bank*	*Grading Status*
1.	Mukrang SHG (Rabha Group)	3000.00	1,91,000.00	AGBB, Serfanguri Branch	1:1
2.	Daogafu SHG (Bodo group)	6000.00	6,45,000.00	AGBB, Serfanguri Branch	1:2
3.	Laimwan SHG (Bodo group)	750.00	2,67,000.00	AGBB, Bhowraguri Branch	1:2
4.	Maidangshri SHG (Bodo group)	2000.00	1,53,000.00	AGBB, Bhowraguri Branch	Nil
5.	Ranjali SHG (Bodo group)	4000.00	8,97,000.00	AGBB, Serfanguri Branch	1:2
6.	Udangshree SHG (Bodo group)	3200.00	79,000.00	SBI, Salakati Branch	1:2
7.	Laimwan Ishanshali SHG (Bodo group)	1800.00	32,000.00	AGBB, Kokrajhar Branch	1:1
8.	Maoriya SHG (Bodo group)	3600.00	69,000.00	SBI, Balagaon Branch	Nil
9.	Purnima SHG (Bodo group)	500.00	32,000.00	AGBB, Kokrajhar Branch.	Nil
10.	Bidinta SHG (Bodo group)	2200.00	1,10,000.00	AGBB, Kokrajhar Branch	1:1
	All Groups	27,050.00	24,75000.00		

Source: Field Study.

APPENDIX-II

Table-A
Distribution of Literacy Rate, Sex-Ratio, Percentage of Female Population, Percentage of ST Population to the Total Population Percentage of ST* Female out of Total ST Population in India/N.E. States/Kokrajhar District, 2001.

Sl. No.	*India/States/ District*	*Literacy Rate*	*Sex-Ratio*	*% of Female Population*	*% of ST Population to the Total Population*	*% of ST Females Out of Total ST*
1.	India	65.38 (54.16)	933	48	8.19	49.43
2.	Arunachal Pradesh	54.3 (43.5)	893	47	64	50.07
3.	Assam	63.3 (54.6)	935	48	12.4	49.27
4.	Manipur	70.5 (60.5)	978	49	35	49.49
5.	Meghalaya	88.8 (86.7)	935	48	95	49.6
6.	Mizoram	62.6 (59.6)	972	49	85	50
7.	Nagaland	66.6 (61.5)	900	47	88	48.52
8.	Sikkim	68.6 (60.4)	875	47	20.6	49
9.	Tripura	73.2 (64.9)	948	49	31.1	49.23
10.	Kokrajhar District	51.6 (42.4)	943	48.53	33.7	49.45

Figs. in the bracket represents female literacy.

* ST: Scheduled Tribe.

Sources: 1. Basic Statistics NER, 2006, NEC, Shillong, Meghalaya.
2. Women Men in India, 2004, GOI.
3. Fact sheet on Women in India, 2005, NIPCCD.

Table-B

Distribution of Work Participation Rate (2001), Unemployment Rate in Per cent (1999-2000) for India/N.E. States and Kokrajhar District

Sl. No.	*India/ State/Dist.*	*Work Participation Rate (Main + Marginal)*			*Unemployment Rate (in %), 1999-2000*			
					Rural		*Urban*	
		Male	*Female*	*Total*	*Female*	*Male*	*Female*	*Male*
1.	India	51.93	25.68 R-30.98 U-11.55	39.26	1.5	2.1	7.1	4.8
2.	Arunachal Pradesh	50.6	36.5 R-41.3 U-17.2	44.0	0.1	0.9	10.0	1.4
3.	Assam	49.9	20.7 R-22.1 U-10.6	35.8	11.9	4.7	22.3	9.1
4.	Manipur	48.1	39.0 R-41.5 U-32.2	43.6	2.5	2.4	10.3	7.4
5.	Meghalaya	48.3	35.1 R-N.A U-	41.8	0.3	0.5	6.8	3.4
6.	Mizoram	57.3	47.5 R-54.5 U-40.5	52.6	0.5	2.1	2.6	4.4
7.	Nagaland	46.7	38.1 R-42.5 U-15.6	42.6	3.8	3.0	10.8	9.3
8.	Sikkim	57.4	38.6 R-40.6 U-21.7	48.6	2.0	3.5	10.0	6.7
9.	Tripura	50.6	21.1 R-22.9 U-12.4	36.2	4.6	0.8	8.8	5.5
10.	Kokrajhar District	48.0	25.2 R-26.3 U-10.3	37.0	–	–	–	–

Sources: 1. Women Men in India, 2004, GOI.
2. Fact sheet on Women in India, 2005, NIPCCD.
3. Basic Statistics NER, 2006, NEC, Shillong, Meghalaya.

Table-C
Physical Performances Under Sampoorna Grameen Rozgar Yojana During 2003-04

Sl. No.	*India/ States*	*SGRY-I Man Days Generated (in Lakh)*			*SGRY-II Man Days Generated (in Lakh)*		
		Total	*Women*	*% of Women*	*Total*	*Women*	*% of Women*
1.	India	4463.43	1198.14	26.84	4096.81	1077.98	26.33
2.	Arunachal Pradesh	2.33	N.A.	0	10.8	2.95	27.31
3.	Assam	299.48	34.72	11.59	337.72	37.55	11.12
4.	Manipur	7.29	2.35	32.24	6.71	1.38	20.57
5.	Meghalaya	14.21	5.09	35.82	20.16	6.06	30.06
6.	Mizoram	2.78	N.A.	0	7.39	1.77	23.94
7.	Nagaland	126.23	N.A.	0	9.45	N.A.	0
8.	Sikkim	4.59	1.52	33.12	3.62	1.45	40.06
9.	Tripura	76.38	20.21	26.46	50.58	13.46	26.61

Source: Women Men in India, 2004, GOI.

Table-D
Distribution of Swarn Jayanti Gram Swarozgar Yojana (SGSY) Physical

Sl. No.	*States*	*Members Covered Under SHGs*	*Number of Individual Swarozgaris Assisted*
1.	Arunachal Pradesh	21	121
2.	Assam	26305	212
3.	Manipur	635	05
4.	Meghalaya	488	11
5.	Mizoram	290	87
6.	Nagaland	0	0
7.	Sikkim	388	393
8.	Tripura	641	0
	Total	28768	829

Source: Basic Statistics of NER, 2006, NEC, Shillong, Meghalaya.

15

Essence of Micro Credit and Industrial Potentials

D.K. BHATTACHARYA

Introduction

This chapter emphasizes on the need for a comprehensive Micro-Credit Policy to achieve sustainable development for a free enterprise regional economy having absolute liberty in small entrepreneurial activities. In particular, economic development should lead to achieve a better standard of living for majority of the people and it obviously include eradication of mass poverty and hunger, spread proper and effective education and culture, augment social, political and economic stability inside the country and finally establish peace in the mind of the social inhabitants. The importance of the study, on regional economic development is always felt in the inequitable world. In recent periods under Globalization, the inter and intra regional inequalities have gone up sharply and in this context, this chapter aims at analyzing the present state of the economy of Nadia, West Bengal through her traditional handloom industry, providing a large number of people and prescribing for extending the scope of Micro-Credit facilities, mainly to expedite all-round regional development by exploring regional potentials. It also aims at representing its position in the state of West Bengal and India.

Our entire chapter has been classified into six broad sections. These are accommodated in the following order:

- *(a)* Meaning of economic development.
- *(b)* Concept of Micro-Credit and its necessity to meet capital scarcity specially in economically backward regions.
- *(c)* Micro-Credit Scenario in India and West Bengal.

(d) Potential of Micro-Credit led growth in the traditional handloom Industry of Nadia a District.

(e) Other Industrial Potentials in the District of Nadia, West Bengal.

(f) Our policy prescriptions and conclusions.

Meaning of Economic Development

By economic development of a society we mean such change that can improve mainly the basic standard of living of the people in general and it obviously include increase in real per capita income, eradicate mass poverty and hunger, especially among the downtrodden and at the same time spread proper and effective education and culture, augment social, political and economic stability inside the country and finally establish peace in the mind of the social inhabitants. In the process of achieving these objectives production in various fields (mainly in agriculture and industry) are to be raised upto the level of expectation and it undoubtedly requires finance. As we know very well that the third world countries along with their many problems scarcity of capital is perhaps the greatest one and they again are found to suffer from unbalanced type of growth process. Availability of institution finance is undoubtedly not upto the expectation there. It naturally comples the willing entrepreneur to seek for an alternative source which are non-institutional and/or regional level sources. Prof. Yunus experiencing these phenomenon in a small village of Bangladesh through for a parallal solution, which today has been popularized as micro-finance all over the world.

Concept of Micro Credit

The present era of Liberalized, Privatized and Globalized (LPG) world, economic policies could not actually materializes the very objective of reducing proverty and inequality in the distribution of income and wealth among the people. More specifically, it is observed that the inequality in the distribution of income and wealth across the low and middle income countries has become greater than that in the high income earning industrialized countries of the world. As a result, the gap in the level of well being among the people of different countries is getting wider. Thus globalization has failed to provide the very objective of reducing income inequality and poverty among the people across the brother. Rather it has enhanced regional inequality significantly and thereby reduced the well being of the common people. It thus induces us to think for development in some other way and we fell the necessity of adopting the development policies for the specific regions of a country supported by that parallel lines of finance marked as micro-finance earlier. Our idea through this tiny effort is to concentrate on grass route planning on the belief, if the under developed regions of a country are developed in the desired direction set by the planners, we can turn the unbalanced type of growth into a balanced one through regionalized growth process and finally reap all the benefits of all round development. We think, only thorough this kind of areawise, need based, regional Development process, can arrest the increasing poverty and inequality among the people, what we call Regional Rural development and it, of course, require adequate credit facilities. We have a mind to have a case study for the Nadia district of West Bengal concentrating on her famous traditional handloom industry which has a chequered past there.

Capitalizing the experience of Bangladesh the Government of India, has also realized the essence of micro credit and thereby inducing regional authorities like Panchayat, Municipalities rural and commercial banks, NGOs of various fileds etc. to pursue the very policy of area-wise, need based regional development specially by mobilizing micro-finance. Some examples in this context are—SEWA Bank acting in remote areas of Gujarat, SPANDAN in Karnataka and Andhra Pradesh, BASIX concentrating in the both rural and urban areas of Andhra Pradesh, Maharashtra, Chhattisgarh, Orissa and in many other regions of South India, MYRAD in Karnataka and Tamil Nadu, SHARDA in Andhra Pradesh, Karnataka and Tamil Nadu, CASHPOR in U.P., Bihar, Rajasthan, Jammu and Kashmir Orissa etc. In West Bengal also we find the efficiency of this policy being supported principally and financially by the State-Government and to make it strengthened a separate Ministry has been set up and started functioning to expedite the very objective of regional development through Micro-finance. A number of successful organizations like CARE, SPADE, BANDHAN, SIPRO, PRADAN etc. are found functioning remarkably even in its remote rural areas and also in towns. These agencies are sometimes formulating their policies in their own fields and sometimes are interlinked with other organizations and also with the State Government to achieve better results. They are very often found to make collaboration among themselves.

Micro-Credit Scenario in India and West Bengal

In India the Cooperative Credit Society Act 1904 should be taken as the pioneering effort in the way of mobilizing micro-credit programmes. The Integrated Rural Development Programme (IRDP) launched by the Government of India in 1980 was, no doubt, an attempt for paving the way to reach the poorest of the poor. However, the linkage in between the SHGs and the formal banking system in 1991-92 by NABARD through pilot projects actually did a lot in this perspective. Large amount of loans have been distributed to ever increasing right persons and organizations since then. Separate departments were set up by the NABARD in its head office in Mumbai in June 1998 and simultaneously it advised in its regional offices all over the country to set up Micro Credit Innovation Cells mainly to expedite the desired credit creation process by a number of preplanned ways. To make it practically possible a special fund initially to the tune of Rs. 100 crores in the name of Micro Finance Development Fund has been created by the NABARD. The SHG programme has registered remarkable achievements in our country. At present the total number of families embrassed under SHG's (10,79,091) cover is Rs. 1.67 crores, 90 per cent of whom were women group. It may also be represented as feminization of micro finance bank in India. At present 560 banks are participating in the entire programme of which 48 are Commercial Banks, 194 are Regional Rural Banks and the remaining 316 are Co-operative Banks.

The State of West Bengal is also not lagging behind in this perspective. We find various agencies like NGOs, Banks, Financial Insitutions, Co-operatives and Government departments etc. are sometimes separately and sometimes jointly promoting SHG in the state. More specifically different models are found functioning here. A district-wise progress in the number of SHGs are their members are shown below in tabular forms:

Table–1
Year Wise District Wise Number of SHGs

Sl. No.	*District*	*2000*	*2001*	*2002*	*2003*	*2004*	*2005*	*2006*
1.	Coochbehar	320	707	1094	1481	1868	2255	2642
2.	Jalpaiguri	142	665	1188	1711	2234	2757	3280
3.	Darjeeling	455	490	525	560	595	630	665

Contd...

Sl. No.	*District*	*2000*	*2001*	*2002*	*2003*	*2004*	*2005*	*2006*
4.	U. Dinajpur	415	683	951	1219	1487	1755	2023
5.	D. Dinajpur	817	918	1019	1120	1221	1322	1434
6.	Malda	574	815	1056	1297	1538	1779	2020
7.	Murshidabad	1201	1943	2685	3427	4169	4911	5653
8.	Nadia	3171	4262	5353	6444	7535	8626	9717
9.	N-24 Pgs.	2787	4269	5751	7233	8715	10197	11679
10.	S-24 Pgs.	5163	6703	8243	9783	11323	12863	14403
11.	Howrah	1853	2037	2221	2405	2589	2773	2957
12.	Hooghly	3602	5264	6926	8588	10250	11912	13574
13.	Midnapur	10900	15450	20000	24550	29100	33650	38200
14.	Bankura	1035	2326	3617	4908	6199	7490	8781
15.	Purulia	501	559	617	675	733	791	849
16.	Burdwan	1086	2136	3186	4236	5286	6336	7386
17.	Birbhum	646	1083	1520	1957	2394	2831	3268
18.	West Bengal	34668	50310	65952	81594	97236	112878	128520

Source: Study Report on SHGs in West Bengal.
Conducted by: State Institute of Panchayat and Rural Development (SIPRD) Kalyani, West Bengal.

Table–2
Year Wise District Wise Number of SHGs

Sl. No.	*District*	*2000*	*2001*	*2002*	*2003*	*2004*	*2005*	*2006*
1.	Coochbehar	3200	7070	10940	17772	22416	29315	39630
2.	Jalpaiguri	1420	6650	11880	20532	26808	35841	49200
3.	Darjeeling	4550	4900	5250	6720	7140	8190	9975
4.	U. Dinajpur	4150	6830	9510	14628	17844	22815	30345
5.	D. Dinajpur	8170	9180	10190	13440	14652	17186	21345
6.	Malda	5740	8150	10560	15564	18456	23127	30300
7.	Murshidabad	12010	19430	26850	41124	50028	63843	84795
8.	Nadia	31710	42620	53530	77328	90420	112138	145755
9.	N-24 Pgs.	27870	42690	57510	86796	104580	132561	175185

Contd...

Sl. No.	District	2000	2001	2002	2003	2004	2005	2006
10.	S-24 Pgs.	51630	67030	82430	117396	135876	167219	216045
11.	Howrah	18530	20370	22210	28860	31068	36049	44355
12.	Hooghly	36020	52640	69260	103056	123000	154856	203610
13.	Midnapur	109000	154500	200000	294600	349200	437450	573000
14.	Bankura	10350	23260	36170	58896	74388	97370	131715
15.	Purulia	5010	5590	6170	8100	8796	10283	12735
16.	Burdwan	10860	21360	31860	50832	63432	82368	110790
17.	Birbhum	6460	10830	15200	23484	28728	36803	49020
18.	West Bengal	346680	503100	659520	979128	1166832	1467414	1927800

Source: Study Report on SHGs in West Bengal.
Conducted by: State Institute of Panchayat and Rural Development (SIPRD) Kalyani, West Bengal.

At a glance on the tables given above we observe a clear steady increasing trend in the number of SHGs and their members.

The SHG BANK Linkage programme launched (initiated) by the NABARD taken as a pioneering effort in our country in February, 1992 can be studied through the following Table-3.

Table–3
Growth of SHG-Bank Linkage Programme (1992-2001)

Year	*Number of Groups*	*Amount of Loans (Rupees in Crores)*
1992-1993	255	0.289
1993-1994	620	0.650
1994-1995	2,122	2.440
1995-1996	4,757	6.058
1996-1997	8,598	11.840
1997-1998	14,317	23.760
1998-1999	32,995	57.070
1999-2000	114,775	192.870
2000-2001	263,825	480.870
2001-2002	461,478	545.46

Source: Financing Agriculture–Journal of Agricultural Finance Corporation Ltd., April-June, 2002, Vol. 34, No. 2.

It may be mentioned that by linking SHGs with formal banks both the banks and SHGs were benefited. It was no charity by banks. The involvement of SHGs with banks reduced the high transaction costs of Banks (for providing small credit to the poor beneficiaries). What is more important is the fact that due to this linkage programme the problem of physical collateral (which the poor people have already access to) was overcome. In the case of microfinance monitoring the loan usage and enforcement are done both at individual and group levels. The group helps in monitoring and enforcing repayment from each member. If any member defaults, he/she has to pay penalty in the form of ostracism and loss of social prestige. Thus through the loans are given without any formal security, they involve social collateral.

Micro Credit-led Growth in the Handloom Industry of Nadia, West Bengal

Situated in the heart of Bengal Delta and enclosed by the Ganga or the Bhagirathi on the east, the district of Nadia has an area of 3927 square kilometer and a population of 46,03,756 (2365054-Male and 33,38,702 Female), density of population 1172 per square kilometer (*Source:* District Statistical Handbook-2002). The district is predominantly a rural one. It is included in the presidency division, landlocked by the District of Murshidabad on the North and North-east, the district Rajsahi and Kustia of Bangladesh on the east and north east while the district of 24-parganas (N) stands on the South and South-east boarder. The river Bhagirathi forms the Western boundary with the city of Nabadeep Mayapur (Famous Iscon Temple) situated on its bank. Geographically, the district stretches from north to south with an irregular shape.

Though the district is essentially an agricultural one, a considerable portion of her working population is engaged in various small industrial persuits. An interesting feature to be noted here is that more men are engaged in household industries than in any other part of the State. Hand-weaving being the main household industry (occupation), a considerable number of weavers concentrate is this district. Every 15th male worker can be found employed in the household industries (mainly hand-weaving) where as this ratio is barely 30 per thousand in the entire state (*Source:* Last population census). Of the traditional industries it is to be mentioned that the Cotton Weaving activities flourished here towards the end of the

18th and at the beginning of 19th century and provide employment to a good number of people in the part. Practically speaking the traditional cotton-weaving here received a set back with the gradual increase in the cost of raw material, the introduction of mill-made and synthetic cloths, scarcity of inadequate finance and above all change in the tastes and fashion of the people which turned demand for away from the traditional hand-women products.

Let us low represents a clear picture on categories of workers by sex comparing the last two census reports for the district.

Table–4
Distribution of Population According to Categories of Workers by Sex, 1991 and 2001 in the District of Nadia, West Bengal

Industrial Categories	*Population (Number)*			*Percentage of Total Population*
	Male	*Female*	*Total*	
A. Total Main Workers	1029267 (1220646)	80564 (187427)	1109831 (1408073)	28.81 (30.59)
1. Cultivators	322477 (291921)	3131 (25964)	325608 (317885)	8.45 (6.91)
2. Agricultural Labourers	287744 (342511)	17225 (32922)	304969 (375433)	7.92 (8.15)
3. Household Industries Mainly Handloom	154584 (87319)	35812 (97597)	190396 184916	4.94 (4.02)
4. Other Workers	264462 (584466)	24396 (154581)	288858 (739047)	7.50 (16.05)
B. Marginal Workers	5435 (85571)	14931 (123637)	20366 (209208)	8.52 (4.54)
C. Non-workers	955139 (1058837)	1766761 (1927638)	2721900 (2986475)	70.67 (64.87)
Total Population (A + B + C)	1989841 (2365054)	1862256 (2238702)	3852097 (4603756)	100.00 –

Source: Census of India, 1991-2001.

N.B., *2001 Census Figures are in brackets.*

The table represented above shows that about 30 per cent of the total population residing in the district are engaged in various industrial and agricultural activities and they are termed as main workers. Among these main works almost 5 per cent of the district population are performing household industrial activities (mainly hand-weaving). Though the percentage of marginal worker is negligible here. Surprisingly enough a large proportion of the population more than 70 per cent shown in the Table were found to be non-workers and they mainly comprise of children, women, old and invalid unproductive people. In the course of filed investigation we have observed that mainly the scarcity of working capital, lack of adequate marketing facilities and insufficient supply of hank yearn and other ingredients are the three basic hurdles responsible for the gradual deterioration of the traditional Cotton textile industry in the district. We just reiterate our previous statement of failure of institutional finance supplement the necessity of working capital in the district to rejuvenate the handloom industry and prescrible for the availability of micro finance revolution for it.

It is to be noted that the our State Government have felt the necessity or nourishing the handloom industry and took step forward by taking its own effort, basically by offering required finance, directly or advicing agencies like NABARD, Commercial and Rural, Banks, Local Municipalities and Panchayats to be as such possible for the weavers. The figures indicated above implies the direct effort by the Government itself, initiated through the Zonal office of Sanitpur and Nabadweep. They mainly cover the handloom activities of the entire district where the important centres and located at Ranaghat, Fulia, Chakda, Kuj, besides Santipur and Nabadweep.

Other Industrial Potentials in the District

The district of Nadia has a leading agricultural sector, though not much developed in nature and it engage a good number (693318) of people (15.06%) both directly and indirectly (according to the last census report). It also has wide possibilities for setting-up a number of other industries in it like:

(i) Production of mango is a pride for this district but unfortunately mango gardens are gradually reducing in number mainly for unplanned construction of housing and other commercial a census and also for developing quick temporary drainage facility specially in flood affected areas. It deserves attention for the local authority and require appropriate measures against it. We can also think for preparing various attractive food items from mango, litchi, nut etc. specially in the years of their bumper crops and thus

initiative active SHGs for setting up food processing industry in the remote rural areas of the district.

The same idea can also be exploited in the case of beautiful flowers available here.

(ii) The two decentralized sectors of the Textile industry i.e., Handloom and Powerloom sectors together have enough potentials to grow here. All possible steps must be taken for the improvement of these two sectors in this district.

(iii) The clay model industry of Nadia is very famous all over the country. More and more varieties of clay models have to be prepared that can satisfy demand and attract people of various tastes, incomes and regions. At fluent people are usually fond of keeping beautiful clay models as show pieces in their dwelling houses. Models of distinguished categories are to be prepared and marketed in larger numbers to satisfy preference of those people. The expert potential of this industry needs to be explored at the same time.

(iv) Sweets of Nadia district have its own name and fame all over the country. "Niquti" and "Sarvaja" of Santipur and Krishnanagar Sweet-Curd of Nadawipt requires no special introduction to the Sweet lovers. People from different corners usually visit this place to collect quality sweets from the renowned pockets of the district specially for their special occasions like Markage etc. The quality and size of sweets have to be improved to attract people of different tastes, preferences and habits. Availability of pure raw materials necessary for this industry at nearby location to keep their production costs (compared to other districts) at a low level. Manufacturers and traders operating under this industry must exploit this advantage properly and by producing and supplying quality products at a competitive price they can minimize cost and maximize revenue and thereby earn highest profit. Under the new patenting system under WTO, location specifications for these products may be patented. With improved packaging and preservation system there is also possibility of export of these items like carved 'resogollas' etc.

Our Policy Prescriptions and Conclusions

We finally prescribe the following propositions to augment SHG led growth of micro finance in the district:

1. To face the basic hurdle of capital scarcity in view of inadequate institutional finance, micro credit programmes must be strengthened for the weaving people in the district under consideration.
2. Traditional hand-women articles must be substituted by better quality products giving proper importance on the changing tasters and preferences of the present generation.
3. We think, it is the right time to think for diversifying the handloom products mainly to supplement the needs of the other countries so as to expand our export market with these articles.
4. It will not be unwise to mention here that to meet the changing tastes and preferences of the ever growing consumers and for broadening our export market the old wooden machinery (handloom) with which production is still carried on, deserves a radical structural change. The scientists and technicians must come forward to give it a new shape so as to make it more productive, less labour absorbing and finally worthy of releasing better quality of products to compete the global market.
5. Besides finance, the member of SHGs should be given proper training so that they can become fit in the home and the markets abroad.
6. To become fit in the financial market also, the literacy rate and the basic education relating to the handloom industry must be given to the members of SHG. This will strengthen the group activity.
7. The organizer initiating these SHG should also think for taking necessary programmes that can maintain the physical and mental health of the SHG members.

We finally conclude saying that the availability of finance without collateral must not be the only objective of micro credit revolution, the organizers forming SHGs must import such lesson among the SHG members that can improve their sense of united fraternity and step up ethical consciousness among these marginal workers. They will automatically find their way to enter into the main stream of the society through various self help group programmes. We think, it will not be an impractical thinking that this micro credit revolution, if really materialized will lead all development programmes both in under-developed and developing countries in the very near future. We remember in this context the famous opinion of Prof. A.K. Sen that 'entitlement' of the down trodens in a society to the available social avenues can originate and improve their productivity from grassroot level and at the same time create their 'ability' to achieve a better standard of living.

REFERENCES

The World Development Report (2000-01), Micro Credit Summit, 1997, Draft Declaration and Plan of Action.

Montgomery, R. (1996), 'Disciplining or Protecting the Poor? The Microfinance Promise" Journal of Economic Literature, Vol. 37, No. 4.

Report of the Study conducted by SIPRO, Kalyani, W.B. in September, 2001.

Sen A.K. – Poverty and Famine.

Sen A.K. – Economics and Ethics.

Rahman Amine 1999 "Micro-Credit Initiatives for Equitable and Sustainable Development: Who pays"? World Development 127(1).

Bandhyopadhyay D., Yugandhar B.N., Mukherjee A. (2002), Convergence of Programmes by Empowering SHGs and PRIs, Economic and Political Weekly, June 29.

The Workshop on the Study Report on MF in W.B. – Published by CARE, W.B., Kolkata – 19, dated 22nd July, 2005.

Swalps Bitta Barta, Vol. 4-5.

Report published by the office of the H.D.O., Santipur, Nadia, 2007 and Discussion with the H.D.O. Santipur on 21.05.2007.

Dua, D.R. – Small Industries and Handicrafts.

APPENDIX–I

Nadia–Profile of the District

Geographical Location

The district lies in between 22°53′ N to 24°11′ N Latitude and 88°09′ E 88°48′ E Longitude. It is surrounded by the District Murshidabad in the North, Bangladesh in the East, 24-Parganas in the South and *Bardhaman* and *Hooghly* in the West.

Her Important Statistics

1.	Area	:	3927 Sq.Km.
2.	Population	:	4603756 (2001)
3.	Density of Population	:	1172 per Sq. Km.
4.	Growth of Population	:	19.51 (1999-2001)
5.	Rivers	:	Bhagirathi, Jalangi, Churni, Ichamati
6.	Agricultural Crops	:	Paddy or Rice, Jute, Wheat, Sugar Cane and Oil Seeds
7.	Literacy Rate	:	68.55 per cent (2001)
8.	Educational Institutions	:	*(a)* No. of Colleges 15+2 B.Ed. *(b)* No. of Schools– PRI–7193 SEC–3819 HEC–4429 **Total 15501 (2001-02)**
9.	Main occupation of the people	:	Weaving (Handloom + Powerloom), Agriculture and Clay Models, Sweet and Utensils etc.

APPENDIX–II

Important Cities and Well Known Places: Of Nadia, W.B.

Krishnanagar is its *District Head Quarter* whereas Clay-industry is internationally famous. Famous poet and the dramatist *Dijendralal Roy* and his son Dilip Kumar Roy, the famous singer were born here. *Nabadwip*, remaining in the western part of the *Bhagirathi*, is a holy ancient centre of Sanskrit Culture. Both Nabadwips and Santipur are famous for Rash Festivals and the birth place of lord SRI CHAITANNAY DEB and hence a holy religious place for the *Baishnabs*. The well-known temple of *Mahaprovu* at *Mayapur* is an added attraction here. *Palasi* is a place of historical interest in the district. *Santipur*, another holy place in the district for *Baishnabs*, is included under *Ranaghat* Sub-division and also famous for handloom cloths of unparallel quality. Fulia is the birth place of *Kirtibas*, the author of *'Bengali Ramayana'* and a centre for Handlooms. A well-planned modern city has been developed at Kalyani mainly with the individual initiative of Late *Dr. Bidhan Chandra Roy*, the Chief Minister of West Bengal. *Bidhan Chandra Krishi Viswa Vidyalaya Abd University of Kalyani* are the two well known universities established here. A large dairy and well known centre of milk production and distribution has been set up by the Government of West Bengal here at *Haringhata*. Bethnadahari is known for its deer santnary. Sivnibas is famous for its Shiva Temple Ghoshpara is well known for Satimar Mela.

16

Financial Inclusion through Commercial Banking Sector

MITHILESH K. SINHA

Introduction

The inclusion is one of the buzz words of the world financial system today. "Financial Inclusion" has been discussed in banking circles in recent years with the main objective of providing banking services at an affordable cost to the poor and weaker sections of the society. It, the latest in the terminology of development literature, is replacing "Micro Finance." The idea of financial inclusion is echoed in the Annual Policy Statements of the RBI and also enforced by the finance minister in his budget speech for the year 2006-07 in terms of revamping the system and working out of a plan "for designing and delivering credit to every household that seeks credit from lending institution financial inclusion is an important policy goal both from the perspective of realization of growth opportunities as well as improved risk management for poor households. With the growing importance of Indian economy in international arena, there is a need for strengthening the forces of inclusive growth in the country.

Financial inclusion was envisaged and embedded in credit policies in the earlier decades also, though in a disguised form and without the same nomenclature. The role of the banking sector in financing rural households was envisioned in the 1950s, in pursuance of the recommendations of the RBI survey, viz., All-India Rural Credit Survey (AIRCS), which observed that "Agricultural credit fell short of the requirements, was not of the right type, did not serve the right purpose and often failed to go to the people." Despite the insignificant role played by cooperatives in financing rural households at that time, a proactive role for cooperatives was suggested stating that "Cooperation has failed, but cooperation must succeed." Commercial banks were also inducted in the 1970s into the ambit of financing agriculture and other priority sectors. Ever since, both commercial and cooperative banks have been financing the unorganized segments, holding a major share in institutional finance.

During the last two years, the idea of financial inclusion has been further brought to the forefront; it is echoed in the Annual Policy Statements of the RBI and also reinforced by the Finance Minister in his budget speech for the year 2006-07 in terms of revamping the system and working out a plan "for designing and delivering credit to every household that seeks credit from lending institutions."[1]

In this chapter, an attempt to make to examine the following issues at length. *(i)* Does India mainstream banking industry have the capacity, to address the issue of financial inclusiveness? *(ii)* Does Para banking (microcredit, self-help groups) increase the cost of providing credit to under-banked groups? *(iii)* Can access to cheap credit be widened by marshalling the traditional social order like the moneylenders, or would it undermine the cause? Section I of this chapter gives the meaning of Financial Inclusion and its access to more people. Section II of this chapter gives a brief review of the credit policies and developments in the banking sector in terms of enhancing the flow of institutional credit to priority sectors. Section III is devoted to examine how inclusion, a business imperative. Section IV emphasizes the suggestions which need to be addressed to deepen financial inclusion.

II

What is Financial Inclusion?

Inclusion is the term used to delineate the extent to which all sections of a society have access to the formal financial system. By financial inclusion, we mean the provision by the financial system, of financial products and services at an affordable price, to those who have been financially excluded. In other words, financial inclusion, at a minimum, may be interpreted to mean the ability of every individual to access basic financial services which include savings, loans and insurance in a manner that is reasonably convenient and flexible in terms of access and design and reliable in the sense that the savings are safe and that insurance claims will be paid with certainty (Mor and Ananth: 2007).

Financial inclusion, according to the Reserve Bank of India, is delivery of banking services at an affordable cost to the vast sections of disadvantaged and low-income groups who tend to be excluded from the formal financial system. While the RBI speaks of financial inclusion, its target is essentially the poor people who have not yet been brought into the mainstream of formal banking culture.

Chief Characteristics

An inclusive financial sector, on the other hand, is defined as one that offers a range of financial services to the entire active population. It is characterized by *(i)* competition among financial service providers; *(ii)* a wide range of financial service providers; *(iii)* sustainability with respect to the permanence of access to financial services; *(iv)* legal and regulatory environments that are built to ensure the integrity of the financial sector and access to financial services.

Access for More People

While the macro level paradigm is relatively abstract, bankers' point of view is more concrete. In the search for profitability, financial institutions need to reduce operational cost. That means more of viable accounts which in turn implies exclusion of several sections of the society from the banking net. Including a larger number would mean more accounts and more people getting involved in banking services, which may have positive social implications as well.

The transformation problem is universal. Many countries have tried to experiment with interventions, both institutional and policy-related, in the U.K., the government established a framework for ensuring enhanced financial inclusion by setting up a Financial Inclusion Fund of 210 million pounds over three years, and a Financial Inclusion Task Force to oversee its progress. A platform for collaboration between local governments and the financial institutions also was set up in order to ensure that everyone had access to financial services.

In India, the RBI has issued guidelines for banks to enhance the level of financial inclusion in their areas of operation, in a time=bound manner. Recently, the Central Government appointed the C. Rangarajan Committee to look into the whole gamut of issues in this context.

Financial inclusion is not an end in itself. Having a bank account or insurance coverage *ipso facto* does not mean an enhancement in the economic position or well being of a person. On the one hand, it acts as a facilitator. It should help in some way the process of economic development and also lead to a change in the pattern of income distribution. Developing countries need to develop mechanisms that ensure that poverty is not exacerbated by lack of access to financial services. People need information and advice when they get into debt. Such information and guidance can best be delivered by appropriate mechanisms. Such mechanisms in turn will reinforce the demand for credit. Indian banks, flush with funds, need to act according to this logic.

Large institutional intervention, as in the form of micro finance, has taken place. But this bad more of a bandwagon effect than contributing to the dynamics of the economy. Large employment oriented rural programmes, such as SGSY, REGP and PMRY, still suffer from absence of backward and forward linkages.

The conventional "credit-technology-market" should undergo a major change in favour of innovative organizational initiatives. It is in this context that the relevance of meaningful business development services arises.

III

Inclusiveness of Commercial Banks in the Past Decades: Experiments

Ever since Independence, the flow of credit to the poorer sections of society has been a key policy concern. Among the institutional initiatives, Development Finance Institutions (DFIs) stand as a major development. With the liberalization of economy and of the financial sector, a major shift in emphasis took place, from institutions to banking technologies.

There is a significant divergence in perspectives on the economies of banking in India. This conflict operates at several levels. The debate on credit-deposit ratio is also based on such a perspective. While the sociology of financial inclusion is agreed by all, the historical experience of banking in the country deserves a detailed examination. In the 1990s, with the introduction of prudential norms, there was a significant focus of banks on viable accounts. Such a policy shift, alternatively, implied a tendency towards exclusion.

How inclusive the commercial banks have in the past decades should be viewed with reference to three distinct time phases, viz. (1) The period from 1951 onwards till the nationalization of commercial banks in 1969; (2) The post-nationalization period till 1991-92; and (3) The subsequent period characterized by the enforcement of measures to enhance the financial strength of commercial banks in the era of globalization and liberalization. In the first phase, cooperative banks were inducted into the sphere of financing agricultural credit in the late 1950s, when it was found by the AIRCS that non-institutional sources, particularly moneylenders, were the main source of finance to this sector. A major part of the credit from the commercial banks was oriented towards the private corporate sector, and commercial banks did not undertake the risk of financing agriculture and allied activities (Rao: 2007).

In view of the inadequacy of cooperatives in financing agricultural credit, commercial banks were brought into picture, after their nationalization in 1969, to cater to the needs of the priority sectors like agriculture, small-scale industries, etc., with social objectives coming to the forestage. The branch licensing policy of the commercial banks was geared to open branches in rural and semi-urban areas, backward regions of the country and unbanked states on a liberal basis, with a view to reduce the inter-regional disparities in provision of banking facilities. The number of offices of commercial banks showed a phenomenal increase from 8,262 in 1969 to 60,220 in 1991. The average population per branch of 64,000 in 1969 improved to 14,000 in 1991. The share of rural and semi-urban branches, which formed 63 per cent of the total number of branches in 1969, increased to 77 per cent by 1991.

As opening of branches per se did not ensure adequate credit utilization of deposit resources in the respective regions, a Credit-Deposit (CD) ratio of 60 per cent was stipulated for rural and semi-urban branches to ensure that there was no migration of credit from rural to urban areas. As credit to priority sectors need not flow to the lower strata of occupational groups, the concept of "weaker sections" in priority sectors was introduced to safe-guards the interests of this group. Targets were also laid down for the priority sectors – priority sector advances should constitute 40 per cent of aggregate bank advances. Similar targets were laid for ensuring flow of credit to "agriculture and allied activities" and the weaker sections thereof and "rural artisans, village craftsman and cottage industries" within the small-scale industrial sector.[2] Regional Rural Banks (RRBs) were inducted into the banking scene in 1975 with a view to further inhance the flow of credit to rural areas, with particular references to small and marginal farmers, labourers, artisans, small entrepreneurs. The branch licensing policy of the commercial banks, with a thrust on opening of branches in rural and semi-urban areas, credit policy measures to enhance the flow of institutional credit to priority sectors and the weaker sections threof, and the multi-agency approach to rural credit financed the rural sector in a big way in the second phase. An element of subsidization for some of the priority sectors was also introduced during this phase, linking concessionality in interest rates with the size of advances, though the number of such slabs of loan sizes was reduced from time to time.

The third phase, the era of banking sector reforms, which was an integral part of economic reforms, has continued since 1991-92 and with a view to augment the financial strength of the commercial banks. These measures covered a gradual reduction in the Cash Reserve Ratio (CRR) and the Statutory Liquidity Ratio (SLR) to enhance loanable funds of the commercial banks, introduction of prudential norms such as the Capital Adequacy Ratio (CAR), provisioning for bad and doubtful debts, recapitalization of banks, deregulation of interest rates and linking markets rates to SLR investments in government securities. Credit deposit ratios in the post-reform period were generally in the range of 50-60 per cent, much lower than those in the 1980s. The balance sheet structure and the portfolio behaviour of commercial banks had undergone radical changes during this period. In particular, the differential in interest rates between credit and investment in government securities, which were linked to market rates, got narrowed down; commercial banks deployed funds in risk free government securities on a larger scale, in preference to lending to the real sectors of the economy. The credit obligations to the priority sectors continued despite these constraints.

The reduction in SLR and CRR, which were aimed at enhancing loanable funds of the commercial banks, did not, ipso facto, raise the CD ratios, in view of the opportunity costs foregone with reference to lending and investments. The cost of loanable funds also underwent changes — the interest rate differential between priority and non-priority sectors narrowed down, reducing thereby the hitherto prevailing interest subsidy to the priority sectors. The linkage between interest rates and size of loans with different slabs was removed in the mid-1990s. Effective April 1998, only two slabs were made effective, the cut-off point being Rs. 2 lakh. For credit limits over Rs. 2 lakh, banks were allowed the freedom to fix their lending rates, while for credit limits less than or equal to the cut-off point, the lending rate was not to exceed the Prime Lending Rate (PLR).

The third phase of the time period was associated with high interest rate regime up to 1997 and softening of interest rates during the latter period. Thus it may be observed that the interest element subsidy for SBA was abolished, and the differential in the cost of funds between the SBA and the Large Borrowal Accounts (LBA) tended to become narrower.[3] The coverage of the priority sectors too underwent substantial modifications in the 1990s with many new sectors and segments added that would indirectly affect the share of credit to the traditionally deemed priority sectors when the concept was first introduced.[4] The branch expansion of commercial banks, which showed considerable expansion in rural and semi-urban areas in the first two phases, did not show similar trends in the third phase of the time period. The share of branches in the two categories declined over a period of time, with a concurrent increase in the share of urban and metropolitan branches. This phase was also characterized by mergers and amalgamation of banks, diversification of activities of commercial banks and conversion term-lending institutions into banks. The share of priority sectors moved in the range of 37-39 per cent of the total non-food credit in recent years. The CD ratio was in the range of 50-60 per cent in the third phase, lower than that observed in the previous two phases.[5] The progress of commercial banking at different time points in the three phases mentioned above, is presented in Table 1.

It may be observed that there was a considerable widening and deepening of credit by commercial banks over the decades. Even so, the moot question is how far the policies adopted from time to time enabled the weaker sections of different occupational groups in accessing institutional credit, and whether the reliance on non-institutional sources has been reduced accordingly. The results available from the All-India Debt and Investment Surveys (AIDIS) of the NSSO revealed several interesting features. At this juncture, mention may be made of two innovations, viz., microfinance initiated

Table–1
Progress of Commercial Banking (Scheduled Commercial Banks)

	1969	*1981*	*1985*	*1991*	*1995*	*2000*	*2001*	*2002*	*2003*	*2004*	*2005*
No. of offices of which rural	8262	35707	51385	60220	62367	65412	65919	66190	66535	67188	68355
And semi-urban	5175 (62.6)	26127 (73.2)	40001 (77.9)	46550 (77.3)	46345 (74.3)	47141 (72.1)	47159 (71.5)	47127	47162	47212	47485
Population per Office ('000s)	64	19	15	14	15	15	15	16	16	16	16
Share of priority Sector advances (per cent)	15.0	35.6	39.9	39.2	35.8	37.4	38.5	38.2	37.1	38.8	38.1
Deposits as per cent of national income	15.5	34.4	39.4	48.1	51.7	53.5	58.9	60.7	65.3	68.5	68.3
Credit-deposit Ratio	77.5	65.5	66.1	60.6	54.7	53.3	53.5	53.8	56.9	56.1	64.9
Investment-Deposit ratio	29.3	35.1	35.4	37.7	38.6	36.6	37.1	38.7	41.3	43.8	41.6

Source: Reserve Bank of India: Publications on Basic Statistical Returns of Scheduled Commercial Banks in India.

by the National Bank for Agriculture and Rural Development (NABARD) in 1992, and the Kisan Credit Cards (KCC) scheme introduced in 1998, which were oriented towards enhancement of timely and cost-effective credit. KCCs are issued to farmers by banks on the basis of their landholdings to purchase agricultural inputs whenever needed. As per the AIDIS, 2002-03, only 2.6 per cent of rural households and 0.2 per cent of urban households reported to have a KCC – the average amount of credit was Rs. 16,270 per rural household and Rs. 16,933 per urban household. The survey of SBA, 2004 conducted by the RBI[6] furnished details of credit outstanding against KCCs. According to this survey, about 19 per cent of the SBA used KCC with a share of 18 per cent of the total credit outstanding against SBI – the average outstanding credit was Rs. 26,284.[7] As the data on landholdings are collected from the cultivator households applying for KCC, it would be useful to evolve an information system linking the landholdings and KCCs, with a view to examine how far farmers with different sizes of landholdings benefited from the scheme.

During the last decade, microcredit provided by banks emerged as a major policy tool of financial assistance in the area of rural credit, particularly to the poor sections of society. The linkage of Self-Help Groups (SHGs) with banks initiated by NABARD in 1992 showed progress over time, the details of which are given in Table 2. Several initiatives and strategies have been adopted by NABARD to fine tune the working of the system and further widen the reach of this finance to the poor. This is also placed under the ambit of the priority sectors. The SHGs financed by the banks accounted for hardly 1-2 per cent of the total number of SBAs in recent years, with a share of hardly 1-4 per cent of the total outstanding credit against SBAs, though the average amount per SHG progressively increased from Rs. 16,815 in 1999-2000 to Rs. 42,626 in 2004-05.

NGOs and SHGs are another category of financial intermediaries in the informal financial sector, assisting the household sector through borrowings from banks. Even though the above data throw light on the reach of microcredit to the rural poor, it is necessary to further develop information systems in this area by collecting data on the sources and uses of funds and also the interest rates charged by these intermediaries. The National Statistical Commission (NSC) recommended that a survey on financial aspects of NGO and SHGs involved in microfinancing should be conducted by NABARD at quinquennial intervals.[8]

Table–2
SHG-Bank Linkage Programme

	Total SHG Financed by Banks (Cumulative) (1)	*Bank Loan (Cumulative) (Rs.) (Rs. Crore) (2)*	*Average Amount Per SHG (1) as Per cent of (2)*
1999-00	114.78	193	16815
2000-01	263.83	481	18231
2001-02	461.48	1026	22233
2002-03	717.36	2049	28563
2003-04	1079.09	3904	36179
2004-05	1618.48	6899	42626

Source: Reserve Bank of India, Trend and Progress of Banking in India, 2004-05.

Cottage and Small-Scale Industries: Perspectives on Inclusive Policies

The commercialization of agriculture, as also technology intensification, has resulted in the creation of substantial surplus labour in the agricultural sector.

The results of the Economic Census-2005 show that:

1. Employment growth in the non-farm sector is much lower than that in the Number of enterprises; and
2. Average employment itself declines (The average today is 2.9%, during 1980-90, it was 2.84%).

For decades, financial services provision to the under-saved was regarded as synonymous with credit delivery to the rural areas, predominantly for the purpose of agriculture. Very few programmes focused on micro enterprises, or encouraged diversification away from agriculture. This led to a focus on merely geographical expansion to rural areas, where bank branches offered credit in sizes, which were too large to be made use of by the very poor, rather than a suite of products designed to cater to the needs of this segment. These practices in turn led to a high default. The present models of credit delivery themselves are constrained and are not adequate from the point of view of enterprise creation. The first constraint relates to the orientation of institutions, as also the overall pooling environment of multiplying SHGs. Secondly, both SHG-Bank linkage model and the MFI-Intermediation model should grow by overcoming their internal constraints and inconsistencies.

Agriculture: Perspectives on Inclusive Policies

Credit to the agricultural sector has improved over time. Moreover, interventions such as RIDF, as also several institutions interventions have helped to deepen the flow of credit to the agricultural sector.

Financial Inclusion: An Insurance Perspective

In the absence of insurance, many rural borrowers are unable to cover production and price risk, which in turn leads to defaults on loan. While insurance coverage has been introduced in several forms, both in agriculture and non-farm activities, it is necessary to deepen the system. But such initiatives need to be based on a deeper understanding of the sub-sectors themselves.

One needs to examine these major trends in this context:

1. *Blurring of Insurance and Banking*
   While a progressive blurring of the banking and FDI activities has been an emerging trend since the second half of the 1990s, the most recent trend has been one of banks increasingly entering the insurance business.
2. *Insurance Companies Entering into Strategies of Inclusion*
   Changes introduced in the design and delivery of insurance products, to some extent, has helped enhance the coverage of such products.
3. *Penetration of Micro Insurance*
   Micro insurance is a system by which, people, businesses and other organizations make payments to share risk. Access to insurance enable entrepreneurs to concentrate more on growing their business, while mitigating other risks affecting property, health, or the ability to work.

MFIs are increasingly entering micro insurance, going beyond conventional credit and savings services. Formal insurance is a regulated industry. On the other hand, micro insurance is often a form of liquidity management and risk pooling. But between the two, there is an array of opportunities that need to be explored.

Though the outreach and depth of banking in India has increased over the years, the socio-cultural and certain institutional issues could not lead to 100 per cent financial inclusion even in about fifty years. With the growing importance of Indian economy in international arena, there is a need for strengthening the forces of inclusive growth in the economy.

IV

Financial Inclusion, A Business Imperative

The hikes in interest rates are beginning to bite. On a year-to year basis, credit growth in October 2006 was 28.6 per cent compared to growth of 31 per cent previous year i.e. 2005. So, credit growth shows signs of slowing down. But credit is still likely to grow at a rate higher than the Reserve Bank of India's preferred figure of 20 per cent.

The challenge for banks is two-fold. One, to garner deposits to sustain credit growth as the India story continues to unfold. Two, to increase yields on loans in the face of growing disintermediation. Banks can best meet the two challenges through greater financial inclusion.

Banks are doing their bit to increase deposit growth. Deposits grew at 17.8 per cent in 2005-06 compared to 16.6 per cent in 2004-05. But deposit growth is not adequate to keep pace with the run away growth in credit. Credit growth has outpaced deposit growth in both absolute and percentage terms.

Thus far, banks have managed to sustain credit growth by other means: liquidation of government and other securities, increased borrowings and increase in retained earnings. But these can help the banks only so far. Banks' holdings of government securities has come down from the peak of 42.7 per cent of liabilities in 2004 to 29.8 per cent, not far from the mandatory requirement of 25 per cent. Borrowings can be expensive. Retained earnings can fund only a small proportion of credit demand.

The composition of deposits is equally a concern. Short-term deposits constitute nearly half the total deposits in the banking system. The latest Report on Trend and Progress in Banking notes this but its comments are intriguing. The Report says, "With low short-term interest rates, banks are able to mobilize resources at lower cost. ......In the Indian context, it is observed that foreign and private sector banks have relatively high share of low-cost deposits. Incidentally, these banks groups also have high profit margin and low NPA levels."

One hope that this is not meant to convey that reliance on short-term deposits offers a magic route to high profitability. Such deposits are cheaper, of course, but they expose banks to interest rate risk. The saviour banks have found ways to manage the risk. One is to have a high proportion of current and savings accounts. Another is to have a high ratio of fee to fund-based income. In general, however, the present order of reliance on short-term deposits can be lethal. Let the RBI examine the impact on banks' profit of a 100 basis point increase in interest rates and publish the results in the form of a frequency distribution table without naming the banks.

Banks need to mobilize more deposits, especially stable deposits. They need to do so in the face of a flight of deposits to capital market and other instruments. Offering higher interest rates on deposits is the soft option. The harder option is to reach out to the rural and semi-rural areas through appropriate innovations in products as well as delivery channels.

This is a more attractive option in the long-run because it would help banks access savings and current account deposits. These are low-cost deposits but they are also stable unlike short-term deposits. Reaching out to under-served segments or financial inclusion is thus an imperative on the liabilities side (Mohan: 2006).

It is equally an imperative on the asset side> Many of the best borrowers have already exited the banking system or will borrow from banks only at the meanest rates – 75 per cent of loans are today being made at sub-PLR rates. Banks could shrug this off thanks to cheap deposits and the opening up of the retail market. They can not do so much longer. B borrowers whom they can charge more will have to be found – and this means reaching out to the SME and rural segments.

The RBI has tried to foster greaer inclusion by giving branch licences mainly in underserved areas and recently by reworking priority sector norms. A better way of doing so would be banks towards putting in place systems for measuring risk-adjusted return on capital (Raroc) for every borrower.

Today banks focus on large corporates and the retail sector and ignore the rest because they are not in a position to measure Raroc. Once they begin to Raroc, they will see the attractiveness of other business segments. They will come to realize that financial inclusion is a business imperative.

V

Ways to Deepen Financial Inclusion

Recognizing the importance of financial inclusion, several policy interventions have been undertaken to address this in the Indian context. The most important of these include the expansion of state-owned banks into rural areas and the creation of specialized rural finance institutions such as the Regional Rural Banks (RRB) and cooperative banks. Despite these well-intentioned efforts, the state of access to finance leaves much to be desired. Design aspects of the financial system architecture are crucial to universalizing access.

1. One key requirement is an environment that promotes the emergence of sustainable financial service providers to work in under-served markets. The traditional view in credit, especially in these markets, has been that the originator of loans is also required to manage the implied credit risk of these activities. The dilemma posed by this in the context of serving poor households and rural India is that entries best suited to 'originate' such as MFIs and other NBFCs and not-for-profit companies are not in a position to raise capital in the quantum required to back the underlying scale of lending.
2. There should be a separation of the origination and risk warehousing functions, making a case for numerous thinly capitalized local entities that specialize in understanding customer needs and running cost-effective operations which in turn are backed by financial institutions/banks with the ability to diversify risks and raise capital. This separation will permit the optimum use of scarce capital in the system without compromising on scale of outreach. This insight is equally pertinent when thinking about making access to savings universal, where the recent Banking Correspondent Act permits partnerships between banks and non-bank entities.
3. The optimum scale of originating entities is an important aspect of design; it must be large enough to afford investments in robust operating systems but contained enough to reap the benefits of local knowledge. Also, in order to encourage entrepreneurial providers to emerge in these markets, they must be able to fully meet the cost of providing services on an ongoing basis. Regulation that takes the form of price caps, for instance, is antithetical to this notion.
4. There are also important regulatory considerations in financial inclusion. We need regulation that is outcome-driven and model-neutral. In other words, rather than

encourage specific configurations such as, say, cooperative banks, regulation should be focused on encouraging diversity of approaches to deepening access. The outcomes that regulators should care about are: *(a)* Whether access to financial services is universal, *(b)* Whether such access is of a quality that is acceptable (here, quality is used to cover aspects such as lender-borrower relationship and features of financial services offered), and *(c)* Whether providers are sustainable and meet certain governance norms. Regulation must not for favour, either by way of diluted capital adequacy norms or direct subsidies, one or the other model for reasons beyond these.

5. The role of the government in financial inclusion is much debated. The biggest contributions lie in creating systemic infrastructure that takes the form of unique identification numbers, payments systems, credit bureau and electronic auction markets that stimulate market activity as a whole as opposed to more interventionist approaches that promote specific institutional types (Mor: 2007).
6. Affordable financial services must include not only need-based credit, but also insurance services, payment and remittance facilities, and, in due course, financial advice. Mindset aspects include promoting trust and financial discipline in the rural populace and a revised sense of opportunities amongst bankers.
7. So far, rural operations of commercial banks have not been as commercially lucrative as operations in the more developed urban and metro centres. Their performance in terms of asset quality and composition has not been much better than that of the RRBs, Rural Cooperative Banks and PACs, all of whom had the rural growth mandate, but floundered because of weak technology, low capital bases, inadequate human resources, lack of professional skills and exclusion from reforms. For commercial banks, hitherto, finance to the rural sector has been of small value and largely by way of dispensing government sponsored schemes, which have had abysmally low recovery percentages. The growth of NGOs, coupled with the SHG movement, has brought about a radical change in views. Recovery rates of over 90 per cent have made such finance a very acceptable

and sought after proposition. Added to this, the new-found interest of corporates in rural India present entiring possibilities, particularly in investment credit.

8. While access to credit is important and vital, other issues of viability, servicing and pricing need to be addressed so as to encourage and expand the outreach that the new model has brought in. In a situation where credit is asset based, i.e., ownership of assets commanding accessibility to credit, equitable distribution of credit is a major challenge. One other major constraint in taking financial services to the unbanked is the transaction costs which are much higher on account of the small ticket size, geographical spread, lack of quality manpower and intense supervision required. While technology can be a mitigator to some extent, I believe cost-effective inclusive growth can be realistically achieved only if we include the existing operators who are in the field, such as the NGOs, local business facilitators and possibly even the moneylenders, who have first-hand knowledge of the credit risks and consumption needs of persons, speak the local language and are available dawn to dusk (Ali: 2007).
9. On the path of inclusive growth, the government can definitely contribute by way of enabling policy and legislative support. A case in this is the adoption of the model APMC Act.

NOTES

1. No. 13, March, p. 11211. See the Annual Policy statements of the RBI (2005a, 2005b, 2006a) and the budget speech of the Finance Minister for 2006-07. The various aspects of financial inclusion are covered in a speech by Leeladhar, V. (2006). Also see Box 5.3 on financial inclusion in RBI (2006b).
2. For further details on the targets and sub-targets, refer to RBI (1983) and Das Gupta (2002).
3. This switchover is based on the recommendation of the Committee on Financial System (CFS) (Chairman: M. Narasimham), which recommended total deregulation of interest rates, i.e., interest rates were to be determined by market forces without subsidizing the small borrowal accounts at a relatively low cost.
4. For details refer to Notes on Tables in Vol. 34 of the RBI publication Basic Statistical Returns of Scheduled Commercial Banks in India, March 2005. As per the definition given therein, there are 16 segments

that come under the purview of the priority sectors. These are repeated for ready reference: (1) agriculture and allied activities, (2) small-scale industries including loans for setting up industrial estates, (3) small road and water transport operators, (4) small business, (5) professional and self-employed persons, (6) retail trade, (7) state-sponsored organizations for scheduled castes/scheduled tribes, (8) education, (9) housing, (10) self-help groups (SHGs)/non-government organizations (NGOs), (11) consumption loans granted under the consumption credit scheme, (12) net funds provided to sponsored RRBs, (13) advances to software industry units having credit items upto Rs. 1 crore, (14) advances to food and agro-based processing sector which do not satisfy small-scale industry norms, (15) credit offered to weaker sections under different schemes, and (16) investment in venture capital.

5. The year 2005 was an exception, as the non-food credit growth in this year emanated from sectors other than agriculture and industry, particularly housing, small road transport operators and retail loans. See Box III 2: "High Credit Growth: Is it a Cause of Concern?" discussed in RBI (2005a).
6. In tune with the changes in credit policy, the information system on BSR on banking statistics is suitably changed. All borrowal accounts, each with a credit limit of Rs. 2 lakh or less are classified as small borrowal accounts from March 1999 onwards. For accounts with a credit limit above Rs. 2 lakh each, truncated distributions according to different classificatory characters are presented in the volumes brought out annually by the RBI. Surveys in respect of small borrowal accounts are conducted by the RBI periodically, and provide useful adjunct for the BSR data on banking statistics.
7. The SBA survey of the RBI provided useful information on the number of KCC accounts and the outstanding loan amounts, whereas the RBI publication Trend and Progress of Banking in India gives only the number of credit cards agency wise without reference to credit.
8. See GoI (2001) for a detailed discussion on these aspects in the chapter on 'Informal Financial Sector Statistics.'

REFERENCES

Mor, Nachiket and Ananth, Bindu (2007): "Inclusive Financial Systems: Some Design Principles and a Case Study," Economic and Political Weekly, Vol. XLII.

Rao, K.G.K. Subba (2007): "Financial Inclusion: An Introspection" Economic and Political Weekly, Vol. XLII, No. 5, February, p. 355.

Mohan, T.T. Ram (2006): "Inclusion, a Business Imperative" The Economic Times, November 30.

Mor, Nachiket (2007): "Making Financial Markets More Inclusive," The Economic Times, January 23.

Ali, Mahpara (2007): "Making Financial Markets More Inclusive," The Economic Times, January 23.

17

Inclusive Finance: Shining SBI

AMALESH BANERJEE

I

How can we attain inclusive development with the support of finance? Finance changes hand. Finances accumulates and through exchange it serve as a fundamental agent of building block. The mechanism is accumulation and investment in productive functions in which the people take part as productive agent. Thus inclusion of people in the development activities take place. When the financial system extend financial support to the marginalized, and under previlized segments of population they obtain effective participation in the process of production and distribution. From the early stage of our planning the government tried to redirect our colonial financial structure in the interest of capital formation and for the benefit of the rural segment of population. That the vast section of our population remain outside the formal financial structure has been emphasized by the Rural Banking Commission and the Rural Credit Survey Committee. Hence the first attempt to develop an inclusive financial structure was the formation of the State Bank of India by nationalizing the Imperial Bank in June 1955, on the basis of recommendations of the Rural Credit Survey Committee. Urge for this nationalization move came from two fronts, first is the rapid capital formation under the public sector and second is the urgent need of extension of banking services to the rural sector in order to relief the farmers from the clushes of private moneylenders and to provide then with necessary capital for rapid production. The first and the second five year plans specifically held out those objectives. Hence the SBI and seven, subsidiaries (of the State Banks of seven princely states) together has became a strong organization entrusted with the task of transforming the hitherto capitalist commercial banking structure to a community banking organization. The SBI family has thus began its march towards a country-wide inclusive banking system. The second attempt to develop an inclusive banking structure was the Reserve Bank of India's unique task of two short-term and long-term agricultural loans for extension functions. Here we briefly bring out the SBI's financial inclusive functions over decade and the corresponding issues. Section II presents the story of its growth in the first decade, the geographical inclusiveness is treated here. The Section III presents the first 25 years growth. Section IV examines the functional inclusive of second 25 years of the basis and the resource Section V state the concluding words.

II

First Decade

The outstanding success of SBI during the first decade has encouraged the Government subsequently in 1969 to nationalize a host of commercial banks. On the recommendation of All India Rural Credit Survey Committee (AIRCSC) the SBI has ventured to become truly all-inclusive banking structure over the decade. In three successive stages it has set up a large number of branches in the unbanked and rural backward regions. The seven subsidiaries are the Central Banks of Seven earlier princely states, namely, the State Banks of Bikaner and Jaipur, Hyderabad, Mysore, Indore, Patiala, Saurashtra and Travancore. This integrated banking structures has taken up an extensive rural credit and development programmes as envisaged by the Rural Banking Enquiry Committee. All-India Rural Credit Enquiry Committee has suggested a strong, integrated, state-sponsored, state-owned commercial banking which is a new pattern in Indian commercial banking structure. Thus since 1955 when the SBI has come into being by nationalization of the former Imperial Bank, the commercial banking structure has extensively spread over different corner of the country in order to extend the financial services to the rural people, particularly to relief them from the age old debt burden.

The SBI group has taken up extensive branch expansion programme in these phases. By the end of 1964 the SBI had set up 140 branches most of these offices were set up in rural unbanked areas. By the end of 1964 the state-associated sector shared one-third of total schedules commercial banks of which more than forty per cent were in rural areas.

The achievement of the first decade of the SBI group is not only geographical extension but also extension of rural credit. Cooperative institutions received extension credit support. Side by side, in the first decade, the SBI group has taken up a number pilot schemes for development of small and medium enterprises and extension of small and medium term credit. The SBI group is the pioneer in extending micro-credit facilities to the under privilized section of population.

A very significant aspect of financial inclusion is to bring the rural people, the savers, in the banking system. Financial intermediation has been very successful. Mobilizing rural saving through branch expansion and extending those to the investors is a very significant function. The SBI group through extension of rural branches mobilized rural deposit and extended credit to the small enterprises has been rapidly transforming the rural economy. This process of rural financial inclusion has contributed to rural development and reducing regional imbalances. SBI's policy of assisting loan to the rural industries has facilitated rapid rural industrialization.

This success story of SBI has emboldened the Government to nationalize the top commercial banks in 1969 and subsequently.

III

First 25 Years

After bank nationalization and SBI has started a new course of rural development with financial support to small enterprises. Thus the SBI group and financial inclusive has become identical. SBI is truly a symbol of inclusive growth; it has grown along with the economy over the century. On 2 June, 1806. The Bank of Calcutta started operation. It was redesignated as The Bank of Bengal in 1809. As the economy grew two other Banks emerged – The Bank of Bombay (in 15 April 1840) and the bank Madras (in July 1st 1843). These three banks were controlled by The Presidency Banks Act of 1876 and came to known as Presidency Banks. The Presidency Banks were merged in 27 January, 1921 into the Imperial Bank of India which was a quasi-central bank.

With the formation of the RBI in 1935 the Imperial Bank has shed the central banking functions. When the SBI came into being on 1st July, 1955 by converting the Imperial Bank, it has been doing the treasury function of the Government. Being integrated with seven subsidiaries the SBI has become truly inclusive and wide extensive. In 2005 with its current market capitalization at Rs. 45000 crores SBI's global ranking is 82 and in Asia its ranking is in the top 20. The SBI thus proceeded on an extensive base and encouraging the various kinds of economic activities and the various economic and social groups.

After nationalization of large number of commercial banks in 1969 the SBI group has become the leader in the financial sector. By extension of country-wide branches, and mobilization of resources the SBI has supported various kinds of economic activities. In this section we consider the structural inclusiveness by setting up branches in rural and urban area, by setting up Regional Rural Banks (RRBs). In the next section we shall see the banks' success in the area of micro finance, community services, personal banking and advance to priority sector. By 1997-98 (Table 1) the Public Sector Banks occupied 90.4 per cent branches but the SBI group shared 26.4 per cent of all branches opened by Public Sector Banks. By June 30, 2007 the rural branches (Table 2) of SBI group is 36.7 per cent out of the Group's total branches. The Semi-urban centres occupy 29.6 per cent of the groups' branch total (14058).

SBI has set up in 2004 different segments like Corporate Banks Group, National Banking Group, International Banking Group, Associates and subsidies.

SBI Corporate Group consists of five Strategy Business Units (SBU) viz.: Corporate Accounts Group (CAG), Leasing SBU, Project Finance SBU, Mid Corporate Group and Stressed Assets Management Group (SAMG). While CAG cover the forex bills, pre-shipment and post-shipment vendor, Finance Group for Industry majors, the Project Finance SBU focus on core and infrastructure sectors like power, telecommunication, oil and gas, roads, bridges, ports and urban infrastructure. This indicates how the SBI Group is extending to inclusive advances for development of the economy.

SBI's personal banking, community services, priority sector lending, particularly to the weaker sections, micro finance to self-help groups, small and medium enterprises and agricultural finance are the special areas through which rural indebtedness is reduced, employment and income are generated.

In recent years SBI linked—SHG Group and the Regional Rural Banks (RRBs) are striking examples of inclusive finances which the Gorwala Committee particularly recommended for the SBI in 1955.

SBI has sponsored 30 Regional Rural Banks (RRBs) which are spread over 102 districts in 16 states with a net work of 2350 branches out of the total (14506) branches of SBI by end March 2005 (Table 2). By end March 2005, the aggregate deposits and advances of the SBI sponsored RRBs stand at Rs. 8794.14 crores and Rs. 4333.00 crores respectively. The appendix gives this details of this second tire banking of the SBI.

Agricultural Banking Business

At a time when the Government of India through its budget 2008-09 has waived Rs. 71 thousand crores debt of rural farmers throughout the country, we must remember that SBI has been formed in 1955 with the principal objective of releaving the farmers from the debt burden which caused thousands of farmers to commit suicide throughout the country.

Success of SBI has encouraged the government end in 1969, 14 major commercial banks were nationalized. After of 25 years of operation in 1980, the bank accounted for 28.9 per cent of the total priority sector advances of all scheduled commercial banks. In 1980 SBI has set up 44 Agricultural Development Branches and the strategy of village adoption helped to accelerate the power of assistance to agriculture from Rs. 88 crores in June 1969 to Rs. 1,110 crores in 1980. The Bank's advance to agriculture accounted for 17.7 per cent of its total advances at the end of 1980. Thus exceeding the goal of 16 per cent laid down by the Government to be achieved by 1985.

The SBI has become lead bank in 77 lead districts out of the 77 lead districts, 71 are industrially backward and mostly situated in hilly tribal regions. The lead bank prepared credit plan for these 71 districts. Agricultural development branches extend credit facilities to village development boards. The bank geared up its branches to revitalizing activities under the 20 points economic programme (Revised).

The SBI has completed 25 years in 1980 and fifty year in 2006. Here we briefly assess the achievements of the Bank in two periods. Under the first twenty five years bank's support to the agricultural in rural areas was significant. During the first twenty five year the bank supported the small and marginal farmers in their cultivation weaving, housing construction. All public sector banks' advance to priority sector was 14.5 per cent of total advance in 1969, but increased to 43.0 per cent in March 2001. (Table 5) 25 years' achievement may be assessed from the following highlights. Growth of SBI during next 25 years is shown below.

SBI Year of Growth at the End of the Year

(Rs. Crores)

	1955	*1960*	*1965*	*1969*	*1970*	*1975*	*1980*
Paid up Capital or Reserve	12	13	16	20	21	76	214
Deposits other Accounts	226	576	735	1227	1441	3598	9636
Advances	106	232	481	841	1115	2501	7213
Total Agri. Advance				92	122	241	1110
Small Scale Industries				7	24	52	304
Expense from Investment	117	300	264	358	448	1100	3024
No. of Offices	497	907	1276	1673	2122	3831	5605

Concluding Overseas Offices.

Source: SBI Annual Report 1980.

We have seen so far that the mission of financial inclusiveness with which the SBI has been tested considerable during the quater century of its financial service to the nation. The twin objectives of the government at the time of late eighties ware to reduce the inflation which reached at 29.8 per cent in 1979 and the implementation of 20 point programme.

In May 1980, the RBI switched over from M1 (currency with the public, demand deposits with banks and the deposits with the RBI) as masure of money stock to M3 (agg. Monetary resources adding time deposits to M1).

SBI has substantially extended credit for the achievement of 20 point programmes. Success of the nationalised banks in general and SBI in particular has encouraged the authority to nationalise some other banks. In April 15, 1980, the Government of India nationaled 6 scheduled commercial banks, whose individual time and demand deposits exceeded Rs. 200 crores with that the number of public sector banks rose to 28 accounting for about 91 per cent of total deposits and advances of commercial banks in the country.

Banks success where in agriculture; branch expansion and credit depreciation to the weaker section and small scale industries. Agricultural development branches (144) village adaption scheme and Gramodaya Scheme Integrated Rural Development Scheme of the SBI have been very successful. At the end of 1980 the bank has set up 15 RRBs. Which extended credit at concetional rates. During 1980 the bank formulated second round of credit plan or all its 77 lead districts. On the basis of 20 point programme the bank assisted bonded labourers to break away from their slackles by providing them productive activities. Under various schemes, the bank assisted cobblers, sweepers, scarangers, bulkers, bone collectors, mobile barbers, works – man, quarry workers, barter traders no mads. Thus the SBI Group has shown the line of success during the first 25 years of its existence. Against this backdrop lot us see the nature of financial inclusion practiced by the SBI during the second quarter century of its services to the nation. From 1981 onwards there has been a significant change in India economic environment. Government policy of economic reform has come into play. Financial sector has also been changed substantially element of competition has been inducted. Commercial banks are also, is some extent, allowed to play the competitive game. Hence during this 25 years of (1980-2006), when the SBI completes 200 years of its existence from origin, the original structural and functional inclusiveness of the bank has been intensified further. We can examine the progress of these fasets over this quarter century. To name those areas of functions: *(a)* Agricultural Credit, *(b)* Credit for small scale and medium enterprises, *(c)* Credit for community development, *(d)* Capital market extension and *(e)* Micro-finance extension.

IV

Second 25 Years

We have already seen the branch expansion programme of the SBI. The SBI group now occupier 25.7 (Table 1) of total commercial bank branches. By 2007 rural branches of SBI group are 38 p.c. of its total branches.

Agriculture still remains the achilles hill of Indian economy Green revolution has passed over. With low productivity, low investment, dedt-ridden farmers are virtually still in the vicious cycle of poverty. Over crowded farming is facing no profit and the farmers are committing suicide every day.

Punjab, the pioneer of Green revolution is now in a dire state. About 30 per cent people are below poverty level. Return from agriculture is declining, bebt is increasing and the cost of production is rising. Under this state of situation farmers' are committing suicide.

Against this situation extension of agricultural credit by commercial banks is very urgent. The bank made record increase in agriculture advances, Rs. 9814 crores during the year 2004-05. SBI has also come out with extensive programme of micro-finance. On the occasion of International year of micro-finance (2005). SBI has been very active in SHG-Bank-Credit Linkage. During 2004-05 the Bank financed 1,69,025 SHGs, with aggregated disbursements of Rs. 696.58 crores taking the cumulative number of SHG credit linked to 343691 with cumulative disbursement of Rs. 1,311,45 crores. SBI is the first commercial bank to be assigned the status of Self-Help Promoting Institute (SHPI). SHG programme has resulted not only economic development but also women empowerment, lessening of social tensions and eradication of social evil like illiteracy.

Contract farming is a viable alternate mode for financing crop loans under tile-up arrangement with corporate/MNC for production of high quality produce with assured marketing arrangement in 2004-05 the bank recorded impressive performance by extending finance to 6,31,006 farmers with aggregate disbursement of Rs. 703.87 crore.

In recent years the SBI group made impressive progress in extending credit to the weaker sections of the community (Table 6). Percentage of weaker section credit to net bank credit of the SBI and the subsidiaries indicates a good record of financial inclusion of the RBI group. State Bank of Mysore (SBM) has a consistent record of around 11 per cent of net bank credit extended to the weaker section. State Bank of Patiala (SBP) also has the same record.

Another aspect of financial inclusion is the community services banking. As a responsible and responsive corporate citizen. SBI seeks to reinvest part of its profit in various community welfare projects to improve the quality of life of the poor, neglected, weaker and down-trodden sections of society. SBI also gives donations to Relief Funds, under children Welfare Funds and to NGOs for the benefit of the under privileged, handicapped and challenged children.

Obviously the priority sector lending and community services have some element of risk. The extent of non-performing assets of SBI group is also notable (Table 3 and 4).

SBI has thus shown an impressive growth and it is the leading commercial bank in Indian sub-continent. The highlights of the operations of the Bank is shown below.

SBI Current Growth Index

	March, 2005	*March, 2004*
Paid up capital and reserves and surplus (Rs. crores)	24,072	20,231
Deposits (Rs. crores)	3,67,048	3,18,619
Advances (Rs. crores)	2,02,374	1,57,934
Number of domestic branches	9,102	9,039
Capital – Adequacy Ratio %	12.45	13.53
Net NPA (%)	2.65	3.68
* Return on Average Assets (%)	0.99	0.94
* Return on Equity (%)	18.10	18.19

* For the year end 2004-05, 2003-04.

Source: SBI Annual Report—2005.

Conclusion

SBI has been created with the spirit of expansion of inclusive finances. Extension of bank credit to the rural areas and to the farmers and neglected section were the prime objectives. Reducing the farmers' indebtedness and rejuvenating the small and medium enterprises were the priority task of SBI. The success of the SBI in this area of inclusive finance has encouraged the authority to further extend the area nationalized banks. The current phenomenon of micro-finance extension is also a part of the SBI finance. The SBI has extended to the corporate area of capital market and foreign countries. But its functions of inclusive finance to the farmers, and poorer section of community is a shining record even after fifty years of its operation. It has shown the last metal by waiving agricultural loans of 25 lakhs farmers as per the Government of India policy of loan waivers to the extent of Rs. 71,000 crores.

Table-1
Branches of Bank Groups (Percentage)

Name of Banks	*2003-04*	*2002-03*	*2001-02*	*2000-01*	*1999-00*	*1998-99*	*1997-98*
Public Sector Banks (27)	88.5	89.2	89.5	89.5	90.3	90.3	90.4
SBI Group	25.7	25.9	26.3	26.2	26.3	26.3	26.4
SBI	17.0	17.3	17.6	17.5	17.6	17.7	17.8
7 Sub of SBI	8.7	8.7	8.7	8.7	8.7	8.8	8.6

Sources: Economic and Political Weekly—Money and Banking. March 19-25, 2005, Table-19.

Table-2(A)
Distribution Com. Bank Branches in India Bank Group and Population Group-wise

Bank Group	*No. of Banks*	*As on June – 30, 2006*				
		Rural	*Semi-Urban*	*Urban*	*Metro*	*Total*
State Bank Group	08	5143 (37.1)	4103 (29.6)	2491 (17.9)	2142 (16.4)	13879 (100.00)
Nationalized Banks	19	12903 (37.6)	7211 (21.0)	7135 (20.8)	7050 (20.6)	34299 (100.00)
RRBs	96	11456 (70.01)	2471 (17.0)	514 (3.5)	35 (0.4)	14496 (100.00)

Source: Trend and Progress of Banks in India, 2006-07.

Table-2(B)
Distribution Com. Bank Branches in India Bank Group and Population Group-wise

Bank Group	*No. of Banks*	*As on June – 30, 2007*				
		Rural	*Semi-Urban*	*Urban*	*Metro*	*Total*
State Bank Group	08	5159 (36.7)	4150 (29.5)	2564 (18.2)	2185 (15.5)	14058 (100.00)
Nationalized Banks	19	12990 (36.7)	7504 (21.2)	7557 (21.3)	7361 (21.3)	35412 (100.00)
RRBs	96	11444 (78.9)	2481 (17.1)	522 (13.6)	59 (10.4)	14506 (100.00)

Source: Trend and Progress of Banks in India, 2006-07 .

Table–3
Net Non-Performing Assets as Percentage of Total Assets and as Percentage of Total Advances

Banks	*2002-03*	*2003-04*	*2004-05*	*2005-06*	*2006-07*
Scheduled Commercial Banks	1.90 (4.40)	1.20 (2.90)	0.92 (2.00)	0.67 (1.22)	0.58 (9.01)
Public Sector Banks	1.93 (4.53)	1.28 (2.99)	0.95 (2.06)	0.72 (1.32)	0.82 (1.05)
Nationalized Banks	2.16 (4.74)	1.40 (3.14)	0.91 (1.85)	0.64 (1.16)	0.53 (0.92)
State Bank Groups	1.58 (4.12)	1.09 (2.70)	1.01 (2.23)	0.88 (1.63)	0.79 (1.32)

Figure in brackets as for net advances percentages.

Source: Reports on Trend and Progress of Banking in India, 2006-07, Table- 27 and 28.

Table–4
Non-Performing Assets in Advances to Weaker Section Under Priority Sector (End March, 2007)

Advance to Weaker Section of which NPA (amount in Crores)

Banks	*Total*	*Amount*	*Per cent*
Public Sector Banks	78,844.69	5,181.15	6.57
Nationalized Banks	51,599.75	3,456.75	6.70
SBI Group	27,244.93	1,724.40	6.33

Source : As Table–1 (Table–30A)
Trend and Progress of Banking in India 2006-07.

Table–5
Advances to the Priority Sectors by Public Sector Bank (PSB), Amount Outstanding (Rs. Crores)

(in percentage)

	June 1969	*March 1998*	*March 1999*	*March 2000*	*March 2001*
1. Agriculture	5.4	15.7	16.3	15.8	15.7
(a) Direct	1.3	13.0	12.9	11.8	11.1
(b) Indirect	4.0	2.8	3.4	4.0	4.6
2. Small Scale Industries	8.5	17.5	17.3	15.6	14.2
3. Other priority sector advances	0.7	8.7	9.9	12.2	11.8
4. Total priority sector advances	14.6	41.8	43.5	43.6	43.0
5. Net Bank Credit	3016	218219	246203	292943	340888

Source: Trend and Progress of Banking 2000-01, Appendix Table 11-14.

Table-6
P.C. of Weaker Section Credit to Net Bank Credit of SBI Group

	2001	2002	2003	2004
SB of Bikaner and Jaipur (SBJ)	3.68	7.22	7.91	6.86
SB of Hyderabad (SBH)	7.42	7.79	6.33	4.38
SBI	7.68	10.01	5.78	7.2
SB Indore (SBI)	8.47	6.96	7.55	6.35
SB Mysore (SBM)	11.75	10.90	10.85	10.04
SB of Patiala (SBP)	10.01	10.02	9.4	10.03
SB of Sourastra (SBS)	4.02	5.73	5.7	4.18
SB of Travancore (SBT)	12.16	10.74	6.29	4.95

Source: Economic and Political Weekly March 19, 2005, p. 1232.

NOTES

We have seen the general achievement of the SBI in respect of inclusive finance. Over last few decades SBI has done series of pilot projects in respect of the priority sector. It has also made evaluation of these projects from time to time. Those evaluations provide some idea of the nature and intensity of the problem. On the basis of these evaluation the bank formulates new action programmes.

(*a*) As early as 1978, the bank has brought out an evaluation of the Banks' credit to the weaker sections. The bank has extended credit to several weaker sections such as conch shell bangle making, auto-cycle rickshaw puller, bel metal craft, basket making etc. The verification shows interesting results. The magnitude of over dues, varies from one to another. The study of Dhanbad and Purnea of Bihar shows that loans were granted by the Agricultural and Rural Development Branches (ARDB) of the bank. Repayment of loan are satisfactory, and wilful default in limited.

(*b*) Similarly evaluation report from Ambala District (Punjab) of the financing schemes of Deep Tubewells indicated that these schemes emply benefited the farmers both in terms of output and employment. One important benefit is that farmers were saved from taking loans from moneylenders.

Two other outstanding features are – IRDP loan and the District Credit Plan.

(*c*) The challenging IRDP of the Central Government to alleviates rural poverty has received full support from the SBI. SBI assisted 17.5 lakhs of beneficiaries with Rs. 403.06 crores of credit during the Sixth plan. A study of beneficiaries in 13 districts from 12 states in 1987, indicated healthy shift of the farmer from the less remunerative agriculture and allied activities to some of the more productive activities under the village and cottage industry segment and the tertiary sector. About 50 per cent, families which had been bellow the poverty line when they received assistance, have crossed the poverty lines.

(*d*) SBI had prepared district (credit plan under its Lead Bank Scheme (77 out of 407 districts in the country) first in 1974-75.

The evaluation study of the Parbhani district of Maharashtra conducted in 1980-81, revealed some intersect oral and intrasectoral unevenness in the targets achieved in respect of industries and services segments. However, the study showed that notable improvements took place in the agricultural sector in terms of increase in area under irrigation, area under H Y Vs of crops, use of fertilizers, yield level of crops etc. This study indicated that the impact of loans extended to the small business and small industries segment were very beneficial.

These notes reflect briefly the nature of inclusive finance extended by the SBI much ahead of present call for that. Thus SBI is the leader and pioneer in respect of inclusive credit extension.

APPENDIX

SBI—Sponsored RRBs

30 RRBs are spread over 102 districts in 16 states with a network of 2350 branches.

1. Alakananda Gramin Bank.
2. Arunachal Pradesh Rural Bank.
3. Bastar Kshetriya Gramin Bank.
4. Basti Gramin Bank.
*5. Bikaner Kshetriya Gramin Bank.
6. Bilashpur - Raipur Kshetriya Gramin Bank.
7. Bolangir Anchalik Gramya Bank.
8. Bundelkhand Kshetriya Gramin Bank.
*9. Couvery Grameena Bank.
10. Damoh-Panna-Sagar Kshiling Gramin Bank.
11. Ellaqui Dehati Bank.
12. Ganga Yamuna Gramin Bank.
*13. Goleonda Grameena Bank.
14. Gorakhpur Kshetriya Gramin Bank.
*15. Jamnagar Rajkot Gramin Bank.
*16. Junagadh Anirdi Gramin Bank.
17. Ka Bank Nongkyndong Ri Kshi Jaintia.
18. Kakátiya Grameen Bank.
19. Kalahandi Anchalika Grammya Bank.
*20. Kalpatharu Grameena Bank.
21. Koraput Panchabati Gramya Bank.

22. Krishna Grameena Bank.
23. Langpi Dehangi Rural Bank.
*24. Malwa Gramin Bank.
25. Mangira Grameen Bank.
*26. Marwar Gramin Bank.
27. Mizoram Rural Bank.
28. Nagaland Rural Bank.
29. Nagarjuna Grameen Bank.
30. Palamara Kshetriya Gramin Bank.
31. Parvatiya Gramin Bank.
32. Pithragarh Kshetriya Gramin Bank.
33. Raigarh Kshetriya Gramin Bank.
34. Smastipur Kshetriya Gramin Bank.
35. Samgameshwara Grameena Bank.
36. Santhal Parganas Gramin Bank.
37. Shivpuri – Guna Kshetriya Gramin Bank.
*38. Sri Ganganagar Kshetriya Gramin Bank.
*39. Sri Saraswathi Grameen Bank.
*40. Sri Satharahanas Grameena Bank.
41. Sir Visakha Grameena Bank.
*42. Srirama Grameena Bank.
*43. Surendranagar Bhyavnagar Gramin Bank.
*44. Vidisha Bhopal Kshetriya Gramin Bank.

* Shared 14 Grameen Bank were sponsored by Associated Banks of SBI.

Part–IV : DECENTRALIZATION AND GANDHIAN ECONOMICS

18

Decentralized Planning for Inclusive Growth

S.N. TRIPATHY

An attempt has been made in this chapter to focus on concepts and issues pertaining to implementation of decentralized planning in the context of tribal development, with the special objective of inclusive growth. It assesses the experiments in and the policies on decentralized planning as well as summarizes the inferences drawn from the analysis.

This chapter also portrays the critical issues involved in the process of democratic decentralization to the tribal community who are not only marginalized but also been excluded in the process of planning.

After independence it was conceived that there should be transformations in the social structure, and the concept of welfare state was supposed to promote socio-economic development on a large scale and accorded more priority on social justice. The block level plan or village level plan or the local plan or grassroot plan or the decentralized planning—are the usual terms, which we found a rationale in terms of participation of the people for whom plans are actually meant. A practical planner has been entrusted with the responsibility of solving localized problems, development of certain segments of the population, striking a harmonious blending between mobilization of resources and optimum utilization of social overhead capital. Before we delve deep to the issue of local planning in the context of tribal development, we may focus on the background of the decentralized planning in India.

Background of the Decentralized Planning During the Plan Period

In the Industrial Policy Resolution of 1948, we accepted mixed economy as an economic system and subsequently accorded importance to planning as an instrument of fulfilling the socio-economic objectives. In the evaluation processes of planning in India, we experience that on 15th March 1950 Planning Commission was established. National Development Council was set up in 1952 to strengthen and mobilize the efforts of the nation in support of the 5-Year Plans.

The Balwantrai Mehta Committee (1957) recommended the constitution of statutory elective local bodies with the necessary resources, power and authority devolved on them and a decentralized administrative system working under their control. The Dantwala Committee (1977) emphasized the block level planning. The Ashok Mehta Committee (1978) in the context of implementation of rural development programmes, insisted on the institutional design for Panchayati Raj. The Hanumantha Rao Committee called for the involvement of the people in the planning and implementation of development schemes. The Krishnamurthy Committee (1985) recommended the revival of the Panchayati Raj system so that related to planning; implementation and monitoring of rural development could be assigned to it. The Singhvi Committee (1986) suggested measures for reorganizing villages to make village panchayats more viable. Thus, various committees appointed by the Government of India as well as different State Governments, recommended decentralization of power and responsibilities to the lowest level. Planning has been a flexible process, subject to corrective actions based on changing assessment of both resources and needs. It is therefore, in case of local planning, if the planners succeed in drought-proofing a part of a location which may further lead to transfer the geographical and economic dimensions of locality to an anticipated level, there by further viable alternations can be incorporated in the future plans or programmes of the local planning.

Over and above, the Five Year Plans of the Central Government too advocated decentralized planning. Specific to a small and homogeneous geographical unit or location has been formed a distinctive feature of planning since its inception. The community development programme emphasizing on decentralization of development efforts aimed at the development of block/taluka. Intensive agricultural programme and Panchayati Raj bodies which emerged in 1960s intended to be local specific approach.

The Fifth Five Year Plan (1974-79) document envisaged that every state would bring out a supplement to their documents giving details of the rationale for resource allocation, sectoral allocation of outlay and physical target for each district. This was expected to realize and also lay a firm foundation for rationalization of planning process at the district level through subsequent reorientation of plans according to the local needs and the revision of physical contents of district plan in the light of annual performance. Besides many area specific and beneficiary-oriented programmes like the Desert Development Programme, Drought—Prone Areas Development Agency and Marginal Farmers and Agricultural Labourers Project, etc. were introduced. These were the centrally Sponsored Programmes on sharing basis without integration and co-ordination with other rural development programmes. Planning has been a national intervention on behalf of a public agency in the overall decision-making process. Similarly, the Ninth Five-Year Plan (1996-2000) mentioned that the states are required to endow the Panchayats with such powers and authority, which enable them to function as institutions of self-government as envisaged in the constitution.

Mobilization of own resources by the Panchayats was seen as the important priorities in the Ninth Plan. To enable the Panchayats to prepare the plan for economic development and social justice, they must be backed with adequate finance, personnel and administrative supports. Tenth Plan Approach has aptly remarked that democratic decentralization not an end in itself but a process for harnessing energies of people for bringing about social transformation. We have noticed that both Central and State Government grants to local governments are specific and 'tied' to particular purposes. Despite recommendations of State Finance Commissions the system of grant to local governments in most of the states has not been rationalized and suffers from inadequacy and uncertainty.

Much emphasis has been placed on decentralized planning, on the immediacy to the people for whom plans are drawn up, and on the involvement of the people in the planning process. Surprisingly, scanty attention has been paid in subsequent guidelines to organizing people for implementing plans. Plan statements cannot be merely indicative; rather they have to be translated into concrete activities well adapted to the realities of the region. Control over various regional resources will be largely in the hands of the people. If the totality of resources has to be allocated in an optimal fashion for the development of the region, then the cooperation of those who control the resources becomes necessary. Since we are concerned about the resources and the development of the region as a whole, we must consider the people of the region as a whole. It, therefore, becomes necessary to emphasis on the role of the organizations of the people in the planning process.

Since the concerns of district planning so widely overlap those of area planning, one would have expected considerable debate on this issue. There should be some discussion on the role of administrators and politicians. To be sure, the process of planned development needs administrators to implement it and politicians to represent and articulate the interests of their clients. It has been, however, necessary to highlight the role of the organization of the people per se in this process if area-specific programmes are to be followed.

Tribal Sub-plan: An Approach to Decentralized Planning

In the context of tribal development plans, specifically targeted to tribal concentrated regions, usually we notice Integrated Tribal Development Programme (ITDP) or Tribal Sub-plan Approach, Drought Prone Area Programme (DPAP), National Rural Employment Guarantee Programme (NREGP) and a series of interventions are made targeting the tribal poor.

Article 46 of the Constitution of India places a special responsibility on the state to "promote with special care the educational interests .... of the Scheduled Tribes." The exploitation, social, political and economic of the tribals is as much an integral part of our history as it is of many other contemporary societies. To expect, therefore, that the needs of the tribals in the developmental context would be treated differently and considered more urgent than those of the rest of the population is wholly realistic. It is with the intention of meeting these needs that the tribal sub-plan was promoted as a part of the Fifth Five Year Plan.

The concept of having a separate tribal sub-plan makes sound sense on various grounds. Firstly, the tribal population is concentrated in certain geographical pockets through out the country. Secondly, these areas have been, by and large, depleted of natural resources over a period of time. Thirdly, the population composition of these areas is fairly homogeneous, in so far as the non-tribals have been living apart from the tribals. It would, therefore, be necessary to draw up plans which are specific to these areas and which would cater to the needs of the local populace. Such plans would then represent a combination of the resource and need-based approaches.

It would be worthwhile to bear in mind the criteria that such plans need to fulfill in order to be effective. It has been proposed that tribal development will imply *(a)* development of technology, *(b)* emergence of new structure, and *(c)* emergence of new social values and attitudes. However, caution has been advocated, lest the traditional fabric of tribal life be destroyed before a new pattern emerges. One could take issue with such a formulation of the criteria. In the first place, we must ensure that technology, appropriate or otherwise, will not be anticipated to yield results in the absence of a reform of agrarian relations. While it has been true that a very large majority inhabiting such areas is tribal, it is equally true that the small resident non-tribal minority (and often, even non-residents), along with a tiny number of tribals, control formally or informally, the economic activities.

The principal impediment to the utilization of whatever resources that is available is not necessarily the availability of a technology but the existence of an agrarian structure that condemns the tribals to a life of exploitation. The plans for tribal areas could thus be initiated with an intention of rectifying this situation. The question of internal social structures, values and attitudes has been intrinsically connected with the external structure. The internal structure should be such that it should be strong and resilient enough to accomplish the task. To hold up some structures as ideal types and impose them upon the tribals, depicting them as result of the development process, has to be both facile and somewhat inconsistent.

Any plan that contemplates merely the injection of large dose of finances into tribal areas necessarily overlooks this dimension: Such influxes could well end up strengthening the existing structure. The converse, of course, is not true. A good workable plan needs finances, but it has to be coupled with other activities. What has been to be anticipated from tribal plans is that in addition to effective area plans in so far as using resources are been concerned, they should, as a prerequisite for the operation of area plans, attempt basic institutional changes. Instead of regarding politics as a residual factor to be tolerated as nuisance value, the planned change must emphasize the scope of the political economy. The problem of eradicating poverty has been a serious phenomenon in India, but what introduces an element of difference, and hence the need for a different approach in tribal areas, has been the fact of exploitation. But, based on our experience, we can provide some insights relating to the reasons why such plans could not percolate benefits to the target group which were intended at their initiation.

General backwardness of tribal communities, illiteracy and lack of awareness, lack of social mobility, inefficient planning, planning not addressed to the felt needs of the local tribes, are some of the reasons. Hence, the above mentioned points must be kept in view while formulating local planning and thus, a flexible approach should be adhered to in implementing the lessons gained in the field experience or experiments with closer involvement of people in the planning process. What has been required in case of block planning or local planning is to investigate local resources and the extent of their utilization.

As already been pointed out the major concerns of planning could be listed as resource identification, allocation, and mobilization. For area planning, as has been discussed above, the question of allocation refers, however, only to activities and not regions. The crucial questions are, therefore, those relating to resource identification which would help generate alternatives and mobilization. The planning process can be indicative or innovative, or both and allocative or adaptive or both. For an area planning approach, it would be necessary to stress the innovative and the adaptive aspects.

In its approach to local planning in a broad national framework, the planning has to involve local NGOs and finally, the administrators, politicians, and local inhabitants, in determining the felt needs of the people, mobilization, and allocation of resources, inflow of funds from the block level or from other funding agencies.

The need for integrated local area plan, beyond on specific endowments and needs of each area, was started from the beginning of planned development in 1950's. The Constitutional 73rd and 74th Amendments mandated local planning at village panchayat, intermediate panchayats and district panchayat levels etc. Ensuring that panchayats and municipalities are involved at the planning stage has been an important objective of the panchayati raj ministry-driven programme. In fact, the money can be utilized only where Panchayati Raj Institutions are in place and functioning.

The Constitution of India has delegated powers to Panchayati Raj Institutions to form local self-government and to undertake developmental programmes. Relevant data sets at the district level and below are therefore essential for panchayati raj members as they are expected to participate more and more in planning and the programme implementation.

National Rural Employment Guarantee Act (NREGA) and Excluded Tribals

Participatory plans drafted by these two institutions will be consolidated into the district plan by the district planning committee. This would reflect all the financial resources available in the district and ensure their optimal use, without delay, diversion, duplication and leakage. With regard to local planning, an important effort has been to increase agricultural productivity and thereby increase farm incomes and employment as a major instrument for poverty alleviation. These will need to be supplemented by special targeted programme aimed at improving the welfare of vulnerable groups in rural areas. Employment programmes in rural areas have been the most important of these anti poverty programmes and India has a long history of such programmes. A number of employment generation schemes had been initiated in India, especially since the mid-1960s, in order to help the poor raise their income levels through additional employment. Most of the initial schemes were tentative and limited in scope. At the end of the 1970s, an attempt was made to rationalize these schemes into two comprehensive nationwide schemes – the National Rural Employment Programme (NREP) and the Rural Landless Employment Guarantee Programme (RLEGP). The operation of these schemes left much to be desired; assets created were usually not economically productive, felt needs of the people were not reflected, funds did not go where they were most needed, the system of project approval was inefficient and time-consuming, and the states tended to use the funds allocated for the programmes for other purposes. All this led to the replacement of NREP and RLEGP with a single scheme - the Jawahar Rozgar Yojana (JRY) towards the end of the 1980s. JRY, a nationwide programme, is funded jointly by the Central (80%) and State (20%) Governments. Allocation of funds is based on a formula designed to ensure that the distribution of funds corresponds to the distribution of the poor across the regions. Part of the funds (less than 25%) allocated to a state are earmarked for two sub-schemes of JRY: Indira Awaas Yojana—a scheme for building houses free of cost for the weaker sections (Scheduled Castes, Scheduled Tribes and Liberated Bonded Labour), and the Million Wells Scheme for constructing dug-wells free of cost for small and marginal farmers. Of the remaining funds, 80 per cent goes to village panchayats and the balance to the district authorities.

The villages Panchayats are free to decide on the use of funds, except that 22.5 per cent must be devoted to works that directly benefit the weaker sections of society. Funds allocated to the district, however, must be spent in accordance with a given schedule, including an individual beneficiary scheme for the Scheduled Castes and the Scheduled Tribes. Significantly, 10 per cent of the funds are to be allocated for the maintenance of assets already created. The choice of community assets to be built is not restricted.

Assets that may be owned by a group of individuals can be included in the works if they result in a flow of income for the group. Land development in small and marginal farms is also permissible if the owners are in the poor category, as are works for identified poor individuals among the weaker sections.

The responsibility for identifying and executing works rests at the district level with the District Rural Development Agency or the Zila Parishad (district Panchayat) and at the village level with the village Panchayat. The latter is empowered to take up any project that has been technically appraised and approved by the Panchayat Samiti (block Panchayat). To avoid deviation and malpractice, the village Panchayat is required to prepare muster rolls in detail for the labour employed and display them at a public place. For all works under JRY, the wage paid is the minimum wage as prescribed under the Minimum Wages Act. Two kilograms of food grains at subsidized rates are also made available to the workers.

All works undertaken are included in the Annual Action Plan. Priority is required to be given to incomplete works from the previous plan. At the village level, the plan has to be discussed in the village

Panchayat and care has to be taken to ensure that top priority is given to works benefiting the weaker sections of the community. The village Panchayat must also report on the progress of work to the Gram Sabha (village assembly) at least twice a year. The National Rural Employment Guarantee Act (NREGA) has been enacted which provides assurance of up to 100 days of employment at the minimum wage to each household in rural areas wishing to make use of it. The employment would be provided on projects chosen by the elected village councils and the guidelines specify that top priority should be given to irrigation and water management schemes. Unlike earlier employment programmes, this scheme included a guarantee in the sense that if employment cannot be provided, unemployment compensation will be provided at least 25 per cent of the wage. Although the programme opens to each household, actual demand for employment is expected to be limited to households below the poverty line. Together with other special programmes relating to provision of housing for the poor, old age insurance, and schemes for supporting self-employment, this programme will provide an element of social security that should help to reduce poverty.

Backward Regions Grant Fund (BRGF)

In recent years to ameliorate the socio-economic situation in the backward regions of our country the Backward Regions Grant Fund (BRGF) has been implemented. The Backward Regions Grant Fund has been designed to redress regional imbalances in development. The fund will provide financial resources for supplementing and converging existing developmental inflows into 250 identified districts, so as to:

(a) Bridge critical gaps in local infrastructure and other development requirements that are not being adequately met through existing inflows.

(b) Strengthen, to this end Panchayat and Municipality level governance with more appropriate capacity building, to facilitate participatory planning, decision-making, implementation and monitoring, to reflect local felt needs.

(c) Provide professional support to local bodies for planning. implementation and monitoring their plans improve the performance and delivery of critical functions assigned to Panchayats, and counter possible efficiency and equity losses on account of inadequate local capacity.

Integrated development will commence with each district undertaking a diagnostic study of its backwardness by enlisting professional planning support. This will be followed by preparing a well-conceived participatory district development perspective plan to address this backwardness during 2006-07 and the period of the Eleventh Five-Year. The Panchayats at the village, intermediate and district level, referred to in Part IX of the Constitution, will undertake planning and implementation of the programme, in keeping with the letter and spirit of Article 243 G, while the Municipalities referred to in Part IX A will similarly plan and implement the programme in urban areas in conformity with the letter and spirit of Article 243 W, read with Article 243 ZD of the constitution.

The BRGF aims to take participatory governance and big funds to 250 backward districts. The fund will pump in a minimum of Rs. 10 crore annually into each of the 250 identified districts during the Eleventh Plan period (2007-12) to bridge critical gaps in district planning, implementation and development. Another Rs. 5 crore will be dispensed annually according to the population or area covered, as some districts are large. The fund covers all districts where the National Rural Employment Guarantee Scheme is being implemented, and all districts mentioned in an inter-ministerial task group report on backwardness constituted by the Planning Commission of India.

While Bihar accounts for the maximum number of districts to be covered under the fund (36), Uttar Pradesh comes next with 34; Madhya Pradesh has 24, Jharkhand 21, Orissa 19, Maharashtra and Rajasthan 12 each, Andhra Pradesh 13 and West Bengal and Assam 11 each. Several other states have also been covered. The fund has been expected to help mitigate regional imbalances – a key area of concern cited by the Planning Commission in its mid-term appraisal of the Tenth Five-Year Plan (2002-07) – and contribute towards poverty alleviation in backward districts. The BRGF it has been anticipated that will eventually replace the Rashtriya Sam Vikas Yojana (RSVY), which was scheduled to be wound up in 2006-07, and will take care of all districts covered under the RSVY.

The 'Percolation effect' never worked and much of the developmental expenditure never reached the poor in spite of its sizeable increase over the years. The *'trickle down theory'* didn't address the issues of poverty and unemployment, particularly in the rural areas. It has been felt that growth by itself could not be a panacea for all economic ills of the country. Growth processes came to be considered as much important as growth itself. The planners and policy makers do realize that development efforts in rural areas could be successful only if the development design rests on the foundation of people's participation. It was conceded that rural development strategies could realize their full potential only through the motivation and active involvement of the rural community starting from the grassroots level with special emphasis on the least advantaged. In a country with such a vast geo-political and cultural diversity there is a need to decentralize governance and encourage active participation of people at all levels.

Community development has come to occupy the center stage of planning of many countries. According to Community Development Review, Community development has been a process of social action in which the people of a community organize themselves for planning and action, define their individual needs and solve their problems; execute their plans with a maximum reliance upon community resources; and supplement these resources when necessary with services and material from Governmental and Non-Governmental agencies outside the community.

Decentralization refers to ensuring the participation of people at the lowest level in self-governance and investing power an authority at their disposal so that they determine the direction and the destiny of development of their own community. In nutshell, effective decentralization implies enlisting local resources, identifying local needs, ensuring local participation, enabling local planning, and effecting local execution and finally carrying out local assessment. It is through this all around and multi-level democratization of governance, communities are assured of all-round development.

Effective decentralization, though has been a political process, has been aimed at bringing about economic development and equality and ultimately ensures restructuring of society. Planning has been considered as a method, which can ensure economic growth, promote harmony among different sections of people and pull down the discord among the human institutions within a society.

Thus, there has to be a change in the attitude of officials, experts, elected representatives and the people at large. India's complex geographical, social and cultural landscape necessitates for multi-level planning further, justifying for a planning—which must be people based especially, at the local levels. Moreover, economic equality and social justice are conditions indispensable for the survival of democracy. The objectives of Indian planning have been not only the growth of the economy, but also to make the economy self-reliant, and finally, to ensure that the operation of the economic system should not result in the concentration of wealth and means of production.

But if one examines fifty seven years of decentralization process carried out in India, there are more failures than success stories. India has been a federal state and hence, powers and functions of center and state have been defined by the constitution. Economic and Social Planning has been in the concurrent list of the Central Government But vital areas of development such as education, public health, land, irrigation, agriculture, electricity, local government and a wide range of activities under industries and transport fall within the State list.

A review of the Indian scene brought to light the reality that decentralization and people's participation has become more of a slogan than an action plan to be enacted. During the last 57 years, the virtues of decentralized planning have been repeatedly glorified by the planners but no serious endeavours have been made to practice the same in its true sprit. Attempts at micro planning have been halting and half-hearted while a technological top-down approach prevailed all the time. The process of planning from below which was said to be inoperative, basically centralized in nature and as such could not succeed to bring about the desired changes in the living conditions of the rural poor of India and particularly the tribals.

Decentralized Planning Tribals

In our country tribes constitute more than 8 per cent of the total population, are languishing in the midst of poverty and backwardness. The tribals reside in forests and inaccessible hill areas and maintained their survival oriented culture. The agents of the new order represented by traders, moneylenders, and contractors entered to the tribal regions and exploited them. They provided money lending and took away their fertile lands as a result of which, the tribal proceeded to interior parts of forest. Tribal peoples being illiterate and unskilled are mostly belonging to the labouring community as they eke out their living through manual labour and wage earning. They are the exploited, indebted, and marginalized communities.

Devoid of life supporting system, the tribals have to (more than 90%) cultivate the poor quality of land paucity of land, work as agricultural labourers to eke out a living. These tribal labourers are the victims of myriad forms of exploitation by the highly inter-locking non-tribals axis of power that dominates the land, credit and input markets. As a result, the tribes migrate as construction workers, which require unskilled manual labour. They live in an inhuman condition devoid of all the human rights. Restoring to wage labour and seasonal migration is widely adopted livelihood strategies of tribals in Gujarat.

The resultant marginalization of millions of people threatens the fabric upon which our democracy has been founded. Apparently, people reposing their faith elect the representative who is supposed to protect their interest and safeguard their livelihoods. But the irony is that we behold a different scene when we find the tribal pockets, as the delicate foundation is shaken as their voice is not heeded.

Excluded Marginalized Tribals and their Dependence on Agricultural Sector

In remote forest areas tribes mostly adopt shifting cultivation as a method of agriculture. Known by different names in tribal India, shifting cultivation is called as 'Jhum' in the North East, Kurao and Khullu in Bihar, Waler in Gujarat, Penda, Bewar and Duhiya in Madhya Pradesh, Kunri in Tamil Nadu, Bringa, Podu, Dahi and Koman in Orissa. The land use system is specially restricted within hill slopes below 1000 meters, where we notice high rainfall with low density of population. Depending upon physiographic, rainfall, temperature, soil and density of population shifting cultivation as a suitable method of land use has been practiced in tribal India for centuries. Thus, shifting cultivation is an age-old method of land use, a piece of land is selected, most of the trees and bushes are cut down and set on fire after exposing them to sun. On this land a variety of mixed crops is grown generally for two to four years. Subsequently, the shifting cultivators abandon the plot and search for another plot for such type of cultivation (Tripathy, 1998).

Agriculture being the backbone of the tribal economy and land being the prized possession in tribal areas shifting cultivation is adopted in the absence of large plain land holdings. In view of the large percentage of tribal cultivators engaged in such ruinous practice of shifting cultivation the adverse effects are to be analyzed so as to suggest remedial measures to mitigate the problems arising out of shifting cultivation(Tripathy, *ibid.*).

Forests have both physiological and physical effect on the temperature attendant upon the plant growth. The forests reduce the temperature of the earth because plants transpire water and secondly, because of the Sun's heat are absorbed in the process of evaporation. By reason of its composition living plant substance cannot become heated by the sun's rays. It follows that effect of forests during the growing season is to lower the temperature of the earth and by reducing absorption of heat by earth's surface it lowers the soil temperature and correspondingly reduces evaporation. Forests not only moderate the intensity of heat in summer as a general rule but also modify the extreme cold of winters. Effects of forests on temperature of a region are highly beneficial to men and animals. By diminishing the velocity wind, forests held to decrease wind erosion. They differ much ameliorate the severity of wind by virtue of physical obstruction they offer (Tripathy, *ibid.*).

In nutshell, shifting cultivation results in indiscriminate deforestation in large scale which is followed by soil erosion and the ruination that erosion brings in its wake for vast and rich tracts is a greater ruination.

The extreme poverty compelled many tribals to sell or mortgage their lands to the people of the plains. As a result of which, the tribes of the region were driven to inaccessible forests and hill areas where they maintained their survival-oriented culture. The agents of the 'new order' represented by traders, moneylenders and contractors didn't leave them there either. The outcome of this oppressive 'new order' was that the 'tribal poor' have found themselves exceedingly indebted and alienated from most of their land except for a few pieces of eroded land strips (Tripathy, 1991, pp. 35-36).

Thus, the tribals from time to time deprived of their fertile lands and were subjected to ruthless exploitation by the invading people which have resulted in the hill men's flying in greater and greater wilderness. The infiltration of people from the plains continues resulting in depriving the hill men of the good lands they reclaimed (Tripathy, 1998, p. 232).

Government intervention, spread and expansion of transport and communication, involvement of NGOs, seasonal out-migration of tribals significantly contributed in breaking the isolation of tribals from the non-tribals (Chaudhury, 2004, p. 112). Construction of roads, establishment of industries, and mining activities disrupted the settled tribal properties leading to landlessness, homelessness, joblessness, food insecurity, loss of access to common property resources and social disruption. Thousands of families have been involuntarily displaced from their age—old traditional habitat, and tribes constitute about 40 per cent of the total project displaced population (Fernades, Walter, 1994).

Because of displacement, the oustees underwent an acute psychological, physical, economic trauma as well as identity crisis. The oustees face untold problems due to multiple displacements. The inhuman tragedy and plight of oustees of Hindustan Aeronautics Limited (HAL), Hirakud Dam Project can be well conceived as instances of multiple displacement. The HAL oustees displaced during 1960s for the first time, constrained for displacement in 1980s second time due to Upper Kolab Multi-purpose dam project. Similarly, the oustees of Hirakud Dam Project who were displaced in mid-1950s and resettled in Brajarajnagar area of Jharsuguda district (Orissa) confronted displacement for the second time because of construction of the IB Thermal Power Station in the late 1980s (Tripathy, 2003, p. 193).

Further, it has been observed that during the last 50 years in various dams about 6 crores population have been displaced, out of which 4 crores have virtually become beggars in the streets. On the contrary, these dam projects because of improper utilization of dam water only 10 per cent of agricultural land in India could be irrigated for yielding crops (Tripathy, 2003 p.188).

The researcher has observed that displacement of tribals in project areas resulted in untold misery as the life supporting system of the tribals the common property resources land, forests etc. are snatched away from the tribals by the politicians, engineers and contractors. Most of tribal lands are cultivated as decided by village's chief through community farming. The simple, illiterate, poverty stricken tribes do not know the entitlement of land or 'Pattas'. The procedure of getting land right or 'patta' is so difficult that a tribal farmer cannot get it so easily. Moreover, the Mahajans, businessmen, traders advance loans to needy, poverty-stricken tribals in the mortgage of their land. Ultimately, land alienation takes place in tribal areas. Though the tribals cultivated the land but mostly the 'Pattas' (registered land deed) remain with the non-tribals, traders and contractors. Thus, due to development project a lion's share is taken by non-tribals.

The backwardness of the tribal regions, widespread poverty of the tribals and problems of integrating them with the mainstream of civilization etc., are the stumbling blocks in the path of tribal development. Thus, the tribals in India continued to remain socially, economically and educationally backward and are languishing at the bottom of the socio-economic ladder. For generation together they are residing in inaccessible forest and hilly areas. Their geographical isolation and impoverished economy have made them object of exploitative economic and trade practices of non-tribal living or entering areas. The powerful exogenous forces of moneylenders, contractors, officials having their link with political personnel and police could exert dominant control and gratify the selfish greed of exploiting the tribals. The poverty stricken, illiterate, innocent, simple tribals fail to withstand the countervailing exogenous forces and becoming prey to all types of exploitation (Tripathy, 2007).

Towards Inclusive Growth of Tribals

Notwithstanding the constraints in the effective implementation of decentralized planning in rural India, new hopes have been kindled that an honest implementation of the provisions of the 73rd and 74th Amendments to the Constitution would initiate a genuine process of decentralized planning with the total involvement of local self-government institutions with their newly acquired constitutional status. In the context of tribal development, it is to be noted that effective decentralization for community participation and community development cannot be achieved unless; the entire social, political, economic and cultural foundations and principles of the tribal community are not taken into consideration. Moreover, the traditional patterns of local self-rule have to be respected and not only technical but also humane elements need to be built into the decentralization processes and policies. Effective decentralization is not just limited to community development or tribal development alone; it is the participation of tribals in the development process.

The basic local institutions for participatory planning in India have been set up. However, these institutions ought to have adequate autonomy as units of self-government so as to decide on the local needs and priorities and design and implement the necessary action. The challenge of making this new phase of decentralized planning successful depends on the commitment of the political leadership, bureaucracy and the people themselves. The State Governments have the responsibility of transferring schemes as provided in the 11th Schedule of the Constitution and also of transferring corresponding funds to the Panchayats. Similarly, the staff available for the implementation of schemes related to these subjects should also be placed under the control of the Panchayats. Sufficiently clear and workable regulations have to be framed to streamline the inter-tier relationships and functions of each tier.

The change which has been initiated by the Seventy-third Constitution Amendment needs to be managed and sustained effectively through innovative strategies. Panchayats have been empowered by this Amendment. Access to and effective control over resources is a critical component of this empowerment. The real issues of such access are knowledge and awareness of the needs of the people, legal rights, and availability and accessibility of social and economic resources. These changes in procedures and organizations have as yet not fully taken place as envisaged in the legislation. It also requires restructuring relationships, including looking at gender issues at both the micro and macro level. A culture of equality has to be evolved not only between men and women representatives but also between officials and non-officials manning the decentralized development structure.

Eliminating poverty requires the reduction of isolation and social exclusion. Thus, there is a need to provide access to infrastructure and services to the rural mass so that they can build their assets, reduce vulnerability and develop sustainable livelihood. As the factors affecting rural access are interactive and cannot be considered in isolation, an integrated approach is most suitable for effective accessibility planning. Integrated Rural Accessibility Planning (IRAP) is a need-based multi-sectoral, sensitive methodology for local level planning. It pertains to the improvement of the living and working conditions and aims at ensuring that the available investments are directed towards the most urgent needs of rural communities, for access to basic goods, social and economic services and employment opportunities.

The district has been recognized as the basic unit for decentralized planning functions. Operationalizing the concept of district planning requires functional local institutions. The District Planning Committee is the statutory authority for preparing plans for local development area planning. The involvement of the people in the planning process is necessary to take into account their felt needs, to mobilize local resources, to increase the speed of implementation by securing the people's cooperation, to increase the acceptance of the plan and projects and also to bring about a change in the power structure in people's institutions in favour of the poor.

PESA and Democratic Governance

Decentralization has been often conceived as a political process where by administrative authority, public resources and responsibilities are transferred from Central Government Agencies to lower level organizations, community based organizations or Non-Government Organizations (NGO's) (Crook and Manor, 1998).

Democratic decentralization also implies that there will be greater political participation of local people by which there will be improvement in the quality of life of the people especially the marginalized and tribals.

Government and other public bodies both at the center and the states even in the district and block levels have emerged with gigantic and ambitious programme for the development of the backward communities in general and the tribal people in particular. Their obligations have been made explicit through plans and programmes to improve the socio-economic conditions of those who belong to Scheduled areas.

Article 244 and 244A read with Fifth and Sixth Schedules of the Constitution outline in detail the powers, privileges, rights and responsibilities of the President, Union Government and the Governors regarding the scheduled areas. In addition to Article 46 of Part IV Directive Principles of State Policy of the Constitution which states that "The State shall promote with special care the educational and economic interests of the weaker sections of the people and in particular of the scheduled castes and the scheduled tribes, and shall protect them from social injustice and all forms of exploitation" there are about 20 other Articles which prescribe the whole framework for regulatory and development functions of the state relating to the scheduled tribe population of the country. In addition to the above, special provisions for scheduled tribes have also been made through certain Acts and orders which are protective and ameliorative in nature. Exempting the scheduled tribes from Hindu Succession Act 1956, Hindu Adoption Act 1956 and Hindu Marriage Act 1956, special provisions have been made for their family and land rights. Thus, the customary marriage and succession rules of the scheduled tribes have remained largely untouched. Laws protecting land rights of the tribal communities have recognized their traditional rights over it and restricting its alienation to non-tribals. Most of the State Governments have taken legislative and executive measures in order to protect tribal lands. Moreover, the national policy on tribal development emphasizes on developing the tribals along the lines of their own genius and encouraging in every way their own traditional arts and culture, respecting tribals' rights to land and forests, and working through and not in rivalry to their own social and cultural institutions. Looking at the legislative history it would, thus, be clear that right from the inception of the colonial administration, the scheduled areas were treated distinctly from other areas. The tribals were protected from exploitation; their rights and title to enjoy the lands, their occupation and their autonomy, culture and ecology, were preserved; infiltration of the non-tribals into tribal areas was prohibited. Even the migrant non-tribals were prohibited to purchase the lands in scheduled areas from the tribals except with the prior sanction of the officer appointed by the Government in that behalf (Das, 2005).

The latest Panchayat Extension to Scheduled Areas (PESA) Act 1996 has made it mandatory for the States having scheduled areas to make specific provisions for giving wide ranging powers to the tribals on matters relating to decision-making and development of their community. Technically, when the Act refers to extending the provisions of Part IX of the Constitution to the fifth schedule areas; politically, it gives radical governance powers to the tribal community and recognizes it's traditional community rights over local natural resources. It not only accepts the validity of "customary law, social and religious practices, and traditional management practices of community resources," but also directs the State Governments not to make any law which is inconsistent with these. Accepting a clear cut role for the community, it gives wide ranging powers to Gram Sabhas, which had hitherto been denied to them by the lawmakers of the country (Das, *ibid.*).

Supreme Court Ruling on Forests

The Supreme Court ruling on forest land and the subsequent note of the MOEF seeks to evict all communities residing within forest lands. This is like the Sword of Damocles that can drop at any time on a forest village, and threaten their livelihood (Das, *ibid.*)

Tasks for Civil Society

In discussing PESA, we need to keep in mind that the central point of concern here is the well being of the tribal community. At this point of time, despite PESA as also several other protective measures; there is extensive violation of the very fundamental rights of the tribal people in this country. The state till now does not even accord them a human status, and persists in being the major violator of all laws and constitutional provisions in the tribal regions. If civil society is concerned about these, then it should begin an informed and massive questioning, challenging the state to be lawful and deliver what it undertakes to. There are many means of doing this, and if all get together, then surely these means can be found and applied (Das, *ibid.*)

The Bhuria Committee Report laid down the final framework. It was legislated through PESA Act 1996. This Act made it mandatory for the states having scheduled areas to make specific provisions for providing wide-range of powers to the tribals for their development. The Act recognizes traditional customary rights over local natural resources. It accepts the validity of customary law, social and religious practices of community resources. It emphasizes the role of Gram Sabhas.

The political philosophy of PESA Act contains the essence of decentralization with empowerment, as expressed in the words of Jha (1999, p. 14), "it will correct the distortions in the democratic processes that are affected by the logic of a structured society." The basic feature of the Act is that it recognizes the traditional form of self-governance as well as concedes to its potentialities in setting the grassroot society in the direction of desired development. But the implementation part involves problems. The political elite and bureaucracy, who form dominant part of the state system, do not easily allow any legal correction of the injustice made towards the marginal section of the population. This is because they think that it may loosen their control on ruling power.

The protective aspects have aimed at the preservation of their unique cultural traits, their rights on land and forests and safeguarding against the inhuman exploitation. The developmental aspects have unfolded various welfare measures for the physical, mental and environmental enrichment and ultimately to accelerate the development of tribal economy.

It empowered villages to protect community resources, control social sector functionaries, own minor forest produce, manage water bodies, give recommendations for mining leases, be consulted for land acquisition, identify beneficiaries for poverty alleviation and other government programmes and have a decisive say in all development projects in the villages. It empowered villages to protect community resources, control social sector functionaries, own minor forest produce, manage water bodies, give recommendations for mining leases, be consulted for land acquisition, identify beneficiaries for poverty alleviation and other government programmes and have a decisive say in all development projects in the villages.

With regard to the tribals, the situation has found completely different. But the hostile administration reserves some scope for manipulation as the customary laws, social and religious practices and traditional management practices are not codified.

Section 4(M) of PESA authorizes the Gram Sabha to act in all areas where the tribals face threat to their survival and welfare because of their continued exploitation. The PESA creates legal space for direct community action, and therefore, PESA directly confers ownership to the Gram Sabha on Minor Forest Produce (MFP) which has been a support for their survival. But it has been observed that this right has been neglected or violated rather than adhered to. The commercial value of MFP has been appreciated resulting in the nationalization of MFP and thereby optimizing the state's revenue.

It is unfortunate to note that people go through several elections but they never anticipate that their representative will confer any benefit to them. There has been limited transparency or openness in the processes that go in a block or panchayat. The relationship of master and beggar-slave has been reinforced in almost every interaction between the tribal people and government officials. It has been observed that the major loophole being the provisions of proxy decisions if a Gram Sabha does not take place the first time due to lack of quorum. As a matter of fact, most of the Gram Sabha meetings are passed through proxy in tribal regions. Even where a Gram Sabha is conducted, few are aware of their right and responsibilities. Signatures of the village members are forged to provide the evidence that there is sanction at the village level, and no body questions as the tribes in their villages find it too difficult to pursue the violations. Because the tribes know that any complain will involve them several trips to the urban areas, loss of their daily wage and thus, ultimately their livelihood. If in proper procedure the village meeting is conducted, the genuine beneficiary list prepared in the Gram Sabha can be manipulated at panchayat samiti level.

Thus, despite PESA, as well as several other protective legislations in the tribal regions of our country, there has been extensive violation of fundamental rights and human rights of the tribal people.

However, the initial experiences show that there were few hindrances in achieving decentralized governance, some of which are gradually disappearing. One in this direction is the politicians and bureaucrats at the higher echelon of governance were usually reluctant to relinquish power to the lower levels but the scenario is changing gradually.

The second hindrance lies in the inability of the poor peasants to make their voice heard in the face of elite domination of the traditional power structures. The ingrained problem of elite domination can hardly be resolved, unless the poor themselves can exercise enough bargaining power and be organized so that their collective voice can be audible to the irrigation executives and bureaucrats.

It is lamentable fact that the purpose of the PESA Act has not been completely understood either by the political leaders or by the bureaucracy. People at large are also not aware of the provisions of PESA act except in those areas where the NGOs are seriously working with the people.

The Act clearly prohibits the state to make any law, which would not be in consonance with the customary law, social and religious practices and traditional management practices of community resources. It has clear provisions that the 'Gram Sabha'or the panchayats at the appropriate level shall be consulted before making the acquisition of land in the schedule areas for development projects. Such consultation and consent of the 'Gram Sabha' is mandatory on the part of the Government much before the settlement and rehabilitation of persons affected by such projects in the schedule areas.

Thus, PESA aims at ensuring significant protection against any arbitrary, discriminatory, and motivated action of the state relating to land acquisition and resettlement and rehabilitation (R and R) in tribal regions. It has been revealed that the local administration in league with the company officials was indulging in deliberate falsehood. In the consultation of 'gram sabha' the method adopted is dubious as the consent was obtained through coercion and brutal force (Das, 2003, 4432).

If the tribal identity could be taken away, the main plank of their protest movement could be removed. All the restrictions on tribal land alienation would vanish in to air. Corporate bodies would be free to enter into land transaction at their will with no legal impediments. Whether the local administration is acting on its own or at the behest of the corporate magnates remains an open question (Das, 2003, Bandyopadhya, 2004).

Conclusion

We must realize that in our country, more than 600 millions of people depending on agriculture, there can be no alternative to building agriculture—sound agrarian base on which to develop the whole range of location specific, nature bound livelihoods. For greater equity in development, we need to forge a development strategy that takes into account the immense social, ecological diversity benefiting the tribal labourers who are in the grip of unemployment accompanied by acute distress and poverty (Sundram and Tendulkar (2003), Mukhopadhay and Raja Raman (2007).

It has been observed that non-recognition of tribes over resources and restrictions on their use, alienation tribes from the means of production, denial of due entitlement of labour, distressed payment of wages, and misappropriation of funds, have kept the tribal labour in the web of misery and starvation. In tribal dominated states in India, the life support system of the local tribes has been snatched away by non-tribals and state institutions. As a result, tribal movement originated in fierce struggle of their rights (Tripathy, 2000).

In spite of adequate provisions in the Articles 164, 244, 244(A), 278, 330, 332, 334, 335, 338, 342 and fifth and sixth schedules of the constitution aiming at development and protection of interest of tribals, the powerful exogenous forces of moneylenders, contractors, officials having their link with political personnel and police could exert dominant control and gratify the selfish greed of exploiting tribals. The poverty stricken, illiterate, innocent, simple tribals fail to with stand the countervailing exogenous forces and becoming prey to all types of exploitations (Tripathy, 2003, p. 39).

Despite the vast expansion of the formal credit system in India, the dependence of the rural poor on moneylenders continues in some areas especially for meeting emergent credit requirements. Such dependencies pronounced in the case of marginal farmers, landless labourers, petty traders and rural artisans belonging to the socially and economically backward classes and the tribal population particularly in the resource-poor areas (Tripathy, 2007).

Strong leadership and political will are the necessary conditions for facing the challenge of enabling the local self-government institutions to become effective instruments of social and economic development of rural areas.

It can be inferred from the analysis that notwithstanding the plethora of Acts and legislations passed with a view to providing social justice and ameliorating the living condition of tribals, there has been an inefficient functioning and implementation of Acts in the tribal regions of India.

The benefits of development has not percolated to the local tribal people, rather adversely affected their life style, leading to the violation of human rights, miserable living standard of tribals, restricted the community rights over natural resources, and finally, culminated to identity crisis of the tribals.

In order to put the decentralized planning on track for tribal development and for inclusive growth, strengthening the planning machinery at different tiers of panchayats, integration of rural and urban areas, people's participation etc. is required. In order to bring about socio-economic changes ameliorating their condition in tribal areas, appropriate policy strategy mainly the provisions of PESA should be strictly adhered to.

Stating that the arming of tribals to fight exploitation and policing their protests have been responsible for their growing sense of alienation and isolation, the government has come out with a draft policy to uplift this marginalized section of the population.

The Indian Government has released a draft national policy on tribals to address the issue of developing this section of the population in "an integrated and holistic manner." For the first time since the formation of the Indian republic, 60 years ago, the Ministry of Tribal Affairs released the draft document whose aim is to "uplift the tribals who have been facing acute poverty, alienation from land and lack of livelihood opportunities," in many parts of India. The document was released in New Delhi on July 21, 2006.

The policy will address issues such as the enhancement of human development indicators among Scheduled Tribes (STs) to bring them on a par with the general population, improvement of infrastructure in tribal areas, tribal control over the natural resource base, displacement and resettlement, and the equitable distribution of wealth and opportunities among tribals.

The policy also provides for regulatory protection, socio-economic and political empowerment, increased livelihood opportunities, improved governance and administration, preservation of tribal cultural and traditional rights and knowledge, and protection of tribal traditional knowledge in the intellectual property rights regime.

Steps will be taken to ensure that the benefits granted to ST communities are evenly spread among all ST communities, and, if so warranted, those populations that have caught up with the general population be de-scheduled. A time-bound programme will be initiated to identify the needs of nomadic tribes and their development.

The National Tribal Policy 2006 outlines several new and continuing initiatives for accelerating the pace of welfare and development of tribal areas in the country. An institutionalized monitoring mechanism will be put in place at both the national and state level. Powers will be given to local communities to monitor and oversee the programme's planning and implementation.

The policy itself will be updated periodically. To make it a living document, the Cabinet Committee on Tribal Affairs (CCTA) will be asked to review the policy every three years and redefine its objectives and guiding principles, if necessary, and accordingly recast the strategy to address any new challenges that may emerge (The Indian Express, July 22, 2006, www.indlawnews.com, July 21, 2006).

In this context, the initiative of the Ministry of Rural Development of the Government of India and UNDP project has been mention worthy. The ministry has inked a four-year project (2003-07) in November 2004 'Social Mobilization around Natural Resource Management for Poverty Alleviation' with UNDP.

People especially those who are poor, land less and asset less encounter severe difficulties in securing credit for productive purposes, building community assets, accessing technical knowledge in areas like agriculture, forestry, water management, health, and availing benefits from poverty alleviation schemes and programmes. Often, the poor do not get access to the relevant information, new knowledge or skills. The poor are constrained by an environment characterized by in-efficient local institutions and hierarchical administrative machinery. All this results in shrinking the pool of opportunities for promoting sustainable livelihoods, thereby, perpetuating poverty. The shrinking and continuously degrading natural resource base of the poorest community is a major cause of concern as it threatens their exiting resource base while other livelihood opportunities are not emerging at the same time. The social mobilization approach offers potential for encouraging effective participation of the poor – especially women amongst them in their own development.

The project is being executed by Ministry of Rural Development in 11 drought-prone districts across the states of Jharkhand, Orissa and Rajasthan and is reaching out to 4300 women's groups in 2400 villages. The project is designed to support national efforts articulated in the Government of India's 10th Five Year Plan (2002-07) that relates to empowerment of communities for poverty alleviation through a process of social mobilization and gender equality.

The 'Citizens' Report on the MDGs' has been released at the UNDP Hall, New Delhi, a set of developmental targets adopted at the turn of the century by 189 member countries of the United Nations as part of a global pact to end extreme poverty and hunger, and ensure greater access to health, education, equality and peace in the world by 2015, adds a new dimension towards inclusive growth.

It has to be admitted that disparities in land ownership, employment, health and education are serious challenges across the country. While initiatives like the NREGA, NRHM and the recent Forest Rights Act can play an important role in the achievement of the MDGs, provisions for Women's Reservation in Parliament, Right to Education and Social Security for the Unorganized Sector need to be taken out of cold storage and acted upon immediately.

Notwithstanding these policy measures, so long as skewed distribution of wealth exists, unabated rampant corruption prevails, capitalists and multi-national nexus with administration and politicians persist-inclusive growth will remain as an illusive concept.

Entitlements can be achieved only if people are politically and administratively empowered to access their rights. We need to focus on institutions of inclusive governance to ensure inclusive growth.

REFERENCES

Bandyopadhyay, D., (2004), Rayagada Story Retold Destitute of Development, Economic and political Weekly, January 31, p. 411.

Chaudhury, S.N. Tribal Leadership in Panchayats: A study of their profile, performance and plan (2004), in Sah D.C. and Sisodia Yatindra Singh edited," Tribal Issues in India," Rawat Publication, Jaipur.

Crook, R., and Manor, J., (1998), Democracy and decentralization in South Asia and West Africa, Participation, Accountability and Performance, Cambridge, Cambridge University Press.

Das, Vidya, (2003), 'Kasipur Politics of Underdevelopment,' Economic and Political Weekly, January 4.

Das, Vidya, (2005), PESA: A Reality, National consultation on PESA Act AGRAGAMEE, Kashipur, Rayagada, Orissa.

Fernades, Walter, (1994), Development Induced Displacement in Tribal Areas of Eastern India, (Research project Sponsored by Indian Council of Social Science Research , New Delhi) p. 24.

Jha, S.N., (1999), 'Introduction' in S.N. Jha and P.C. Mathur edited 'Decentralization and Local Politics', New Delhi, Sage Publication.

Tripathy, S.N., (1998), Shifting Cultivation in Tribal Orissa in self-edited "Tribals in India: The Changing Scenario," Discovery Publishing House, New Delhi.

Tripathy, S.N., (2000), Glimpses on Tribal Development, Discovery Publishing House, New Delhi.

Tripathy, S.N., (2003), 'Impact of Development Induced Displacement on Tribals, in the Self Edited "Economic Development and Problem of Displacement," Anmol Publication, New Delhi, pp. 35-41.

Tripathy, S.N., (2003), 'Problems of Displacement and Development, in the self edited "Economic Development and Problem of Displacement," Anmol Publication, New Delhi, p. 188.

Tripathy, S.N., (2007), Tribal Development: Issues and Policy Options Anmol Publication, New Delhi.

Sundaram, K. and Suresh D. Tendulkar, (2003), Poverty among social and Economic groups in India in 1990's, Economic and Political Weekly, December-13.

Mukhopadhay, A. and I. Raja Raman, (2007), "Rural Unemployment 1999-2005: Who Gained who Lost?' Economic and Political Weekly, July, 28.

19

Democratizing Planning for Inclusive Growth: Reform in West Bengal Panchayats

D.K. GHOSH

India started its march in the path of planned development with the launching of the First Five Year Plan. The Planning Commission was set up in March, 1950 by a Resolution of the Government of India. The First Five Year Plan defined the scope of the work of Planing Commission in following words:

> *"The Constitution of India has guaranteed certain Fundamental Rights to the citizens of India and enunciated certain Directive Principles of State Policy, in particular, that the State shall strive to promote the welfare of the people by securing and protecting as effectively as it may a social order in which justice, social, economic and political, shall inform all the institutions of the national life, and shall direct its policy towards securing, among other things:*
>
> *(a) that the citizens, men and women equally, have the right to an adequate means of livelihood;*
>
> *(b) that the ownership and control of the material resources of the community are so distributed as best to subserve the common good; and*
>
> *(c) that the operation of the economic system does not result in the concentration of wealth and means of production to the common detriment."*

In the First Five Year Plan the declared objective of the National Government was "to promote a rapid rise in the standard of living of the people by efficient exploitation of the resources of the country, increasing production, and offering opportunities to all for employment in the service of the community."

After more than fifty-seven years of planning, the Government is now talking about inclusive growth. The Eleventh Five Year Plan (2007-12) has the approach paper with the title "Towards faster and More inclusive growth." The first hand observation made by the Approach Paper is that, "it is true that economic growth has failed to be sufficiently inclusive, particularly after the mid – 1990s." For alleviating the weak spots in the planned development, the Eleventh Five Year Plan attempts to design the plan in such a way so that poverty can be reduced appreciably with a focus on bridging the various divides persisting in our society. The Approach Paper identified a number of divides fragmenting the society. These can be listed as follows:

(i) Divide between the rich and the poor;

(ii) Divide between those who have access to essential services such as health, education, drinking water, sanitation etc. and those who do not;

(iii) Divide between those belong to other castes and those groups of people who have hitherto been marginalised in the process of development, such as, scheduled castes/scheduled tribes, some minorities etc.;

(iv) Divide between the males and females in the matter of enjoying the fruits of development and joining the mainstream of activities;

(v) Divide between urban and rural areas where urban areas have better access to basic amenities and infrastructure development.

Inclusive growth approach tries to address these divides with a view to making the society more egalitarian than it is at present. These divides prompt us to take up the present study, with special emphasis on the measures initiated by the Government of West Bengal to revamp the panchayat system for making it more pro-people, especially pro-poor. The reason behind considering the rural areas of West Bengal is that more than 72 per cent of total population in the State live in this segment. For the last thirty years since 1977 an alliance of left parties has been governing the State. The dormant panchayat system was also awakened by this State Government immediately in the next year (1978). The revival was made through elections to all three panchayat bodies at village, block and district levels. Since then, the State Government has brought many amendments to the West Bengal Panchayat Act, 1973 for democratising the activities of three tier-panchayats. Particularly after sixth panchayat general elections in the year 2003, the State Government made some amendments to the West Bengal Panchayat Act, 1973 with the purpose to broad base their activities with close involvement of local people. This is the case of constitution of Gram Unnayan Samiti at each village constituency of the gram panchayats.

In the framework of law, Gram Panchayats (village tier), Panchayat Samitis (block tier) and Zilla Parishads (district tier) function to achieve economic development and secure social justice for all within their respective jurisdiction. Securing social justice itself connotes inclusive growth as any discrimination implies distortion of inclusiveness. Everywhere in rural West Bengal there are panchayats and all of them are guided by the West Bengal Panchayat Act, 1973 and its subsequent amendments. But they function differently and the outcome of different programmes has wide variations. The panchayats have the responsibilities to prepare a development plan for the five-year and an annual plan for each year. As per provisions of the law, in the plans thus prepared, the demands of the local people are to be reflected. The plans have their origin in the meeting of village constituencies known as gram sansads. If these demands can be addressed adequately by the panchayats in implementation process, it is expected that development benefits can reach the poor effectively. According to the West Bengal Panchayat Act, the panchayats have been given the functions to implement schemes for economic development and social justice.

With this background, the present study has been taken up with two broad objectives. First is to portray the existing divides in promotion of literacy and propagation of education, particularly primary education; and in access to basic minimum needs like drinking water and sanitation facilities. Non-availability of district-disaggregated data in respect of primary health care facilities debars us from including health sector in this study. In the health sector, the panchayats are primarily involved with preventive and promotive health care. Extension of toilet facilities and provisioning of safe drinking water comes under preventive health care, however. With the introduction of National Rural Health Mission, the State Government decentralises the functioning of health system in the rural areas for the purpose of efficient delivery of services. The involvement of the panchayats is also augmented toward this end. In the first section the existing divides between scheduled castes, scheduled tribes and non-scheduled castes/tribes; between males and females; and rural and urban areas are depicted with district level data. The second section deals with a number of measures introduced by the Government of West Bengal for democratising the functioning of the panchayats at different tiers. These were incorporated in the West Bengal Panchayat Act through different amendments. Section three discusses the planning process followed at district level. In general the process starts from the gram sansad (village constituency) and culminates into District Planning Committee when the district plan is formulated. Panchayat plan is an integral component of a district plan.

I

Literacy rate is the commonly used comprehensive indicator for reflecting the achievement of education sector. According to the census definition, literacy rate is the proportion of literates to total population in age group of 7 years and above. Census defines, literacy as the ability to read and write with understanding in any language. For being literate, it is not necessary to possess any formal education or minimum educational standard. Even with this definition subscribing minimum requirement, the total literacy rate for West Bengal in Census 2001 comes out to be 69.22 per cent. In Table 1 district wise data of literacy rate for the scheduled castes and scheduled tribes are given along with the total literacy rate. The literacy rate of scheduled tribes is the lowest. The same trend was there in 1991 Census also.

From Table 1 it can be seen that higher literacy rates are achieved in the districts located near Kolkata (at a tentative distance of 130 kilometers). Only exception is Darjeeling where Siliguri is a highly urbanised agglomeration. The overall rate varies from as high as 81.31 per cent in Kolkata to as low as 48.63 per cent in Uttar Dinajpur (2001). According to census 2001, among the scheduled castes around 50 per cent are still illiterate while among the scheduled tribes this figure is about 64 per cent. Disparities in literacy rate between SC and non SC/ST and between ST and non SC/ST are also quite high. For measuring these disparities, the following simple index can be used (Chakraborty and Ghosh, 2000):

$$\text{Disparity index between SC or ST and Non SC/ST} = \frac{\text{Per cent literate among SCs or STs}}{\text{Per cent literate among non SC/ST}} \times 100$$

Table–1
Total Literacy Rate: 1991-2001

District	*1991*			*2001*			*Growth Index*		
	All	*SC*	*ST*	*All*	*SC*	*ST*	*All*	*SC*	*ST*
Burdwan	61.88	29.59	20.58	71.00	44.22	34.90	1.147	1.494	1.695
Birbhum	48.56	21.97	11.77	62.16	37.95	25.32	1.280	1.727	2.151
Bankura	52.04	21.81	26.77	63.84	35.92	42.16	1.226	1.646	1.574
Midnapur	69.32	43.74	32.24	75.17	53.54	39.26	1.084	1.224	1.217
Howrah	67.62	36.65	35.28	77.64	53.08	45.57	1.148	1.448	1.291
Hooghly	66.78	33.23	22.31	75.59	48.10	38.37	1.131	1.447	1.719
North 24 Parganas	66.81	44.59	20.50	78.49	61.79	38.92	1.174	1.385	1.898
South 24 Parganas	55.10	40.46	20.00	70.16	57.90	36.08	1.273	1.431	1.804
Kolkata	77.61	49.67	49.27	81.31	63.39	69.18	1.047	1.276	1.404
Nadia	52.53	37.35	18.68	66.55	54.55	34.22	1.267	1.460	1.831
Murshi-dabad	38.28	26.16	14.40	55.05	40.86	28.87	1.438	1.561	2.004
Uttar Dinajpur	34.58	24.33	10.73	48.63	40.41	22.55	1.406	1.660	2.101
Dakshin Dinajpur	46.40	29.04	17.66	64.46	45.22	34.90	1.389	1.557	1.976
Malda	35.62	27.02	12.78	50.71	42.17	26.08	1.423	1.560	2.040
Jalpaiguri	45.09	33.42	17.95	63.62	51.97	35.47	1.410	1.555	1.976
Darjeeling	57.95	37.96	32.49	72.87	52.60	47.31	1.257	1.385	1.456
Cooch Behar	45.78	33.30	26.46	67.21	54.47	46.27	1.468	1.635	1.748
Purulia	43.29	25.12	22.30	56.14	37.40	35.66	1.296	1.488	1.599
West Bengal	57.70	34.27	22.37	69.22	50.13	36.14	1.199	1.462	1.615

Source: Census 1991 and Census 2001 Reports.
Note: Growth Index = Value in 2001/Value in 1991.

The index measures the performance of one group relative to the other group. If literacy among SCs is low relative to that among non SC/ST, the index will have a low value, less than 100. The disparity index value will reach the value 100 when literacy rate among the two groups become equal. Therefore any deviation from the value 100 can be considered as a measure of disparity between the groups. Higher the value of disparity index, lower the disparity against the deprived group. On the basis of census 2001, the disparity index of literacy between SC and non-SC/ST is 72.42 per cent; in 1991 it was 59.39. The interpretation is that in spite of reduction in disparity during the period 1991-2001, a long way has to be covered before reaching the goal of no disparity. In this way, the disparity index of literacy between ST and non-SC/ST can also be calculated. On the basis of Census 2001, this value is found to be 52.21 indicating huge disparity; in 1991 it was 38.76 per cent.

Female literacy rate reflects the status of women in a society. Judging by this indicator, there exists substantial disparity everywhere. It is a reflection of male-female disparity also. This is not at all desirable so far as the question of equality is concerned. One important feature of census 2001 is that for the first time since independence, the absolute number of female illiterates in the country decreased. Female literacy rate as a whole was boosted and it showed faster increase in comparison to male literacy rate. In spite of this encouraging trend, the male-female gap in literacy and in attainment of education in different levels is still high. It requires to move with sustained efforts to fulfil the goal of universalisation of elementary education. In Table 2, district wise female literacy rates for scheduled castes and scheduled tribe population are given vis a vis overall female literacy rate. This comparison is made with a view to reiterating the hypothesis that even within the females they are not equal.

From Table 2 it must be acknowledged that the female literacy rate improves in West Bengal irrespective of castes and tribes. But the disparity index of female literacy rate is higher than that of total literacy rate in both the cases of comparison between SC and non-SC/ST, and ST and non-SC/ST. On the basis of census 2001, the value of disparity index of female literacy rate taking into consideration SC and non-SC/ST is found to be 66.07 per cent as against 72.42 per cent for the overall literacy rate. The value of disparity index nearer to 100 indicates more equality i.e. less disparity. Within the females of SC and non-SC/ST there exists more disparity than the overall population. If the disparity index of female literacy rates (2001) of ST and non-SC/ST are calculated, value will be 40.30 per cent which is lower than the value (52.21 %) calculated with the respective total literacy rate of ST and non-SC/ST population.

Table–2
Female Literacy Rate: 1991-2001

District	*1991*			*2001*			*Growth Index*		
	All	*SC*	*ST*	*All*	*SC*	*ST*	*All*	*SC*	*ST*
Burdwan	51.46	19.89	11.70	61.93	33.63	23.54	1.203	1.690	2.011
Birbhum	37.17	12.78	4.48	52.21	27.39	14.75	1.404	2.143	3.292
Bankura	36.55	10.57	11.43	49.80	22.69	26.50	1.362	2.146	2.318
Midnapur	56.63	31.88	19.65	64.63	42.06	25.74	1.141	1.319	1.309
Howrah	57.83	26.73	25.98	70.93	44.65	36.88	1.226	1.670	1.419
Hooghly	56.90	22.67	10.96	67.72	38.42	27.08	1.190	1.694	2.470
North 24 Parganas	57.99	34.19	10.52	72.13	53.55	28.08	1.243	1.566	2.669
South 24 Parganas	40.57	27.15	9.86	59.73	46.51	24.97	1.472	1.713	2.532
Kolkata	72.09	40.79	36.44	77.95	55.51	60.22	1.081	1.360	1.652
Nadia	44.42	28.54	10.01	60.06	46.56	24.52	1.352	1.631	2.449
Murshi-dabad	29.57	19.37	8.29	48.33	32.74	20.08	1.634	1.690	2.422
Uttar Dinajpur	22.85	12.56	4.29	37.16	28.77	13.87	1.626	2.290	3.233
Dakshin Dinajpur	35.33	18.32	8.98	55.12	34.84	24.63	1.560	1.901	2.742
Malda	24.92	16.05	5.20	41.67	31.96	15.95	1.672	1.991	3.067
Jalpaiguri	33.20	21.37	9.98	52.90	41.60	25.51	1.593	1.946	2.556
Darjeeling	47.84	27.12	25.33	63.92	42.35	39.08	1.336	1.561	1.542
Cooch Behar	33.31	21.75	15.24	57.04	44.22	36.31	1.712	2.033	2.382
Purulia	23.24	10.60	8.49	37.15	21.81	19.53	1.598	2.057	2.300
West Bengal	46.56	23.35	12.04	60.22	39.79	24.27	1.293	1.704	2.015

Source : Census 1991 and Census 2001 Reports.

Note: Growth Index = Value in 2001/Value in 1991.

Education is considered as the fundamental human right; it is the gateway to the enjoyment of other human rights for an individual. On December 10, 1948 the General Assembly of the United Nations adopted and proclaimed the Universal Declaration of Human Rights.

Our country is a signatory to this Declaration. Following this historic measures, the Assembly called upon all Member countries to publicise the text of the Declaration and "to cause it to be disseminated, displayed, read and expounded principally in schools and other educational institutions, without distinction based on the political status of countries and territories." Article 26 of this Declaration states:

"1. *Everyone has the right to education. Education shall be free, at least in the elementary and fundamental stages. Elementary education shall be compulsory. Technical and professional education shall be made generally available and higher education shall be equally accessible to all on the basis of merit.*

2. *Education shall be directed to the full development of the human personality and to the strengthening of respect for human rights and fundamental freedoms. It shall promote understanding, tolerance and friendship among all nations, racial or religious groups, and shall further the activities of the United Nations for the maintenance of peace.*

3. *Parents have a prior right to choose the kind of education that shall be given to their children."*

Emphasis on free and compulsory primary education was very much in our Constitution since its proclamation on 26th January, 1950 (Article 45 of the Constitution). With the passage of the Constitution (Eighty Sixth Amendment) Act, 2002 the content of this Article was replaced by the words: "The State shall endeavour to provide, within a period of ten years from the commencement of this Constitution, for free and compulsory education for all children until they complete the age of fourteen years." 86th Amendment Act, 2002, inserted the Article 21A into the Constitution where it has been laid down that the state would frame an appropriate law for operationalising the pledge of the Constitution in the Directive Principles (Article 45). It is necessary to point out that the Constitutional provision for making free and compulsory education for a particular age group is not the same as the right to education. The right to education is something broader and requires the State to fulfil certain obligation particularly in relation to making education available and accessible and then to make it acceptable and adaptable to the masses. Alongwith the universalisation of primary and elementary education, it is also urgent to ensure the quality of education imparted. Availability of trained teachers at the primary level may provide an indication about the quality of education delivered.

Even the plan documents express doubts about the achievement of the country in the field of education. The remarks of Tenth Five Year Plan can give an evidence:

> *"India's educational development is a mixed bag of remarkable successes and glaring gaps. Out of 200 million children in the age group of 6-14 years, 42 million children do not attend schools. There are problems relating to high drop-out rates, low levels of learning achievements and low participation of girls. Coupled with it are various systematic issues like inadequate school infrastructure, high teacher absenteeism, large scale teacher vacancies, inadequate equipment like teaching–learning material etc. The policy focus and public intervention in provisioning of educational services has not been given the attention it deserves."*

For bridging the gaps in elementary education, the Government of India launched the programme Sarva Siksha Abhiyan (SSA) in the year 2000-01. SSA is designed as a time bound programme to provide elementary education to all children in the age group 6-14 years by 2010. This is an initiative on the part of the Union Government to achieve the goal of universalisation of elementary education in partnership with the State Governments, local bodies in the rural and urban areas and through community participation. A different challenge that may come up in the process of fulfilling the targets of universalisation of elementary education is the access to basic education in favour of the so far un-reached segments and weaker section people located in far-flung areas.

Age group data from census 2001 show that there is a huge gap in case of girls also in the matter of their enrolment in educational institutions. In Table 3 the age group situation is depicted. Age group coverage of girl child can indicate the extent of deprivation of women from their early childhood. Sex ratio calculated for each age group of persons attending educational institutions gives an idea about the bias against girl child. The common practice in particular among the poor households is to prefer boys over girls for schooling.

From Table 3 it can be revealed that for every age group in formal school system, scheduled caste and scheduled tribe girls have less scope for attending schools in comparison to their non SC/ST counterparts. The neglect is not only between the castes and tribes,

Table-3
Girls Attending Educational Institutions: West Bengal (2001)

Age Group	*Total Female Population*			*Attending Institutions*		
	Non SC/ST	*SC*	*ST*	*Non SC/ST*	*SC*	*ST*
6 years	632301	219768	63229	232580 (36.78)	78491 (35.71)	18108 (28.64)
7 years	634095	232004	57975	482666 (76.12)	157279 (67.79)	31215 (53.84)
8 years	730510	261576	69243	557119 (76.26)	190839 (72.96)	38995 (56.31)
9 years	559983	197506	48371	466829 (83.36)	155450 (78.70)	30472 (62.99)
10 years	821550	290538	72724	657740 (80.06)	214557 (73.85)	40929 (56.28)
11 years	474583	156625	33413	400397 (84.37)	120457 (76.90)	20548 (61.49)
12 years	769617	273816	68883	587847 (76.38)	181078 (66.13)	33836 (49.12)
13 years	547205	183978	39987	414438 (75.74)	116499 (63.32)	19480 (48.71)
14 years	628471	213870	48524	421328 (67.04)	115067 (53.80)	19477 (40.14)
Total	5798315	2029681	502349	4220944 (72.80)	1329717 (65.51)	253060 (50.37)

but it remains very much within the castes or tribes. The fact that a girl child is discriminated can be easily corroborated if sex ratio of attendance is calculated. Here these ratios are calculated separately for the rural and urban areas for each district. Rural-urban divide in attendance is also very prominent. In urban areas, women have better privileges for getting enrolled in formal education system. Table 4 presents the results.

Table 4 shows that in Purulia and Bankura districts, the sex ratio is very much depressing both in the rural and urban areas in comparison to the better off districts like Howrah, North 24 Parganas and Hooghly. Low sex ratios in Malda and Murshidabad districts are mainly due to predominant Muslim population where the thrust on female education seems to be very much feeble. As a consequence, women are not widely favoured to come out and register in formal educational institutions.

Table-4
Sex Ratio of Attendance in Educational Institutions: 2001

District	*All*			*SC*			*ST*		
	R + U	*R*	*U*	*R + U*	*R*	*U*	*R + U*	*R*	*U*
Burdwan	820	818	822	753	745	774	729	730	728
Birbhum	786	782	830	693	684	826	650	649	670
Bankura	747	739	851	638	631	774	664	664	750
Midnapore	857	856	865	811	806	859	681	675	852
Howrah	945	1001	893	926	930	918	832	845	827
Hooghly	931	962	872	878	876	889	805	789	1048
North 24 Parganas	889	913	869	842	834	858	757	732	873
South 24 Parganas	887	885	897	815	811	862	720	708	880
Kolkata	878	-	878	825	-	825	763	-	763
Nadia	873	866	899	825	820	853	748	734	858
Murshidabad	862	863	855	749	737	824	689	678	913
Uttar Dinajpur	752	742	803	738	735	772	618	615	691
Dakshin Dinajpur	868	862	900	831	829	853	795	792	858
Malda	806	796	913	740	731	854	628	644	720
Jalpaiguri	864	856	901	873	872	881	786	787	737
Darjeeling	873	872	874	842	835	868	867	844	978
Cooch Behar	874	869	924	860	858	895	791	782	887
Purulia	647	626	805	575	562	671	559	557	661
West Bengal	854	848	869	801	794	840	711	703	818

Source: *Census 2001 Report.*
Note: *R = Rural, U = Urban, R + U = Rural and Urban together.*

For meeting the basic needs of human being, Minimum Needs Programme (MNP) was introduced during the Fifth Five Year Plan. The programme essentially indicated an investment in human resource development. The components of MNP were elementary education, adult education, rural health, rural water supply, rural roads, rural electrification, rural housing, environmental improvement of urban slums and nutrition. To the list of eight components, during Seventh Five Year Plan three more items were added. These were rural domestic energy, rural sanitation and public distribution system. In view of the shortfall in ensuring the basic minimum standard of life for all sections of the people, "a bold initiative was taken by the Chief Ministers Conference held in July 1996 to ensure access of all to certain Basic Minimum Services (BMS) in a time bound manner" (Ninth Five Year Plan, Vol. II). According to Ninth Five Year Plan document, the basic minimum services are of paramount importance:

> *"The Conference endorsed the seven basic minimum services as of paramount importance in securing a better quality of life for the people, especially those residing in rural areas. Further, it observed that it would be in the best interests of the country, if time-bound action plans are formulated to secure full coverage of the country with these seven basic services by 2000 AD. This was essential for the rapid growth of the economy and for social justice and hence, these basic services were to constitute the core of the social sector development plan."*

Seven basic services are reproduced below from Ninth Five Year Plan :

(i) 100 per cent coverage of provision of safe drinking water in rural and urban areas;
(ii) 100 per cent coverage of primary health service facilities in rural and urban areas;
(iii) Universalisation of primary education;
(iv) Provision of Public Housing Assistance to all shelterless poor families;
(v) Extension of Mid-day Meal Programme in primary schools, to all rural blocks and urban slums and disadvantaged sections;
(vi) Provision of connectivity to all unconnected villages and habitations; and
(vii) Streamlining of the Public Distribution System with focus upon the poor.

National Human Development Report (2001) mentions that if a household has access to drinking water supplied from a tap or a hand pump/ tube well situated within or outside the premises, it is considered as having access to safe drinking water. Census 2001 identified eight sources of drinking water; but all are not safe for use. The sources are tap, hand pump, tube well, well, tank/pond/lake, river/canal, spring and any other sources. In Ninth Five Year Plan, the Union Government made following commitment in respect of drinking water and sanitation facilities:

> *"Drinking water supply and sanitation facilities are very important and crucial for achieving goal of 'Health for All'. The Government is committed to provide drinking water to every settlement in the country within five years. The Government has also decided to go all out to achieve the goal of expansion and improvement of sanitation facility".*

Tenth Five Year Plan (2002-07) envisaged 100 per cent coverage of rural and urban population with safe drinking water as per the stipulated norms and standards on a sustainable basis. With reference to rural water supply, Tenth Five Year Plan stipulated that safe drinking water would be provided to all habitations by March 2004 with the highest priority to the not-covered habitations. It was also mentioned in Tenth Plan document that "it should be ensured that scheduled castes/scheduled tribe population and other poor and weaker sections are covered fully on a priority basis." The stipulated norms of supply of safe drinking water is delineated below in the words of the Report of the Steering Committee of Tenth Five Year Plan on drinking water and sanitation :

> *"The stipulated norms of supply would be 40 lpcd of safe drinking water within a walking distance of 1.6 kms or elevation difference of 100 metres in hilly areas, to be relaxed as per field conditions applicable to arid, semi-arid and hilly areas. At least one hand pump/spot source for every 250 persons to be provided."*

The State Government have the primary responsibility for providing drinking water to these inhabitants. Since the passage of the Constitution (Seventy Third Amendment) Act, 1992 and incorporation of the Eleventh Schedule in the Constitution, panchayats have been entrusted with the responsibility of providing drinking water to the local residents of the villages under their jurisdiction. Similarly, in the urban areas, the municipalities are responsible for supply of safe drinking water.

Following the distribution of households on the basis of location of the source of drinking water, it can be observed that the households in urban areas are in comfortable position than those living in the rural areas. For example, of the total rural households, only 23.40

per cent have the source of drinking water located within their premises; whereas in case of urban areas, this percentage is 53.43. If scheduled caste households are considered exclusively, the corresponding percentages are 22.52 in rural areas and 38.68 in urban areas. For scheduled tribe households, the percentages are 9.70 and 38.50 in rural and urban areas respectively. These data are enough to reflect the deprivation of scheduled tribe households in getting a source of drinking water within their premises. Of the scheduled tribe households in rural areas, 23.76 per cent have to collect drinking water from a distance of more than 500 meters. In case of the scheduled caste households in rural areas, this percentage is 20.60. Taking total rural households, the proportion of households fetching water from a distance of more than 500 meters is 20.44 per cent. This fact also indicates the deprivation of ST families in rural areas. In Table 5, taking Census 2001 data, a distribution of households is made on the basis of location of sources of drinking water. Divide between SC/ST and non SC/ST is prominent. A large number of SC/ST families are compelled to walk more than half a kilometer several times in a day to collect drinking water. Mostly women and girl children have to bear the burden of collecting and carrying water.

Table 5 shows that non-scheduled caste/scheduled tribe households have locational advantages, regarding the sources of drinking water. 36.39 per cent non SC/ST households have the sources located within their premises – this indicates that they do not have to move outside for collecting water. Considerable progress in respect of supply of drinking water has been achieved in West Bengal by implementation of different projects through the panchayat in rural areas and municipalities in the urban areas. From Table 5 it can be seen that in case of ST households collecting water from a distance more than 500 metres, there are only six districts where proportion of households are more than the state average. The districts are Bankura, Midnapore, South 24 Parganas, Malda, Darjeeling and Purulia. Of these six districts, Bankura, Midnapore and Purulia are in the western plains of the State which is marked as relatively underdeveloped in comparison to the eastern and central plain districts like Howrah, Hooghly and Burdwan. South 24 Parganas district has geographical dis-advantages, as major part of Sunderban region is located in this district.

Table–5
Distribution of Households on the Basis of Location of Sources of Drinking Water: 2001

District	*Non SC/ ST*			*SC*			*ST*		
	I	*II*	*III*	*I*	*II*	*III*	*I*	*II*	*III*
Burdwan	41.65	44.19	14.15	14.20	64.59	21.21	9.22	69.17	21.61
Birbhum	19.94	63.13	16.92	5.14	75.66	19.20	2.47	80.80	16.73
Bankura	22.28	56.20	21.51	5.94	69.62	24.44	2.51	70.77	26.72
Midnapur	12.69	61.41	25.90	5.74	65.48	28.78	6.09	66.42	27.48
Howrah	23.33	55.58	21.08	9.39	65.45	25.16	26.57	51.45	21.98
Hooghly	38.51	49.73	11.75	11.30	71.63	17.07	8.76	73.72	17.52
North 24 Parganas	55.62	32.66	11.72	41.89	41.11	17.00	26.17	54.93	18.90
South 24 Parganas	9.93	60.67	29.40	6.10	61.64	32.26	6.88	57.44	35.68
Kolkata	64.32	28.80	6.88	41.00	44.32	14.68	50.54	38.90	10.56
Nadia	63.56	28.42	8.01	57.97	32.29	9.74	33.84	52.55	13.61
Murshi-dabad	31.73	52.57	15.70	21.75	59.37	18.88	13.02	67.69	19.29
Uttar Dinajpur	43.10	47.35	9.55	45.95	46.10	7.95	28.66	58.64	12.70
Dakshin Dinajpur	37.95	49.28	12.77	19.94	64.72	15.34	7.37	73.75	18.88
Malda	31.97	52.88	15.15	17.68	60.51	21.81	6.41	65.06	28.53
Jalpaiguri	51.17	35.75	13.08	46.10	39.27	14.62	24.02	57.45	18.52
Darjeeling	37.32	32.21	30.47	36.54	38.75	24.71	19.92	48.16	31.92
Cooch Behar	72.13	20.50	7.37	65.49	25.27	9.24	60.73	27.74	11.53
Purulia	13.58	57.19	29.23	5.81	63.79	30.39	3.01	64.68	32.31
West Bengal	36.39	46.87	16.74	25.63	54.47	19.90	13.51	63.52	22.97

Source: Census 2001 Tables H-8, H-8 SC and H-8 ST.

Note: I -> Within premises, II -> Near premises, III -> Away. All figures are in percentage.

The coverage of safe sources of drinking water has rural-urban divide also. If a household has access to drinking water supplied through pipes and tap or a hand pump/tube well located within premises or outside the premises, it is considered that the household has access to safe drinking water. 89.3 per cent households in West Bengal have got such access. From census data, households having access to tap, tube well/hand pump are added to determine the coverage of safe drinking water. Table 5(a) shows the access of households to safe drinking water.

Table–5(a)
Proportions of Households Having Safe Drinking Water, 2001

District	*Non SC/ST*		*Scheduled Caste*		*Scheduled Tribe*	
	Rural	*Urban*	*Rural*	*Urban*	*Rural*	*Urban*
Burdwan	93.59	83.58	94.12	77.49	88.07	71.75
Birbhum	87.95	77.65	89.46	88.75	76.20	89.68
Bankura	72.10	75.23	75.28	85.17	46.30	78.36
Midnapur	89.18	82.70	84.15	84.93	54.14	68.60
Howrah	99.12	94.21	99.19	94.35	98.54	94.13
Hooghly	98.73	97.65	99.26	97.74	99.21	98.28
North 24 Parganas	99.05	98.01	98.82	97.58	98.39	97.15
South 24 Parganas	99.38	98.39	99.11	98.34	98.67	97.59
Kolkata	-	98.72	-	97.98	-	98.30
Nadia	98.79	96.67	98.97	98.12	98.62	97.77
Murshidabad	98.28	98.17	98.62	97.95	96.71	98.64
Uttar Dinajpur	92.05	97.43	95.99	96.55	95.71	98.08
Dakshin Dinajpur	96.99	97.51	95.77	98.14	93.20	99.05
Malda	91.96	98.13	76.58	98.50	45.62	98.18
Jalpaiguri	49.53	59.11	35.51	49.94	61.36	62.70
Darjeeling	41.88	48.15	31.55	50.02	29.92	59.19
Cooch Behar	89.80	95.06	81.58	90.34	84.69	95.68
Purulia	38.70	72.40	50.56	83.54	38.06	73.68
West Bengal	89.87	92.84	86.07	90.67	67.75	86.91

Source: Tables on houses, household amenities and assets, Census of India 2001, West Bengal series.

Note: All figures are in percentage.

From Table 5(a) inequity in access to safe drinking water can be realized. In calculating the proportion of households having safe sources, wells are not considered as in general they are open wells. Covered wells are accepted as safe sources. Of scheduled caste households, 11.82 per cent use wells as source of drinking water; for scheduled tribe households, this percentage is 26.34 and in case of non SC/ST, the corresponding percentage is 7.70. This means, the better off households have higher access to safe sources of drinking water than the poor households—there is not much difference whether they reside in urban areas or in rural areas. For the poor and unserved population, efforts are being initiated through taking up of more rural water supply projects under Accelerated Rural Water Supply Programme and through installation of deep well and hand pumps. Next to safe drinking water, access to toilet facilities is important from health point of view of an individual. This access is discussed with district level data available from census.

Expanding access to sanitation is a moral and ethical imperative in view of human dignity and privacy. The practice of open defecation, though very serious from the point of view of environmental pollution and health hazards, is not yet considered as ill-practice. In 1986, the Government of India launched the Central Rural Sanitation Programme (CRSP) for construction of sanitary latrines in the rural areas. In this programme there was provision of 100 per cent subsidy for scheduled castes, scheduled tribes and landless labourers. The programme was revised in March 1991 to set an integrated approach to rural sanitation. In 1999, the programme was again restructured to launch Total Sanitation Campaign (TSC) for making the programme demand-driven.

Census 2001 provides data on households having 'no latrine'. On the basis of 'no latrine' figures, Table 6 is constructed taking both the rural and urban areas. This table reflects a dissatisfied status of coverage. Millennium Development Goal is to halve the proportion of people without sustainable access to basic sanitation by 2015. In this respect, the achievement is far away from desirable standard.

From Table 6 it can be seen that in case of scheduled tribe households, only 18.41 per cent have their latrine within their houses. Of 135717 ST households living in urban areas, 93264 have their latrines. The coverage is 68.71 per cent. If scheduled caste household are considered, there also urban areas have better coverage than the rural areas; for example, of 782483 urban scheduled caste households, 562200 households have their latrines – the coverage is

71.85 per cent. This signifies that the rural areas are predominantly featured with low coverage of latrine facilities in the rural areas. For this reason, Total Sanitation Campaign is concentrated in the rural areas. In districts with high proportion of scheduled tribe population, very few scheduled tribe households have this amenity. In district like Purulia, only 2.22 per cent ST households have latrine, for SC households it is only 5.06 per cent. With presentation of the scenario of pervasive divides in basic human needs, the next section discusses the various measures initiated in recent years by the State Government to make the panchayat more pro-people.

Table–6

Households Not Having Latrine Within their Houses: 1991-2001

District	*1991*			*2001*		
	Non SC/ST	*SC*	*ST*	*Non SC/ST*	*SC*	*ST*
Burdwan	55.68	88.50	93.26	44.09	81.24	87.32
Birbhum	84.17	96.64	98.52	76.95	94.29	97.03
Bankura	87.85	97.58	98.34	81.46	96.01	97.73
Midnapore	87.17	96.12	98.43	62.55	82.18	92.65
Howrah	46.69	76.72	49.93	33.83	63.30	29.57
Hooghly	46.65	84.22	91.80	31.67	71.10	80.45
North 24 Parganas	34.68	57.38	69.96	20.65	32.79	50.78
South 24 Parganas	72.67	84.43	86.33	54.68	64.00	64.50
Kolkata	03.83	15.40	13.73	3.59	08.72	06.85
Nadia	60.40	72.80	87.83	44.85	46.59	71.07
Murshidabad	86.13	91.33	96.78	76.07	80.39	87.53
Uttar Dinajpur	79.95	92.79	97.77	76.91	82.12	92.95
Dakshin Dinajpur	79.93	92.78	97.78	64.77	84.82	94.72
Malda	85.21	91.32	98.34	76.69	80.30	94.03
Jalpaiguri	55.86	86.79	89.09	44.25	73.97	74.26
Darjeeling	51.34	73.60	81.70	32.02	56.53	62.05
Cooch Behar	74.40	93.37	87.27	60.37	80.11	70.00
Purulia	88.18	95.91	98.23	86.04	94.94	97.78
West Bengal	65.83	83.39	92.17	48.90	69.18	81.59

Source: Census Reports 1991 and 2001.

Note: All figures are in percentage.

II

With the incorporation of the Eleventh Schedule in the Constitution after the passage of the Constitution (Seventy Third Amendment) Act, 1992, the panchayats have been entrusted with planning and implementation of programmes related to 29 subjects listed in the schedule. Of them, there are primary education, provisioning of drinking water and toilet facilities, primary health, poverty alleviation etc. In West Bengal for introducing decentralisation in the function of the gram panchayats, the State Government introduced a new section (Section 32A) in the West Bengal Panchayat Act, 1973 through an amendment of the Act in 1997. The purpose was to delegate power to the sub-committees comprising the members of the gram panchayat. The section was further amended in 2003 for delegating additional powers to the sub-committees and specifying their functions distinctly in the Act and Rules framed thereunder. The Section 32A made the provision that subject to direction as may be issued by the State Government in this behalf, a gram panchayat shall as soon as may be within three months from the first meeting of the gram panchayat, constitute upa-samitis (sub-committees). Presently the State Government has approved constitution of following five upa-samitis:

(i) Artha-O-Parikalpana Upa-Samiti (Finance and Planning Sub-Committee);
(ii) Krishi-O-Pranisampad Bikas Upa-Samiti (Agriculture and Animal Resource Development Sub-Committee);
(iii) Siksha-O-Janaswasthya Upa-Samiti (Education and Public Health Sub-Committee);
(iv) Nari, Sishu Unnayan-O-Samaj Kalyan Upa-Samiti (Women, Child Development and Social Welfare Sub-Committee); and
(v) Shilpa-O-Parikathama Upa-Samiti (Industry and Infrastructure Sub-Committee).

Sub-section 3 of Section 32A, specifies the provision regarding formation of sub-committees. The pradhan and the upa pradhan shall be the ex-officio members of all upa-samitis. Every upa-samiti shall consist of members ranging from 1 to 3 depending on the size of the gram panchayat. Only exception is the Artha-O-Parikalpana upa-samiti where the heads of other upa-samitis shall be the members. The head of a upa-samiti is known as Sanchalak (coordinator). Apart from the gram panchayat members in upa-samitis, the West Bengal

Panchayat Act has the provision to include members appointed by the State Government by any general order or special order. The West Bengal Panchayat Act mentions two categories of persons from whom the State Government can make the appointment. These two categories are:

(a) from among the officials of the panchayat bodies having jurisdiction, the State Government or any Statutory Board, Corporation or Organisation or any individual official receiving grant, financial assistance or remuneration from the State Exchequer, and

(b) any person having any specialized knowledge about the locality or any area of activity.

By a general order issued in the month of September 2004, the State Government made the appointment of different village level officials of functional departments to the upa-samitis. For example, two key employees of a gram panchayat, namely, the Executive Assistant and the Secretary have been appointed as members in Artha-O-Parikalpana Upa-samiti. This upa-samiti is responsible for preparation of the budget and formulation of perspective and annual plans of the gram panchayat.

Regarding Sanchalak, the West Bengal Panchayat Act makes the provision that "members of such upa-samiti shall elect one member from among themselves in such manner as may be prescribed to act as Sanchalak for such upa-samiti." Within the framework of law, the Sanchalak is responsible for convening the meetings of upa-samiti and coordinating function of members of the concerned upa-samiti. Every upa-samiti has been empowered by the State Government to prepare schemes and perform the functions of the gram panchayat in relation to the subjects allotted to the upa-samiti within the budgetary provisions of the gram panchayat. To this effect, the Sanchalak has the responsibility to prepare and place report of actions taken or proposed to be taken relating to the upa-samiti, to the pradhan and the gram panchayat. This is a continuing process. The spirit of constitution of upa-samitis is that the gram panchayat as a body will discharge its responsibilities through the upa-samitis. Under Rule 66 of the West Bengal Panchayat (Gram Panchayat Administration) Rules, 2004, the subject matters on which the upa-samiti of a gram panchayat shall deliberate upon and deal with are specified against each upa-samiti. The distribution of subject matters among the upa-samitis is made keeping in view 29 subjects enlisted in the Eleventh Schedule of the Constitution.

Simple counting of the subjects as mentioned in Rule 66, gives following distribution:

Upa-Samiti	*Number of Subjects*
Artha-o-Parikalpana	14
Krishi-o-Pranisampad Bikash	14
Siksha-o-Jana Swasthya	12
Nari, Sishu Unnayan-o-Samajkalyan	5
Shilpa-o-Parikathamo	6

Regarding the powers of upa-samiti, the West Bengal Panchayat (Gram Panchayat Administration) Rules, 2004 delineates clearly in Rule 67 that the upa-samiti shall be responsible for implementation of the works and schemes of the gram panchayat and those assigned to it by different departments of the State Government. The financial limits to which an upa-samiti is competent to execute works and schemes undertaken by the gram panchayat shall be fixed by the gram panchayat or by the State Government from time to time. The present norm is that an upa-samiti can spend upto Rs. 25 thousand without the approval of Artha-O-Parikalpana upa-samiti for implementation of any scheme related to the subjects assigned to the concerned upa-samiti. The Artha-O-Parikalpana upa-samiti can give approval to any scheme of value upto Rs. 1 lakh for every upa-samiti. These financial limits have been set by the State Government for quick implementation of schemes. For any scheme of value exceeding Rs. 1 lakh, the Artha-O-Parikalpana upa-samiti has to take the approval of the general body of the gram panchayat.

The State Government has created District Council for Panchayat in each district (Section 214A of the West Bengal Panchayat Act). The leader of the recognized political party in opposition having the largest number of members directly elected with the reserved symbol of such recognized political party in the zilla parishad is the chairperson of this Council. If there is no member in opposition, then the zilla parishad members shall elect one member out of them. This District Council, according to sub-section 2(a) of the Section 214A, "can examine the accounts of the panchayats within its territorial jurisdiction, in relation to the budget approved by the Panchayats concerned for the expenditure to be incurred by such Panchayats, the annual report of such Panchayats and such other accounts of such Panchayats as the District Council may think fit." The visits of District Council to the gram panchayats are, however, few and far between.

The panchayats being a political entity, the persons within these bodies should have a minimum level of knowledge to realise the inner dynamics of the system. It is not sufficient to know the guidelines of the programmes; rather it is necessary to know how a system functions in close association with political and social contents. Because of this gap even with so much of investments, everywhere we have to encounter deficits, distortion and dys-functionalities. This is certainly different from the picture of ideal democratic state. The panchayat members can overcome the short falls if they are allowed to function with adequate political and bureaucratic support. The local political leaders dictate the panchayats and the bureaucracy in different tiers make the panchayats overburdened with orders and guidelines. Practically, none of them truly guide the panchayat members with care and sympathy.

For augmenting people's participation in the activities of the panchayats, through an amendment of the West Bengal Panchayat Act in the year 1994, the State Government brought in the concept of gram sansad. According to the definition of the West Bengal Panchayat Act, gram sansad means a body consisting of persons registered at any time in the electoral rolls pertaining to a constituency of a gram panchayat. In this case, West Bengal went one step ahead of the provision made in the 73rd Amendment for evoking people's participation in the panchayats. All electors in a constituency of a gram panchayat are the members of a gram sansad. In respect of the meetings of gram sansad, the Act in Section 16A makes two provisions: *(i)* every gram panchayat shall hold within its local limits an annual and a half yearly meeting for each gram sansad at such place, on such date and at such hour as may be fixed by the gram panchayat; and *(ii)* the annual meeting of the gram sansad shall be held ordinarily in the month of May and the half-yearly meeting of the gram sansad shall be held ordinarily in the month of November every year.

Apart from these two meetings, the West Bengal Panchayat Act keeps a provision that a gram panchayat may hold extra-ordinary meeting of a gram sansad at any time if the situation so warrants or if the State Government, by order, so directs. Regarding quorum of the gram sansad meeting, the provision of the West Bengal Panchayat Act is that one-tenth of the total number of members shall form a quorum for a meeting. If there is no quorum available in such meeting, the meeting shall be adjourned, and held at the same place and hour on the seventh day after the date of the original meeting. For the adjourned meeting, the required presence of the sansad members has been fixed at one-twentieth of total members. But in the West Bengal Panchayat Act, there is no provision for ensuring minimum presence of women in the gram sansad meetings. The general trend is that women attendance in these meetings is low.

For giving local people pre-eminent importance, the Act makes the provision that a gram sansad shall guide and advise the gram panchayat in regard to the schemes for economic development and social justice undertaken or proposed to be undertaken in the gram panchayat area. Gram panchayats implement wage employment programmes like Sampoorna Grameen Rojgar Yojana, West Bengal Rural Employment Guarantee Scheme (WBREGS); housing programmes like Indira Awas Yojana and Pradhan Mantri Gramodya Yojana, social security schemes like National Old Age Pension Scheme (NOAPS), National Family Benefit Scheme (NFBS), National Maternity Benefit Scheme (NMBS) renamed as Janani Suraksha Yojana. Infrastructure development schemes under finances from Eleventh and Twelfth Finance Commissions and untied fund of the State Government are also implemented by gram panchayats. All these programmes have specific guidelines and the panchayats have to fulfill those conditions. Gram sansads have the responsibility to identify or lay down principles for identification of *(i)* the beneficiaries for these programmes, and *(ii)* the schemes which are required to be taken on priority basis for economic development of the villages under their jurisdiction. In addition to identification of schemes and beneficiaries, the gram sansads have been given following responsibilities also:

(i) to mobilize mass participation for community welfare programmes and programmes for adult education, family welfare and child welfare; and

(ii) to promote solidarity and harmony among all sections of the people irrespective of religion, faith, caste, creed or race.

The essence of the importance of gram sansads can be viewed from the Annual Administrative Report, 2003-04 of the Department of Panchayats and Rural Development, Government of West Bengal:

> *"The main function of Gram Sansad is to guide and advice the gram panchayat in regard to the schemes for economic development and social justice, identification of beneficiaries for various poverty alleviation and food security programmes, constitution of one or more beneficiary committees for ensuring active participation of people in implementation, maintenance and equitable distribution of benefits of one or more schemes in its area. A Gram Sansad may raise objection to action of Pradhan or any other member of gram panchayat for failure to implement any development work properly. Further, it is mandatory for a gram panchayat to place in the meetings of Gram Sansad, the budget and audit report of the accounts of Gram Panchayat for deliberation, recommendation and suggestion of Gram Sansad."*

For attaching importance to the gram sansad meetings, the State Government through an amendment in the West Bengal Panchayat Act in the year 2003 has made it obligatory on the part of a gram panchayat to act upon any recommendation of a gram sansad relating to prioritization of beneficiaries for assistance under a programme or regarding a scheme which will be of importance for the gram sansad. If a gram panchayat has to take decision that recommendations of a gram sansad cannot be implemented or are not acceptable under the framework of the law, this decision has to be placed by the gram panchayat in the next meeting of the concerned gram sansad. For strengthening gram sansads, the State Government places enormous weightage on convening these meetings with wide publicity among the public. The purpose is to bring all sections of people in these meetings and to deliberate freely. It is expected that these measures can boost up the process of functioning at local level toward holistic development of the area.

In compliance with the Constitution (Seventy-Third Amendment) Act 1992, Section 16B of the West Bengal Panchayat Act has the provision for holding the gram sabha meeting in every gram panchayat. Members of all gram sansads in a gram panchayat are the members of the gram sabha. The provision of the law is that every gram panchayat shall hold within its local limits an annual meeting of the gram sabha ordinarily in the month of December every year after completion of the half-yearly meeting of the gram sansads in November. In many cases the gram panchayat cannot complete the gram sansad meetings within November; then the gram sabha meeting has to be deferred to January or even to February. Attendance of one twentieth of the total number of members shall form a quorum for a meeting of a gram sabha. No quorum shall be necessary for an adjourned meeting of a gram sabha. The adjourned meeting of a gram sabha shall be held at the same time and place after seven days. As gram sabha jurisdiction is the same as the gram panchayat, a meeting of the gram sabha shall be presided over by the pradhan (Chairperson of the gram panchayat) or in his absence by the upa-pradhan (Vice-Chairperson).

For strengthening decentralization and involvement of people in the process of development, the State Government by an amendment of the West Bengal Panchayat Act in the year 2003 took decision to constitute a Gram Unnayan Samiti (GUS) in each gram sansad. As specified in the Act, a Gram Unnayan Samiti shall ensure active participation of people in implementation; maintenance and equitable distribution of benefits with respect to such subjects as may be prescribed. In the Act it is provided that the Gram Unnayan Samiti shall be accountable for its functions and decisions to the gram sansad in which it is constituted. The gram sansad in turn shall exercise its power and authority in this behalf in such manner, as may be prescribed by the State Government. The West Bengal Panchayat (Gram Panchayat Administration) Rules, 2004 in Rules 72, 73 and 74 give the details about the formation and functions of a GUS. For the formation of Gram Unnayan Samiti, an extra-ordinary meeting of the gram sansad (Rule 71) shall be convened by the gram panchayat. For this meeting clear fifteen days notice is to be given specifying the date, time and venue of the meeting. The venue should be in a place within the jurisdiction of the gram sansad. Provision of the Gram Panchayat Administration Rules, prescribes that wide publicity shall be arranged by the gram panchayat for this extra ordinary meeting of the gram sansad. The presence of at least one-fifth of the members of a gram sansad is fixed as a quorum for this meeting. In case of an ordinary meeting of a gram sansad the quorum is one-tenth of the total members. The extra-ordinary meeting thus calls for presence of more members. If due to low attendance of gram sansad members, the meeting becomes adjourned, that adjourned meeting shall be held on the 7th day after the date of the first meeting and the attendance of at least one tenth of the total members of gram sansad shall require for the quorum. Rule 72 of the Gram Panchayat Administration Rules, 2004 denotes the membership pattern of a Gram Unnayan Samiti. In this samiti, possible representation of all sections of people in a village is sought to be ensured. Let us narrate the category of membership prescribed in this rule:

(i) The member or members of the gram panchayat elected from the particular gram sansad will be ex-officio member(s). There may be two-seated constituency in a gram panchayat. In that case both the members elected from the constituency will be the ex-officio members. Member of the gram panchayat will be the Chairperson. If there are two members, then the member senior in age will be the Chairperson.

(ii) The person or persons securing the second highest votes in the last panchayat election 2003 will be member(s). This provision has been made to ensure representation of the opposition political party in GUS.

(iii) Not more than three representatives from non-government organizations, either registered or otherwise recognized by the State Government and other community based organizations like the Samabay Krishi Unnayan Samiti (SKUS), Village Education Committee, Anganwadi Centre, etc. will be included as members. In all these community-based organizations, local people are closely involved and participate in different activities. They themselves run their organizations with facilitation from the panchayat and related departments. The purpose is to dovetail their expertise in the process of development in the gram sansad area. Only condition is that the persons should be the members of the gram sansad, that is, should be a voter of that village constituency.

(iv) Membership has been given to the self-help groups functioning in the gram sansad area for at least six months, having a bank account and all the members of the group being members of the gram sansad. The underlying condition is that such membership shall remain restricted to three self-help groups of which at least two shall be from the women led self-help groups. Self-help groups are considered because in rural areas they are prominently coming up as vehicle for social mobilisation, in particular among women.

(*v*) One government employee is made the member. The employee may be serving in any department or may be retired. Only eligibility condition is that the employee should be a member of the gram sansad.

(*vi*) One teacher, serving or retired is made the member, provided he or she is the member of the gram sansad.

In addition to these categories, there shall be another 10 members or one per cent of the total members of the gram sansad whichever is higher. These members are to be elected from among the remaining members of the gram sansad. The stipulation is that not less than one-third members of the Gram Unnayan Samiti shall be women. This provision again reflects the government intention to include women in decision-making fora.

Gram Unnayan Samiti, in fact, has been made the executive arm of the gram sansad. The planning process in the rural areas starts from this gram sansad. In the sansad meeting, the local people express their demands for the benefit of their area. Getting the demands, in technical term plans of the gram sansads, the gram panchayat concerned collate and prioritize them according to the availability of funds in different programmes. In West Bengal, implementation of all rural development programmes is entrusted to three tier panchayats. District Plan is an integrated depiction of panchayat plan and municipality plan. The next section discusses some facets of the district plan and the process of planning.

III

In the foreword of the Approach to the Eleventh Five Year Plan for West Bengal by the Chief Minister, the vision of the State Government is well depicted. To quote from the document:

> *"Our approach to the 11th Five Year Plan is to ensure an inclusive growth of the economy at a faster pace. The core objective will be to accelerate a pro poor growth process on a sustainable basis through creation of employment opportunities. The all round human development will be our vision for the plan. The success of our land reforms programme and firmly entrenched democratic decentralization will ensure our total commitment to the vision."*

With the effect of the Constitution (Seventy Fourth Amendment) Act, 1992, the Government of West Bengal passed the West Bengal District Planning Committee Act, 1994 for formation of District Planning Committee in the district. The Chairperson of the Zilla

Parishad has been made the Chairperson of the District Planning Committee. For the formulation of a district plan, the State Government classified all subjects into eleven sectors and placed the subjects under them. All these subjects take care of inclusive development in rural and urban areas. Then the schemes are placed under the appropriate head. These schemes are proposed by the panchayats for the rural segment and by the municipalities for urban areas. In Table 7 the sectors and heads of district planning are presented to have a comprehensive view of the subjects taken up for planning in a district.

Table–7
Sectors and Heads of the District Plan

Name of Sector	*Name of Heads*
1. Agriculture and Allied Sectors	*(i)* Crop husbandry, *(ii)* Horticulture and food processing, *(iii)* Soil and water conservation, *(iv)* Animal husbandry, *(v)* Fisheries, *(vi)* Co-operation, *(vii)* Any other agricultural project
2. *(a)* Rural Development	*(i)* Special programmes for rural development, *(ii)* Rural employment generation, *(iii)* Land reforms, *(iv)* Other rural development programmes
(b) Urban Development	Urban development programmes
3. Special Area Programme	Other special area programmes
4. Irrigation and Flood Control	*(i)* Minor irrigation, *(ii)* Drainage
5. Energy	*(i)* Electricity, *(ii)* Non-conventional source of energy, *(iii)* Integrated Rural Energy Programme
6. Industry and Minerals	*(i)* Cottage and small scale industries, *(ii)* Food processing industry
7. Transport	*(i)* Roads and bridges, *(ii)* Road transport, *(iii)* Inland water transport
8. Science, Technology and Environment	*(i)* Information technology, *(ii)* Environment, *(iii)* Forestry and wild life

Contd...

Name of Sector	*Name of Heads*
9. General Economic Services	*(i)* Civil supplies,
	(ii) Tourism
10. Social Services	*(i)* General education,
	(ii) Literacy and adult education,
	(iii) Technical education,
	(iv) Sports and culture,
	(v) Youth welfare,
	(vi) Art and culture,
	(vii) Health,
	(viii) Water supply and sanitation,
	(ix) Housing,
	(x) Labour welfare,
	(xi) Other social services
11. General Services	*(i)* Capacity building

From the sectoral classification of the subjects for planning, it can be seen that the coverage is universal. Each local body is responsible for implementing development and welfare schemes located within its geographical jurisdiction. In a district plan broadly there are two types of schemes, namely, *(a)* local body schemes and *(b)* line department schemes. Local body schemes are those schemes which are to be implemented by each tier of the panchayats or the urban bodies in the district. For specific determination of the schemes, the State Planning Board defined schemes on the basis of their location: "schemes that cover more than one gram panchayat will be categorized as schemes of the panchayat samiti having jurisdiction over the gram panchayat concerned, while those that cover more than one panchayat samiti will be categorized as schemes of the Zilla Parishad having jurisdiction over the panchayat samiti concerned." If there are schemes covering more than one urban local body in a district or an urban local body and a block tier panchayat then those schemes will be included under line department schemes. Schemes covering more than one district, according to the guidelines are included under State Sector Schemes. As District Planning Committee is the authority at district level for plan formulation, the State Planning Board gives instruction that "in all cases where the line department has a state or a district sector schemes, it will invariably intimate the district planning committee and take into consideration its views in finalising the schemes." In democratic and decentralized planning process it is usual that the decision making authority rests with the elected representatives. For technical support and other associated functions, the Government Officials in different line departments will only act as facilitators in the process. On this logical background, the State Government deputes its employees at different levels of the local bodies. The process is termed as devolution of functionaries. Making plans successful from the viewpoint of its implementation and outcome, the adequate devolution of functionaries is essential along with devolution of functions and funds. The Zilla Parishad, panchayat samiti and urban local bodies have a certain set up of employees to implement schemes and functions assigned to them. Only at gram panchayat level, the existing staff strength seems to be not so sufficient to cope with the works entrusted to them. The opinions of the Expert Committee on Planning at the Grassroots Level may be quoted here to explain the nature of a district plan :

> *"The object of district planning is to arrive at an integrated, participatory coordinated idea of development of a local area. An essential step in this direction is to ensure that each panchayat at any level or municipality is treated as a planning unit and the district plan is built up through consolidation and integration of these plans as well as by considering the development of the district as a whole."*

As mentioned earlier, in West Bengal, the planning process in the rural areas originates from the gram sansad. Generally in November meeting of the gram sansad the demands are placed, discussed and recommended to the gram panchayat for consideration in gram panchayat plan. On the basis of the principle of subsidiarity, projects and activities which can be implemented at the gram panchayat level should be included in gram panchayat plan. From the gram sansad, only the lists of names of schemes for different programmes and locations are raised. In case of individual benefit oriented programmes, such as Indira Awas Yojana for house construction and augmentation of existing houses, the gram sansad prepares lists for the prospective beneficiaries. The West Bengal Panchayat Act in the sub-section (3) of Section 19, inserted through an amendment in the year 2003, makes it obligatory on the part of the gram panchayat to accept the recommendation of a gram sansad, if it is not otherwise impossible.

In democratizing the process of planning, the State Government places enormous importance on the people's options. Utmost efforts are made to respect them. Through an amendment of the West Bengal Panchayat Act in the year 2003, the State Government created a Block Sansad in every panchayat samiti and a Zilla Sansad in every Zilla Parishad. All members of the gram panchayats pertaining to the Block and all members of that panchayat samiti are the members of the Block Sansad (Section 115A of the Act). Likewise, Pradhans of all gram panchayats in a district, Sabhapatis, Sahakari-Sabhapatis and Chairpersons of standing committees in panchayat samitis, and all members of the Zilla Parishad are the members of the Zilla Sansad (Section 163A of the Act). Unlike gram sansad, only people's representatives are the members of these sansads. Demands and aspirations of the local people are represented through their elected representatives at village, block and district panchayats. The West Bengal Panchayat Act clearly defines the functions of the Block Sansad and the Zilla Sansad. It will be relevant here to quote the provision of the Act in respect of the block sansad:

> *"The Block Sansad shall guide and advise the Panchayat Samiti for all matters relating to development including preparation of annual plan and budget, implementation of development programmes, schemes or projects and for undertaking such activities for economic development and for ensuring social justice as are undertaken or proposed to be undertaken by the Panchayat Samiti..." (Sub-Section 5 of Section 115A of the Act).*

For the Zilla Sansad, the functions are laid down in the Act in similar language. Only replacement is the words 'the Zilla Sansad' in place of 'the Block Sansad' and 'Zilla Parishad' in place of 'Panchayat Samiti.' These two sansads are constituted for making functioning more democratic and furthering the process of decentralized decision making.

Keeping in view the broad objective of inclusive growth in the Eleventh Five Year Plan, the State Planning Board introduced the components of 'gender plan' and 'children plan' in a district plan. The purpose has been explained in the Approach to the Eleventh Five Year Plan for West Bengal:

> *"In tune with faster and more inclusive growth the State would have distinct and focussed Gender Plan to ensure address of the gender related issues, programme outreach and level of social and women empowerment. All cross sectoral issues under Gender Plan would be coordinated and convergence of programme initiatives*

ensured in partnership with civil society both at the State level and also at the decentralized levels. To this end there would also have decentralized Gender Plan under District Plan and also to all tiers of the Panchayat and the Municipality/Corporation plan."

So far experiences go, gender plan component is included in district plans prepared by the district planning committees. But in the ground below, this concept is yet to be conceptualized by the grassroots decision makers. Education, health, promotion of livelihood and dissemination of livelihood related options including wage employment and self-employment, mobilization of social supports etc. are included in the gender plan. The main intention is to intensify the need based delivery mechanism at all levels and to reduce gender discrimination in different sectors.

In case of Children Plan, the approach of the State Government is expressed in this way: "For the children of today and tomorrow, the State Government would build up children—specific support system for our children to grow as citizens of future India keeping in consideration the rights of the child and also the need for faster and more inclusive growth." In this plan, education, health care including routine immunization of all children, provision of child labour etc. are included as components. However, appropriate sensitization of the decision-making persons is yet to be grounded with full thrust. There may be some isolated efforts.

In Lieu of a Conclusion

From the discussions on different measures unleashed by the Government of West Bengal for revamping the panchayats, it is clear that all these were taken for democratizing their activities. It is true that the panchayat representatives are elected by people. Involvement of local people in all affairs of the panchayats, however, is not generally evolved. Considering the reality, several provisions are incorporated in the West Bengal Panchayat Act for ensuring people's participation in the functioning of the panchayats. Achieving inclusive growth is very much in the West Bengal Panchayat Act as social justice cannot be secured without inclusive development. It is doubtful whether the elected representatives in the panchayats and officials at the field level are fully aware of the different facets of inclusive growth. In the guidelines of different rural development programmes, there are specific components for benefits of the so far disadvantaged sectors like scheduled castes, scheduled tribes and women. Even after such obligation, the coverage does not satisfy the requirement. As a consequence the chasm simply widens instead of being bridged. Planning exercise at the gram panchayat level can do justice to the disadvantaged people if this exercise is done fruitfully and effectively. The common practice is to comply the orders from above with proforma report. Gram Panchayat plan contains only lists of schemes and names of persons to be benefited under different programmes entrusted to the gram panchayats for implementation. No participatory assessment is practiced, even if the provisions are there in the West Bengal Panchayat Act. It is true that the State Government in West Bengal is very much keen on making the panchayats pro-people. In reality, this is not being executed effectively and efficiently. For inclusive growth, it is of very much necessity that the State Government provides adequate untied funds to the panchayats for meeting critical gaps in their jurisdictions. Most of the funds provided to the panchayats for implementation of centrally sponsored and central sector programmes are tied in nature. The panchayats have no autonomy in the process of implementation. This calls for urgency of untied fund.

Lack of proper database at gram panchayats is a serious limitation in the planning process. This often compels adoption of adhocism in plan formulation. As planning denotes organizations of future activities in rational manner, lack of database often influences the local level policy makers to adopt irrational practices.. For example, in the lists of beneficiaries, in place of needy and indigent villagers, better off persons are included (the debates over inclusion of families in below poverty line lists bear such evidences). Even the existing divides are not well captured in the database available at village and block level panchayats. Sufficient improvement is necessary in this front for designing plans reflecting the reality. For achieving inclusive growth this is an essential step also.

REFERENCES

Chakraborty, G. and Ghosh P.K. — Human Development Profile of Scheduled Castes and Scheduled Tribes in Rural India: A Benchmark Survey Published by National Council of Applied Economic Research, 2000.

Department of Panchayats and Rural Development, Government of West Bengal — Annual Administrative Report, 2003-04.

Development and Planning Department, Government of West Bengal – Approach to the Eleventh Five Year Plan for West Bengal, 2007.

Planning Commission, Government of India:

(i) Ninth Five Year Plan, Volume II.

(ii) Tenth Five Year Plan, Volume II.

(iii) Report of the Expert Group on Planning at the Grassroots Level, 2006.

(iv) Towards Faster and More Inclusive Growth—An Approach to the 11th Five Year Plan, 2006.

20

NGOs for Inclusive Development

P.K. ROY BARMAN

In order to give special thrust on economic development the government has laid emphasis to establish Special Economic Zone (SEZ) in different areas of the country; the zones are in the process of identification. Simultaneously the concept of inclusive growth has also been conceived in a larger dimension. It is a fact that total development of a country like ours mostly depends on the implementation of the concept of inclusive growth covering more than 70 per cent of geographical area of our vast country and the population as well. The civil society and the Non-Government Organisations (NGOs) play a pivotal role so far as inclusive development is concerned. The study on the issue has been made from the view point of the prevailing economic condition of West Bengal *vis-a-vis* the human resource development of the state. The results of the study are presented in the following sections;

I. Introduction
II. Scope of the Study
III. Civil Society, Innovative NGOs and Challenges
IV. Inclusive Development through NGO
   (i) Thrust on Income Generation
   (ii) Thrust on Literacy and Education
   (iii) Thrust on Health Care
   (iv) Thrust on Micro Credit
V. Concluding Observations

I

Introduction

Development of a nation depends on the human resources, the

endowment of natural resources and the attainment of technological skill. Given the natural resources and the technological advance at a point of time, the development of the nation then virtually is a function of human resources. It is the quality of human resources that determines the economic growth of a nation. Human resources play a significant role in economic growth of India. But this resource remains undeveloped in different aspects. Illiteracy, ill health and low level of income are our constant agony. The nation is trapped in a low level equilibrium. The rate of growth of our economy has been very low in spite of many decades of planning. Under the Five Year Plans Governments, both central and state level, have spent huge financial resource through budgetary allocation. This has yielded some good results, but still a huge problem remains, which the government alone cannot solve.

Development through administrative set up has a standard pattern. The proposals and programmes for development are formulated at higher level, which often appear to be inconsistent with the diversified character of the ground realities. This results in implementation gap. Over a period of time, therefore, there develops a hiatus between the set objectives and the realized benefits.

The standard pattern of proposals for welfare programmes of the government requires to be flexible and continuously adaptable. But the nature of administration does not allow it to happen occasionally. The NGOs are civil society organizations, which spring up from the spontaneous inspiration and imagination of the civil society. It is, therefore, more likely that the NGOs reflect the many-sided aspirations and the views of the different segments of the society.

Fifty years of our planning has provided the lessons that huge problem of under-development of the society cannot singularly be tackled by centralized planning and development agencies set up by the government. NGO programmes of different characters, extensively working at the grassroot level, can tackle the local problems in a more significant way. However, it is to work within the decentralized framework of our democratic administration.

Theories of social welfare furnished principles of efficient allocation of resources in order to have optimal social welfare. Welfare economists work extensively to find out the direction of social progress through the social reform organizations. The NGO study is perfectly consistent with the theoretical set up of welfare optimization of the society.

This study attempts to make an assessment of the importance of NGOs in our society as to how far they are efficient in contributing to the objective of inclusive development so also the human resource development in West Bengal.

II

Scope of the Study

A significant part of the State of West Bengal is relatively more backward economically and also less advanced in terms of human development. There are regional imbalances in the districts. It is worth mentioning that in terms of more obvious indicators of human development, the state is somewhere in the middle of all Indian states. Per capita State Domestic Product in West Bengal in the late 1990 was just above the national average. Per capita consumption expenditure in 1999-00 (according to National Sample Survey Organization) in West Bengal was Rs. 572. According to the Planning Commission, the incidence of poverty in West Bengal in 1999-2000 is such that 27 per cent of the population are below the poverty line, which was marginally higher than the national average of 26 per cent. However, it was more rurally concentrated; 84 per cent of the absolutely poor population in West Bengal live in rural areas, compared to 74 per cent in India as a whole. Literacy and education indicators in West Bengal are well below the expected level that could be achieved during the last two and half decades under a new administrative set up. The aggregate literacy (at 69% in 2001) was marginally above the national average of 65 per cent. Only 63 per cent of children in West Bengal in the age group of 7 – 14 years were literate in 1991 compared to all – India proportion of 64 per cent. Human development in West Bengal presents a mixed picture and this picture is further complicated by the variation across the districts in the state. This regional imbalance is the resultant effect of the prevailing socio-economic conditions. There is no denial of the fact, that State Government is giving much efforts for redressal but government requires an extended hand to supplement it's effort. There is ample scope to study the problems from various points one of which is implementing agency and a supervisory body acceptable to the State Government. It is also worth examining what role can NGOs play in human resources development in West Bengal. The qualitative improvement of the factors that contribute to the human development can take care of narrowing the regional imbalances.

Government of West Bengal has an administrative network upto the field level to transmit the plans and programmes of different activities in respect of health and literacy development. But the government does not have required infrastructure to reach the common people of different socio-economic profile upto the remotest part of the state. In order to face such a situation it is expected that NGOs can add to extension services rendered by the government. The NGOs, when formed in the remotest part of the state, establish good rapport with the local population and as such they know better about the health and literacy of the people. So these NGOs can be accepted as media or agencies through which government can reach people; and the NGOs can lend support for implementation of the programme.

Non-Government Organization (NGOs) generally works with local people's organization. They work through local people. NGOs help local people to organize activities in a more or less formal manner, which is very important part of participating approach. Such type of integration of working with people is a goal for development agencies and also is a right of local people. It helps to increase effectiveness, enhancing communication, mobilizing local resources and exchanging local cooperation It is also meant to develop access of local people to NGO resource and services and expand distribution of benefit of any schemes and project. The aspect of building local organization empowers local people, boosting their capacity to act for themselves in many practical ways in the locality. Such type of organization ultimately helps local people to find equality within local leadership. It will be convenient if example of Bangladesh is cited here where the poorer men in Bangladesh have control over the sources of irrigation that was needed by farmers. In this process they were able to negotiate for satisfactory payment with the better-off farmers. Local organizations are thus seen as a vehicle to stronger civil society by helping local people or even in participating with government and NGO themselves. In order to achieve these various traits of quality, sustainability and greater equality, NGOs act for creating of initial awareness to group formation and resourcing and finalizing as a local organization.

III

Civil Society, Innovative NGOs and Challenges

Economic reforms now pursued for economic advancement may provide for a new thinking to our economic institutions. But the development of the country largely depends on structured non-economic set up of the society. For historical and administrative reasons the structure of the society remains fragmented, passive and often inoperative. Hence to activate the civil society suffering from various types of these social and cultural drawbacks, innovative organizations should be encouraged. NGOs of various types are important institutional assets, which can overcome these drawbacks. In the present study we like to stress upon this important aspect of organization and possibilities of civil society as reflected in the formation and functioning of the NGOs. In the civil society some functions are carried by the people in unorganized manner. These social functions are for welfare of mankind. The society should come in an organized way for specific purposes of development. Once this is done in an organized way, it adds to the developmental system of the society. The examples of puja committee, "haz" committee can be cited to substantiate this statement. These are formed sporadically and spontaneously. Once these are organized they can perform better. We can also take the examples of football club. These are the clubs which have hardly any organized attempt throughout the year for development of the game. They also have hardly any systematic and organized attempt for improvement of skills of players. Even in the country as a whole no organized attempt is observed to have taken by the club or association for improvement of the skill of the players. In reality no contribution is made by the club and even by All India Associations of different games and sports. No fruitful scheme on that score is in existence. One may wonder how many NGOs have devoted to development of the games. It is also evident from the results of World Olympic that no creative effort has been made by the government for development of the games in the country. Is it not the responsibility of civil society also? But, however, in West Bengal there are organized societies, which by their own effort and application of mind develop the skill and aptitude for drama and theatre etc., some even have reached the national and international height. Civil society has always independence; creativity of the civil society will continuously find expression in the formation of social organization of various complexions. Even now-a-days in the era of science, a section of people is charged with superstition of various nature and misconception in respect of peripheral phenomenon of human life. Only organized effort to create awareness among the people can eradicate the superstition, misconceptions, misgivings and orthodox beliefs. This requires efforts and penetration and awareness among the people, which can be performed by organized social units. These superstitions are mostly found among the illiterate people who having no proper education and motivation always become prey to superstitions and as such to so called well wishers of the section of the society. Government cannot weed out such superstition from the mind and thought of the people. Only the organized society, so to say social organization, can bring this people out of treacherous fold. Educated person of the society has to play the pivotal role to wipe out the tentacles of such dangerous superstitions. Government by way of enactment of any law or provision cannot fight against such human enemies; only the society without enforcement of any law can do it. There lies the responsibility of NGOs. They can transform the status of such illiterate people through continuous motivation and innovative ideas, thoughts and examples. These are the challenges to be confronted by a civil society and can be overcome by a sensible and committed social organization.

NGOs have a relatively long history, but their numbers and profile rose significantly during the past decade. In India voluntary action is not new. Historically, individuals and associations helped the poor and destitute among crisis. For instance, kitchens were set up by the rich and affluent during the famines to provide food to the destitutes etc. Social reformers initiated and sustained movements against certain types of social practices such as "sati", "bride-price" and for widow "re-marriages" etc. Most of the reform activities and movements were led by concerned and like-minded upper caste individuals who had been exposed to western education. Some examples are the Atmiya Sabha (1815) and Brahmo Samaj in Bengal. Swaminarayan Sect and Manohar Dharma Sabha of Gujarat, the Prarthana Samaj and Hindu Dharma Sabha in Maharashtra and Arya Samaj in the North. The work of these organizations formed mostly on recognizing the access of "untouchables" to education and worship and the access of women to education for a better social status within Hindu society.

The Christian Missionaries did considerable work relating to charity, welfare and provision of services. Decades ago, two American Missionaries called Dr. and Mrs. Spencer Hatch, devoted their energies to YMCA programme for impaired poultry and bee keeping for honey in the Marthondam Taluk of Trivandrum. Another missionary called Dr. Leonard Elmbirst from U.K. in collaboration with Rabindranath Tagore, worked on rural reconstructions and made Shantiniketan as a pioneering institution. Sundaram (1986) observed, a large number of Christian Missionaries established educational institutions, hospitals and the charitable institutions for the poor. In the zeal to recruit converts, the Missionaries brought educational and health service to the poor even in the rural areas.

The significant development started taking place in India and across the world by 1990s. NGOs had become popular with government and aid agencies in response to certain developments in economic and political thinking (Edwards 1995 and Hulme 1996). The development policy of World Bank, bilateral and multi-lateral agencies and aid transfers from then onwards have come to be dominated by what is referred to as "New Policy Agenda", which gives a prominent role to the NGOs in poverty alleviation and in development of civil society (Robinson 1993). The agenda has mainly two elements; economic and political. The aid agencies prescribed that Indian Government should gradually reduce its role in service provision and development, and leave the task to the NGOs as these are seen as cost effective and efficient providers. Seemingly the role of Government has changed from police state to welfare state and subsequently to a development state. Correspondingly, NGOs had undergone various generations of change role such as charity, relief, welfare, development and empowerment. The role of various development organizations is basically complementary and hence development partnership is inevitable for the furtherance of the cause of development. The role expected from NGO is complementary but distinct from government, business and informal groups. The NGOs in India have contributed handsomely towards social activities through their intense campaigns, people's mobilization programmes and effective network.

In the process of participation of NGOs in different activities especially economic activities by themselves and through the Self-

Help Groups (SHGs) organized by the NGOs, the NGOs are directly and indirectly playing role in development of people of the country and different states as well. Whatever contribution is made by the NGOs, it creates an impact on the development of human resource of the country in different ways viz., education health, sanitary, housing, childcare, mother care, nutrition etc. NGOs are the voluntary agencies that come to the help and aid of government.

IV

Inclusive Development through NGO

Government of West Bengal is providing various types of extension services coupled with financial package for economic growth *vis-à-vis* development of human resources. As stated earlier many NGOs of different types have come to supplement the government efforts. Although the growth and generation of NGOs are sporadic and spontaneous they are playing some roles of their own. Theses social organizations require to be properly designing, guiding and utilizing for social welfare. NGOs are not self-sufficient, neither from the viewpoint of economic condition nor organizational and administrative set up. They are to depend on government and other philanthropic institutions, which come forward for paving the way for infrastructural development required for human development and management as well. As stated, it is a fact that these organizations can penetrate into the areas where government cannot operate in the process they can establish rapport with common people and can understand very closely to earn people's confidence. This confidence goes a long way to create an atmosphere where human resources can be better treated and utilized in desired manner. This is virtually the offshoot of group dynamism where gradually a sense of belongingness and cohesion develop there-by generating a concept of "instinct of herd." This instinct of herd acts as a catalyst to accelerate the social activities of the NGOs. It is an established fact that NGOs can bring substantial change in spheres of life be it social, economic, cultural and value system of human being. We can cite examples of Ramakrishna Mission, Bharat Sevashram Sangha, Missionaries of Charity etc. It gives us to understand that human resources when properly directed with the principle of motivation can bring a remarkable change in the society.

The role played by the NGOs is primarily a voluntary one; the natural instinct is the driving force. But the core quality of NGO is the behavioural aspect along with value perception and value system. These are the motive forces where the values are not identical. NGO's attitude predisposes oneself to value one's thought plan. In some cases effort may be directed to amassing money. In other places NGO values service to the mankind and strives to achieve that. Such understanding of values and service to mankind can be from personal angle, attitude and social environment. There may exist a duality in an NGO consisting of value of individual or group or vice versa. According to Indian thought, in real perspective the blending of moral values and the capability of individual or society can bring about a substantial social structure for development. People can contribute to the formation of NGOs for successful performance of their function. The integral part of a good value system is commitment. When the NGO's value system is clear, it becomes a lot easier to make decision and commitment. Lack of commitment along with lack of devotion destabilizes relationship and lead to insecurity and causes failure of the organization. Now-a-days it is observed that in some NGOs there is renewed interest in integrating human values for transformation into an effective organization. They are to understand to whom they owe loyalties.

(i) Thrust on Income Generation

NGOs provide funds and physical support with non-profit motive to the members of SHGs organized by them – NGO. With the objective of raising income level of the member beneficiaries, the NGOs have identified economic activities of various types namely agriculture, animal husbandry, village industries, small trading, small business and small scale industries etc. for the members and they have been provided financial support by way of bank credit and credit from the NGO itself. SHGs themselves also raise funds by thrift and lend it to their members. While studying the level of income generation the concept of per capita domestic products of the beneficiaries has been applied and in order to find out the variation due to NGOs intervention the per capita domestic product of the beneficiaries during pre NGO support and post NGO support has been considered. In order to collect data 100 beneficiaries under each NGO of such 10 NGOs have been randomly selected. An example of how NGOs help the members of SHGs can be seen from the table on next page.

Table–1
Per Capita Domestic Product of the Beneficiaries of the Areas Studied (Pre and Post NGO Support)

(Rs.)

NGOs	*Number of Beneficiaries*	*Pre NGO Support*	*Post NGO Support*	*Increase*	*% of Increase*
1	100	12132.25	13905.20	1772.95	14.61
2	100	11750.18	12810.21	1060.03	9.02
3	100	13610.20	14845.20	1235.00	9.07
4	100	12525.15	13538.19	1013.04	8.09
5	100	11920.10	13110.20	1190.10	9.98
6	100	12527.15	13987.18	1460.03	11.65
7	100	11889.25	13015.25	1126.00	9.47
8	100	11985.20	13705.15	1719.95	14.35
9	100	13275.18	14498.12	1222.94	9.21
10	100	13392.39	14832.60	1440.21	10.75
Average	100	12500.71	13824.52	1324.03	10.59

Source: Field Study.

The table represents per capita domestic product of the randomly selected beneficiaries of the areas identified for study. It is evident from the above table that with the intervention of NGO through financial help in the manner of micro credit the beneficiaries have been able to raise the per capita income by adopting various activities the increase of per capita income in each case ranges from lowest Rs. 1013.04 to highest Rs. 1772.95. It is considered, given proper guidance and support per capita income will go high. In this study each beneficiary has been taken as a unit and accordingly the domestic product has been worked out.

In course of study it has been observed that the beneficiary has either taken up the activities individually or on the basis of "cluster approach" of one type of activity. Cluster approach has helped successful implementation of the schemes and marketing of the product as well. It has also been observed that while arranging for financial support the NGOs have also arranged for formulation of economically viable projects and post credit supervision for end use of fund with training support wherever necessary. The surplus

Table-2
Per Capita Consumption Dimension of the Areas Under Study
Per Capita Monthly Consumption

(Rs.)

NGO	*Pre NGO Intervention*	*Post NGO Intervention with Financial Help*
1	415.75	550.25
2	426.85	495.69
3	375.26	415.25
4	385.70	425.10
5	375.20	405.50
6	398.25	430.35
7	415.50	460.15
8	385.15	425.50
9	407.15	485.00
10	290.25	335.75
Average	387.51	444.29

Source: Field Study.

Table-3
Poverty Dimension of the Area Under Study
(Poverty Ratio) – (%)

NGO	*Poverty Ratio Pre NGO Intervention*	*Post NGO Intervention*
1	15.25	12.50
2	27.15	23.75
3	19.90	15.05
4	59.85	52.15
5	52.50	44.80
6	29.75	25.10
7	19.60	16.20
8	28.50	23.75
9	28.10	22.05
10	76.51	71.25
Average	35.71	30.66

Source: Field Study.

generated out of economic activities have helped to increase the per capita domestic product and the standard of living and generation of surplus fund to meet the emergent need of the family.

(ii) Thrust on Education and Literacy

The literacy rate is generally considered as one of the important indicators of the development of population and the educational level of a population is seen as an important determinant of quality of life. The tenth five-year plan observes: "Performance in the field of education is one of the disappointing aspects of India's development strategy. Out of 200 million children in the age group 6 to 14 years, only 120 million are in schools and net attendance in the primary level is only 66 per cent of enrolment. This is completely unacceptable and the tenth plan should aim at a radical transformation in this situation." Literacy is the widely used and most comprehensive indicator for reflecting achievement in respect of education sector. Literacy rate, according to the Census definition is the proportion of literates to total population in the age group of 7 years and above.

Table–4

Literacy Percentage During Pre and Post NGO Intervention

NGOs	*Number of Beneficiaries*	*Aggregate Literacy Rate (%) Pre NGO Intervention*	*Aggregate Literacy Rate (%) Post NGO Intervention*	*Change in Literacy*
1	100	64.6	57.8	3.2
2	100	50.7	56.7	6.0
3	100	48.6	55.8	7.2
4	100	75.6	79.7	4.1
5	100	63.8	67.9	4.1
6	100	54.1	59.2	5.1
7	100	59.6	66.2	7.4
8	100	72.2	76.9	4.7
9	100	71.2	76.8	5.6
10	100	61.1	67.7	6.6
Average	100	62.15	67.47	5.32

Source: Field Study.

In view of above the NGOs are playing a constructive role. The "Abhijan" scheme, which has been, introduced by the government has already given a thrust on increasing literacy in the rural and semi urban areas. The efforts made by NGO in this area have become an added contribution to make the people literate thereby increasing the literary percentage of particular area which ultimately adds to the achievement of the state. The following table shows how NGOs have contributed to literacy percentage and schooling etc. This indicator has been studied in relation to Census literacy rate of the population of area under study and school enrolment rate as well.

Primary School Enrolment

Progress in literacy and education is dependent upon the propensity of children to go to school and also to complete the primary level education. But it has been observed during study that lack of progress can become self-reinforcing, in terms of reducing the incentives among children to carry on with schooling when the parents are not educated. It has also been observed that enrolment ratios of children in primary schools tends to be strongly related to the educational level among adults in the same household. This is also true of West Bengal where studies indicate high correlation of both enrolment and attendance with parental literacy rate and with parents' education levels. The data in relation to central literacy rate of area under study and the actual school enrolment rate on the basis of study form the education index of the particular area. The school enrolment rate of the areas under study is given in the following table.

Table–5
School Enrolment (rate %) of the Areas Under Study in Pre and Post NGO Intervention

NGOs	*School Enrolment Rate*			
	Pre Ngo Intervention	*Post NGO Intervention*	*Increase*	*Increase in Percentage*
1	66.51	70.54	4.03	6.06
2	52.53	58.59	6.06	11.54
3	50.55	57.61	7.06	13.97
4	78.50	84.58	6.08	7.75
5	66.49	73.57	7.08	10.65
6	56.55	63.61	7.06	12.48

Contd...

NGOs	School Enrolment Rate			
	Pre Ngo Intervention	*Post NGO Intervention*	*Increase*	*Increase in Percentage*
7	63.56	68.61	5.05	7.95
8	75.57	81.62	6.05	8.01
9	74.52	79.56	5.04	6.76
10	64.58	70.65	6.07	9.40
Average	64.94	70.89	5.95	9.17

Source : Field Study.

It is evident from the table that school enrolment rate has increased due to intervention of NGOs; the growth varies from lowest 4.03 to highest 7.08.

It has been observed during field study that in terms of social and caste categories the level of literacy among persons of age 7 years and above in the schedule tribe households is uniformly lower as compared to all other social categories. The problem of illiteracy is particularly acute among rural women from schedule tribe household with 70 per cent of them being non literate. Children who have never been to school tends to be concentrated in lower income schedule caste/ schedule tribe groups. Another important parameter studied is age wise school attendance ratio (%) influenced by the intervention of NGO; the data given below represent the position of all the areas studied served by all the NGOs taken together.

Table–6
Age Specific School Attendance Ratio

Pre NGO Intervention

Areas	*6-10 Years Age*			*11-13 Years Age*		
	Boys	*Girls*	*Children*	*Boys*	*Girls*	*Children*
Rural	60	56	58	69	65	67
Semi Urban	69	63	66	71	67	74

Post NGO Intervention

Areas	*6-10 Years Age*			*11-13 Years Age*		
	Boys	*Girls*	*Children*	*Boys*	*Girls*	*Children*
Rural	69	62	66	76	74	75
Semi Urban	76	68	72	79	73	76

Source: Field Study.

The table shows the positive growth of attendance ratio with the counselling of NGO.

Table-7
Dropout Rate in (Percentage) from School at Primary Level and Secondary Level

	Pre NGO Persuasion			*Post NGO Persuasion*		
	Boys	*Girls*	*Children*	*Boys*	*Girls*	*Children*
Primary level	5	6	6	2	4	3
Secondary level	25	28	27	20	21	22

Source: Field Study.

As discussed above when school enrolment is an important indicator of literacy another important issue is the rate of dropout from school, especially in the early stages of education. It is given in the following table in aggregate of all the NGOs – served areas under study. It is evident that there has also been decreased in school dropout rate due to persuasion by the NGOs.

It deserves mention that IIM (Kolkata) in conducting a study in relation to literacy and education level of West Bengal found that the dropout of rural children is 3 per cent compared to around 27 per cent of children from secondary level.

The typical reasons of dropout as studied are lack of interest in education, inability to meet expenses, distance of the school from home and the need to attending to domestic and other household duties. As per Human Development Report of West Bengal 2004 the dropout rates tend to be higher in 10-14 years of age, at around 18 per cent.

From the above table it is also evident that with the involvement of NGO in the literacy programme the school enrolment rate, age specific school attendance and dropout rate in percentage from school at both primary and secondary level have changed favourably.

(iii) Thrust on Health Care

The performance of NGO in respect of health care has been studied considering the life expectancy of the population of the areas under study, which is represented, in the following table:

Table-8
Life Expectancy (Pre and Post NGO Intervention)
(Average of 5 Years)

NGO	*Maximum*		*Minimum*	
	Pre NGO Intervention	*Post NGO Intervention*	*Pre NGO Intervention*	*Post NGO Intervention*
1	69	71	30	32
2	67	69	25	29
3	65	67	25	28
4	70	71	25	26
5	65	68	24	26
6	67	70	26	27
7	68	68	27	28
8	61	68	25	26
9	64	67	25	27
10	64	67	26	28
Average	66.0	68.6	26.0	28.0

Source: Field Study.

Like attainment in education, health attainment is also a very crucial for achieving respectable level of inclusive development. It is the normal expectations that State Government ensures its population a healthy life, which provides with a reasonable life span. Tenth Plan reinitiates the assurances given in eighth plans. The Tenth Plan observes "improvement in the health status of the population has been one of the major thrust areas in social development programmes of the country." There are many indicators to assess the health attainment of the citizen.

(iv) Thrust on Micro Credit

The performance of selected SHGs under supervision of 10 different NGOs under report are given below in the table both in respect of credit availability and surplus generation:

In course of study it revealed that:

(i) Individual loans are very useful for women empowerment. These loans are mostly used for production purposes resulting in income generation and not for consumption proposes as are commonly believed.

Table–9
Availability of Loan by Individual Members of SHG

(Rs.)

SHGs Under Selected NGO	*Use of Credit*		*Total*
	Production	*Consumption*	
1	6000	1000	7000
2	3000	Not availed	3000
3	1500	500	2000
4	4000	500	4500
5	4600	1000	5600
6	3500	500	4000
7	4600	1000	5600
8	4500	1000	5500
9	5000	1000	6000
10	5500	1000	6550
Total	**42200**	**7500**	**49700**

Source: Field Study.

(ii) The groups borrow fund at lower rate of interest and relend to members at higher rate of interest to cover expenses of the SHGs including risk premium.

(iii) NGOs play a very positive role in establishing forward and backward linkages, mobilizing resources and arrangement for marketing of SHG –products.

Table–10
Incremental Income Earned by Individual Members of SHGs

	Range of Monthly Incremental Income			
	Rs. 100-250	*Rs. 250-300*	*Rs. 300-500*	*Above 500*
1	-	Yes	-	-
2	-	Yes	-	-
3	-	Yes	-	Yes
4	-	-	Yes	-
5	-	-	-	Yes
6	-	Yes	-	-
7	-	-	-	Yes

Contd...

	Range of Monthly Incremental Income			
	Rs. 100-250	*Rs. 250-300*	*Rs. 300-500*	*Above 500*
8	-	-	Yes	-
9	-	-	Yes	-
10	-	-	Yes	-

Source: Field Study.

V

Concluding Observation

Civil society everywhere is organized by association or body of the people. In the early stage of the social development social bodies used to play dominant role in the management of society. Even today the replica of that social management is found in tribal society. The developed social system of the public administration has been evolved as a determinate authority. The public administration is of different complexion—democratic, autocratic and dictatorial etc. However in a democratic system public administration is supposed to work for the people because the administration is run by the people and it is composed of the people. It is essential to combine the public administration and the NGOs in order to fill up the gap in social development task. NGO programme has now, therefore, become an essential part of human development agenda and inclusive growth of the economy.

In our study of NGOs in West Bengal we have seen large number of NGOs are engaged in social development work. Indeed NGO can be a pioneer, mediator, facilitator and a catalyst. We have found that when the NGOs properly work with commitment and devotion to the specific cause of inclusive development they can serve as an effective alternative agency in the development process. However there are small and sporadic NGOs, which are continually emerging in a pluralistic society. Although they can serve as pivotal role in attaining human well-being this is not always so. Many NGOs are not upto the mark of standard social organisation. They suffer from inefficient management, doubtful financial accountability and are committed to religion or metaphysical conduct of the life. NGOs in such cases tend to be bias and unscientific in their approach to social development.

The NGO-set up should, therefore, be regulated in a system of decentralized administrative mechanism. Panchayat should be associated with the NGOs so that the human development functions of the NGOs are under constant in view of people's representatives. NGOs play crucial role in formation, linkage and stabilization of SHGs. They have succeeded where the micro credit institutions have failed. It is encouraging that NGOs take the initiative to promote the SHGs in collaboration with and cooperation of the NABARD and bank. The SHGs, therefore, can penetrate among the common mass where the NGOs operate. In this respect panchayat renders very positive help to form the SHG units.

NGO cannot be an alternative to the government but it can, when properly conducted and aligned with public administration, supplement government development works.

REFERENCES

Amin, R. and Li Y., 1997, "NGO promoted Women's Credit Programme, Immunization Coverage, and Child Mortality in Rural Bangladesh, in Women and Health, 26(1), pp. 71-87.

Amin, R. and others, 1994, "Poor Women's Participation in Income Generation Projects and Thin Fertility Regulation in Rural Bangladesh – Evidence from a Recent Survey" in World Development 22(4), pp. 555-56.

Bernard, A., Helmich, H. and Lehning, P.B., 1998, Civil Society and Industrial Development, OECD Development Centre, Paris, OECD.

Bhatt, Anil, 1995 Voluntary Action in India – Role, Trends and Challenges, Economic and Political Weekly, Volume 30, No. 16, April 22, Bombay.

Blair, Harry, 1998, Civil Society, Employment, Democratic Pluralism, and Poverty Reduction: Delivering the Goods at National and Local Levels, Rawat Publication, Jaipur and New Delhi.

Cernea, Michael M., 1988, NGOs and Local Development in the World Bank, Washington, Discussion Paper 40.

Chatterjee, Biswajit and Dilip Kumar Ghosh, 2001, In Search of a District Development Index, State Institute of Panchayats and Rural Development, Kalyani, West Bengal.

Choudhury, A. Kumar, 2006 – NGOs and their Role in Poverty Alleviation, Indian Institute of Management, Kolkata.

Edward, M. and D. Hulme, 1996. "International Development NGOs; Legitimacy, Accountability, Regulations and Roles." A discussion paper for the Commissions on the Future of the Voluntary Sector and the British Overseas Aid Group, London: BOAG.

Government of India, 1992, Eighth Five-Year Plan 1992-97 Document, Planning Commission, and New Delhi.

Government of West Bengal 2004, West Bengal Human Development Report, Development and Planning Department.

Guha Roy, Samir and Sen Kasturi, 2002, Patterns of Health and Utilization and Expenditure; A Household Survey in India; West Bengal 1999, ISI, Kolkata.

Kallur, M.S. , 1992, "Income and Employment Generation" through IRDP for Rural Development in India", The Asian Economic Review, Vol. XXXIV, August, No. 2, pp. 340-58.

Kulkarni, V.M. , 1969, Voluntary Activities in a Developing Society, IIPA, New Delhi, p. 9.

Ministry of Finance, 1998, Economic Survey, 1997-98, Government of India, New Delhi.

Mukherjee N. and D. Bandopadhyay, 1993, New Horizon for West Bengal's Panchayats, Report submitted to the Department of Panchayat, Government of West Bengal.

Mukhopadhyay, Rabindranath, 2002, Tribal Education: The Case of West Bengal, Background Paper submitted for West Bengal State Development Report and Perspective 2007-08, Kolkata, May.

Ninth Five-Year Plan, 1997-2002, Government of India, Vol. 1, pp. 238-40.

Rahman, A. 1986, Impact of the Gramin Bank on the Nutritional Status of the Rural Poor, Bangladesh, Dhaka, Institute of Development Studies.

Robinson M., 1993, Governance, Democracy and Conditionality: NGOs and the New Policy Agenda, in A. Clayton (ed.), Governance Democracy and Conditionality: What Role for NGOs? Oxford, INTRAC.

Rao, D.V.R. , General Editor V.K.R.V. Rao, "Panchayats and Rural Development."

Ron, A., 1998, "NGOs in Community Health Insurance Schemes": Examples from Guatemala and the Philippines." ILO Paper Geneva, pp. 1-19.

Sarkar, Pranab and Mukherjee, Debesh, 2000, NGOs and India's Health Sector, Deep and Deep Publications, New Delhi.

Sundaram, S. and Moulasha, K. , 1994, "Child Adoption in India: An Overview," Yojana, Vol. 38, No. 10, June 15, 1994, pp. 26-27.

Sen, M., 2000, Self-Help Groups and Micro Finance: An Alternative Socio-Economic Option for the Poor, Deep and Deep Publications, New Delhi

The PROBE Team, 1999, Public Report on Basic Education in India, Center for Development Economics, Oxford University Press, 1999, p. 106.

Wahid, A.N.M., 1994, January, "The Gramin Bank and Poverty Alleviation in Bangladesh: Theory, Evidence and Limitations," in American Journal of Economics and Sociology, 53(1), pp. 1-17.

Yunus, M., 1998 a, "Poverty Alleviation: Is Economics any Help? Lessons from the Gramin Bank Experience," in Journal of International Affairs 52(1), pp. 47-65.

21

Gandhian Economics of Development

SUKHENDU MAZUMDAR

Gandhian Basics

It is a matter of controversy and a great debate whether we can successfully put the Gandhian economic philosophy into use in the context of Indian economic scenario. Hence, without giving it a fair trial, it would be quite impertinent to say that the Gandhian concept has lost its depth and efficacy. Gandhi was perhaps the only Indian to date who had traveled India covering its every nook and corner and who had far better understanding of the people and the economy from its grassroot level to the top. In the Words of Larry Collins and Dominique Lapierre ("Freedom at Midnight") to a country fraught with violence, Gandhi offered an alternative non-violence and civil disobedience. In Churchill's famous phrase, a 'Half-naked fakir' Gandhi crisscrossed his nation on foot and in third-class railway cars to stress his identity with the impoverished masses. He took tea at Buckingham Palace with King Emperor, dressed in the homespun cotton sheet that was his uniform and practiced a life of Spartan simplicity. The symbol of his challenge to the Age of Imperialism was the primitive wooden spinning wheel on which the laboured religiously everyday. Gandhiji, if viewed strictly, was not an economist or a politician in the academic sense of the term. He did never try to shape his principles under any system and yet it can be said with conviction that he is the only one in the world who has brought Economics, Politics, Ethics etc. closer and available to the general mass. It is often said that Gandhiji was not in favour of the use of machines where the labour-intensive system would do. But here lies the fundamental issue that Gandhiji was not against the use of machines as such, rather he wanted that labour should be employed. He was not against the use of large machines if that served the masses. The beauty of the concept is to provide employment to all. So it can be said that time has come that we should attempt to apply Gandhian techniques in the context of Indian economy. Also, it is to be mentioned that Gandhiji was very much keen to see a healthy India emerging out from the healthy and prosperous villages. It is a matter of deep concern that neither the centre nor the State Capitals pay the needed attention towards the villages. India lives in villages and we can bring a drastic change in the village economy by utilizing the untapped resources and by applying labour intensive methods which needs negligible capital. We can broadly divide his economic principles into three or four categories.

Controversy of Large and Small Scale Industries (Spl. Ref. to Khadi and Gramodyog)

The controversy of large-scale and small-scale industries in the realm of Gandhian thought has drawn the attention of many economists, political thinkers and analysts to study the same and scrutinize its applicability. But, Gandhi; at times appeared beyond fathom since he of ten changed his views when the same was felt necessary by him. Truly speaking, he never had a change in his basic principles of non-violence and truth. He believed in the welfare of the entire mankind.

Here it can of course be said that we cannot hold machinery guilty for such exploitations since it is the humans that has made things emerge like that. Hence, the root of the disease in lying elsewhere and not in the machines as has been doubted by the Mahatma. Because a tool in a skilled hand may prove very useful fore the welfare of the people and the same may become a terror if goes to the wrong hands. So the balanced and judicious use is the answer.

Gandhi felt that the capitalist process would make the richer more richer and the poor poorer. The impact of industrial process on our economy as felt by M.S. Patwardhan, "India's high cost Industrial sector has harmed the country in more ways than one. It has added to inflationary forces, impeded exports, reduced the rewards of high savings and investment ratio and slowed down economic growth." However, without inflationary does the economic growth does not get the forward push and the doubt as expressed by Gandhi and as expressed in favour of the same by Patwardhan may not be that serious if things are exercised in a balanced way.

But again the same Gandhi did talk in favour of machines as has been reflected when he says, ".... I know that my own body is nothing but an extraordinarily delicately constructed machine. The spinning wheel is also a machine.... I am not fighting against machinery as such, but the madness of thinking that machinery saves labour."

Again, Gandhiji was not against the large-scale or small-scale industries as such; rather his concern was that of peace and harmony in the society. He wanted that labour should get its due place in the system. Thus we find a thread of harmony existing in his concept linking the large-scale, small-scale and the cottage industry. It is hoped that his concept can be blended with the three successfully. Truly speaking, Gandhi had no problem in accepting the functioning of the large-scale industries if the same is required for the existence of the human beings. Gandhi had accepted the production of Singer Sewing Machines with the plea that the same should be gainfully employed and that might have been the root cause which prompted him going against the labour-saving device. In the villages where people remain unemployed during the off-season or sometimes for the whole year, there the upliftment is possible, only through the establishment of small and cottage industries. So he stressed on the Swadeshi movement and establishment of Charkha at every household so that the people remain absorbed in some occupation for the year round. His idea of Charkha is a uniqe concept with may a purposes. It can be established at a very low cost and with minimum of technical problem. Also, it would provide employment to all who aspire for. Another striking point was that it was a powerful medium which had a magical power to unite the whole nation into one soul. So the dual purpose was of politically uniting the country and then giving the people economic freedom. Thus Gandhi's Charkha and Khadi concept seem to be powerful enough to tackle the unemployment problem (including disguised or seasonal) and provide livelihood to millions. However Gandhi had to face severe criticism from many including the then Stalwarts Gurudev Rabindranath Tagore. Many did not see any utility in the concept as it failed to appeal them. But Gandhi was firm in his approach and continued his mission of non-violent and peaceful struggle till the end of his life. His remarks in Young India clearly asserts the same:

> "Khadi was once the dress of the nation at large ...... There are instances of whole villages taking a legitimate pride in

the fact they had to import nothing but salt in the whole round of six seasons. With such conditions, there could be no drain, no exploitation and therefore, no para-raj (others rule)." It's a pit that we have failed to produce 13 yards of cloth per head per year. But India is capable of producing her entire requirements through hand-weaving and hand-spinning and this venture can provide employment to millions. Hence, Swadeshi principle can bring an end to the problems of India's poverty. He was out and out a true patriot and a practical person. He could not accept the idea that our valuable national wealth should be misused or there should be any improper exploitation and at the same time he was eager to use the Swadeshi to arrest the exploitation of our national wealth. He observes, "It is the greatest delusion to suppose, that the duty of Swadeshi begins and ends with merely spinning some yearn anyhow and wearing khadi made form it. Khadi is the first indispensable step towards the discharge of Swadeshi dharma to society. But one often meets men, who wear khadi, while in all other things they indulge their taste for foreign manufactures. Such men cannot be said to be practicing Swadeshi. They are simply following the fashion."

Regarding the villages it can be opined that our villages can turn to self-sufficiently at ease provided they stop looking to the cities for every petty issue. In fact it is the villages that hold the key to prosperity and in reality the cities cannot survive without the active co-operation of the villages. If Gandhian concept is applied with some modification, we can turn our villages self-reliant and can reap a better-quality of life with minimum of expenses. Things produced in the villages are environment friendly and they can be produced with simple technical know-how and with simple tools and with less capital. Thus with some efforts on our part we can raise the village economy to glory. Here we can enumerate below few which can help change the village economic scenario quite effectively.

1. Ghanis and Kolhus to be used to produce Oil and Gur.
2. Vegetable and fruit production should be increased which can help the people to consume as well as to supply outside.
3. Better quality of cartel-breeding and scientific method of dairing to be introduced.

4. Improved methods of production for cotton, grains, sugarcane, soyabean etc. to be applied.
5. The use of Dhenki and Chakki to be revived for husking paddy, grinding wheat and breaking pulses etc.
6. Agricultural tools can be manufactured by the villagers themselves and the same can be improved gradually.

It is to be understood that there is virtually no conflict between the large-scale and small-scale industries and in practice, there are different areas of production which can be judiciously divided between these two sectors.

Agrarian Re-organization

It is clearly understood to all that agriculture is the basic feature of our economy and its developments in the right direction is important since it provides food to all and employment to many. In fact, more than 60 per cent of population are engaged in agriculture alone. If the food problem is kept under control, many other ills of the economy can be faced successfully. Gandhiji wanted that we should use very simple methods of production and must not go for the use of chemical fertilizer. He knew the defect of such chemical fertilizers which in turn renders the land lifeless with many ills. He was rather in favour of using organic manures since the same had manifold benefits. He always advocated simple and natural methods which would suit the villagers and in turn yield better result. We are aware that human excrete can be used as a rich fertilizer and still we hesitate to make use of the same. But simply wasting the same invites diseases and pollutes the environment also. Prof. Brultini in 'The Use of Waste Materials,' writes, "Nitrogen derived from the 2,84,000 residents of Delhi is sufficient to fertilize a minimum of 10,000 and a maximum of 95,000 acres." So it clearly shows that if there is a will there is a way. We only need to apply things in the Gandhian way and work seriously. Gandhiji used to belive that 'all lands belong to Gopal.' To him actual tillers are the real owners of land. And without the active cooperation of the tillers/peasants land cannot give forth anything. Gandhiji suggested that land can be held in cooperation of the both the tiller and the landlord. This will certainly save labour, capital, tools, etc. In the worlds of R.K. Prabhu, "Cooperative farming of his conception would change the face of the land and banish poverty and idleness from their midst. All this was only possible if people became friends of one another and as one family. When that happy event took place there would be no ugly sore in the form of a communal problem. "If such solid measures are taken, hunger can be tackled quite easily.

Gandhiji discussed at length about how to make use of human waste and cowdung which are of very high potential to increase the production to a substantial level. He even suggested the use of 'kachra' (farm waste) so that minimum of efforts can offer maximum of return. The following very simple but useful items can be made into compost:

> Weeds, stools of jawar, rape, black and green-gram, sugarcane crash, stalks of cotton, maize and sugarcane, fallen leaves of trees, uneaten resides of grass, straw, jwar and other fodders.

These are easily available and immensely useful. Gandhi suggested even the use of household waste by digging pits near compost area where some 50 to 60 gallon tins of water can make one cart-load of compost easily. If the farmers want they can make use of cattle-urine also as fertilizer.

It's cheap and useful. In fact, natural fertilizers are very simple to use and yet produce invaluable result. But the age is of science and mechanization everywhere and we are inclined to it also. Mechanization can be a terrible snare as it makes it possible the kind of soil exploitation which has led to desert formation on a scale hitherto unparalleled. Problems are gradually mounting up and things are going out of hands needing immediate treatment in a soothing manner. However the Gandhian remedial measures can be applied with care and here we take up some of the measures:

(a) The load of population is being felt in the economy as well as in the land and there has been repeated fragmentation of holdings and in resultant rendering it quite unfit for cultivation. Hence, the remedy is to resort to cooperative farming. This can go a long way in solving the problems of agriculture as a whole.

(b) In Indian agriculture another problem is of water. The monsoon is very much uncertain and it always concreates havoc in the shape of either flood of famine. So to tackle the vagaries of nature alternative arrangements should be made in the shape of irrigation by cutting canals etc. in addition,

where the canal irrigation is not possible, we can resort to wells, tubewells etc.

(*c*) Due to rain or drought, the soil erosion is a common feature of Indian agriculture. To stop the same, tree plantation is a must. And to improve the fertility of soil, we should go the natural way only and should apply the natural manures which would remain the solid quality as well as the fertility.

(*d*) In the agricultural scenario there are lot of problems crippling the entire process. The farmers are basically poor and have small land holdings and they cannot invest money the way it is required. Here the solution lies in the shape of cooperative farming. It can meet most of the requirement as is felt.

(*e*) At times when situation became abnormal, or need help then the State intervention becomes necessary. However, Gandhiji himself was not much interested in the State intervention becomes necessary. However, Gandhiji himself was not much interested in the State intervention as it creates various types of problems.

(*f*) Sometimes it is necessary that reclamation of land be made. But in this the Government has to come forward and do the needful.

Labour and Capital

It is found that Gandhi's views on labour and capitals not same as that of Marx and other capitalist ideologists. He advocated the universal method of non-violence and peaceful approach which he believed to be fit enough to deliver the goods and reach the core of things.

Labour is the prime source of wealth. It is crystal clear that wealth of the society cannot be created without the active cooperation of the labour. Hence, the use of capital is possible when the same is used by labour only. Thus, it is obvious that capital is at the mercy of labour and the labour is not under the capital, rather is the master. Gandhiji was not confined with this only and he felt it very seriously that labour should have a say in the management also. Otherwise there will be undue exploitation leading to deprivation. He has been very clear in his outlook as we find him opining in 'Young India', "It is vital to the well being of the industry that workmen should be regarded as equal with the share holders and that they have, therefore, every right to possess an accurate knowledge of the transaction of the Mills."

Gandhiji felt that labour and capital should have peaceful co-existence and the role should be of supplementary nature and has to be back and call of one another. However, Gandhi was cautious enough of the imbalance of wealth in the society and that is why he did not approve of any one acquiring more than one's requirement. And here lies his idea of Trusteeship which would bring a sophisticated change in the society. These days a common feature to be witnessed in the industrial arena is of labour unrest inviting all-round trouble in the entire social fabric. " It is unfortunate that till recently study of the human side of labour has been criminally neglected and this had led to the present tensions, distrucst and ill-will in the industrial sphere."

Gandhiji was not in favour of unlimited material and luxurious type of life. It was his life's realization that such things would not bring peace or real happiness in life. That is why, according to him, the wage for labour should be of just living wage. He has clearly said in his Young India, "I have always said that my ideas is that capital and labour should supplement and help each other. They should be a great family living in unity and harmony."

Conclusion

To sum up it can be safely said that the real judge is the time and time alone. Unless his concept is tested full and a practical approach is taken, we cannot negotiate their importance and suitability. It is strongly hoped and felt that his concept would prove its mettle in the coming days ahead. "It is never too late to mend" goes the wise saying.

REFERENCES

Larry Collins and Dominique Lapierre 'Freedom at Midnight'.

'Young India' dated 12th October, 1951.

Patwardhan M.S., "Modernization of Indian Industry."

Gandhi M.K., "Economic and Industrial Life and Relations."

"Young India" dated 9th July, 1919.

Gandhi M.K., "Navajevan Publishing House, Edn.

"Harijan dated 15th March, 1935.

Gandhi M.K. – India's Food Problem' compiled by R.K. Prabhu.

Gandhi M.K. – 'Food Shortage and Agriculture' – End. 1949.

'Young India' 16th February, 1921.

Gupta S.S. "The Economic Philosophy of Mahatma Gandhi.

Young India dated 20th August, 1925.

22

Inclusive Growth of Rural India

RAM NARESH THAKUR

I

Our country is divided into two parts India and Bharat i.e., the nation of the rural people and India represents urban people. The major part of the poor consists of rural poor. The government data shows that there became only 8 per cent decrease in the number of persons of below poverty line between 1993-94 to 2004-05. That means the poverty reduces in the very slow rate i.e., 0.75 per annum. In 1993-94 the ratio of the persons of below poverty line in the total population was 36 per cent, which reduced upto 28 per cent in 2004-05. It is wonder that the 'poverty line' is not the line of 'poverty' but it is the 'line of hunger'. The line of extreme poverty. The U.N.O. recognizes $ 2 (Rs. 90) per capita per day expenditure as 'poverty line' and 32 per cent persons come under this line in India. Unemployment has also been increasing rapidly. In 1993-94 the 'rate of rural unemployment for men' was 5.6 per cent which increased upto 9 per cent in 2004. In the same span of period the 'rate of rural unemployment for women' was also 5.6 per cent which increased upto 9.3 per cent. In the same way this rate of unemployment of urban male became 8.1 per cent increasing from 6.7 per cent between 1993-94 to 2004. This rate, became 11.7 per cent increased from 10.5 per cent for the urban female. This rate is the incident of that very period when the market value of the total shares listed in the share market became Rs. 16,98,428 crore (in 2004-05) increased from Rs. 1,88,146 crore (in 1993-94).

In other hand during the financial year 2005-06, there became tremendous increase in the number of such persons having more

Table–1
Rural-Urban Unemployment Rate

	Rural Unemployment Rate (in %)		*Urban Unemployment Rate (in %)*	
	Male	*Female*	*Male*	*Female*
1993–94	05.6	5.6	6.7	10.5
2003–04	09.0	9.3	8.1	11.7

Table–2
Market Value of Total Shares Listed in The Share Market (in Rs. Crore)

1993–94	1,88,146
2003–04	16,98,428

than $ 10 lac (more than > Rs. 5 crore) financial assets e.g. shares, bonds, saving bonds etc. This speed is the second biggest in the world. Such persons are 83,000 in number. This number was 61,000 in 2003 and 71,000 in 2004. These 83,000 persons are the owners (lords, masters) of $ 290 Arab i.e. at least the financial assets of Rs. 14,00,000 crore. These 83,000 big persons have grip over the 40 per cent of Gross Domestic Product (GDP) of India on the market value. These 83,000 big persons covers only 0.01 per cent of total adult population of India.

Table–3
Rapid Increase of Billionaires

2003	61,000
2004	71,000
2005	83,000
2007	1,00,000

The leaders of the nations are in hurry to go forward at any cost, but they are not ready to leave the neo-liberal policies. This is only the 'so called reform' which is in the roof of such tremendous unemployment due to which the public health facilities has deceased to the negligible point. Rural life is infested with epidemics, illness and ill health. Malnutrition has become the main problem. One, out of two children, dies due to malnutrition. This is the same 'reform' due to which more than a lac persons were compelled to do suicide in Andhra Pradesh, Karnataka, Maharashtra, Punjab and other states during previous fifteen years of globalization era. It is the same 'reform' due to which thousands of farmers and peasants are over thrown from the ownership of their land. It is the same 'reform' due to which the 'Special Economic Zones (SEZ)' are being established which will throw lacs of workers in the ditch of unemployment.

In the 11th Five Year Plan government will spend heavy amount of money on 'poverty eradication.' The number of big cars and other vehicles will be increased on the roads. There will be increase in the magnificent buildings of thousands of people. There will be good management for the luxuries of future generations of some persons. Some pieces of loafes will reach to the poors also. But will there by any qualitative change really in the lots of those poors? The 'Eradicate poverty' or 'Garibi Hatao' slogans or stunts of the governments could not remove the poverty and the soil-rooted truth of the 'rural India' or the 'real India'. Any government could not take any chronic or stable step to save the existence of the rural India'. It could not change the fate of those people facing always with horrible poverty, unemployment, hunger, malnutrition and illness etc. The share market of the country is creating new records daily, the foreign exchange stocks are increasing day by day, growth rate is focusing of development, the condition of industries is better than before, the profits of some companies increased upto 50 per cent. The Tata Steel is taking over the four times big British-Dutch Company 'CHORUS'. The prosperousness of the industrial sector of urban India is visible on the screen. But the 'face of the rural India' is not such. Whatever the government is doing is not for 'the welfare of rural India'. What ever the government is doing is not for 'the Welfare of rural India, not for the development of rural India,' not to attract 'the rural people of India', but to attract 'the innocent poor voters related with villages'. This is the real agony. In the remote villages poors are being poorer cn the cost of some rich people. The gap of disparity is widening day by day. Our Prime Minister says, 'there will not be a poor person in coming 20 years'. But the reality is such that the Planning Commission has prepared the 11th Plan (2007-12) in such a way that our agriculture will be prosperous in future five years if one crore farmers will adopt other professions leaving agriculture. That means 20 lakh farmers should tell good bye to agriculture each year. What will be the employment/profession of those 20 lakh farmers leaving agriculture every year ? The Planning Commission has no answer to this question. Those one crore farmers will add the number of large volume of unemployees waiting from before. The Planning Commission of India can not have the different views except the eminent economists, the planners of the policies of globalization. The majority of the rural people are facing with the regular increasing problems. They are struggling for the 'crisis of existence' only. The inequality of 'urban growth rate' and 'rural growth rate' of 8 and 2 per cent respectively tells the real story of rural India. The Planning Commission of India is of opinion that the 'slow growth rate' of agriculture cannot be increased in comparison of that of industries. Hence the suicide made by the farmers is impossible to be prevented. It is only why the Planning Commission suggests farmers to leave the profession of agriculture.

Cost and Price Disparity of Agricultural and Industrial Goods

What will be fate of those rural people or farmers who will march to urban areas in search of jobs? What will be of their basic amenities of life? The price of every commodity (except agriculture) has increased 200 to 300 times in respect of 1978. There is no sequence of balance in 'cost determination' and 'price fixation', nor the government has any control/ interference/ command to it. Really it is only the central profit of 'the conspiracy to break the rural economy'. It is impossible to be checked by the governments governed by the industrialists/ entrepreneurs and capitalists. So a farmer, a common rural Indian cannot afford to buy industrial goods. He lacks the purchasing power (entitlement) to purchase the industrial produces. In other hand he has to sell agricultural goods/ produce on cheap prices. The difference of 'initial cost' and 'selling cost' of agricultural goods is rarely 1.5 to 2 times, whereas this goes upto 10 times in the case of industrial goods (Produces). If the cost or steel is Rs. 30 per kg, but its utensils of reputed companies are sold Rs. 300 per kg. But in villages if the cost of the raw material of any matter (e.g. soil pot) is Rs. 100, the pot will be sold in Rs. 150 per kg maximum. Thus the cottage/household industries are being smashed by the big industries.

The lives of the crores of people of rural India is worsening for maintaining the 'growth rate' of few crores of people of urban India. The development models of western/ developed (south) countries will not be suited for the proper development of rural India. We should think properly for the 'existence of rural India'.

Table–4
Incidence of Poverty Line–Social and Occupational Group (Rural)

Incidence (%)

Category	*Very Poor*		*Poor*	
	1993–94	*1994–00*	*1993–94*	*1994–00*
ST	22.1	17.0	50.2	44.2
SC	21.7	11.5	48.3	35.3
OBC	NA	7.0	NA	25.5
Occupation				
Agricultural Labour	26.2	14.1	54.4	38.7
Non-agricultural Labour	15.2	8.7	42.2	27.2

Source: Computed using NSS 50th Round Data on Household Consumer Expenditure.

The occupational composition of the rural poor varied across the states. In general, in the developed states poverty was highly concentrated among agricultural labour households and, in contrast, in the backward states poverty extended to other occupations groups, including the self-employed in agriculture. For instance, in Punjab, Haryana, Maharashtra and Andhra Pradesh agricultural labour households constituted more than 60 per cent of the rural poor in 1999-2000, but they constituted less than 16 per cent in Rajasthan and 28 per cent in Assam.

Among the social groups, SCs, STs and backward castes accounted for 81 per cent of the rural poor in 1999-2000 whereas they were considerably less among the rural population. The poor among the SCs in rural areas were concentrated in Uttar Pradesh, Bihar and West Bengal. They comprised 58 per cent of the poor among SCs. In urban areas, Madhya Pradesh and Uttar Pradesh accounted for 41 per cent of the poor among the SCs. The incidence of poverty among SCs was high in Bihar, Madhya Pradesh and Uttar Pradesh in both rural and urban areas. In terms of income poverty and other indicators of human development also such as education, health etc. the STs are at the bottom. The increasing concentration of poverty among tribals who suffer from multiple deprivations is a matter of concern.

The percentage of ST population among the rural poor has been increasing fast. It increased from 14.8 in 1993-94 to 17.5 in 1999-2000. The increase was mainly on account of the comparatively slower reduction in the incidence of poverty among the STs. The percentage of poor among the STs declined from 50 in 1993-94 to 44.2 in 1999-2000 whereas for all rural population it declined from 37 to 27. Bihar, Gujarat, Madhya Pradesh and Maharashtra together accounted for 75.5 per cent of the poor amongst STs in 1999-2000. It is noteworthy that nearly 30 per cent of the poor were located in Madhya Pradesh. The poverty levels of STs in rural areas were high in Orissa (73%), Bihar (59%), Madhya Pradesh (57%) and West Bengal (50%) and in urban area, in Orissa (59%), Karnataka (52%), Andhra Pradesh (46%) and Bihar (43%). Even in the 21st century the world is predominantly rural, especially the developing world. In spite of fast growth urbanization and industrialization, a vast majority of people in the world development report 2000-01 estimates, about 69 per cent of the people of the low income countries live in rural settlements and in South Asia the figure stands at 72 per cent. Rural development has emerged as a distinct field of policy and research in the last three decades and is almost at the top of the agenda in national policies of the developing countries of Asia, Africa and Latin America.

Poverty alleviation has been one of the guiding principles of the planning process in India. The role of economic growth in providing more employment avenues to the population has been recognized. The growth-oriented approach has been reinforced by focusing on specific sectors which provide greater process. The various dimensions of poverty relating to health, education and their basic services have been progressively internalized in the planning process. Central and State Governments have considerably enhanced allocations for the provision of education, health, sanitation and other facilities which promote capacity-building and well-being of the poor. Investments in agriculture, area development programmes and afforestation provide avenues for employment and income. Special programmes have been taken up for the welfare of Schedule Casts (SCs) and Scheduled Tribes (STs), the disabled and other vulnerable groups. Anti-poverty programmes that seek to transfer assets and skills to people for self-employment coupled with public works programmes that enable people to cope up with transient poverty, are the third strand of larger anti-poverty strategy.

The Targeted Public Distribution System (TPDS) protects the poor from the adverse effects of a rise in prices and ensures food and nutrition security at affordable prices. Our efforts at reducing poverty are less effective. Despite completion of many anti-poverty programmes, there is not commensurate decline in poverty. The incidence of income poverty has declined from about 36 per cent in the early nineties to some where around 25-30 per cent but yet the pick-up in growth has not translated into a commensurate decline in poverty. India continues the low ranking of 127 in 2005 also in Human Development Index (HDI).

As far as income poverty is concerned, the Planning Commission (1987-88) estimated that 29.9 per cent live below the poverty line, out of which 33.4 per cent in rural areas and 20.1 per cent in urban areas. However, the World Bank Report has envisaged that although the poverty rate has declined in India, yet the actual number of people living in poverty continued such that the country has more than 320 million live in adject poverty unable to muster an income equivalent to the $1 a day needed to buy basic foods. It has also been further depicted in the report that 'the poverty imposes an oppressive weight on India, especially in the rural areas, where almost three out of four Indian and 77 per cent of poor live.'

Table–5
Estimates of Poverty

	Poverty Ratio (Per cent)			*Number of Poor (Million)*		
Year	*Rural*	*Urban*	*Combined*	*Rural*	*Urban*	*Combined*
1973-74	56.4	49.0	54.9	261.3	60.0	321.3
1977-78	53.1	45.0	51.3	264.3	64.6	328.9
1983	45.7	40.8	44.5	252.0	70.9	322.9
1987-88	39.1	38.2	38.6	231.9	75.2	307.1
1993-94	37.3	32.4	36.0	244.0	76.3	320.3
1999-00	27.1	23.6	26.1	193.2	67.1	260.3
2007 (target)	21.1	15.1	19.3	––	––	––

Source: Economic Survey 2003-04 and Planning Commission .

The rural-urban gaps in the poverty estimates are also of interest. Looking first at the base year (1987-88), the rural-urban gap based on adjusted estimates in much larger than that based on official estimates. Indeed, the latter suggest no difference between rural and urban poverty in that year. This is hard to reconcile with independent evidence on living conditions in rural and urban areas, such as a life-expectancy gap of about seven years in favour of urban areas around that time. The incidence of poverty is high among the scheduled castes, schedule tribes, landless general castes, backward caste labourers, petty vendors, marginal farmers, landless women headed households and dalit minorities.

Table–6
Percentage Distribution of Persons

Below Poverty Line by Occupation Groups-Statewise, 1993-94 and 1999-00

State	*Year*	*Artisans*	*Agri-cultural Labour*	*Non-Agri-cultural Labour*	*Self-Employed in Agriculture*	*Others*	*Total*
Andhra	1993-94	7.8	51.3	7.3	19.2	14.3	100.0
Pradesh	1999-00	10.5	63.9	4.6	18.5	2.5	
Assam	1993-94	9.6	28.7	15.5	40.2	6.0	100.0
	1999-00	15.2	27.8	20.6	28.6	7.8	
Bihar	1993-94	11.0	46.9	3.7	32.2	6.3	100.0
	1999-00	12.3	46.5	6.3	26.4	8.5	
Gujarat	1993-94	7.6	49.2	9.1	18.8	15.3	100.0
	1999-00	7.1	59.1	10.8	19.1	3.8	
Haryana	1993-94	14.3	32.1	18.8	29.4	5.4	100.0
	1999-00	17.2	50.3	22.2	6.6	3.8	
H.P.	1993-94	7.9	4.3	17.6	65.8	4.4	100.0
	1999-00	12.5	8.0	34.1	40.6	4.8	
Karna-	1993-94	12.6	54.2	2.9	28.5	1.8	100.0
taka	1999-00	8.8	59.7	4.2	24.7	2.7	
Kerala	1993-94	13.3	35.0	23.2	11.2	17.3	100.0
	1999-00	14.6	46.7	25.4	7.6	5.8	
Madhya	1993-94	5.2	45.2	4.8	42.8	1.9	100.0
Pradesh	1999-00	6.2	51.2	6.1	34.0	2.4	
Maha-	1993-94	5.1	48.9	6.6	19.1	20.4	100.0
rashtra	1999-00	5.5	66.4	4.1	20.6	3.3	
Orissa	1993-94	14.2	45.2	5.3	30.8	4.4	100.0
	1999-00	8.2	55.9	4.2	26.6	5.1	

Contd...

State	*Year*	*Artisans*	*Agri-cultural Labour*	*Non-Agri-cultural Labour*	*Self-Employed in Agriculture*	*Others*	*Total*
Punjab	1993-94	12.4	64.3	11.2	7.7	4.4	100.0
	1999-00	11.1	66.0	10.5	5.2	7.1	
Rajas-than	1993-94	9.4	14.1	27.9	42.4	6.2	100.0
	1999-00	9.2	16.0	22.3	47.8	4.7	
Tamil Nadu	1993-94	8.2	61.4	9.5	16.0	4.8	100.0
	1999-00	10.0	65.5	9.5	9.7	5.4	
Uttar Pradesh	1993-94	14.0	26.5	6.0	49.5	3.9	100.0
	1999-00	17.2	29.9	6.9	40.1	5.9	
West Bengal	1993-94	18.3	44.1	13.7	21.5	2.5	100.0
	1999-00	20.4	55.4	5.5	15.4	3.1	
Other States & Union Terri-tories	1993-94	9.6	21.1	16.8	43.6	8.9	100.0
	1999-00	3.2	33.2	13.5	38.7	11.4	
All India	1993-94	11.2	40.7	8.4	33.2	6.5	100.0
	1999-00	12.3	46.8	7.6	28.1	5.3	

Source: Computed from NSS 50th Rounds Data on Household Consumer Expenditure.

Table–7

Percentage Distribution of Persons Below Poverty Line by Caste-Statewise, 1993-94 and 1999-2000

State	*Year*	*ST*	*SC*	*OBC*	*Others*	*Total*
Andhra Pradesh	1993-94	15.4	31.6		53.0	100.0
	1999-00	15.6	35.0	41.3	(49.4) 8.1	
Assam	1993-94	13.3	9.3		77.5	100.0
	1999-00	15.4	12.5	18.8	(72.1) 53.3	
Bihar	1993-94	10.1	26.5		63.4	100.0
	1999-00	9.5	28.1	50.4	(62.4) 12.0	
Gujarat	1993-94	30.8	18.0		51.1	100.0
	1999-00	43.1	13.8	29.3	(43.1) 13.8	
Haryana	1993-94	–	47.2		52.8	100.0
	1999-00	–	55.4	36.9	(44.6) 13.8	

Contd...

State	*Year*	*ST*	*SC*	*OBC*	*Others*	*Total*
Himachal	1993-94	9.2	79.1		61.7	100.0
Pradesh	1999-00	2.7	41.9	10.7	(55.4) 44.7	
Karnataka	1993-94	11.7	32.5		57.0	100.0
	1999-00	11.6	30.0	36.6	(58.8) 21.9	
Kerala	1993-94	2.2	14.9		81.0	100.0
	1999-00	4.5	16.4	59.3	(79.1) 19.8	
Madhya	1993-94	41.4	19.5		39.0	100.0
Pradesh	1999-00	42.9	16.0	36.0	(41.0) 5.0	
Maharashtra	1993-94	18.1	22.0		59.9	100.0
	1999-00	31.7	17.7	28.5	(50.6) 22.1	
Orissa	1993-94	36.0	18.5		45.5	100.0
	1999-00	41.1	22.4	26.4	(36.4) 10.0	
Punjab	1993-94	–	74.9		25.1	100.0
	1999-00	–	78.7	17.1	(21.4) 4.3	
Rajasthan	1993-94	28.8	26.4		44.5	100.0
	1999-00	36.5	23.7	27.5	(39.8) 12.3	
Tamil Nadu	1993-94	2.7	34.6		62.7	100.0
	1999-00	2.6	48.5	46.1	(48.8) 2.7	
Uttar Pradesh	1993-94	0.8	33.7		65.5	100.0
	1999-00	1.4	34.6	47.6	(64.1) 16.5	
West Bengal	1993-94	12.4	35.1		51.5	100.0
	1999-00	10.6	30.1	4.3	(59.3) 55.0	
Other States	1993-94	52.7	12.6		34.7	100.0
and Union	1999-00	39.4	13.5	13.3	(47.1) 33.8	
Territories						
All India	1993-94	14.8	27.6		57.6	100.0
	1999-00					

Note: Figures in parenthesis include OBC also.

Source: Computed from NSS 50th and 55th Rounds Data on Household Consumer Expenditure.

II

Incidence of Rural Poverty in India

In fact, poverty of the worst kind was seen in the institution of slavery in India. It has been recorded that slavery has a continuous component of the social and economic life of ancient India. Historical records in India prove that a vast majority of Indians were always in poverty.

The first economist who attempted to study poverty in India was Dadabhai Naroji, who stated his views on Indian poverty in his book entitled, 'Poverty in India, in the year 1988. After Dadabhai Naroji, it was Gandhi who made a serious attempt to fathom the depth of Indian poverty and seriously thought of ways and means to ameliorate the distressing situation. Another important work in this area is of C.N. Vakil who published a book entitled 'Poverty and Planning in 1963, and this study found out the reasons for poverty in India as lack of adequate work for vast majority of the agricultural population during the off-season, the social system which made one person bear the burden of supporting a large family, faulty educational system etc. In 1962, the Government of India appointed a study group to make a thorough study of poverty in India and prepared a report on, it and the group estimated that a total of 59.4 per cent of Indians were below the poverty line in 1960-61.

Table–8
Some other Estimates of Poverty in India (Head Count Ratios)

	NSS/Year	*Rural*			*Urban*		
		Dutt	*Gupta*	*S. Tendulkar*	*Dutt*	*Gupta*	*S. Tendulkar*
27	October 72–September 73	55.4	NA	57.2	45.7	NA	47.0
28	October 73–June 74	55.7	NA	56.2	48.0	NA	49.2
32	July 77–June 78	52.6	NA	54.5	40.5	NA	42.3
38	January–December 83	45.3	45.6	49.0	35.7	40.6	38.3
42	July 86–June 87	38.8	NA	45.2	34.3	NA	35.4
43	July 87–June 88	39.2	39.1	44.9	36.2	38.2	35.1
44	July 88–June 89	39.1	NA	42.2	36.6	NA	34.8
45	July 89–June 90	34.3	33.7	36.7	33.4	36.0	34.8
46	July 90–June 91	36.4	35.0	37.5	32.8	35.3	35.0
47	July 91–December 91	37.4	NA	40.1	33.2	NA	34.8
48	January 92–December 91	43.5	41.7	46.1	33.7	37.8	36.4
49	January 93–June 93	NA	NA	44.2	NA	NA	38.9

Contd...

NSS/Year		Rural			Urban		
		Dutt	Gupta	S. Tendulkar	Dutt	Gupta	S. Tendulkar
50	July 93–June 93	36.7	37.3	39.7	30.5	32.4	30.9
51	July 94–June 95	41.0	38.0	43.6	33.5	34.2	34.1
52	July 95–June 96	37.2	38.3	40.1	28.0	30.0	23.7
53	January 97–December 97	35.8	38.5	38.3	30.0	33.9	31.0
54	January 98– June 98	NA	45.3	44.9	NA	34.6	31.6

Abhijit Sen, 'Estimates of Consumer Expenditure and its Distribution – Statistical priorities NSS 55th Round', Economic and Political Weekly, December 16, 2000, Table–I.

Table–9
Poverty Estimates Based on the 55th NSS Round (Year–1999-2000) (Per cent)

Reference	All India	Rural	Urban
40 day recall	26.10	27.09	23.62
07 day recall	23.33	24.02	21.59

Source: Planning Commission, Results reproduced in Government of India, Ministry of Finance, Economic Survey, 2000-01, Table 10.5, p. 194.

Table–10
Percentage of Rural Urban Population

Years	Sector	Male	Female	Persons	% of Rural and Urban Population
1951	Rural	153444642	145199739	298644381	82.71
	Urban	32083820	30359889	62443709	17.29
	Total	185528462	175559628	361088090	100
1961	Rural	183504095	176794073	360298168	82.03
	Urban	42789106	36147497	78936603	17.97
	Total	22629301	212941570	439234771	100
1971	Rural	225319943	213725732	439045675	80.09
	Urban	58729333	50384644	109113977	19.91
	Total	284049276	264110376	548159652	100
1981	Rural	270910547	252956003	523866550	76.67
	Urban	82463913	76998634	159462547	23.33
	Total	353374460	329954637	683329097	100

Contd...

Years	*Sector*	*Male*	*Female*	*Persons*	*% of Rural and Urban Population*
1991	Rural	324321614	304370062	628691676	74.29
	Urban	114908844	102702168	217611012	25.71
	Total	439230458	407072230	846302688	100
2001	Rural	381141184	360519109	741660293	72.22
	Urban	150135894	135219060	285354954	27.78
	Total	531277078	495738169	1027015247	100

Table–11
Male and Female Literacy Rates by Rural-Urban Division (in %)

Years	*Rural Male*	*Rural Female*	*Urban Male*	*Urban Female*	*Male*	*Female*
1951	19.02	04.87	45.60	22.23	27.10	08.86
1961	34.30	10.10	66.00	40.50	40.40	15.35
1971	48.60	15.50	69.80	48.80	45.96	21.97
1981	49.60	21.70	76.70	56.30	56.38	29.76
1991	57.90	30.60	81.10	64.00	64.13	39.29
2001	71.40	46.70	86.70	73.20	75.85	54.16

Source: Economic survey 2001-02, Economic Division, Ministry of Finance, Government of India.

Although the above data shows the rates of literacy both of the rural and urban areas, despite rising figures of illiteracy much higher in rural women than in urban women.

Causes of Rural Women Backwardness

The major causes of rural women's backwardness are:

- Illiteracy
- Poverty in Rural Area
- Child Marriage
- Burden of Homely Works
- Population Overloading
- Lack of Natural and Human Resource in Rural Area
- The Biased Vision of Society
- Social Exploitation
- Poor Health Rate

- Least Health Care
- Dowry System

III

Health Disparity in Rural and Urban Sectors–The following data shows the wide gap in the health measurement of rural and urban sectors.

Crude Birth Rate (CBR) – Crude Birth Rate (CBR) means number of births in a year per thousand. In rural India Crude Birth Rate (CBR) has always remained higher than the urban India.

Table-12

Trends of CBR in India

Year	*CBR Per 1000 Population*		
	Rural	*Urban*	*Combined*
1971	38.9	30.1	36.9
1976	35.8	28.4	34.9
1981	35.6	27.0	33.9
1986	34.2	27.1	32.6
1991	30.9	24.3	29.5
1996	29.3	21.6	27.5
2001	27.1	20.3	25.4
2002	26.6	19.9	25.0
2004	25.9	0.19	24.1

Source: SRS Bulletin, various years.

In terms of Annual growth rates of CBR, its tanks in states had severe deviation from national average during the period of 1992-04. In the said period states like Punjab, Himachal Pradesh, Andhra Pradesh, Maharashtra and West Bengal fared well in reducing the CBR growth rates. But the picture of backward states like Bihar is very gloomy where reduction has been just less than 1 per cent (32.30 in 1992 to 30.2% in 2004). Some how this picture of Bihar reminds us of various factors like poverty, illiteracy, semi-feudal and unchanging nature of society and aversion to adopt new ideas and norms according to the changing needs of emerging era. It may be mentioned here, that most literate state Kerala stands at the rank one in terms of annual growth rate falling from 17 per cent in 1992 to 15 per cent 2004.

Crude Death Rate (CDR)

The Crude Death Rate (CDR) is defined as the number of deaths in a year per 1000 of the mid year population. It reflects the declining trends in the CDR. The overall CDR declined from 14.9 in 1971 to 7.5 per cent in 2004. The rate of reduction in rural areas from 16.4 to 8.2 per cent which is higher than that in urban areas (from 9.7 in 1991 to 5.8% in 2004). But the CDR figure in rural areas (8.2% in 2004) is still higher than that in urban areas. This rural-urban dichotomy speaks a lot about varying economic status and health facilities for the rural as well as urban population.

Table–13

Rural-Urban Trends of CDR in India During 1971-2004

Year	*CDR Per 1000 Population*		
	Rural	*Urban*	*Combined*
1971	16.4	9.7	14.9
1976	16.3	9.5	15.0
1981	13.7	7.8	12.5
1986	12.2	7.6	11.1
1991	10.6	7.1	09.8
1996	09.7	6.5	09.0
2001	0.91	6.3	08.4
2002	08.7	6.1	08.1
2004	08.2	5.8	07.5

Source: SRS Bulletin, various years.

All India average death rate was 7.50 per cent in 2004. The highest percentage of such rate being in Orissa (9.60%) followed by MP (9.2%) UP, Assam (8.8%) and Bihar (8.1%), TN is equivalent to national average. Remaining 11 states among these 16 major states had percentage lower than the national average. The inter states variations are also noticeable. Comparatively richer states have CDR below than the national average. Again the figure in Kerala is the lowest at 6.1 per cent in 2004 where as poorer states like Orissa, MP, UP, Assam and Bihar exceed the national average. Needless to say, these states provide very poor health facilities to their population.

In terms of Annual growth rates of CDR, its ranks in states and deviation from national average during the period of 1992-2004 varies. Some states like Rajasthan, UP, MP and Bihar had in better reducing the CDR growth rates during year 1992 to 2004. The CDR growth of Kerala, Punjab, Himachal Pradesh, Andhra Pradesh, Maharashtra and West Bengal are better than national average.

Infant Mortality Rate (IMR)

The Infant Mortality Rate (IMR) is defined as the number of infant dying in a year per 1000 lives births during the year. IMR was reported to be 79 per 1000 live births in 1991-92 and now it has reduced to 58 per 1000 live births in 2004. The main causes of death are disease of circulatory system, infections and parasitic diseases, injury, poisoning, pre-natal conditions, and diseases of respiratory system. The main constraints are low literacy and income levels, socio-cultural beliefs and practices and suboptimal utilization of health facilities. The infant mortality rate is also called the infant death rate. In the past, infant mortality claimed a considerable percentage of children born, but the rates have significantly decline in the West in modern times, mainly due to improvements in basic health care though high technology and medical advancements have also helped. Infant mortality rate is reported as number of live new borns dying under a year of age per one thousand live births, so the IMRs are different in different states, which can be compared.

Infant Mortality Rate is an explicit indicator of health status and especially the women and child care which is the direct outcome of economic well-being of the people and success of government intervention. It is affected by factors like immunization programmes, pre-natal and post-natal care facilities for institutional delivery etc. Poor people are more likely to live in massive over crowded areas without clean water and sanitation or in distant rural areas, also without clean water and sanitation. As a result, they have a larger propensity to have diarrhea, cholera, or typhoid fever, (Martine - 2005). According to UN's Children Funds, diarrhea is one of the three main causes of child mortality (the other two are malnutrition and respiratory infections) (Sachs–2001).

Poor people are more likely to live far away from doctors and hospitals. They are more likely to have less education and hence understand the need to seek doctors or other kind of help. It has been widely documented that on of the key determinants of child mortality in literacy of mothers. Educated mothers, for example, understand

Table–14
Infant Mortality Rate (Per Thousand Live Births)

Years	*Rural*	*Urban*	*Combined*
1971	138	82	129
1981	119	62	110
1991	98	53	80
1992	85	53	79
1993	82	45	74
1994	80	52	74
1995	80	48	74
1996	77	46	72
1997	77	45	71
1998	77	45	72
1999	75	44	70
2000	74	44	68
2001	72	42	66
2002	69	40	64
2004	64	40	58

Source : SRS Bulletin, Registrar General of India, Various Years.

the need for hand washing, for the use of soap, for the need to drink of clean water. (Kiros & Hogan–2001).

Her is declining trends during the last 35 years. IMR in India from 129 per thousand live births in 1971 to 58 in year 2004. The percentage decline in IMR in the period 1971-81 was 14.7 between 1981-91 it was 27.3 per cent. This period was the remarkable period in the history Indian health sector. The rural urban variations can also be seen. In case of rural areas, the IMR declined form 138 per thousand live births in 1971 to 64 in 2004 whereas the figure in the same period reduced from 129 to 58 per thousand live births in 2004 in urban areas.

However, in the period between 1991-2004 this declined to around 22 per cent. Inter states variation can be seen here. Kerala shows the lowest IMR at 12 in 2004, while Maharashtra, TN, Delhi, Uttaranchal, Jharkhand, Punjab, Karnataka and HP have met the national goal of reducing the IMR to 58 by 2004. The major states such as MP (79), Orissa (77), UP (72) and Rajasthan (67) are still far behind the national average.

IV

The Gloomy Future

The Indian market is very large and it is expanding by leaps and bound, but the retail shop-keepers of villages are being deprieved of their share in the retail market day by day. The policy of privatization, liberalization and globalization has made the access/approach of the rural farmers in the market decreased. The rural poors are being poorer. The computer and mobile has become not only important but essential commodities also. After all these commodities are beyond the approach of the rural people. The rural farmers are being labourers day by day. The holding of land is very small and there is fragmentation and sub-division of holdings. Thus the productivity becomes decreased. The peasants are living in worse condition in Karnataka, Andhra Pradesh, Maharashtra and Punjab. In previous ten years 1 lac 40 thousand farmers suicided. Employment and income avenues are being shrinked day by day due to globalization policies.

The peasants are restless. Their movement is against social and economic disparity and lack of opportunity of employment. Rural India is facing 'Crisis of Existence'. More than 400 'Special Economic Zones' are being created, which will destroy the villages, poors, farmers and their agriculture. In Ganganagar, Hanumangarh and Bikaner districts the prosperous farmers reserve the canal water in their grip with the linkage of malafide nexus of corrupt bureaucrats, whereas the poor farmers and their regions face the water scarcity.

The development of rural economy is linked with the base of social castes, religious systems and my orthodox practices which make the villagers unaware and ignorant towards their share/right/benefit in the economy. The 'Vicious circle of poverty' is very strong. The development of villages is possible only by eradicating those defects. The rural poors will themselves change the face of rural India and will decide their destiny.

REFERENCES

Datt. G. and M. Ravallion (1998), "Why Have Some Indian States Done Better than Others at Reducing Rural Poverty ?' Economics, Vol. 65, No. 1:17-38.

Hashim S.R. (1999), 'Employment and Poverty : Some Emerging Policy Issues', A Quarterly Journal of the Indian Society of Labour Economics, Vol. 42, No. 1.

Krishnan I.N. (1992), "Population Poverty and Employment", Economic and Political Weekly, November, 14.

Mathur, A. (1998), 'Employment, Equity and Growth', Presidential Address Delivered at the 39th Annual Conference of the Indian Society of Labour Economics at Thiruvananthapuram (January 2).

Mehta, J. and S., Venkataman (2000), 'Poverty Statistics : Bermicide's Feast'. Economic and Political Weekly, Vol. 15, No. 35.

Minhas, B.S.L.R. Jain and S.D. Tendulkar (1991), 'Declining Incidence of Poverty in the 1980s : Evidence *versus* Arts Facts'. *Economic and Political Weekly, Vol. 26* : 1637-82.

National Sample Survey Organization (2000). *Report No. 455 (55/10), Employment and Unemployment India, 1999-2000. Key Results, NSS 55th Round, July 1999 – June 2000 (Dec.)*

____________________ (2001). Draft Report No. 458 (55/10/2). Employment and Unemployment Situation in India, 1999-2000. Part I and II, NSS 55th Round July 1999–June 2 (April).

Palmer-Jones, R. and K. Sen (2001), "On India's Poverty Puzzles and Statistics of Poverty', *Economic and Political Weekly* (January 20) : 211-17.

Planning Commission of India (1993), *Report of the Expert Group on Estimation of Proportion and Number of Poor,* Perspective Planning Division, New Delhi.

Rao, C.H. Hanumantha and H. Linnemann (1996), *Economic Reforms and Poverty Alleviation in India,* Sage Publication, New Delhi.

Sen, A. (1996), 'Economic Reforms, Employment and Poverty—Trends and Options', Economic and Political Weekly, Vol. 31 (September): 2459–78.

Sethi, A.S. (2001), "Globalization and the Emerging Pattern of Consumption Expenditure—The Indian Experience", *The Journal of Income and Wealth,* 23(2) : 145-60.

________________ (2003), 'Determinants of Poverty at the Global Level with Special Reference to India', in the 86th *Annual Conference Volume of the Indian Economic Association* : 480–91.

________________ (2005a), 'Poverty at the Global Level with Reference to India', in K. Nageswara Rao (ed.), Poverty in India : Global and Regional Dimensions (New Delhi, Deep & Deep Publication Pvt. Ltd.) : 03-23.

________________ (2005b), 'Inter-Sectoral Linkages in Haryana's Income—A Temporal Analysis', Artha Vijnana, Vol. 45, Nos. 3-4 : 147–60.

Sethi A.S. and P.S. Raikhy (2002), 'Economic Development and Poverty—An International Experience' Anvesak, 32 (2): 27–37.

Thakur, R.N. (2002), The Economy of Kerala; Human Development, Social Progress and Economic Crisis, IEA Volume, Special Lecture, University of Trivandrum.

Thakur, R.N. (2004), The Economy of Uttar Pradesh, Bright Past and Gloomy Future, IEA. Volume, Special Lecture at B.H.U., Varanasi.

Thakur, R.N. (2002), For the Future of Prosperous Bihar, Souvenir, Economic Association of Bihar Conference, Samastipur College, Samastipur.

Thakur, R.N. (2005), Globalization and Poverty, the World Panorama, Poverty Alleviation in the Third World, Ed. S.R. Singh, A.P.H. Publishing Crop. New Delhi.

Thakur, R.N. (2003), Poverty, The Progeny of Progress, IEA Conference Volume, Kolhapur.

Thakur, R.N. (2005), Poverty and Sustainable Development (Vol. I), Ed. R.K. Singh, Abhijit Publication, New Delhi.

Thakur, R.N. (2005), Employment, Poverty and Development : During Economic Reforms, Economic Reforms in India, Ed. R.K. Singh, Nagaland University, Abhijit Publication, New Delhi.

Thakur, R.N. (2007), Economics of Growing Rural-Urban Disparity, Souvenir, U.G.C. Sponsored National Seminar, Samastipur College, Samastipur, Bihar, 9-10, February, 2007.

23
Inequality

RAKESH A. JOSHI

Introduction

Of the 6.5 billion people on this earth, perhaps, 1.5 billion live in absolute poverty—barely able to survive from day to day. What causes the vast differences in the wealth of nations ? Can the world peacefully survive with poverty in the midst of plenty, with agricultural surpluses in America alongside starvation and environmental degradation in Africa ? Which steps can Development Economics suggest to improve living standards of the poor ? What are the responsibilities of rich nations?—These are the alarming challenges faced by the modern economics.

The whole world is divided in two poles —North Pole and South Pole. In the North Pole, most of the nations are rich having less population, while in the South Pole, most of the countries are poor or underdeveloped with heavy population pressure. Many of the poorer nations, being newly independent after 1945, are filled with memories of colonial relationships, and a fierce desire for real development and real independence. The rich North Pole, with 30 per cent of the world's population, has 80 per cent of world's income and wealth. This tremendous imbalance is also seen in the matters like military power, financial power, technological power, industrial and commercial power, food power and even academic power. The underdeveloped and developing nations also feel strongly about the power inequalities that exist concerning the control of the major international organizations like World Bank, IMF and WTO.

Inequalities Within Our Country

In India, the inequalities of income distribution has increased in the rural areas, in the urban areas, between agricultural and industrial sector and as regards a shift of GNP from the more equal rural to the more unequal urban areas. There have been growing inequalities of income and wealth in India during the last 56 years of planned economic development. Prof. Dandekar and Prof. Rath studied the inequalities in economic power. According to them, "the small gains of development seem to be monopolized by the upper middle and richer sections of the society by leaving the lower middle and poorer sections more or less untouched by the process of development."

Redistribution of income in favour of the less privileged classes has not taken place. On the other hand, concentration of income and wealth has increased. Our per capita NNP (at market prices) has increased from Rs. 267 to Rs. 12000 during 1950-51 to 2004-05. But, it does not mean that every Indian gets Rs. 12,000 per year. It is just an average. So many Indians are in debt position, while a few are getting millions of rupees per year.

India has several forms of economic inequality. The three important forms are : inequality of assets, inequality of income and regional inequality. This forms of inequalities are inter-related and mutually reinforcing. For example, inequality of assets reinforces inequality of income. The few, who possess large blocs of income that yield physical and financial assets such as land, buildings, factories, fleets of commercial vehicles, huge deposits with banks, investments in government securities and company shares receive a great deal of income from these – while the many, who possess few such assets receive little income from these sources. Thus, inequality of assets gives rise to inequality of income. RBI survey of assets of rural and urban households for the period July 1991 to June 1992 focuses on the existence of severe inequalities in asset distribution. 51 per cent of the bottom households owned just 10 per cent of the total assets. As against, 9.6 per cent of the rich households owned assets worth Rs. 2.5 lakhs and above accounted for nearly 49 per cent of total assets. Inequality in asset distribution is the main cause of unequal distribution of income in the rural areas. It is also seen that the resource base of 50 per cent of the households is so weak that, it can hardly provide them anything above the subsistence level of income.

Low Level of Living of the Average Indian

As a result of severe income inequality, the level of living of the average Indian is very low. In 2002, the average calorie intake of food was only 2490 as compared to over 3400 calories per day in most of the developed countries. This was slightly above the minimum intake for sustaining life estimated at 2100 calories per day. Since nearly 28 per cent of the Indian population lives below the poverty line, it is very doubtful whether the poor get a minimum intake of even 2100 calories.

According to World Development Indicators, 46 per cent of the child population in India suffers from malnutrition. Nearly 60 per cent of the mothers are malnourished. Even today, 80 per cent of the Indian cannot get safe drinking water. The picture about housing is also bad.

According to the estimates of National Building Organization, the total housing stock was 138 million dwelling units in 2001. Out of this, over 50 per cent houses were either made of mud or unburnt bricks. In urban areas, 35 per cent of the population lives in slums. During the last 10 years, at least 50,000 farmers committed suicides due to bad economic conditions.

Thus, we can note that, due to economic inequalities, most of the Indians do not get basic needs in proper manner, while the pet animals of the few rich persons get luxurious treatment. The main causes of economic inequalities in India are as under:

Inheritance law, inequality in land distribution, concentration of economic power in the private sector, black economy, inequalities in professional training, unemployment and underemployment, faulty taxation, neglect of backward areas, and inflationary trends.

Faulty Fiscal and Monetary Policy

The Indian fiscal policy has lost its progressive character of improving income distribution. Fiscal stabilization and consolidation have further accentuated the shift. The cuts in indirect taxes, mainly in import duties are very useful, but little of this cuts have been passed on to the consumers by way of price reductions. Similarly, the personal and corporate income tax rates have been lowered and certain incomes have been altogether exempted. The resulting accentuation of the regressive character of the direct tax regime is yet another disequalising feature of the supply-side tax policy adopted under L.P.G. policy. The taxation of long-term equity capital gains was abolished, creating a distinctly uncomfortable situation, in which owners of capital are neither taxed on dividend earnings nor on capital gains; while all forms of labour incomes are taxed.

The worst disequalising role with respect to the working of the financial sector is played by the malice of corporate defaults on loans from banks and financial institutions. Recent data on the magnitude of such concerning of bank resources by large companies are shocking and the new securitisation law does not seem to have made a big difference. Over the 1997-2004 period, the bad loans of the banks increased from Rs. 47,300 crore to Rs. 96,084 crore. If the lost interest is also added to this, it reaches a staggering level of about Rs. 3,00,000 crore. Most of the defaulters, who have concerned public money are in the category of big borrowers with each loan exceeding Rs. 1 crore. The amount stuck with the largest single defaulter is Rs. 1227 crore. In most of these cases, no legal proceedings have been initiated and as much as Rs. 11,074 crore have been written off. The banking system's loot has added and abetted the disequalisation process in a big way.

Suggestions to Remove Economic Inequalities

It is a duty of Development Economics to suggest some steps to remove economic inequalities. Having the objective of growth with social justice, Central Government of India and various State Governments have undertaken various steps to reduce economic inequalities. These steps have encompassed personal distribution as also its other aspects like urban – rural inequalities and regional disparities. Some steps were intended to level down the income of the few at the top and other steps were intended to raise the income of the large many at the bottom. During various five year plans, Government implemented various schemes like IRDP, NREP, DRI, RLEGP etc. to generate employment opportunities and to reduce poverty, so that economic inequalities can be reduced. But, the results are not quite satisfactory.

As a development economist, I suggest following measures to decrease economic inequalities:

1. Progressive taxation is essential to reduce economic inequalities. For the last 10 years, we see that, the luxurious

goods and services are becoming cheaper in our country, e.g., the prices of four wheelers, A.C. machines, colour TVs etc. are decreasing; while the prices of essential commodities are increasing rapidly. The rates of indirect taxes on luxurious goods should be increased, and the rates of indirect taxes on essential commodities should be decreased.

2. Redistribution of agricultural land is necessary. Small and marginal farmers should be given more land from rich – big farmers.
3. The industrialization of rural areas with labour intensive production techniques can generate more employment opportunities and thus, we can reduce economic inequalities.
4. It is necessary to create opportunities of self-employment by providing credit to low income groups – both in the rural and urban areas.
5. Self-financed education system has created inequalities in opportunities. The State Governments should give a much greater quantum of grants for education of the poor people, so that they may get good education.
6. The production of primary goods and services should also be increased. More production can control inflation as well as it can generate more employment opportunities.
7. Health services for the poor people should be improved. With good health services they will be able to work efficiently.
8. Due to scarce irrigation and electricity facilities, so many rural people get limited employment during the year. With 100 per cent electrification and 100 per cent irrigation facilities, our farmers can work for the whole year and it will help to reduce economic inequalities by generating more employment. In this context, the completion of Sardar Sarovar Project is essential to solve major economic problems of the states like Gujarat, Madhya Pradesh, Rajasthan and Maharashtra.
9. Social security schemes in the form of pension, provident fund benefits, medical treatment compensation etc. should be expanded, so that the needy people may get more real income.

Above mentioned measures can improve the capabilities of the poor and by that way the economic inequalities would be reduced.

REFERENCES

Datt Gaurav and M. Ravallion, "Regional Disparities, Targeting and Poverty in India" – 1990.

Agarwal R.C., "Economics of Development and Planning" – L.N. Agarwal Educational Publishers, Agra, 2005-06.

Eugene Staley, "Future of Underdeveloped Countries."

Datt Ruddar and K.P.M. Sundharam, "Indian Economy," S. Chand and Co. Ltd. New Delhi, 2005.

R.B.I., "All India Debt and Investment Survey," 1991-92.

Tata Services Ltd., "Statistical Outline of India," 2004-05.

Myrdal G., "Asian Drama."

24

Rural Industrial Diversification and Inclusive Development

AMALESH BANERJEE

Introduction

India is now poised for high growth, tentatively at the rate of 10 per cent. It is estimated that if agricultural growth can be attained at a higher rate of 4 per cent then this high rate of growth of GDP could be sustained over certains period. Agriculture still absorbs 65 per cent of population and of contributes 20 per cent of GDP. Two segements of rural economy are the farming and non-farm activities. In fact the non-farm manufacturing enterprises are important for rural transformation and poverty eradication. A large segment of our rural industries faced decline historically due to neglect. At the same time modern urban industries should set up out sourcing centres in rural areas. The technological diffusion will encourage innovation and encourage them to compete in the market. Rural industrialization thus encompass three stages: *(a)* old village industries, *(b)* new enterprises, and *(c)* out sourcing of modern big manufacturing units in the urban centres training and technological adoption is important. This chapter classifies in the section two the rural non-farm enterprises. In the Section III choice of technology of rural enterprises are concerned. Section V examines the employment potency of the sector in the informal segment. In the Section V micro credit and input supply is examined in order to explain the potentiality of inclusive growth and women empowerment. Section VI seeks to assess the Eleventh Plan agendas in this respect.

Conclusions are offered in the Section VII.

II

Rural Industries – Old and New

India has a long tradition of rural industries. In fact many of our artistic and important rural industries were competed out during the colonial rule. Decline of handicraft is a historical phase during which British products in many cases replaced the Indian handicrafts. Subsequently, after independence village industries received specials treatment and subsidies and quota production. This old generation village industries provided employment and earning opportunities to a large section of marginalized landless rural households. Sericulture, Khadi and village industries, handloom and many such traditional industries belong to this category. Brick making, hushing, bidi making, carpet making, diary, basket making and large number of other such village, industries provided income opportunities to a large section of village non-farming households.

Second set of rural industries which is relatively new include processing and machine tools. This category is extensively using the agro products and makes value addition. With the diversification of agriculture more emphasis is placed on cash crops and value addition. The agro-processing industries are rapidly developing in the agriculturally advanced states. The third category of rural industries is the modern industries rapidly spreading in the rural areas and are being adapted by the skillfull young people of new generation. The big mechanized large industries also make outsourcing to rural skilled young people for complete products at low cost. With the development of rural infrastructure rural centres of production will be further machanised and modernized. The production at low cost and induction of new technology will enhance the productivity and quality of the rural manufacturing and processing units.

Rural transformation has a number of components to be emphasised on priority basis so that rural stagnation and often decline can be arrested. Education, skill formation technological adoption and infrastructure are some of those essential components of that dynamic transformation process of rural economy. With a well though out network of non-farm small and medium enterprises (SME) in the rural sector, the rural economy will be rejuvenated and income generation process will be strengthened.

III

Choice of Technology

All the rural non-farm enterprises classified above must be based on modern technology adoption. Two purposes of the continuous adoption of modern technology are the reduction of cost to reap the benefit of economics of scale and dissemination of knowledge so that innovation can take place at the lower level. It is a dynamic process of on the job learning or what is called 'learning by doing.' The development takes place at a cumulative process. The first phase of technology adoption enables the workers and entrepreneurs to learn the skill. In the successive phases further perfection and larger output take place. Increasing productivity and increasing income is the outcome of the technological adoption and learning-by-doing. One can conceive of, along Schumpeterian line, cluster of innovation and dynamic growth process. Rural non-farm enterprises are thus the strong channel of technological diffusion and transmission. 'Small is beautiful' small rural enterprises can produce diversified products and can as well bring about change in demand pattern.

From pur technical point of view, a lower Incremental Capital Output Ratio (ICOR) is a positive index of growth. Rural non-farm enterprises have the advantage of low ICOR and hence provides an incentive to the enterprises. Low ICOR is an index of low coat economic production with larger employment opportunity. Eleventh Five Year Plan envisages inclusive growth. One mechanism of that strategy is the absorption of SC/ST Dalits and underprivileged section in the growth propelling activities. The development of rural non-farm activities of different description as stated above with modern technological leverage will reduce the average ICOR of the economy and will make it possible to attains the professed inclusive growth.

Current economic growth pattern of our economy has a tendency of over heating. High-tech products produced by multinational companies has the in-built tendency of high-cost and low-employment tendency. With moderate level of productivity in these production the average ICOR tend to be high. Rural non-farm enterprise will serve as an anti-dose in this context. Besides this mechanism will also have high welfare distributional advantage. As the village people, often landless and unskilled, have advantage of being associated with these rural non-farm enterprises their income will increase. The consequent rising income will generate larger demand for urban products. It opens an interlinkage of urban and rural markets of inputs and outputs and employment. Eleventh Five Year Plans' professed policy of inclusive growth with low ICOR is possible through the development of low-tech rural non-farm Small and Medium Enterprises (SME).

The fundamental issue is that India has to break the technological shackle both in the rural as well as urban sector. This is particularly in the rural sector where hundreds of local products are as good as local and national use. Once this technological break-thorough is achieved, the demand pattern of the products will be quite similar and the local produces will have the benefit of larger sale in the extended market. A transition from local to national market through technological breaks through in the rural production structure the small and medium will enterprises will reap the benefit of economies of scale and profit from larger sale.

This will set a stage for higher effective demand in the backward economy for sustained growth.

IV

Employment

Non-farm enterprises and rural employment is basically a bottom-up approach. Traditionally the employment character of these non-farm enterprises is that large number of people with little skill and limited wages and productivity are employed in these activities. Present employment status in the country is such that about 60 per cent labour force is engaged in rural activities of which a large section is in non-farm enterprises. Once agriculture is diversified and farm productivity is increased some farm labour force will be released. This surplus labour force from farm and the annual additional new labour force together will create a vast pool of rural unemployed. Hence the non-farm rural enterprises equipped with modern technique and technology can play an important role in providing employment to the emerging rural workforce. Rural transformation depend on:

- *(a)* quality of agriculture,
- *(b)* rural infrastructure, including irrigation electricity,
- *(c)* extension of non-farm employment in the small and cottage industries,

(d) credit availability. As such a large part of these works including infrastructure, irrigation depend on large scale public investment.

Hence for increasing employment in the rural sector the diversification and modernization of the Khadi and village industries and modern machanised processing and producing industries have to be strengthened.

But the current status of rural employment and poverty condition is a disappointing phenomenon. Both 55th and 61st round of NSS data indicate over an all rise in rural unemployment in 2004-05. For woman work force with little education there has been no improvement, although for men, with some education, there is marginal improvement of employment. The information about rural poverty is also disappointing as per direct estimate of calorie intake (Mukhopadhyay and Rajaram 2007 and Utsha Patnaik 2007). This is contrary to the actual condition of employment and poverty we have in the rural India. Based on 55th and 61 round of NSS data the authors indicated that Neo liberal approach of expenditure reduction has a negative effect on rural employment and poverty estimation.

Against this perspective, the non-farm enterprises deserve special mention. However there are two limitations. One is the expenditure--reduction by the state and the second is the globalization. Small enterprises in all over the country are therated by foreign capital and multinationals. It is essential to increase public expenditure in the rural sector as well as to regulate the unequal competition from the multinationals.

V

Credit and Financial Inclusion

Although there are certain guidelines for rural lending by the commercial banks, the actual volume of credit available to the priority sector is declining under the neo-liberal prescriptions. Financial reform has curbed the commercial banks' priority sector lending and is diverting the bulk of resources to the corporate sector. As on last Friday of March 2007. Priority sector lending of the public sector banks come down to 39.6 per cent compared to 41.2 per cent in 2003 and 43.6 per cent in 2004. Priority sector loans comprises agriculture, small enterprises, retail trade, micro credit, education and housing loans. The SSI and non-farm enterprises together is a small segment of the group. As on last reporting Friday of March 2007, 8 per cent of net bank credit and 20 per cent of total priority sector advances went to the SSI sector. The PSBs are required to operationalise at least one specialized SSI branch in every district and centre with a cluster of SSI units. By the end March 2007 the PSB had operationalised 636 SSI bank branches.

Of the broad group of non-farm enterprises the Self-Half Group (SHG) has now become the most rapidly expanding channel. Bank link SHGs and N.G.O. linked SHGs are extensively empowering the poor, particularly women, in the rural sector. As of and March 2007 around 3 million SHGs are linked to banks, covering a total flow of credit at Rs. 18,040 crores. The rural banking structure is still weak and insufficient. As on March 2005 rural population personal branch inceased from 13462 in 1991 to 16650 in 2005. Moneylenders still have 29.6 per cent share in rural non-institutional loan in the rural population.

Rural-Urban Divide

Table–1
Average Population Per Branch Office

	1991	*2001*	*2005*
Population for Branch	13711	15209	15680
Population for Rural Branch	13462	15667	16650
Population for Urban Branch	14484	14137	13619

Source: RBI Bulletin, March 2007.

Table–2
Region-wise No. of Accounts, 2005

	Deposit (C+S) Accounts		*Credit Accounts*		*Number of Accounts Per 1000 Population*			
					Deposit (C+S)		*Credit Account*	
	Rural	*Urban*	*Rural*	*Urban*	*Rural*	*Urban*	*Rural*	*Urban*
North Region	4130	6677	675	771	338	652	55	71
N.E. Region	3716	5340	702	781	186	281	35	41
Eastern Region	3676	6087	887	693	185	413	45	47
Central Region	4586	6675	859	797	242	375	45	49

Contd...

	Deposit (C+S) Accounts		*Credit Accounts*		*Number of Accounts Per 1000 Population*			
					Deposit (C+S)		*Credit Account*	
	Rural	*Urban*	*Rural*	*Urban*	*Rural*	*Urban*	*Rural*	*Urban*
Western Region	3826	6630	663	1530	262	526	46	121
Southern Region	4549	5571	1577	2121	393	486	136	185
All India	4202	6155	1000	1321	270	483	64	105

Source: As Table—1.

Table–3
Share of Different Agencies in Outstanding Debt of Households (Share of Percentage)

Cedit Agencies	*Rural Household*			*Urban Household*		
	1981	*1991*	*2002*	*1981*	*1991*	*2002*
Institutional of which	61.2	64.0	57.2	60.0	72.0	75.1
corporate SOC/Bank		21.6	27.3		17.2	20.5
Commerical Banks		33.7	24.5		21.6	29.7
Government		6.1	2.3		11.1	7.6
Non Institutional of	38.8	36.0	42.9	40.0	28.0	24.9
which moneylenders		17.5	29.6		10.2	14.1
Total	100	100	100	100	100	100

Source: As Table—1.

Table–4
Financial Inclusion RBB, July 2007

	PC of Savings Deposit to Adult Population 2005	*PC of Credit Accounts to Adult Population 2005*
Northern Region	80	12
North-eastern Region	37	7
Eastern Region	41	8
Central Region	52	9
Western Region	60	13
Southern Region	66	25
All India	59	14

Source: RBB July 2007, p. 1166.

The extent of exclusion from credit market is such that as number of loan accounts constituted only 14 per cent of adult population. In rural areas the coverage in 9.5 per cent against 14 p.c. in urban areas. Regional for thoughts region and or low as 7.8 and 9 per cent respectively in North-eastern, eastern and central regions.

The extent of exclusion from credit markets can be observed from a different view point. Out of 203 million household in the country 147 millions are in rural areas. 89 million farmer household, 51.4 per cent of farm households have no access to formal sources of credit.

Looking at different sources of credit, it is observed that the share of non-institutional sources reduced from 70.8 per cent in 1971 to 42.9 per cent in 2002. However after 1991 with share of non-institutional sources has increased specifically the share of moneylenders in the debt of rural households increased from 17.5 per cent in 1991 to 29.6 per cent in 2007. In the urban areas the share of non-institutional sources has been come down significantly from 40 per cent in 1981 to around 25 per cent in 2002.

There is a wrong perception that credit extended to the SSI units is unremunerative and hence it is a reason for rising non-performing assets of commercial banks. However, there are a number of factors for the inefficient performance of the SSI units. Equally Small and Medium Enterprises (SME) of modern varity are often sinking. However, side by side there is a dynamic and progressive aspect of SSI and SME units that are important for a symbiotic growth of both SME and banks extending credit to them. With a technically viable productivity improvement programmes of the SME units and backward and forward linkage equally to resources base and marketing centres, these units open a vide vista of employment and income generating process. The financing units involved in this process of dynamic growth of the industry will earn profit. The circular flow of credit, output growth and increase in bank deposit will set a vibrant cumulative transformation and growth of the rural economy.

It has another most important aspect of welfare, Credit extended to SSI and SME sector as well as micro finance to micro enterprises opens the possibility of inclusive growth envisaged in the Eleventh Plan. Finance is a tool, and along with other inputs, it can energies and transform the rural sector.

VI

Rural Non-Farm Enterprises and Five Year Plans

Eleventh Five Year Plan (EP) envisages inclusive growth. The inclusive growth programme envisages rural economic programme, both farm and non-farm, so that disadvantaged people in rural area can find alternative employment in the rural non-farm and SME enterprises. Based on NSSO uniform call period, rural poverty is 28.3 per cent. Both in rural and urban area there are large number of sick enterprises. Huge amount of capital is locked up in these units which is an important source for reindustrialization. Rural industriali-zation will further be a strong channel for poverty eradication and development.

Both the Ninth and Tenth Five Year Plan envisaged non-farm industrial development in the rural sector. The decentralized cluster development of rural industries was the agenda of the Ninth Plan. Ninth Plan took up programme for rural industries like textile, village and small Industries, Khadi and village industries, handloom, sericulture, and food processing industries. The Tenth Plan also envisaged more rural/village industry cluster under the National Programme for Rural Industrialisation. The Eleventh Plan in the same line envisaged for inclusive growth during the plan. Inclusive growth aims at encompassing the marginalized people like, SC/ST, landless and poor people, in the rural industrial programme so that their income and employment opportunity is extended. The Tenth Plan envisaged setting up of technology interfaces to serve as information dissemination of and technology adoption centre. Information technology in the rural sector is employment generation is the most important in order to break the stagnation and the vicious circle of incapacity poverty and low productivity. However, no assessment as yet has come out as to the implementation of the programme of the Tenth Plan. Eleventh Plan's inclusive growth agenda should be based on this knowledge-based transformation of the rural economy. It is not the casteist separation but ignorance and lack of enlightenment which is the main hurdle in rural transformation. Working on this front of knowledge dissemination through work in cluster of SME and SSI, will bring about a wave of transformation in the rural economy. To attain the objective of inclusive growth the Eleventh Plan Programme has to work on this line.

In our agenda of rural transformation we can accommodate the current agenda of Special Economic Zone (SEZ). If the SEZ is meant for only high-tech big industrial estates, and rapid industrial development for high growth, it is seriously an attempt of enclave development which has no backward and forward linkage with rest of the productive zone of the economy. With the advancement of science and technology such kind of SEZ is consistant without present stage of technological advance. However, such a SEZ will hardly make possible for inclusive growth and transformation of the rural economy. On the other hand if SEZ is concerned as a separate model in which SME and SSI clusters are developed with the support of modern technology with backward and forward linkage, this will improve the production and productivity of labour working otherwise with primitive tools in isolation. Non-farm enterprises thus can serve as the very effective channel of rural transformation.

VII

Conclusion

Rural transformation with the diversification of non-farm enterprises is an effective channel for dynamic development of the rural economy. Rural industrial structure may be classified in four categories:

(a) KVI and village cottage industries including handloom and sericulture;

(b) agro-processing industries, like dairy, food processing etc;

(c) modern manufacturing enterprises based on modern inputs like factories for agri tools leather industry etc;

(d) out sourcing of urban big industry like by cycle, shoe, silk and information technology. Adoption of modern technology will improve quality and output of the traditional enterprises. These industries are labour – intensive and the capital – output ratio is low.

Credit availability, input and infrastructures supports are essential for diversified development of these industries. The employment potentiality of these industries is larger than our modern high-tech industries. Ultimately it is the productivity that enhances economic growth. Higher growth of rural industries will have multiplier effect on output employment. Poverty will be reduced and inclusive growth will be easier. The Ninth, Tenth and Eleventh Five Year Plans have been aiming at this objective. We can have SEZ of village and rural manufacturing enterprises with backward and forward linkage. This types of second best SEZ will have higher growth potentiality and larger employment. This will transmit technology at the rural sector and will set the stage for dynamic transformation of the rural economy.

REFERENCES

Balakrishnan, Pulapre, Parameswaran, (2007) Understanding Economic Growth in India. A Prerequisite E.P.W., July, 14.

Banerjee, Amalesh, (2007) Economic Reform and Vision of North-East, Kanishka Publishers, Distributors, New Delhi.

Chand, Remesh, S.S. Raju, L.M. Pandey, (2007) Growth Crisis in Agriculture, EPW June-30, July 6.

Goyal, Ashima, (2007) 'Planning for Inclusive, Productivity Growth,' Yojana, April.

Government of India, (2003), Report of the National Commission on Labours Academic Foundation, New Delhi.

Mukhopadhyay, Abhiroop Indira Rajaraman, (2007), 'Rural Unemployment 1999-2005. Who Ganied and Who Lost' E.P.W., July 28, August, 3.

Patnaik, Utsha, (2007) 'Neoliberalism and Rural Poverty in India,' E.P.W., July 28, August, 3.

Vaidyanathan A., (2007) Farmers' Suicides and the Agrarian Crisis, E.P.W., September 23, 2006.

25

Industrialization in Bihar: Prospects of Inclusive Employment Generation in the Global Era

BIRENDRA KUMAR JHA

Introduction

India has entered into the global era since 1991 and it is widely believed that globalization which simply means the integration of the Indian economy with the world economy, has been deemed as the panacea for sloving all problems (Jha B.K. 2005). But its advocates overlook the fact that 'globalization has raised both apprehensions and expectations, more often the former than the latter, in respect of its impact on labour' (Papola T.S. 2004). Employment generation has been one of the principal conerns of development planning the countries. Industrialization is expected to be a helpful instrument in this concern. But the picture which has emerged in the global era is not rosy. The Tenth Plan accepts that there is a widespread unemployment and underemployment in the both urban and rural areas and this is likely to worsen with demographic projections indicating substantial increase in the workfore with about 60 per cent of the population in the 15-59 age group. The Report is the Special Group on Targeting (RSG) Ten Million Employment Opportunities per year over the Tenth Plan period has observed that the present increase in unemployment is primarily due to the declining job creating capacity of growth observed in 1993-94 and that the employment elasticity of the organized sector has come down to near zero essentially due to: *(a)* the phenomenon of nightsizing, *(b)* increasing capital intensity per unit of output, and *(c)* the pattern of growth in favour of capital intensive sectors. The Tenth Plan has estimated the backlog of unemployment around 34.85 million in 2001-2002 and the total job opportunities required during this plan period as 70.14 million. The total employment in the economy increased at an average growth rate of close to 2 per annum between 1977-78 and 1983, 1.5 per cent between 1983 and 1988, 2.2 per cent during 1987-1994 and less than 1 per cent between 1993-94 and 1999-2000 (Vaidyanathan, 2001). The incidence of unemployment, expressed in terms of unemployment as a percentage of the labour force increased from 5.99 per cent in 1993-94 to 7.32 per cent in 1999-2000. Dr. Man Mohan Singh has expressed his belief in these words, 'We are creating a macroeconomic environment in which industry speeds ahead with growth rate of 12 per cent or more, generate more jobs and higher levels of wages and incomes through increased productivity.' This was the moot behind entering into the global era expressed by the then Finance Minister but what happened. Undoubtedly, over past decade, the industrialized economics were the only ones to experience falling unemployment rate while in the other the rate either remained stable or increased. So far as industrial development in India is concerned, significant changes have taken place in the post reform era.

Overhauling of the domestic industrial policy—dismantling of the licence, Permit Raj, substantial amendment of the MRTP Act and complete restructuring of the industrial policy—have led to diversified growth of this sector. Till 2001-02 the overall growth rate, by and large has been decelerating except in the year 1995-96. An assessment of industrial growth dugling the period of Eight, Ninth and Tenth Plan—all three formulated and implemented under the reformist agenda indicates that industrial performance has been below the targeted growth rates. While in the Eight Plan 7.3 per cent of industrial growth against the target of 7.5 per cent was recorded, the Ninth Plan witnesses growth of only 4.9 per cent against the target of 8.2 per cent the industrial growth in the first year of the Tenth Plan (2002-03) at 5.3 per cent was below the target of 10 per cent but from 2002-03 onwards the growth rate has picked up and has attained 8 per cent in 2004-05. This may be a good sign but it is futile to expect that the economic scenario will change for the better. We may recall the history of decline of Indian handicrafts, which had to face high tariffs wall in Britain and even other European countries because these countries developed modern industries earlier. Things in India, however, was not so bad in ancient time. It was not always a poor, underdeveloped country depending on solely on agriculture. The Indian Industrial Commission of 1916-18 presided over by Sri Thomes Holland opened its report with the statement. "At a time when western Europe, the birthplace of the modern industrial system, was inhabited by uncivilized tribes, India was famous for the wealth of her rulers and for the high artistic skill of her creftmen. And even at a much later period, when merchant adventures from the west made their first appearance in India, the industrial development of this country was at any rate not inferior to that of the more advanced European nations" (IICR). But it is the policy of our erstwhile British masters responsible for destroying systematically the industrial base of India. No colonial power helped its colony to industrialize. Hereby Indian should learn a lesson from its past and in the global era it needs to be considered. Foreign investment rarely marked a transfer of capital to India from abroad. The multiplier effects in terms of income, employment, capital, technical knowledge and growth of external economics of these investment were largely exported back to the developed countries (Bose A. 1965). So far Bihar is concerned, it being part of the former Bengal Presidency during the colonial period, was subjected to maximum exploitation. The state experienced the disastrous impact of de-industrialization. No doubt, advocates of globalization drew a very rosy picture and for them India, once upon labeled as the 'Caged Tiger' by the economists during 1990-91 is now heading towards achieving the status of new economic stars of the 21st century with China through integrating its economy with the Worlds' economy. But they are forgetting the fact that the changing world scenario has thrown up new challenges to the very existence of this sector in most cases on the name of efficiency. Competition is supposed to promote efficiency but it has to be amongst equals. And so the impact of globalization in the present scenario of India and Bihar cannot be considered favourable particularly for labour intensive industrial sector which results in enhancement of unemployed labour force. It is but stark truth that the growth rate of G.D.P. including industrial output has been notable but the growth in industrial employment has been discouraging in the global era. "Employment in the organized sector lagged output and, at times, the population, growth rate. This is particularly true of employment in organized manufacturing. The poor performance of organized manufacturing employment relative to output in the 1980s led many to describe the decade as one of jobless growth" (Desh Pande Sharma, Karan, Sarkar, 2004). And the jobless growth has continued till now.

Urge for Industrialization

Industrialization is a synonym of economic development, R.B. Sutcliffe in his book, 'Industry and Underdevelopment Has Observed' Industrialization is in one sense a process which has invariably been the outcome or accompaniment of economic development. In another sense industrialization denotes a set of policies which, more than any other broad set of policies, is seen as a means towards economic development'. (quoted by Suman H.N.P.S. 1977). Of course, industrialization is a major source of accelerating the tempo of economic development of underdeveloped economics. It assumes a special role in underdeveloped regions where per capita output is higher in manufacturing industries than in agriculture due to existence of greater capital intensity, continuity of production, greater specialization and division of labour, less dependence on natural factors, and greater possibility of internal and external economics in manufacturing industries. In agricultural dominated economies like India or Bihar, the role of Industrialization cannot be denied where the marginal productivity of agriculture is very negligible or sometimes negative owing to existence of disguised unemployment. In this case the growth of modern industry can provide employment for an underutilized labour force now bottled up in agriculture as well as in the traditional and the unorganized sectors of non-agriculture pursuits. Industrialized is held to be crucial to development strategy also because it will radiate stimuli throughout the economy and lift it out of stagnation (Myrdal Gynnar, 1972). It is expected to instill a new spirit of rationalism, enterprise, discipline, punctuality, mobility and efficiency. Many happy results are expected to follow as a direct consequence of industrial expansion. And so to boost up the economic status of Bihar and to solve its problems like poverty, unemployment, over population low productivity, low per capita income, regional disparity and so on the necessity for advancing the pace of industrialization in the state can never be disputed. The industrial sector which possesses a relatively high marginal propensity to save and invest contributes significantly to the eventual achievement of self-sustaining economy with continued high levels of investment and rapid rate of increase in income and industrial employment. And so there is clamour for industrialization throughout underdeveloped economies.

Outside Experiences

In England,Germany as well as in USA industrialization solved the problems of a rapidly increasing population. Employment, income and capital grew at an accelerated rate, and for a time, at any rate, it appeared that the Malthusian devil had been chained and the age of plenty had at last dawned. Taking the employment in 1932 as 100, the index of employment in industry had risen within six years to 200 in Germany, 180 in Estionia, 161 in Poland, 153 in Hungary, 151 in Denmark, 142 in Italy, 141 in Finland, 137 in Norway and 117 in Holland. It is because of this industrial development that the percentage of people engaged in agriculture shows a decline in many European countries. Between 1885 and 1925 the ratio of agriculture population to total population in Germany fell from 42.2 per cent to 30.5 per cent between 1910 and 1925, it declined from 22.5 to 19.1 per cent in Belgium, in Switzerland from 64.3 per cent to 40.7 per cent and in Hoalland from 28.4 per cent to 23.6 per cent. During the second and third decades of the century, Norway brought down the ratio of agricultural population from 39.5 per cent to 29.9 per cent and Denmark form 46.5 per cent 30.3 per cent (Nanavati Manilal B. and Anjaria, 1947). It is but true that in the U.S.A., Sweden and other countries, surplus from labour released by mechanization of agriculture did not create any problems of unemployment because it was absorbed by industries which developed in the meantime. (Singh Charan, 1964). The problem of surplus population in by no means peculiar to India and Bihar. It had to be faced in most European countries at a certain stage of economic development. The comparatively high rate of increase in Europe is shown by the fact that whereas the population in European countries increased between 1870 and 1930 by 198 million or 64 per cent that of India increased by 88 million or 31 per cent during the same period (Nanavati Manilal B. and Anjaria J.J., 1947). These populous European countries succeeded in solving their population-problem through industrialization. In India the Famine Commission of 1881 and 1901 had emphasized the need for the development of industries in order to reduce the increasing pressure of population on the soil. Bihar, being one of the most populous state next to Uttar Pradesh before bifurcation which is in the grip of problems like poverty, unemployment, low productivity, disparity.

Bihar Scenario

In a predominately agricultural economy like Bihar which is a demographically sick and economically weak, the key to future development less in reducing the pressure on land an in generating employment in the non-agricultural sector. Certainly, rapid indusrialization which is a generator of growth, by raising income, by cerating and widening employment opportunities and by raising capital formation is the surest prescription for all the ills prevailing in the state like poverty, unemployment, low productivity, low income, high population pressure on land, backwardness and what not. But unfortunately, the industrial scene in Bihar remains murky even after 59 years of independence. The economy of Bihar suffers from the paradox of retarded industrial development and it is very disappointing to take down that after more than five and a half decades of planned development efforts the state is still in groups of non-industrialized region of the country. Whatever be the reasons for the industrial backwardness of the state, lack of natural resources is certainly not one of them. So far as availability of mineral resources is concerned that state having command over 40 per cent total mineral resources, ranks first in the mineral map of India. It has been rightly observed that if a location of industry in India was to be determined from the Weberian concept. Bihar would have witnesses grand stride in indusrialization. Undoubtedly, removal of the backwardness of the state can be possible if we succeed in making it one of the most vibrant economic zones of the country through full exploitation of mineral deposits of Chotanagpur plateau and the agricultural potentials of North and Central Bihar (Jha B.K. 2000). But the picture has changed to a certain extent after bifurcation of the State on 14th November 2000. When all the mines and minerals have gone to Jharkhand and vast expose to fertile soil has come to Bihar. Of course, Jharkhand has gained industry and lost agriculture and Bihar has not industry and gained agriculture. The carving of the new state has taken away roughly 45 per cent of the geographical area and nearly 26 per cent of the population of undivided Bihar. With this, new Bihar is left with a geographical area a approximately 94.16 thousand sq.km. having a population of 82.88 million on Ist March 2001. Bihar has lost 30 per cent of India's copper cool, 20 per cent of India is iron ore, 24 per cent of India is copper ore, 17 per cent of bauxite, 54 per cent of India's mica and 100 per cent pyrites. The state is wholly denuded of entire forest wealth. No doubt, the socio-demographic and economic features of the new state look skewed, unbalanced, and unsuitable for industrialization when we find an unfavourable land-man-ratio i.e., 0.31 acre per capita, on alarming density of population as high as 880 persons per sq.km. after West Bengal (904) and an abysmally low per capita income at around Rs. 2250 at 1996-97 prices. After bifurcation the assets of Bihar come to Rs. 20389 crore but liabilities swell to 3082 crore and thus, the state's liabilities are Rs. 10443 crore more than the assets. But there is no use and no need for breathing of the breast in lamentation. Bihar is fortunate in having the most fertile soil in the world; the state is fortunate in having sufficient natural resources and human capital for industrial development of the state.

The eastern part of India, of which Bihar state is an important constituent has been renowned for its industrial area in the past industrialization in great Britain started with the development of textile industry which faced competition of eastern India particularly Bihar and Bengal states. The household and cottage industries of this region had been very popular. The manufacturing of cloth, ornaments, utensils ornaments of the state was popular. Kautilyas' Arthshastra has clear indications of the fact that the area was not only self-sufficient with regard to the supply of industrial gods but was a major centre of export to foreign countries. In the last decade of the 19th century the coal mining industry started in Raniganj (West Bengal) and Jharia (Bihar now in Jharkhand). TISCO at Jamshedpur, Japla Cement Factory at Japla, Dalmia Nagar, Banjari and Chaibasa were started in the beginning of the century. Bihar was one of the first states where the process of transformation of potential resources into real resources was initiated, and yet it never completed the process of transition whereas many states, starting later with much lesser resources, are much ahead the road to industrialization now. Is it not true that the state was one of the pioneering states in production of sugar. In northern part of the state the location of sugar mills can be seen. It enjoyed the position next to Uttar Pradesh production of sugar and also considering the number of mills located in India. A concentration of mineral based industries at some locations in the districts of Dhanbad. Hazaribagh, Singhbhum, Giridih, Ranchi and Palamau was found. Besides mining, major industries were steel, aluminium, copper engineering, cement, automobiles, chemicals, silk glass and tobacco based industries. Besides the organized industrial units there existed small scale college industries in lakhs in the state. And so Bihar's industrial scene was not bad but the state during the colonial period was subjected to maximum exploitation. Its mineral resources was plundered gearing to the colonial need. Infact every country has faced plundering of mineral resources under alien subjugation.

The degree of industrialization is generally measured on the basis of *(i)* certain minimum percentage of its Gross Domestic Product (GDP) arising in the industrial sector, *(ii)* a certain proportion of the output of the industrial sector to be in manufacturing, and *(iii)* a certain proportion of the population to be employed in the industrial sector. So on the basis of the above three criteria Mr. Sutcliffe has preferred to give the following definition, 'a country 20 per cent of whose GDP arose in the industrial sector of which at least 60 per cent was in manufacturing and which had at least one – tenth of the total population employed in industry would be counted as industrialized. Any country which did not satisfy these three criteria would not.' (Sutcliffe quoted by Suman H.N.P.S. 1977). No doubt, this observation is arbitrary. However, they clearly reflect qualitative structural change in addition to simple quantitative change in the level of output and income but may not focus on whether the structural change towards industrialization will result in alleviation of poverty through creating employment opportunities or not. If we take any indicators, that will show that Bihar is industrially backward. It is but true that being a mineral rich state there existed very little of industry in this region on the eve of independence. Percentage of industrial worker to total working force was about 3 on the eve of independence.

The mainstay of the people of Bihar was agriculture which was highly under-developed. Soon after independence concentrated efforts came to be made at the industrialization of the country but the Indian planning exercises have generally been devoid of any regional consideration. As a result Bihar could not succeed in achieving the rank of highly industrialized states even after 59 years of independence. Since the industrialized regions of developing countries enjoyed considerable external economics, there was a tendency for savings from all parts of the country, by and large to get invested in the industrialized region. The other regions, starved of the investable resources, remained sunk in the quagmire of non development, characterized by a predominance of primitive agriculture in their economic activities, a high level of unemployment, underemployment and distinguished unemployment and a low level of income. Bihar state is one such region in India, which is a developing economy (Pradhan H. Prasad 2000). One of the important factors hampering the growth of industrialization in the state is said to be lack of entrepreneurs. Indigenous entrepreneurs are not many and outside entrepreneurs are not attracted to it. The basic cause of the lack of indigenous entrepreneurs is to be found in the feudal way of life and thinking. The most disappointing fact is that even today outside entrepreneurs have hesitation to investment their capital in this state where kidnapping industrialists have already flourished, Rangdari tax has become common rule. No doubt, poor infrastructure too is also one of important factors hampering industrial growth of the state but in the prevailing law and order scenario of the state even sound infrastructure will fail to attract entrepreneurs of investment in this state.

The strategy for industrialization based on Mahalanobis model was speltout in the following strategy of industrialization words, "If industrialization is to be rapid enough, the country must aim to developing basic industries and industries which make machines to make the machines needed for further development (Bhagavan M.R. 1985). But 'the heavy industries of Bihar are like Palm tree growing higher and higher without giving rise to adequate proliferation' (Jha P.K. 1977). Here by it is worth nothing that what will suit Bihar depends upon the answer to the question as to what do we aim? If we merely at the highest output per person employed, output being positively correlated with capital per head, we must have capital intensive large scale industries on the lines of western industries where this amount is large. But we have three other aims also. Viz. *(i)* to provide optimum employment, *(ii)* to ensure equitable distribution of the national product, and *(iii)* to promote a democratic way of life. And then we should agree W.S. Woytinsky who has observed 'Heavy industry and specially heavy-machine making industry has never been the root and base of economic growth. The basis of economic growth in the early phase of industrialization was agriculture, trade and handicrafts. In all the great industrial power except the USSR and Japan heavy industry grew on the basis of consumer good industries, responding to their demand and adjusting itself to their needs. This refers not only to the United States, Great Britain and Germany but also to France, Italy, Canada and so on! (Quoted by Singh Charan 1972) of course, Woytinsky's observation may prove very inspiring for Bihar's economy which has lost its mineral resources after bifurcation and is facing the problem of unemployment, excess pressure of population on agriculture, poverty etc. Bihar would have moved ahead and would have joined the set of progressive states in India, instead of being at the bottom. This policy which would have increased the real income and employment in the rural areas, would have then provided investable funds and favourable market demand conditions for the industrial and other nonfarm activities but the policies followed on the economic particularly industrial front for past more than five decades, were just the opposite of what were required. One thing more to be considered here is that the main difficulty in the way of development of large scale industries has been the all too meager purchasing power in the hands of a large majority of the people. That alone constitutes on explanation for the phenomenon of over no pollution. Any attempt to increase the purchasing power of the people will have largely to concentrate on agriculture, which affords the main channel of employment to a majority of people. And so a plan which over looks this fundamental consideration, or does not put an adequate emphasis on the development of agriculture cannot be successful in achieving desired result because in the development of an underdeveloped economy like Bihar there is no conflict between agricultural and industrial development. Both are complementary to each other and so there is need to give due emphasis on the development of both sectors – agriculture and industry. In the case of Bihar rural industrialization particularly agro-based industries development may serve our purpose and prove insrumental in providing employment opportunities and thus in eradicating poverty, too. Even the Second Five Year Plan which lauds so much emphasis on heavy industry also goes on to concede. 'In a country like India with vast distances and a large potential market, the demands can and ought to be met through production in efficient, decentralized units. There are other reasons also which weigh in favour of wide diffusion of industry.' Is it not true that despite the iron and steel industry, the people of Bihar have remained poor and, although Punjab has no large industry, by devoting greater attention to agriculture and small scale industries, its people have come to enjoy a higher standard of living than people elsewhere in the country of course, our problem is to retain the advantages of technological progress and at the same time to minimize the social cost in terms of unemployment. Hereby it is worth nothing that even in some of the developed countries like U.S.A. and Japan, the organized sector is loosing importance as creators of new jobs. Recent trends in the GDP spectrum and in the employment structure in selected countries, reveal that in most of the advanced countries, the share of organized manufacturing sector is declining rapidly (World Development Report 89) but unfortunately, we are still trying to follow the traditional path of industrialization in terms of the organized manufacturing activities and so more than 55 years of planned development efforts, rural industries continue to be an insignificant and inefficient activity in rural areas, untracted by the dynamic influence of industrialization efforts.

Rural Industries

No doubt, Bihar has lost its mineral resources to a great explants but there is no reason for Bihar is to be frustrated 'A country' Lewis has pointed out, 'which is considered to be poor in natural resources today may be considered very rich in resources at some later time not merely because unknown resources are discovered, but equally because news user are discovered for the known resources' (Lewis p. 52). Bihar should realize its potentiality for industrialization and at the same time, take lesson from failure of planned efforts of industrialization on national level in the sense it, on the one side increased unemployment and on the other side most of our public industries have become white elephants due to lack of capital. Bihar is a rural agricultural dominated popular. Economy facing widespread unemployment and endemic poverty and so agro-based industries may be instrumental in eradication its poverty and raising standard of life through providing and widening the scope of employment opportunities in non-farm sector. In Bihar at attempt should be made to develop cottage and small industries on the model of Japan where small enterprises occupying a predominant position representing about 99.4 per cent of the total number of establishments in the country and engaging about 80 per cent of the total number of employees. What to talk of Bihar, it is to Mahatma Gandhi's credit that he foresaw the crucial role of rural industries in the economic development of the country and prepared a model with their centre role. Ajit Kumar Sinha (1988) has undertaken a micro level of study of rural industrial units on the basis of stratified sampling method from different representative unit of Bihar and found that the rural industries are far off from the main stream of industrialization efforts.

They are limping with capital shortage and technological backwardness. The conditions of traditional rural industries is worst, though still having dominance over the rural industrial scene in number. There are under the low income trap i.e., low level of income—low level of investment—low level technology and employment—low level of production—low level of income. The non-traditional industries are in comparatively better position, though few in number and have developed in an unplanned manner and without any proper incentive. It is due to the policy makers and the government who do not appear to think in firms of rural industrialization (Sinha Ajit Kumar 2000). Rural industries are most suitable for Bihar not only because these are labour intensive but there are other reasons, too. These industries have also high potential for income generation in the rural area by providing employment. These industries encourage dispersal of economic activities in the rural areas and thus, promote balanced regional development. Besides these rural industries also help protect and promote balanced regional development. Moreover, these industries being environment friendly lead to development without destruction. And so rural industrialization is a key to inclusive rural development and rural prosperity of the state.

Rural industrialization contributes to the development of agriculture which is the backbone of a economy of Bihar and urban industries and without that it would not be easy to solve the problem of disguished unemployment found particularly in agricultural dominated economy of Bihar. No doubt, the level of output produced by the village industries went up from Rs. 1443.27 crores in 1988-89 to Rs. 9228.27 crores in 2003-04. The number of persons employed in these industries increased from 28.83 lakhs in 1988-89 to 62.58 lakhs in 2003-04. Sales have gone up from Rs. 1598.31 crores in 1988-89 to Rs. 10988.17 crores in 2003-04. Thus, during the period 1988-89 to 2003-04 the compound annual growth rate of production, employment and sales was 13.17 per cent, 5.30 per cent and 13.71 per cent respectively (K. Kamalakaran, 2000). In case of Bihar we find that the overall First Five Year Plan provisions for schemes under cottage industries amounted to Rs. 50.03 lakhs and by the end of the first plan the cottage industries provided employment to 1970 persons. In the Second plan the total expenditure went up to Rs. 6.84 crores in village and small industries and 31406 persons got full time employment and 21,666 persons got part time employment in all cottage industries like Khadi industries, village oil industries, hand-pounding rice industries, gur khandsari udyog, bee keeping, palm-gur industry village skin industries, a large number of rural people got full and part time employment. During the Fourth Plan the total expenditure of Rs. 645826 lakhs over the various schemes were incurred under the small and cottage industries which provided employment to 11050 persons. During the Five Year Plan which the total expenditure of Rs. 1098.19 lakhs employment generated for around 1,13,000 persons in village and small industries. Undoubtedly, in plan after plan one discovers adequate emphasis on the need, rationale and concern for accelerating the growth of rural industry. During the 4th plan emphasis was laid on area development by means of growth centres for rural industrialization under the auspices of the Backward Areas Development Programme. Following the recommendations of the Pande working group and the Wanchoo working group, a programme was introduced for providing financial, fiscal and other support (e.g., store purchase facilities, price preferences, quality control, marketing assistance, raw material depots etc.) to private entrepreneurs for locating industrial units in backward areas but in actual effect, many things occurred by default. The Fifth Plan broadened the RIP promoting village and small scale industries primarily to achieves a balanced regional development and to reduce the tendency of concentration of industry in large urban area. Hereby it is worth nothing that was a sharp decline in the growth of industrial production after 1965-66. Since seventies we got plagued with increasing industrial sickness, a phenomenon practically unknown in the modern industrial sector in India earlier. In Bihar about 1.5 lakhs SSI units are registered out of which over 3000 units are reported to be sick or closed for various reasons (Rath. A.R. 1997). Nearly 25 per cent of total registered units in the state are closed which is fairly high compared to many other states of India. There are some working units which are either sick or on the verge of getting so. According to a report of RBI a large number of SSI units (30894) were closed in Bihar March, 1998 (Prasad Umesh 2002). Thus, while the government is striving for development of SSI, sickness among SSI units, on the other hand, is growth at an alarming rate and threatening to cripple the economy of the state. The phenomenon of sickness tends to aggravate the problem of unemployment although the Sixth Plan mainly laid emphasis on employment creation in the village and small scale industries and a sum of Rs. 6805 lakhs was proposed as outlay for development of village and small scale industries. The Seventh Plan laid further emphasis on improving productivity, enhancing product quality, reducing costs and modernization. At the same time, the need to strengthen the programme of ancillarisation for a harmonious growth of the total industrial sector was given importance. The Eight Plan Witnessed the priority for development of village and small industries in order to generate adequate employment for achieving near full employment and alleviation of poverty. The entire policy thrust for the Ninth Plan was involved under the shadow of the WTO economic regime. However, the role of small scale and village industries could not be ignored and incentives for the development of these industries have been provided during this plan period. Undoubtedly, even in the face of strict and difficult economic and other constraints the sector has been able to register impressive growth rates.

With carving of the new state Jharkhand, agriculture and agro-based industries assumes greater significance in Bihar's economy and it is heartening to take down that there is a tremendous scope for development of agro-based industries in new Bihar. The planning has recently identified the following industry groups with high employment potential and low ICOR. They are:

Fish canning and preservation, backery, manufacturer of Sugar and Khandsari, tobacco products, cotton gining, cleaning, printing and dyeing, Khadi, Handlooms textiles, powerlooms, wool spinning and weaving (in units other than mills), dyneing and bleaching of woolen textiles, wine drugs and medicines and batteries, also has high employment content and ICOR is also found not so very high in these cases.

Although an assumption has always been made that economic growth will lead to increase in production and employment, ILO statistics about a number of countries, however bring out the lack of correlation between production and employment growth. And so it is a facility to presume that by recording growth and development, we will be solving the basic problems related to employment. Obviously, the rate of investment and choice of technology determine the growth of employment and so the Planning Commission Suggests that economic growth would be mainly derived from sectors which have high observed and so potential employment content. It is clear that through rural industrialization a large section of population can be offered employment opportunities at the place of their residence. Rural industries have the capacity to correct regional imbalances by initiating industrial activities on dispersed basis in the most neglected, backward inaccessible areas where perhaps large scale sector is unable to penetrate.

Agro Product

Bihar is second largest producer of vegetables and fourth in fruits and has potential of emerging as the sugar bowl of the country. The area of fruit crop is Bihar is estimated to 266824 hectares with annual production of nearly 2833847 tonnes which is more than 8 per cent of the total fruit growing area of our country and 10 per cent of the total production of the fruit accounts for the state whereas the areas of vegetables constitute 596648 hectares with annual production of 9817009 tonnes. On an averages 18 to 10 lakh mt. mango is being produced annually. The major varieties of fruits cultivated in the state including mango, banana, pineapple, guava, litchi, papaya and citrus fruits whereas vegetables like potato, cabbage, cauliflower, brinjal, French beans, tomato, peas, okra and chilies are produced. In spite of the immense potential to become principal industry, the state does not have adequate number of food processing units. What to talk of Bihar only 0.5 to 1.0 per cent of the total production of fruits and vegetables in the country is processed in India whereas processing level in Malaysia is 83 per cent followed by Philippines (78%), Brazil (70%) and USA (60-70%) (Krishna Meeta, 2000). There are other commodities like makhana, lac, silk, leather and its product which give indications that Bihar has sufficient potential for agro-based industries. There is wide scope for development of fisheries, dairy farming, wood industry, carpentry, soap factories, paper industry, sugar industry, tiles, bakery, utensils, khandasari, plastic goods, mat making etc. Dolls of Muzaffarpur are exported to France, West Germany, Canada, Scandinavia etc. The appliqué work products of flok style of Saran and Siwan districts are exported to France and Scandinavian countries. The Munj articles of West Champaran are exported to U.S.A., Japan etc. The Slkki articles of Darbhanga, Madhubani, Samastipur and Siwan district are exported to U.S.A., Canada, Sweden and Japan. The Madhubani folk painting have become very popular in U.S.A., Spain, France, West Germany and Scandinavian countries. (Jha P.K. 1977). Thus, the agro-based industries and other village and cottage industries can play major role in the industrial development of the state and these industries being labour intensive provide employment to a large number of unemployed workforce.

Concluding Remarks

Bihar appears to be one of the first states where the process of industrialization has been initiated very earlier in comparison to other states which have attracted later with lesser resources but overtake Bihar in the race of industrialization. A capital intensive industry like Tata Iron and Steel Company established as back as in 1912 is considered as an important landmark in the industrial history of Bihar, Punjab and Bihar as agriculture based states but Bihar stands in no way with Punjab.

To come on equal footing with Punjab the state is in need developing rural industries particularly agro-based industries which help the development of backward and forward spread effects. Of course, small and rural industries play an important role as far as employment generation is concerned not only by virtue of their labour intensive nature but also due to the fact that the growth in agriculture facilitated by labour intensive in the initial stages but became capital intensive later and was accompanied by reduced labour absorption (Papole, 1982). Similarly, the labour absorbing capacity of large industries is limited and has been declining, may be because of its growing capital intensification and meager purchasing power in the hands of a large majority of the people also stands in the way of development of large scale industries undoubtedly. Agro-based industries develop the purchasing capacity of the people. In view of this small and rural industries enjoy the special patronage from the government. However, despite numerous policy measures during the last five decades small scale industries have remained tiny, technologically backward and lacking in competitive strength. Unfortunately, in the global era, the reforms process which has been under way since July 1991 exposed the small scale industries to greater market competition by taking away its assured market. In view of the increasing competition in the global market Bihar will have to pay special attention to the quality products to be exported at cheaper rates by reducing the cost of production. But at the same time we cannot set aside truth that the economy of Bihar is suffering from the paradox of retarded industrial development is largely on account of poor infrastructural support, low investment, lack of market and above all the corrupt government machinery which is not only corrupt but also lethargic.

For success of labour intensive small scale industries the basic requirements are availability of timely and adequately finance, marketing opportunities, maintenance of quality, timely up gradation of technology and proper management but unfortunately, about 30,000 units out 1.5 lakh registered units tell the true story. No effort can bear fruit so long as the prevailing circumstances in the state are not changed. Even the policy of promotion rather permitting; towards investors of outside states or foreigners proves fruitless in the state where the kidnapping industry is flourishing and Rangdari tax they are compelled to pay for movement of a file in any department of the state Dastori is a normal phenomenon. No doubt, Bihar is not the only state where such type of situation prevails but in this state if presents a very ugly scene. Undoubtedly, one of the reasons behind kidnapping industry or Rangdari tax is unemployment in the young generation and so problems of unemployment and poverty need to be tackled on the priority basis for which rural industrialization particularly agro-based industries in Bihar proves instrumental. As early as in 1929 Nehru said, "If we are to eradicate poverty, we must first do away with this widespread unemployment." But all these are not enough. In the global era we need to be more cautions against the malafied intentions of developed countries which do not like to see our prosperity.

REFERENCES

Jha B.K. (2005) Gandhian Economics Versus Globalization' in Globalization and Contemporary Economic Scenario edited by R.K. Singh.

Jha B.K. (2000) Strategy for Industrialization in BEJ Conference volume.

Jha P.K. (1997) Economics of North Bihar.

Pradhan H. Prasad (2000) India. Dilemma of Development.

Singh Charan (1964) India's Poverty and its Solution.

Sharma Alakh N. and Gupta Shaibal (1987) Bihar Stagnation or Grout.

Mayrdal Gunnar (19) Asian Drama.

Nanavati, Manilal B. and Anjana J.J. (1947) The India Rural Problem.

Papola T.S. (1982) Rural Industrialization. Approach and Potential IJIEA, Vol., 35, No. 3.

Papola T.S. (2004) Globalization, Employment and Social Protection. Emerging Perspective for the Indian Worker IJLE, Vol. 47, No. 3.

Different Conference Volumes of India Economic Association.

Different Conference Volumes of Economic Association of Bihar.

Kurushetra 2006, Vol. 54, No. 7.

Yadava Gorelal 'Industrialization of Bihar' in Studies in Bihar's Economy by N.K. Karna.

Suman H.N.P.S. (1977) Industrial Economics for Under-Developed Countries.

26

Special Economic Zones: Boon or Bane

MITHILESH KUMAR SINHA

Introduction

Special Economic Zones are crucial for generating employment, boosting manufacturing and allowing India to compete with countries like China. The SEZs offer 'the only way forward' in bridging the gap between India and South-East Asia, including China, in terms of manufacturing and employment.

The idea of setting up Special Economic Zones (SEZ) was first conceived by the National Democratic Alliance (NDA) Government at the centre. SEZs are known as 'Urban Enterprises Zones' in the USA and in China they are referred to as 'Special Administrative Regions'. The model in view was the existing Special Export Zones, which were meant to boost country's exports so that the adverse payments balance in the external sector of the economy is reduced to manageable limit. Those zones met with limited success. The idea behind SEZs was to promote industrial growth, encourage manufacturing industries and thereby to promote economic growth, improve Gross Domestic Product (GDP) growth rate, and expand employment. However, the concrete shape to SEZs was provided by the UPA Government through the SEZs Act, 2005. The Special Economic Zones Act of 2005 was passed on 23rd June, 2005 and notified in February 2006 with the objects for the establishment, development and management of the Special Economic Zones for the promotion of exports.

The total number of approvals for SEZs till 10th May 2007, was 257. Out of these 63 SEZs have been notified. On 5th April, 2007, 83 more SEZs were cleared for notification. The 162 SEZs which have in-principle approvals are yet to be cleared by Board of Approvals. Apart from these, 370 proposals are pending with the Government, of which more than 160 have already acquired land.

SEZs are specially demarcated zones where units operate under a set of rules and regulations different from those applicable to other units in the country. SEZ is a region with special tax laws and duty exemptions, permission to have captive power plants and distribute power, therefrom, have their own water and gas supply units.

Broadly SEZ has certain defining features such as special tax incentives; duty free movement of goods and services; world-class infrastructure; construction intensive nature; export orientation; differentiated economic management like relaxations in certain basic restrictions applicable to the rest of the economy; and free inflow of foreign capital (Ranganathan: 2007).

The above are not official definitions, but no one familiar with the concept of SEZ can deny these features. It is important to appreciate that such zones have regulations on the activities carried on, and are not to be mistaken as areas that do not have any form of restrictions. It is often a controlled economic environment for free trade.

The Perspective

According to an article written in 2000 by Robert C. Hayword, Director, World Economic Processing Zones Association (www. Wepza.org), the concept of free economic zones dates back to 300 BC. The author notes that such enclaves were found in the Phoenician city of Tyre in the Greek island of Delos. The city became very wealthy as a result of such policies and was viewed as a challenge to the centralism of the Roman Empire.

According to the Wepza website, more than 2,000 zones are said to exist in over 120 countries. These are found in various countries following all known systems of economic management. They are in high, low and middle-income countries, having capitalist, socialist or communist oriented economies. Such has been the irresistible pull of the concept to promote economic growth.

The evolution of these zones owes to the fact that traditionally governance has sought to apply much rigidity to the way business is conducted and governments have sought to relax this in designated zones to promote specific forms of economic activity.

China was possibly the most closed and authoritarian economic system in the world in the 1970s and early 1980s. It could not liberalize its economy as its political system did not allow it. So, it created pockets of economic freedom in the form of SEZs, which at times exceeded some small countries in their geographical spread. These pockets were a world apart from the rest of the country in terms of economic system and philosophy. Similar is the example of Dubai, a part of the Emirates that almost exists as an SEZ in itself, though it also has also designated areas like the Jebel Ali Zone.

Ironically, world bodies responsible for administering and advocating global policy initiatives such as the IMF, World Bank, OECD and ILO have reservations about the benefits of such exclusive economic enclaves that liberalise selectively but involves costs for the economies in the form of revenue losses and regional imbalances and instead advocate across the board liberalization.

Earlier Initiatives

Around the time the Chinese started their SEZ initiatives in the early 1980s. India pitched in with its nascent export enclaves. Over time the six EPZs were created in places that had access to seaports. Parallely 100 per cent EOU and similar schemes were unveiled. Over the next two decades, there was a plethora of schemes focused on export promotion. The broad strain in all these was tax and duly exemptions with limited relaxation on foreign exchange transactions.

Unlike China, that coupled liberalization in FDI with SEZ initiatives, India missed the opportunity to attract FDI when it made half-hearted attempts to promote export zones. Another stark distinction lay in the fact that the Chinese SEZ involved gigantic infrastructure creation, which attracted its own share of FDI. The China model of SEZ with complete sovereignty in governance was not thought of in India at any stage. The years of fairly muddled and hotchpotch efforts to generate clusters of industries sharing common infrastructure, that delivered very little value in export or growth terms culminated in the policy on SEZ in 2005.

Report Card of SEZ

SEZ ACT 2005	Passed by Parliament in May 2005
Received Presidential Assent on June 23, 2005	
Came into effect on February 10, 2006	

Contd...

No. of valid formal approvals	366
No. of notified SEZs	142
Investment in 142 notified SEZs	Rs. 46,705 crore
Direct employment in 142 notified SEZs	40,153 persons
Expected investment and employment from SEZs (by December 2009) By the 142 notified SEZs as on July 31, 2007	Investment: Rs. 2,83,319 crore Employment: 21,00,000 direct additional jobs
If 366 SEZs become operational	Investment: Rs. 3,00,000 crore Employment: 40 lakh additional jobs
Exports in 2006-07	Rs. 34,787 crore (Rs. 9,301 crore by new-genearation SEZs) Growth of 52 per cent over Rs. 22,840 crore in 2005-06

Figures as on August 29, 2007.

Under the SEZ Act of 2005, the SEZs will have the following incentives:

- The SEZs should have a minimum area of 1000 hectares. Now maximum area of a SEZ has been fixed at 5000 hectares. However, this restriction does not apply to sector specific SEZ. It can be set up even on a small area of 10 hectares.
- Duty free import/domestic procurement of goods for development, operation and maintenance.
- Income tax exemption for a block of 10 years in 15 years.
- 100 per cent FDI is permitted for all investments in SEZs, except for activities listed under the negative list.
- Full freedom to allocate space and built up area to approved SEZ units on commercial basis.
- Self-generation, transmission and distribution of power is permitted in SEZs.
- The developer is authorized to provide and maintain basic services like water, electricity, security, swimming pools, recreation centres, restaurants, hotels etc. on a commercial basis.
- The units in SEZ are free to import without any license.
- The units have income tax exemption—100 per cent for a block of five years and 50 per cent for a block of two years there after.

- Exemption from custom duties on import of capital goods, raw materials, consumables, spares etc.
- SEZ units exempted from sales tax, services tax etc.
- SEZ units may sub-contract part of production through units in other SEZs or Domestic Tariff Area.
- Of the total land acquired for SEZ, now 50 per cent is required to be used for principal processing activities. The other portion can be used for marketing, storage, housing, recreation, even for specialized agricultural operations such as dairying, poultry, horticulture, floriculture etc.
- Normal labour laws enforced by State Government are not applicable to SEZs.

Comparison Between SEZs in China and India

Indian policymakers' ongoing fascination with special economic zones was inspired by China's roaring success with these enclaves of galvanized production. New Delhi has sanctioned close to 200 SEZs.

China's success in attracting oodles of foreign direct investment and becoming one of the top exporting countries of the world hinged on careful implementation of its SEZ policy. More than two decades later, India, too, is trying to tread on the same ground. There are, however, certain fundamental differences in the Indian and Chinese approaches to SEZs, which make it difficult to say for sure that Indian SEZs will be able to recreate the Chinese magic.

Size, location, flexible labour laws and stable policies are the factors primarily responsible for making Chinese SEZs attractive to foreign investors. In India, it the fiscal sops being offered to developers and units, which is the primary driving force.

The Chinese Government started building SEZs way back in 1979. The idea behind the SEZs was to experiment with liberal policies in certain earmarked regions while insulating the rest of the economy from their influence. The government identified huge tracts of land, near the coastal region, and started building mega cities with all required infrastructure. Stringent labour laws applicable in China were relaxed in the regions and foreign investors were wooed with sops and the promise of stability. Although India had a headstart in the direction by building its first export processing zone in 1969 with certain minimum infrastructure and fiscal sops (seven more followed later), it could not muster enough political will to build full-fledged SEZs with foreign territory status in the matters of international trade till the turn of the country. In 2000, former trade minister, the late Murasoli Maran, announced that India should try to replicate the Chinese success story and announced a SEZ policy. However, five years later the SEZ Act was passed by the Parliament, what India had was a policy very different from China's.

As opposed to the six mega SEZs built by the Chinese Government (the largest being Shenzhen built over 49,500 hectares), India opened its doors to private players and allowed sector-specific SEZs to develop on just 10 hectares of land. As a result, India has as many as 28 operational SEZs with about 200 more having received approvals. In China, the government chose the location for SEZs with a lot of thought with all six located near the coastal region. This makes it easier for SEZ units to export their products and import inputs. In India, SEZs are being built all over the country, wherever land can be acquired by developers. This has also led to allegations of land-grabbing and conversion of productive agricultural land by developers.

Flexibility in labour laws, which played an important role in attracting investors, is absent in Indian SEZs. This is one of the prices India is having to pay for the advantages of a federal democratic government.

India has, however, tried to make up for all the disadvantages by offering attractive fiscal sops. Tax holidays for SEZs in India are longer and steeper than those given by China. This had given rise to some dissent from the finance ministry, which had complained that the fiscal loss would be immense. However, the commerce ministry argument that the gains would be larger than the losses had prevailed. One has to now wait and see whether the interest shown in SEZs translates into more jobs, exports and revenue.

Comparison Between SEZs in China and India

	CHINA	INDIA
Number	06	200 approved
Largest	Shenzhen (49,300 hectares)	Reliance Navi Mumbai (1,000 hectares)
Location	Coastal Region	All over the country
Labour Laws	Flexible	Non-flexible
Fiscal sops	Less Liberal	More liberal
Developers	Government	Mostly private initiative

Special Economic Zones: Contemporary Rational

A pertinent question that can arise for consideration is whether the new policy on SEZ has a distinctly different rationale or objective from the approach of the earlier policies that failed to deliver any significant advantage for the cc untry as compared to similar policies of the Philippines, Taiwan or Korea, not to mention China's far superior strategy.

The Indian policy lacks a grandiose purpose either in terms of creating a completely different type of infrastructure or an industry focus that would attract significant foreign capital as in the case of other countries. The investment that is stated to find its way into the new SEZ enclaves would have come any way into the country if the existing schemes of tax holiday as applicable to export oriented units had continued. In fact, the quantum and actually that quantum of investment would have to be much more if other policy liberalization had happened in tandem.

The support for this, rather pessimistic view is found in the fact that out of 267 cases cleared till September 2006 by the Board of Approvals, 133 cases are SEZs of less than 0.4 square miles in area and only about five are of any internationally significant size. The smaller SEZs for IT/ITES (the minimum prescribed area of 10 hectares) constitute nearly 53 per cent of the total approved cases. This exemplifies the fact that no significant large infrastructure creation is either possible or likely to arise, which has successfully been the engine of growth in the SEZ phenomenon across the globe.

The reason for such a large number of projects in the IT sector is fact that income tax benefits for this sector are expiring in March 2009 and by converting or migrating the operations that currently enjoy the tax holiday into SEZs, the industry hopes to enjoy the tax holiday for further periods allowed under the policy. This is an unfortunate and perverse development where the SEZ route is exploited by an industry that neither creates nor requires any significant infrastructure for its operations. These businesses that are currently scattered in different parts of various cities may now congregate into designated SEZs for continuing the tax benefits, adding to the pressure on urban infrastructure.

It could have never been on the wish list of the IT industry that it required continued tax subsidy for its progress, nor was the absence of tax holiday seen as a hurdle in attracting fresh investment in this. Thus the SEZ, which significantly catalysed infrastructure and industrial investment in other countries, may end up creating dismal IT complexes and multi-storied buildings in India with the sole objective of continuing tax exemption. If the tax exemption for software technology park units gets extended, the significant number of SEZ proposals will evaporate. The only logic for the SEZ scheme could be the position adopted that it is more compatible with the WTO regime as compared to other schemes in place. This also is an unverified proposition to serve as the basis for justifying or providing the rationale for the current policy. In fact the current scheme that provides pro rata exemption of income taxes to SEZ units based on export turnover is more likely to be viewed as a subsidy under the SCM clause of WTO and countervailed by the importing countries as it happened in the case of EPZ and EOU units.

To round off the discussion on the rationale for SEZs, it will be profitable to understand the imperatives that seem to exist in other countries that have more successfully adopted this model. One of the key reasons for setting up SEZs was the need to provide a high degree of economic freedom in an otherwise restricted regime. The compulsions could have been either in terms of high duty and tax structure applicable in that country, or limitation on free use of exchange, or freedom for foreign investments.

Another factor that has driven SEZs was the need to relax rigid labour laws which could not be done on a national scale. It is also a fact that countries saw significant benefits in using SEZs for opening up the economy in a limited fashion to handle political oppositions while hoping that technology and skill transferred by the process would have backward linkages to the rest of the economy.

SEZs and Employment

India needs to tackle unemployment if it has to eradicate poverty in the next 25 years. The special economic zones are a vital instrument for generating employment. SEZs will lead to faster growth of labour-intensive manufacturing and services. The zones are expected to employ five lakh people by December 2007. Many SEZs are recruiting people from rural areas and providing them training for operations in the SEZs, as we have seen from the gem and jewellery SEZ in Hyderabad, textiles units in Mahindra SEZ in Chennai and other new SEZs like Nokia, Flextronics, Brandix Apparel SEZ, Divi

Laboratories in Andhra Pradesh and Rajiv Gandhi Technology Park in Chandigarh. If the SEZ policy is carefully and fairly implemented, it would result in creation of lakhs of new jobs for skilled and unskilled workers. The number of managerial jobs would also increase tremendously. By 2009 SEZs are expected to employ 21,00,000 persons and if 366 SEZs become operational, 40 lakh additional jobs will be created (see Report Card of SEZs).

SEZs and Export

The special economic zones are a vital instrument for boosting India's exports. Software exports from Visakhapatnam Special Economic Zone (VSEZ), which were a paltry Rs. 5 crore in 1999-2000, had gone up to Rs. 109 crore in 2005-06. As per the projections, the export turnover will increase to Rs. 265 crore in 2007-08 and Rs. 413 crore in 2008-09. Conservative estimates suggest that the exports will witness a quantum jump and touch the magic figure of Rs. 1,000 crore by 2009-10. Andhra Pradesh has recorded the highest growth rate of 51 per cent in IT exports against the national average of 36 per cent in 2005-06.

Growth of IT at Vizag

Year	*No. of Units*	*Export Turnover (Rs. In Crore)*	*Employment (Cumulative)*
1999-00	16	5	700
2000-01	19	8	1,100
2001-02	20	17	1,700
2002-03	24	22	2,200
2003-04	26	52	2,800
2004-05	37	70	4,500
2005-06	40	109	6,000
2006-07	51	170	9,000
2007-08	63	265	13,500
2008-09	70	413	19,250

Source: The Hindu Survey of Indian Industry 2007 p. 236, cited by Prabhakar Sharma and Santosh Patnaik.

The farm sector cannot support the entire rural population. Industries have a play in eradicating rural poverty. To move people out of agriculture and create new jobs and industrial growth is important. SEZs are a must. SEZs can be helpful in improving the industrial infrastructure, enhancing competitiveness of industries and can prove a boon for absorbing the targeted employment generation in non-agricultural sector. Also concentration of industries in one place may enable common environment protection measures thus enhancing sustainable growth.

We can say that through SEZs we can boost exports, generate employment, create world-class infrastructure, attract FDI and consequently rapid growth will take place.

Implications of SEZs

The SEZ policy has invited criticism from several quarters. The following points are being raised against this policy:

1. SEZs will acquire large tracts of land. Though it is being said that agricultural land or at least land with double cropping will not be acquired. But in the states of Punjab and Haryana, wasteland is very little and no area has a single crop in a year. The area where RIL's Maha Mumbai SEZ is being developed is known as 'rice bowl', of Maharashtra. The Amritsar SEZ is being developed over 1218 acres of land. All of it has two or even three crops a year. Similarly, farmers are up in arms against forceful acquisition of their agricultural land near Barnala by Trident group. With 8 per cent as net sown area, 18.9 per cent cropped area and only 0.34 per cent as cultivable waste (Statistical Abstract of Punjab: 2005), Punjab has no land available for SEZs.
2. Land Ceiling laws do not apply to SEZs. The developers are acquiring large tracts of land through State Governments at cheap rates. The UP Government had given a corporate house 2500 acres of land to set up a power plant which required only 50 acres. Similarly the West Bengal Government has handed over prime agricultural land for Tata Small Car manufacturing unit near Singur. The land was capable of producing three crops a year (Datt: 2006). The project was opposed by farmers which led to violent protests and firing by the police. Spread over an area of 35,000 acres, the Reliance SEZ at Maha Mumbai will be the second largest in the world, after Shenzhen in China. RIL SEZ in Haryana is to be on about 25000 acres of land. Earlier, the Government of India started policies of Free Trade Zones and 100 per cent Export

Oriented Units but none of them could deliver the desired results. The share of exports from these in 2004-05 was a mere 5 per cent of total exports. The Empowered Group of Ministers, in its meeting on 5th April, 2007, limited the land size of SEZs to 5000 hectares. This decision will also be applicable to already notified SEZs.

3. In sector specific SEZs, developers can build 7500 houses, a hotel with 100 rooms, a 25 bed hospital, schools and other educational institutions and a multiplex up to 50,000 sq. metres. In multi product SEZs, they can build with 100 beds, and a multiplex of 2 lakh sq. metres. It means developers are free to use SEZ land to build large urban colonies. For these, the tax free raw materials can be imported from any where in the world. It is feared that if SEZ policy falters, the developers will be happy as only 50 per cent of land is to be used for export promotion units. The rest of the land can be used for real estate purposes.
4. The government is also not totally clear about the policy. The RBI treats SEZs as real estate business for all banking purposes. The Commerce Ministry projects that by March 2008, SEZs will attract investment of about Rs. 1 lakh crore, including FDI of Rs. 2500 crore, and create about 10 lakh jobs. On the other hand the Finance Ministry, fears that by 2009-10, Rs. 1 lakh crore will be the state loss in the form of tax rebates and subsides to the SEZs. With exemption of excise duty (16%), service tax (12.5%), sales tax, stamp duty, electricity duty, octroi etc. the SEZs will not generate any revenue for the states.
5. It is feared that because of huge tax rebates, the existing normal industries will shift to SEZs. It will lead to revenue loss to states. Moreover, about 62 per cent of approvals and 'in principal' approvals for SEZs till date are in IT and ITES sector in which we already have an edge. SEZs will be worthwhile if we are able to bring foreign investment in textiles, leather, agro-processing, engineering or consumer goods. Specially, the investment should be labour intensive.
6. Export orientation of industries with in SEZs is overestimated. Who will benefit out of this? The MNCs and Foreign Governments are happy that we will supply cheaper goods and services for their population. For this, we will use

our nonrenewable resources. The Indian Government has given tax exemption to SEZs to make these products cheaper.

7. If we earn huge amounts of foreign exchange, will we be able to fulfill basic needs of the populace living outside these SEZs, or will it be used to satiate the needs of select few, the ultra rich? The small numbers of such super and ultra rich people use the foreign exchange, so earned, for purchase of imported cars, personal helicopters, or expensive clothes and luxury consumer durable goods from international market.
8. In the SEZ Act of 2005, the definition of manufacturing includes agriculture, animal husbandry, horticulture, floriculture, pisci culture, sericulture etc. It would be perfectly legal for a company, located in a SEZ, to set up huge corporates farms, dairy farms, orchards, etc. especially in the name of export production. With real estate and financial and other services already included in the scope of SEZ, this is the backdoor entry to agriculture (Kabra: 2006).
9. It is being emphasized that SEZs will create a large number of new jobs in manufacturing, financial and other sectors. But nobody can say certainly how many will lose their jobs with the land being acquired and how many will be employed in new set up. At present it appears as a quick fix by power hungry 'netas' who are eager to announce that they have created so many jobs, while their predecessor did nothing on this front.
10. If new jobs are created in SEZs, the workers' exploitation will also accompany this. SEZs are exempt from the application of labour laws e.g., the Factories Act, 1948; the Industrial Disputes Act, 1947; the Trade Union Act, 1926 etc. Thus the Labour Commissioners will have no jurisdiction to inspect SEZs, even to implement safety and environmental norms in these units (Datt: 2006). Moreover, civil suits and criminal cases under the Act, will be tried either by the designated courts (Section 23 of SEZ Act of 2005) or by arbitration (Section 42 of SEZ Act of 2005). Exploitation can be in the form of exhausting work schedules, forced overtime, poor health and safety conditions, no job security, sexual exploitation of female workers etc. Our experience on this front in IT industry is already before us. The workers are not

even allowed to have their unions. So ensuring enforcement of fundamental rights of workers to form associations and unions enshrined in Article 19 (1) © of the Constitution of India will be a paramount task.

11. The immediate brunt of SEZs will be borne by the farming community. Their source of livelihood i.e. land holdings will be lost. In Mahamumbai SEZ, about 1.5 lakh families face eviction. The farmers are against forceful acquisition of their land as seen in Punjab, Orissa, Maharashtra, West Bengal etc. State Government acquires land at a price much lower than the prevailing market price. With low price of their land, the farmers will not be able to buy new land in other areas. Now the government has decided that land for SEZs will be directly purchased by the promoters. In this way, the farmers will get market price of their land.
12. Where will the marginal farmers and agricultural labourers go? Farmers will be compensated for their land but those who do not have land of their own or work on farms have nowhere to go. Some of them may indulge in criminal activities. So farmers and agricultural labourers should be given a stake in SEZs so that they can be able to earn their livelihood.
13. Food security of the nation will be affected with decrease in net sown area.

Conclusion

Despite criticisms SEZs are a useful tool of economic development and growth. There is no doubt that if the SEZ policy is carefully and fairly implemented, it would result in creation of lakhs of new jobs for skilled and unskilled workers. For a harmonious blend of agriculture and industry, we must think of locating SEZs near seaports and airports having better road connectivity. Then there will be no need to acquire agricultural land. We can also think of expanding industries vertically instead of horizontally to save on land requirements. We can say that SEZs are a boon, not a bane for the national economy. They could give a flying start to India's development. That could become an important prop to 11th Five-Year Plan achieving 10 per cent growth rate by the end of the plan period as envisaged in the Plan's Approach Paper.

REFERENCES

Datt, Ruddar (2006), "Special Economic Zones," Mainstream, November 10-16, p. 10.

Ibid., p. 17.

Kabra, K.N. (2006), "Special Economic Zones: A Baneful Package," Mainstream, October 20-26, p. 12.

Ranganathan, V. (2007), "Special Economic Zones: Rationale and Prospects," The Hindu Survey of Indian Industry, p. 24.

Index